英語反意語辞典

A Dictionary of English Antonyms

富井 篤［編］

三省堂

装　　丁　三省堂デザイン室
本文組版　株式会社トップスタジオ

はしがき

「反意語」とは，文字通り，ある言葉（肯定語）に対し，反対の意味を持つ言葉のことである．

ある言葉の反意語を作ろうとする時，我々は，日本語でも，「否」，「非」，「不」，「無」，「未」など，そのうちのどれをつけるか迷うことがしばしばある．このことは英語でも言えることで，英語の場合には，その接頭語の種類が日本語の場合よりもはるかに多く，特に我々日本人にとっては，さらに迷うことがある．

例えば，possible のように，その反意語である impossible がすぐに思い浮かんでくる言葉はよいが，英語の場合，否定を表す接頭辞の種類が多いだけに，英語の反意語を作ることは容易ではない．例えば，symmetry の反意語は？，moral の反意語は？と問われてすぐに正しい反意語を言える人は，そう多くはない．

最近の英和辞典の中には，例えば possible の項を引くと，あまり目立つ書き方ではないが，注意深く探すと後ろのほうに“反対語は impossible”などと書いてある辞書や，決められた記号で表している辞書もある．しかし，すべての肯定語に対して書いてあるわけではなく，皮肉なことに，表示されている言葉は，わかりきった単語ばかりであることが多い．そのため，欲しい反意語が素直に出てきたことは滅多にないというのが実情である．

このような状況において「英語反意語辞典」の必要性を感じ，編纂してみようと思い立ったわけである．

40 年ほど前，脱サラして翻訳の世界にデビューしてから，主に，英文和訳の翻訳をしている際，英字新聞や雑誌を読んだり，英文の文献を読んだりしている際などに，反意語に遭遇すると，その反意語を含む英文全体を丸ごと集め，その英文の中に使われている反意語を，接頭辞を取り除いた肯定語としてアルファベット順に整理していった．

その英例文，正確には反意語の数が 1,500 個くらい集まった時点で，（株）三省堂に書籍化の企画を持ち込み，紆余曲折はいろいろあったが，6 か月後，反意語辞典の編纂が決まり，何人かの仲間を集め，正式に書籍化の作業に着手した．2011 年 6 月のことである．

約 1,500 個の英例文を元に実際の作業をスタートしてみたが

(1) あまりにも技術英文に偏りすぎていたこと

(2) そのため，一般文からの例文を集めなければならなかったこと

それに，1,500 個というかなりの数のコレクションと思ってはいたが，何よりも，いざ，辞書となると

(3) その数は十分ではなかったこと

などにより，スタート後，やや泥縄式の感もあったが，新たな例文を収集しなければならず，協力メンバー 5 人とともに約 1 年間かけてこの収集作業を行なった．その後，辞書としての執筆活動期間が約 1 年間，英文校閲が約 2 か月，そして完全脱稿したのが 2013 年 8 月である．

この種の辞書は，今までになく，一般辞書の，ほんのわずかの隙間を借りて存在してきたものである．これからは，この辞書が，世の多くの方たちの要望に応えることができたら，これに勝る喜びはない．

振り返ってみると，「反意語」に興味を抱き，データを集め始めてから約 40 年，書籍化を視野に入れてから約 5 年，具体的な作業に取り掛かってから 2 年半，やっとここに「英語反意語辞典」が完成したわけである．

これまでに，たくさんの方たちにお世話になった．まず，この辞典の基礎資料となった英文の原著者たちに謝意を表したい．当初，この辞書がまだ海のものとも山のものとも分からない，書籍化検討期にいろいろアドバイスくださった三省堂の柳百合氏，さらには書籍化を決定していただいた西垣浩二氏および坂本淳氏，また，編集作業当初から，新しい英例文の収集，分類，翻訳の各工程を担当していただいた 5 人のメンバー，瀬谷啓一，野崎哲郎，堀合直，山田幹夫，渡辺恵子（50 音順）の各氏，それに，各メンバーの翻訳作業がオーバーフローしてしまった英例文を一手に引き受

けて翻訳していただいた高澤市郎氏，さらには，終盤，接頭辞および接尾辞を徹底的に調査・研究していただいた田神義一氏にこの場を借りてお礼申し上げたい．

最後になってしまったが，もう一人忘れることのできない方に，全体の英文の校閲と接頭辞と接尾辞の解説を担当してくださった，日本在住 50 年，日本語に堪能な翻訳者，Fred Uleman 氏がいる．

我々が収集した英例文は，すべて，ネイティブの書いたものや，アメリカやイギリスなどで出版された文献から採取したものばかりであるが，必ずしも，すべて英例文が辞書に例文として載せることができるほど良い英文であるとは限らない．Uleman 氏は，それらの英例文を，「一度見ればすべて直せる」というものではないという信念のもとに，何回も何回も，時間が許す限り徹底的に校閲してくださり，時には，われわれ日本人メンバーが訳した和訳文の不適切な部分にまで指摘くださった．さらには，反対を表す接頭辞と接尾辞の基本を，われわれとは異なった，独自の視点から解説をしてくださった．心より感謝したい．

2014 年 3 月

編　者	富井 篤，株式会社 国際テクリンガ研究所 代表取締役
スタッフ	瀬谷 啓一，田神 義一，野崎 哲郎，堀合 直，山田 幹夫，渡辺 恵子（50 音順）
翻訳者	高澤 市郎
英文校閲者	Fred Uleman

本書の特長

本書には，次の特長がある．

● 英例文の質が高い

本書で使われている英例文は，そのほとんどが，英米人と思われる人たちが書いた英文やアメリカやイギリスで出版された文献から採取したものである．しかも，それらの英文を，さらにUleman 氏が校閲していただいている．そのため，英語教育の現場や英語学習書によく見られる，「現在，死んでしまっている英文」はほとんどない．

● 反意語の引き方が易しい

配列が，肯定語 ⇒ 接頭辞または接尾辞 ⇒ 反意語 ⇒ 品詞 ⇒ 訳語 ⇒ 英例文 ⇒ 和訳文となっているので，肯定語から反意語にたどり着くのが容易である．

● 接頭辞または接尾辞の学習ができる

肯定語の綴りや肯定語の品詞に接頭辞または接尾辞がどのように変わるか学習できる．

● 新規に反意語を集め，手作りの反意語辞典をつくることができる

この辞書に載っていない新しい反意語をたくさん集めていくことにより，手作りのユーザー反意語辞典に発展させていくことができる．

● 英例文と和訳文を通して英語の学習ができる

すべての反意語に付随しているわけではないが，大部分の反意語については，訳語の後に 英例文 ⇒ 和訳文が付いているので，英語の学習書として使える．

● 索引が充実している

本文は肯定語をアルファベット順に並べているので，巻末に反意語のアルファベット索引と和英索引を用意した．検索に役立てていただきたい．

● **比較的多くの項目を収録してある．**

「肯定語」の数は約 2,300 個，「反意語」の数は約 2,500 個，そして「全項目」の数は約 2,600 個である．

お断りとお詫び

この「英語反意語辞典」は，長い時間をかけ，できうる限り誠心誠意作成したものであるが，いくつかの点で，お断りとお詫びを申し上げなければならないことがある．

● 必ずしも，考えられうるすべての肯定語に対する反意語を網羅しているわけではない

過去 40 年間のうちに「集めた」というよりも「集まった」反意語の例を取り上げているに過ぎない．そのため，収録されている反意語も，1 つの語幹に対して派生すべきすべての品詞，例えば，名詞形，動詞形，形容詞形，副詞形など，をすべて収録しているわけではなく，中には，すべての品詞の例を収録している反意語も多々あることはあるが，どちらかというと，品詞が 1 個であったり，2 個ないしは 3 個である場合が多い．したがって，そのような反意語に出会ったら，反意語がそれだけの数しかありえないというわけではなく，それだけしか，まだ集まっていなかったのだというように理解していただきたい．この点は率直に告白し，読者が，これ以降，ご自身で収集していき，手作りのユーザー辞書を構築していただければ，もちろん我々も改訂時にはさらに新しい反意語を追加する努力は惜しまないが，編者として望外の喜びである．

● 和訳文の品質的拙さが避けられなかった

この辞書を手掛けた当初から，肯定語に対する「反意語」の例示が第一の目的であり，次いでその反意語が使われている英例文の例示が第二の目的であった．だからといって許されることでは決してないが，そのため，英例文に対する和訳文は，必ずしも完全なものではなく，まして，辞書の中の和訳文となると，英例文をどこまで意訳してよいものか，どこまで英例文との関わり合いを持たせるために直訳調を残しておかなければならないか，この点が最後まで問題となっていた．そこに加え，どの分野までカバーすべきか，まず第一に技術系の例文か非技術系の例文かから始まり，同じ技術系の例文であっても，その技術分野そのものが範囲が広く，また非技術系の例文といっても，政治，経済，文学，歴史などなど範囲が広く，執筆担当者 6 人で，まともな対応が難しかったという能力的な限界もあった．きっと，100 点満点に対して 80 点か 90 点の出来でしかないかもしれない．この点は率直に告白し，読者の皆さんのご指導により，改訂を重ねるたびに満点に近づけていこうと思っている．願わくは，この辞書の足りない 10 点とか 20 点を批評する使い方ではなく，80 点か 90 点を評価する使い方をしていただければ幸いである．

● 英例文の分野的偏りが，最後まで完全には払拭できなかった

この辞書の基本データは，編者がほぼ 40 年近く前から英文和訳の翻訳をしたり，英字新聞や雑誌を読んだり，英文の文献を読んだりしている間に収集した反意語に関する英文データである．したがって，どちらかというと，科学技術文から引用した英文データが主流をなしていた．しかし，その後，この「反意語辞典」の編纂が決まってから，技術系と非技術系の英文データのアンバランスを解消するため，各種非技術系の英文情報を収集し，全体のバランスを取るように努力した．しかし，完全にアンバランスが解消できるまでには，どうしてもたどり着くことができず，最後まで，若干の悔いが残っている．これも，これからの改訂と，読者の皆さんのさらなる収集に負うところが多いと言わざるを得ない．

●「英語反意語辞典」の機能を正しく理解してほしい

これは，あくまでも辞書であって，反意語の作り方を解説した参考書ではない．「反意語」というのは，すでに存在している基本の「肯定語」に対し，あるルールに基づいて接頭辞や接尾辞が付けられているもので，すでに「反意語」として定着しているものである．したがって，本書を活用して，新しい反意語を作ろうとしても，その隙間はほとんど残っていないと考えるべきである．

● 1つの肯定語に異なった複数個の接頭辞または接尾辞が付く反意語の処理は便法をとった

このような反意語は，この「英語反意語辞書」の中で，約220個近くある．そのすべてについて解説を加えるということは紙面の関係で無理であり，それよりも，接頭辞や接尾辞を詳細に理解していくと，その意味がないことに気付いた．特に，il, im，ir は意味的には in と全く同じであり，違いは，ただ肯定語の頭の文字によって違うだけであり，in と un も意味は同じ，ニュアンスが若干異なる程度である．そこで，これらすべての接頭辞および接尾辞をできる限り詳細に解説し，それによって接頭辞や接尾辞の差違によって若干変化する反意語を理解していただこうという便法をとった．

当初，この解説は日本語で行おうかと思ったが，辞書全体の英文を校閲くださった Fred Uleman 氏にお願いし，我々日本人の理解だけではなく，ネイティブでなければ理解できないような記述法を採っていただいた．これについては，この後に続く，英文を基調として書かれている「反対を表す接頭辞と接尾辞」をお読みいただきたい．

反対を表す接頭辞と接尾辞

Parts of English words often function much the same as kanji. If you know what 注意 means and what 要 and 不 mean, you can guess what 要注意 and 不注意 mean. 不 can negate all manner of words: 不衛生，不愉快，and 不要, for example.

With English, "ize" can be thought of as equivalent to 化, as in "energize" and "politicize." "En" works the same way in "encourage" and "enable." These are "positive" in the sense that they add a characteristic.

But there are also "negative" parts of words that negate or remove a characteristic. "Un" is an example. "An armed man" is a 武器を持っている男, but "an unarmed man" is a 武器を持たない男（非武装の男）. The "un" makes "unarmed" the opposite of "armed."

This dictionary is an effort to help you understand and use these "negating" prefixes and suffixes. While the dictionary goes by full words, it might help to provide a brief overview here working not from the base word but from the prefix/suffix.

A　This is used in

apolitical 政治に特に関心がない＝ノンポリ
amoral 道徳観のない者，非道徳的（but not "evil"）
atheist（theist＝神を信じる者＝信者；atheist＝無信論者＝無宗教）
But note that not all words that start with "a" are negations. "Apathetic"（無関心）is not the opposite of "pathetic"（惨めな）. "Abase" is not the opposite of "base."

Ab　This is used in

abnormal（normal = 通常；abnormal = 非通常 = 異常な）
abuse（use = 使用する；abuse = 不正に使う or 悪用する → abuse his hospitality もてなしに甘え過ぎる and child abuse 児童虐待）

Anti　can be either "the opposite of " or "opposed to"
Thesis – **Anti**thesis = 理論—反対理論
matter – **anti**matter = 物質—反物質
anti-American = opposed to America and not the opposite of America 反米
Antimonopoly laws are laws against monopolies 独占禁止法
But "antibody"（抗体）is not included here because the "body" that it negates differs from illness to illness.

De　"**De**certify" = to remove a certification（資格を剥奪する）
Debase（a currency）= to remove all or part of the base/basis for the currency. In early times, currencies were actual pieces of precious metal, so "debasing" them meant adulterating/diluting the metal. And because the "base" was cheapened, the currency lost value. When this happens, we can also say the currency lost part of its value and was "**de**valued."
Likewise, something that is operational（has been activated）can be **de**activated.
Derail a project 企画を脱線させる = 軌道から外す
Defund = 資金（融資）を剥がす

Dis　This is usually used not to mean just that the characteristic does not exist but even more to mean that it is removed.
For example, "**dis**arm" is 非武装化.
For example, "**dis**comfort" is to make someone uncomfortable.
For example, **dis**able means to "make no longer able." It is used in phrases such as "disable the firewall" パソコンのファイアー

ウォールを無効にする

Similarly, someone with a **dis**ability 障害者 is someone without a common ability such as walking or seeing.

For example, something that was hidden or "covered" can be **dis**covered 発見される.

However, there are instances where the change is not attributed to an actor.

For example, things that are "**dis**similar" are just "not similar" and there is no nuance of someone's having made them dissimilar.

Similarly, "**dis**appear" 消える can happen spontaneously（the same as "appear" 洗われる can）without human intervention. However, "disappear" can also happen with a human actor and mean "to cause someone/something to no longer be visible" – as a euphemism for "jailed" or "killed" as in "The Pinochet government 'disappeared' thousands of its critics." 反対勢力の数千人を抹消［＝殺害］した.

And of course, "**dis**like" is simply 非好む→嫌う

Dys　is a variation of "dis."

As in a **dys**functional family or system 機能しない.

Free　as a prefix（coming before the base）

Freeform is used to describe a type of poetry that does not follow a strict form. 型に拘らない Yet this is by no means limited to poetry. There are also "freeform sculpture" and "freeform organizations."

Free　as a suffix（coming after the base）

This means "without" as in "sugar-**free**," "gluten-**free**," and "fat-**free**."

Ships can sail up the Thames as far as Central London when it is ice-**free**.

Because tariffs are also called "duties," we have "duty-**free**" 非関税 shops in airports and other areas catering to international travelers.

Il A variant of "in," this is usually used with words starting with "l."

For example, **il**legal（違法）and **il**legible（解読不能）.

Im Another variant of "in," this is used in, for example:

impotent 能力がない→インポ
impractical 非現実的→むちゃ
imprecise 正確でない→不正確
impossible 可能性のない→不可能＝あり得ない
immobile 動けない→不動

In

independent 依存しないもの→独立したもの
inadvertent 意図性のない→偶然な，うっかり
inexact 正確でない→大雑把
inadequate = insufficient 充分ではない→不充分
inappropriate 適切ではない→不適切
incomplete = 不完全 = 未完
innumerable（= countless）数えられない→無数

Note that "**in**valuable" does not mean "not valuable" but means "having more value than can be assessed" = "having immense value." 評価できないほどの価値がある

Ir This is usually used with words starting with "r."

For example, **ir**regular（said of a shape or a procedure that is not regular）and **ir**religious（said of a person who is not religious）.

Less

art**less** 飾らない，作為のない→素朴な，素直な
time**less** 時代に限定されない→時代を超える，永久の
price**less** 値段が付けられない→金で買えない
limit**less** 制限がない→無限
base**less** (= ground**less**) rumor 根拠のない噂→デマ
form**less** fears = 形のない恐怖，漠然とした恐怖

Non

nonsense = sense（感，常識）がない→でたらめ，無意味
nonstop = 止まらない→直行便
nonconformance to standards = 基準に合わない = ムラ
noncompliance = 医者の指示を無視する，命令に従わない
non sequitur（logic that does not follow in sequence）論理の飛躍
non-Japanese = 非日本人，外国人
NPO and NGO（**non**-profit and non-governmental organizations）非営利活動法人 and 非政府組織

Un

Unappetizing（appetizing = 食欲を誘う）食欲を誘わない，まずそう
Unfit（for a job or for human consumption）
仕事の場合はマッチしない（必要な能力がない）→不適
食料品の場合は基準に合わない→食用に不向き，到底食べられない
uncertain 不確定，未定
unvarnished（or **un**adorned）truth 飾りのない→ありのままの真実
unhappy = 非ハッピー→悲しい
uncommon = 非普通→珍しい
unlock 鍵をかけるの逆→鍵を開ける

un-American アメリカらしくない. But is then extended to mean 非国民 as in the House Un-American Affairs Committee.

But because there are so many words that look like this but are not this, we need this dictionary.
For example, import and export do not negate "port" but show the direction the merchandise is transported (im = in, ex = out).

And there are times when this appears to work, but it is working on a base that no longer has currency (if it ever did).
For example, inflation and deflation. The root for "flation" is wind or gas, such that these terms are best understood in terms of a balloon, but there is no such term as "flation," so the "in" and "de" should not be thought of as negating it. Especially since the "in" in "inflation" is to make it bigger and not to remove or negate the "flation."
For example, similarly, even though we have "persuade" (to make someone in favor of something) and "dissuade" (to make someone opposed to something) there is no such word as "suade" so these cannot really be said to modify or change "suade."
For example, "antipathy" is not in this dictionary because there is no word "pathy" in common usage. There is "empathy," which is the opposite of "antipathy," but there is no "pathy."

Finally, please note that there are many words such as "delight," which does not mean 光を消す. It is 喜ばす.
We need to see things in context and realize that not everything that looks like a negation prefixes or suffixes is actually a negation prefix or suffix. As Freud would say, sometimes a cigar is just a cigar.

著者略歴

略歴

1934年 横須賀に生まれる

1974年 アメリカ系産業機械メーカーのチーフエンジニアを経て，翻訳・通訳，語学研究・教育・指導，および執筆活動を開始

1976年 株式会社 国際テクリンガ研究所 設立，現在に至る

主な著書 『技術英語 前置詞活用辞典』，『技術英語 数量表現辞典』，『技術英語 構文辞典』（以上三省堂），『技術翻訳のテクニック』，『続 技術翻訳のテクニック』，『科学技術英語 用法・実例データベース』（以上丸善），『科学技術和英大辞典』，『科学技術英和大辞典』，『科学技術英語表現辞典』，『科学技術英語動詞活用辞典』（以上オーム社），「わかる・使える」実務英語4巻シリーズ（日興企画）など.

所属団体 日本翻訳者協会（JAT　Japan Association of Translators）

SWET（Society of Writers, Editors, and Translators）

日米協会（The America-Japan Society, Inc.）

A

abashed

接頭 (un) **unabashed** *adj* 恥を感じない ▶ an **unabashed** hawk with strong ties to military contractors 軍用契約者と強い結び付きがある厚顔の強硬論者 ▶ The old gentleman continued clapping, with tears in his eyes, quite undaunted and **unabashed**. その老人は涙を流しながら毅然として堂々と[恥を感じず]手を叩き続けた.

abated

接頭 (un) **unabated** *adj* 〈台風などが〉衰えない ▶ Can everything of importance continue **unabated** even when you are not here? あなたがここにいなくても，重要なことはすべて同じように[衰えずに]続きますか. ▶ Environmental degradation rages **unabated**. 環境は相変わらず[衰えないで]急激に劣化している.

ability

接頭 (dis) **disability** *n* 身体障害，心身障害 ▶ Many aids exist to help people with different types of **disabilities**, ranging from weakness in the hands to loss of the use of an arm. 手の機能低下から一方の腕を使用できない場合まで，さまざまな種類の身体障害を持っている人たちを助ける数多くの補助手段がある.

接頭 (in) **inability** *n* できないこと ▶ Another problem is the **inability** to address large memory. もう一つの問題は，大きいメモリーのアドレス指定ができないことである. ▶ Japanese negotiators' seeming **inability** to say "no" is a potential cause of U.S. frustration. 日本人交渉者の，うわべでは「ノー」と言えないことは，米国のフラストレーションの潜在的な原因である.

able

接頭 (dis) **disable** *v* 能力を奪う ▸ Setting the SO register to 0 **disables** auto-answer. SO レジスターを0に設定すると，自動応答は無効になる．

接頭 (dis) **disabling** *n* 無能力化 ▸ The Stark's **disabling** is attributed in part to the fact that its defenses are computer-controlled. スタークの無能力化は，一つには，その種の防御手段がコンピューター制御に依るからである．

接頭 (un) **unable** *adj* ～できない ▸ I'm sorry I was **unable** to let you know in advance. 前もって連絡できずにすみません． ▸ Unless . . . the writer will be **unable** to use his facts to good advantage. ……がなければ，その筆者は事実を十分に利用することができないであろう． ▸ If you are **unable** to insert the plug into the outlet, contact an electrician to replace the outlet. プラグをコンセントに差し込めないようなら，ライセンスを持った電気技術者に連絡してそのコンセントを交換する．

abled

接頭 (dis) **disabled** *adj*

❶障害のある ▸ A **disabled** person confined permanently to a wheelchair will be very familiar with the wheelchair's use. 恒久的に車椅子を離れられない身体障害者は，その使用方法に非常に習熟するであろう．

❷〈コントロールなどを〉失った ▸ Horrified controllers watched the **disabled** aircraft drop to below 10,000 ft and disappear from their radar screens altogether. 管制官たちは，コントロールを失った航空機が1万フィート下に落ち，レーダースクリーンから完全に消えるのをぞっとする思いで見つめていた．

abridged

接頭 (un) **unabridged** *adj* 要約されていない，縮刷版ではない ▸ an **unabridged** dictionary 非縮小版の辞書

absorbent

接頭 (un) **unabsorbent** *adj* 吸収性のない ▶ apatite crystal without including a biological **unabsorbent** material 生体非吸収性材料を含まないアパタイト結晶

accented

接頭 (un) **unaccented** *adj* アクセントのない ▶ Words with accented vowels are sorted after the same words with **unaccented** vowels. アクセントの付いた母音は，アクセントの付かない母音の後ろにまとめられる．

acceptable

接頭 (un) **unacceptable** *adj* 受け入れられない，許容できない ▶ Ship lines must be selected with great care to avoid **unacceptable** results. 船会社は，許容できない結果を避けるために，高度の注意をして選ばなければならない． ▶ As mentioned above, for some applications, delays caused by acknowledgments are **unacceptable**. 前述したとおり，一部のアプリケーションでは，認証によって生じる遅延を許容することができない． ▶ Business ethics are moral principles concerning acceptable and **unacceptable** business behavior. ビジネス倫理とは，ビジネス行動において認められ，また認められない[受け入れられない]，道義原則である．

acceptably

接頭 (un) **unacceptably** *ad* 容認できずに ▶ An alternate circuit has been designed for applications where a broken sense wire would **unacceptably** compromise appliance safety. 代替回路は，センスワイヤが破断すると器具の安全が容認できないほどに脅かされる場合に適用するよう設計されている． ▶ Their main concern is that, choosing to focus on the still **unacceptably** high unemployment level in America, the Fed will lose sight of its mandate to fight inflation. いまだに容認できないほど高い失業率に重点を置くことにより，FRB がインフレと闘うという責務を見失うことになるのが大きな懸念事項であ

る.

acceptance

接頭 (non) **nonacceptance** *n* 不承知, 不承諾, 不受理 ▶ **Non-Acceptance** of a Medical Certificate, etc. 診断書の不受理等

accessibility

接頭 (in) **inaccessibility** *n* 接近［利用］不可能性 ▶ The mountain is known for its **inaccessibility**. その山は到達しにくいことで知られている.

accessible

接頭 (in) **inaccessible** *adj*

❶近づきにくい, 得がたい, よそよそしい ▶ She is **inaccessible**. 彼女は寄りつきにくい人だ.

❷アクセスできない ▶ Certain applications may remain **inaccessible** because of a lack of suitable terminals. 適当な端末機がないために, いくつかの使えるはずのアプリケーションが使えないままになっているかもしれない.

accessibly

接頭 (in) **inaccessibly** *ad* 近づきがたいほどに ▶ **inaccessibly** located or situated 近づきがたい位置か状況にある

accommodated

接頭 (un) **unaccommodated** *adj* 適応していない ▶ Hyperopia, or farsightedness, results from the eyeball's being too short and **unaccommodated** rays focusing behind the retina. 遠視は, 眼球が短すぎて適応していない光線が網膜の後ろで焦点を結ぶことが原因で起きる.

accompanied

接頭 (un) **unaccompanied** *adj*

❶付いていない, 付属していない ▶ Do you have any **unaccompanied** luggage? 別送の［ついていない］荷物はお持ちですか.

❷伴奏なしの ▶ All pieces should be played **unaccompanied**.

すべての曲は伴奏なしで演奏しなければならない.

accomplished

接頭 (un) **unaccomplished** *adj* 遂行されていない ► The task remained **unaccomplished**. その仕事は, 依然として未完成のままだった.

accord

接頭 (dis) **disaccord** *v* 一致しない

accountable

接頭 (un) **unaccountable** *adj* 説明できない, 不可思議な ► an **unaccountable** feeling of well-being 不思議な幸福感

accountably

接頭 (un) **unaccountably** *ad* 説明できないくらい ► She was **unaccountably** irritated. 彼女は, 妙にいらいらしていた.

accounted-for

接頭 (un) **unaccounted-for** *adj* 説明されていない ► All other **unaccounted-for** water is classified as loss and waste. 他の究明されていない水はすべて損失および廃棄物として分類される.

accredited

接頭 (un) **unaccredited** *adj* 認可された, 公認の ► Degrees from **unaccredited** schools are not acceptable. 不認可の学校の学位は認められない.

accuracy

接頭 (in) **inaccuracy** *n* 不正確, 誤り, 間違い ► There are a number of methodological problems here, quite aside from the **inaccuracy** of some of the results. ここには, 結果の不正確さに加えて, 方法論上の問題が数多く存在している. ► Errors due to speedometer **inaccuracy** are unavoidable. 速度計の不正確さによる誤差は避けられない.

accurate

接頭 (in) **inaccurate** *adj* 不正確な ► In most cases, the primary errors are those caused by **inaccurate** guidelines. 不正確なガ

イドラインによるエラーが大半を占めている. ▶ Perceptions of Japanese-U.S. negotiation efforts are often **inaccurate**, which can make the actual negotiating situation even more difficult. 日本人と米国人の交渉の努力を取り巻く認識は多くの場合不正確であり，そしてそれが実際の交渉の状況をさらに難しくしている可能性がある.

accustomed

接頭 (un) **unaccustomed** *adj* 慣れていない，不慣れな ▶ The elderly daughter with **unaccustomed** time on her hands may have difficulty planning her future once she no longer has to care for her parents. 不慣れな時間を手中にしている姉娘は，もはや両親の世話を見る必要がないとなっても，自分の将来を決めるのに困惑することがある.

achievable

接頭 (un) **unachievable** *adj* 達成できない ▶ But the positions themselves range from loony to irrelevant, **unachievable**, and just plain wrong. しかし，姿勢それ自体は，狂信的なものから的外れの，達成できない，単純に間違っているものまで及んでいる.

acknowledged

接頭 (un) **unacknowledged** *adj* 認められていない ▶ an **unacknowledged** emergency 認知されていない非常事態

acquainted

接頭 (un) **unacquainted** *adj* 精通していない

action

接頭 (in) **inaction** *n* 何もしないこと ▶ He is wasting his youth in **inaction**. よい若者が何もせずに年を腐らしている.

activate

接頭 (de) **deactivate** *v*

❶ 〈機械などが〉停止する ▶ The mechanical unit was made to **deactivate** on sensing wheel-spin on the ground. この機械装置は地上のホイールスピンに感応して停止した.

❷不活発化させる，非活性化させる ▶ effectively **deactivate** pathogenic microorganisms 病原微生物を効果的に不活性化する

接頭 (in) **inactivate** *v* 〈機能などを〉止める ▶ This process can **inactivate** certain viruses. この過程によってある種のウイルスを不活性にすることができる.

activated

接頭 (in) **inactivated** *adj* 不活性化された ▶ This medicine is used to reanimate **inactivated** cells. この薬は不活性化された細胞を生き返らせるために用いられる.

activating

接頭 (in) **inactivating** *adj* 不活性化する ▶ White tea was more effective than green tea in **inactivating** bacterial viruses. 白茶は，細菌ウイルスを機能させない点で緑茶より効果的だった.

activation

接頭 (de) **deactivation** *n* 非活性化 ▶ If adhesion failure occurs on a nickel plate, the most probable cause is **deactivation** of the nickel surface. ニッケルプレートの上で粘着しないときは，おおかたの原因はニッケル表面の非活発化による.

接頭 (in) **inactivation** *n* 不活性化 ▶ the gene **inactivation** system 遺伝子不活性化システム

active

接頭 (in) **inactive** *adj*

❶活動しない ▶ He has been quite **inactive** [has kept very quiet] for the last few years. 彼は，この2，3年まったく鳴りをひそめている.

❷不活発な，開店休業状態の，休止中の ▶ The stock market is especially **inactive**. 株式市場は殊に景気が悪い.

❸不活性の，非放射性の，静態の

❹現役でない

actively

[接頭] (in) **inactively** *ad* 不活発に ► retrieve an image without **inactively** increasing the number of corresponding point candidates 無為に対応点候補を増やすことなく画像を検索する

activity

[接頭] (in) **inactivity** *n* 不活発，休止，静止，無為 ► Your session will time out after 30 minutes of **inactivity**. 30分間何もしないと，セッションはタイムアウトになる．

adaptable

[接頭] (in) **inadaptable** *adj* 適応できない ► a hardware debugging mechanism **inadaptable** to an operating system オペレーティングシステムに適応できないハードウエア・デバッグ・メカニズム

[接頭] (un) **unadaptable** *adj* 適合できない ► We possessed some deficiency which made us subtly **unadaptable** to Eastern life. 我々は，東洋の生活に少し適合できない何らかの欠陥を持っていた．

addictive

[接頭] (non) **nonaddictive** *adj* 非習慣性の ► This drug is believed to be **nonaddictive** and less damaging to the health than a hard drug. この薬剤は非習慣性であり，中毒性の高い薬物よりも健康に悪い影響を与えることは少ないと考えられる．

adequacy

[接頭] (in) **inadequacy** *n*

❶ 不適当，不適切 ► The **inadequacies** of these approaches are due to strict adherence to the selection rule. これらの方法が不適当であるのは，選択規則を厳密に守りすぎているからだ．

❷ 不十分さ ► That misunderstanding is attributable to the **inadequacy** of the preliminary negotiations. その誤解は，予備交渉の不十分さを物語っている．

adequate

接頭 (in) **inadequate** *adj* 不十分な，不適切な，不適当な，無力な ▶ Words are **inadequate** to express my grief. 私の悲しみを表現するには，言葉は不十分である．

adequately

接頭 (in) **inadequately** *ad* 不十分に，不適切に ▶ The President was shot because he was **inadequately** guarded. 大統領は警備が手薄だったため撃たれた． ▶ Japanese literature, in spite of its beauty and riches, is as yet **inadequately** known in the West. 日本文学は，その美しさと豊かさにもかかわらず，西洋ではまだ不十分にしか知られていない．

adherent

接頭 (non) **nonadherent** *adj* 非接着性の；剥落する ▶ Rapid corrosion occurs if liquid or volatile corrosives are formed or if the solid compound is **nonadherent**. 液体または揮発液腐食生成物が形成されるかまたは固体コンパウンドが非粘着性であると，腐食が迅速に発生する．

admissible

接頭 (in) **inadmissible** *adj* 許容できない ▶ speculation that was permissible in cosmology but is **inadmissible** in medicine 宇宙論では許されたが医学では受け入れがたい推測

接頭 (in) **inadmissibly** *ad* 許容できないほどに ▶ Heat bridges lead to **inadmissibly** low surface temperatures. 熱橋が許容できないくらい低い表面温度を示すことになる．

adopted

接頭 (un) **unadopted** *adj* 採用されない，管理されていない ▶ The proposed standards were left **unadopted**. 提案された標準規格は，採用されないままになっている．

adorned

接頭 (un) **unadorned** *adj* 飾られていない，質素な ▶ Friends say Kelly prides himself on his **unadorned** bluntness. 彼の友人が言うには，ケリーは飾り気のない無愛想さを誇りにしてい

る.

adulterated

接頭 (un) **unadulterated** *adj*

❶混ぜられていない ► You may soon be able to put eggs back on your menu, **unadulterated** with guilt. 罪の意識が混ざっていない卵がまもなくメニューに戻ってくるであろう.

❷純粋な ► **unadulterated** ethyl alcohol 純粋なエチルアルコール

advantage

接頭 (dis) **disadvantage** *n*

❶不利な立場, 損失 ► U.S. manufacturers will be at a distinct **disadvantage** unless current government policies are reversed. 現在のアメリカ政府の政策が転換されなければ, アメリカの製造業者らが損をすることは明らかである.

❷短所, 欠点 ► Both approaches have their advantages and **disadvantages**. 両方のアプローチが相対的な長所と短所を表している.

advantageous

接頭 (dis) **disadvantageous** *adj* 不利な, 不都合な ► The relatively **disadvantageous** properties of these materials are higher cost, lower temperature resistance, and poorer acid resistance. これらの材料の特性で比較的不利な点は, 価格が比較的高く, 耐温度性と耐酸性が低いことである.

advertence

接頭 (in) **inadvertence** *n* 不注意, 見落とし ► It was another example of her **inadvertence**. それは, もう一つの彼女の不注意の例である.

advertent

接頭 (in) **inadvertent** *adj* 故意でない, 不注意な, うっかりした ► There was an **inadvertent** release of toxic gas. 毒ガスの不注意な放出があった. ► The January 11 accident was the first **inadvertent** ignition. 1月11日の事故が最初の点火ミス

だった.

advertently

接頭 (in) **inadvertently** *ad* 不注意に, 軽率に, うっかり ► I **inadvertently** forgot about that. 私はそれをうっかり忘れてました.

advisability

接頭 (in) **inadvisability** *n* 勧められないこと, 愚かなこと

advisable

接頭 (in) **inadvisable** *adj* 勧められない, 得策でない ► an unnecessary and **inadvisable** action 不必要で賢明でない行動

接頭 (un) **unadvisable** *adj* 勧められない ► That is **unadvisable**. 当を得た策ではない.

advised

接頭 (ill) **ill-advised** *adj* 思慮の足りない ► I do not think that you are **ill-advised**. 私は, あなたは思慮がないとは思わない.

接頭 (un) **unadvised** *adj* 忠告を受けていない

advisedly

接頭 (ill) **ill-advisedly** *adj* 軽率に, 無分別に ► When Labour swept to power in 1997, Tony Blair **ill-advisedly** pledged to clean up sleaze in politics. 労働党が1997年に選挙で圧勝して政権についたとき, トニー・ブレア首相は政治スキャンダルを一掃すると軽率に誓った.

affect

接頭 (ill) **ill-affect** *v* ~に悪影響を与える

affected

接頭 (dis) **disaffected** *adj* 不満のある ► At that time, the board wasn't fretting about a few **disaffected** lawyers. その当時, 委員会は幾人かの不満を抱いた弁護士について気にしていなかった.

接頭 (ill) **ill-affected** *adj* 不満を抱いている ► The people are **ill-affected** towards the government. 人民は政府に不満を抱いている.

[接頭] (un) **unaffected** *adj*

❶ 影響を受けない ► This scatter was attributed to the fracture path running into the **unaffected** base material. この散乱は，影響を受けていない母材に続く割れ目のせいだった． ► The strength of the country remains **unaffected** by the economic crisis. 経済危機によって国力は影響を受けない［衰えることはない］.

❷ 飾らない，気取らない ► **unaffected** behavior 気取らないしぐさ

affection

[接頭] (dis) **disaffection** *n* 不満，不忠実 ► Mary McDonald was one catalyst for the **disaffection**. 不満を助長させた一人はメアリ・マクドナルドであった.

affiliate

[接頭] (dis) **disaffiliate** *v* 関係を絶つ

affiliated

[接頭] (un) **unaffiliated** *adj* 提携していない，加盟していない

affordable

[接頭] (un) **unaffordable** *adj* (高くて)手が届かない ► Even after restructuring, the debt remains **unaffordable**. その債務は，整理を行ってはいるが，まだ返済できる状態ではない［手が届かない］.

afforest

[接頭] (dis) **disafforest** *v* 森林を伐採する

afforestation

[接頭] (dis) **deforestation** *n* 森林の伐採

afraid

[接頭] (un) **unafraid** *adj* 恐れていない

age

[接尾] (less) **ageless** *adj*

❶ 不老の，老いない ► There was an **ageless** quality in his face. 彼の顔は老けなかった.

❷ 永遠の ► The **ageless** pop star bought a $40 million townhouse in New York's Upper East Side. 永遠のポップスターは，ニューヨークのアッパーイーストサイドにある4千万ドルのタウンハウスを買った.

接頭 (non) **nonage** *n* 未成年

aged

接頭 (un) **unaged** *adj* 経年していない，成熟していない ► Aged and **unaged** cheeses are blended to obtain a mild but distinctive flavor. 熟成したチーズと熟成していないチーズをブレンドして，口当たりがよく個性のある風味をもたせる.

agglomerated

接頭 (non) **nonagglomerated** *adj* 塊状になっていない，非凝集の ► The agglomerates are more rapidly soluble than the **nonagglomerated** products. 凝集体は非凝集体よりもはるかに素早く溶解する.

aggression

接頭 (non) **nonaggression** *n* 不侵略 ► They signed a **nonaggression** pact. 彼らは不可侵条約に署名した.

agree

接頭 (dis) **disagree** *v*

❶ 同意しない ► If you vehemently **disagree** with your company's plans for your future, it is probably wise to speak to a lawyer. もし君が，君の将来についての会社の計画に完全に同意しないならば，君自身の弁護士に話してみるのがおそらく賢明だろう.

❷ 一致しない ► Communications specialists **disagreed** on whether or not the French videotex product would be profitable. 通信施設の他の専門家たちは，フランス製ビデオテックス計画が実際に利益を生むものかどうかについて意見が一致しなかった.

❸ 〈気候などが〉合わない，適さない

agreeable

接頭 (dis) **disagreeable** *adj*

❶ 不快な, 不愉快な ▸ He seemed to find even the slightest blurring **disagreeable.** ごくわずかな曇りでも彼にとっては不快なもののように見えた. ▸ The driver was **disagreeable** all the way to the station. 運転手は駅までの途中, 不愉快なことを私に言い続けた.

❷ 好ましくない ▸ In such a case, vibrations may become quite **disagreeable.** このような場合, 振動は実に好ましからざるものとなる.

agreement

接頭 (dis) **disagreement** *n*

❶ 不一致 ▸ There is **disagreement,** however, among producers and processors of UHMWP as to how high "ultra" is. しかし, 超高分子ポリエチレンのメーカーと加工業者の間には「超」とはどのくらいのことを言うのかについて意見はまちまちである.

❷ 合わないこと, 合致しないこと ▸ If you do have a **disagreement** with your boss, rationally explain your side of the argument, make sure he understands what you have said, and then let him make a decision. もし君が, ボスと合わないときは, 論理的に自分の議論を説明し, それを彼が理解したことを確認して結論を出してもらいなさい.

接頭 (non) **nonagreement** *n* 不承知, 不同意

aided

接頭 (un) **unaided** *adj* 助けを借りない ▸ Each crew member will be provided with a comprehensive suite of automatic avionics so she can carry out her mission **unaided.** 乗組員それぞれに, 援助を受けずに任務を遂行できるように一連の自動化された航空電子機器が支給される.

aim

接尾 (less) **aimless** *adj* 当てのない ▸ The infant sleeps most of the time and, when awake, waves his arms and legs in an **aimless** fashion. 幼児は1日24時間のほとんどを眠って過ごし，目が覚めているときには，特に目的もなく手や足を動かしている．

接尾 (less) **aimlessly** *ad* 当てもなく ▶ At that time, I was wandering **aimlessly** through the store. その時，私は，当てもなく店の中をぶらぶらしていた．

aimed

接頭 (ill) **ill-aimed** *adj* 狙いどころが悪い

air

接尾 (less) **airless** *adj*

❶空気のない，風通しの良い ▶ The parachutes would be useless to a craft descending onto the **airless** moon, but a landing mechanism would be indispensable. 空気のない月旅行船にはパラシュートは不要だが，着陸装置は不可欠となる．

❷静かな

alcoholic

接頭 (non) **nonalcoholic** *n* 非アルコール性の ▶ Other causes of chronic hepatitis include alcoholic hepatitis and **nonalcoholic** steatohepatitis. 慢性肝炎のその他の原因としてアルコール性肝炎や非アルコール性脂肪肝がある．

alienable

接頭 (in) **inalienable** *adj* 奪うことのできない，不可分の ▶ The people have the **inalienable** right to choose their public officials and to dismiss them. 人々は，彼らの公務員を選びまた解任する，不可分の権利を有する．

接頭 (un) **unalienable** *adj* (権利などの) 譲渡移転ができない

aligned

接頭 (non) **nonaligned** *adj* 非同盟の，中立の

接頭 (un) **unaligned** *adj*

❶一列になっていない，整列されていない

❷提携していない，加盟していない

❸非同盟の

alignment

接頭 (non) **nonalignment** *n* 非同盟，中立

allocate

接頭 (de) **deallocate** *v* 割り当てを解除する ▶ However, if one process allocates a packet buffer and puts a pointer to it in another process' work queue, how does the first process know when to **deallocate** the buffer? しかし，一つの工程がパケットバッファを割り当て，もう一つの工程の作業待ち行列においてそれにポインタを入れるならば，最初の工程はどのようにしてそのバッファを取り消す時がわかるだろうか．

allow

接頭 (dis) **disallow** *v* 認めない，否認する ▶ The bank may show its first operating loss unless market rates decrease or an international agreement is reached to **disallow** subsidy financing. その銀行は，市場金利が低下するか，また補助金融資を否認するような国際的同意が得られるようなことなどがない限り，初めての営業損失を出すことになろう．

alloyed

接頭 (un) **unalloyed** *adj* 不純物のない ▶ **unalloyed** metal 純粋な金属

alterable

接頭 (in) **inalterable** *adj* 不変の，変えられない ▶ By implications, the right of the first-born is an **inalterable** right. 意味合いからいって，長子の権利は，不変な権利である．

接頭 (un) **unalterable** *adj* 変更できない ▶ "Black" refers to a preset and **unalterable** color value.「ブラック」とは，プリセットされて変更できないカラー値のことをいう．

alterableness

接頭 (in) **inalterableness** *n* 不変性

alterably

接頭 (in) **inalterably** *ad* 変えられずに，不変に

ambiguous

接頭 (un) **unambiguous** *adj*

❶ 曖昧でない, 誤解の余地がない ▶ Make sure the wording is exactly right: **unambiguous,** precise, and standard. 言葉遣いが適切であること, すなわち, 曖昧ではなく, 精確で, そして標準的であることに意を用いること. ▶ The distinction between living and nonliving is arbitrary, though useful and **unambiguous** when transitional states are not under consideration. 物質を生物と非生物に区分するのは恣意的にできるが, 遷移状態が考慮外であるときには有用で曖昧さはなくなる.

❷ 明白な ▶ make target selection easy and **unambiguous** 目標を容易にかつ明白に選択できるようにする ▶ That constituted **unambiguous** insider trading. それは明らかにインサイダー取引であった. ▶ Not only do these signals provide **unambiguous** feedback, . . . これらの信号は明白なフィードバックを送るだけでなく, ….

ambiguously

接頭 (un) **unambiguously** *ad* 曖昧でなく, 明白に, 明らかに ▶ Solid models **unambiguously** define geometry and volume. ソリッドモデルは, 外形および容量を明白に [曖昧ではなく] 表す. ▶ Such gifts are routine in Chinese business, but they **unambiguously** violated Google policy. 中国のビジネス慣習では, そのような贈答は一般的であるが, グーグルのポリシーには明らかに [曖昧ではなく] 違反していた.

ambiguousness

接頭 (un) **unambiguousness** *n* 明瞭さ, 曖昧でないこと ▶ The engineer seeks a writing style that will produce clarity and **unambiguousness.** エンジニアは, 曖昧でなく明瞭さを持たせることができる書き方を求める.

American

接頭 (un) **un-American** *adj* 非アメリカ的な ▶ **un-American**

activities 非米活動

animate

[接頭] (in) **inanimate** *adj*

❶活気のない，生気のない ▸ **inanimate** conversation 活気のない会話

❷生命のない ▸ relating to the lack of consciousness of **inanimate** things 生命のないものの意識の欠如に関して

animately

[接頭] (in) **inanimately** *ad* 活気のない状態で，生気のない状態で

animateness

[接頭] (in) **inanimateness** *n* 生命をもっていないこと

announced

[接頭] (un) **unannounced** *adj* 予告のない ▸ The last **unannounced** visit was in October 2006. 最後の予告なしの訪問は2006年の10月であった.

answerable

[接頭] (un) **unanswerable** *adj* 答えることのできない ▸ **unanswerable** logic 反論できない論法

answered

[接頭] (un) **unanswered** *adj* 答えのない ▸ The big question — what causes autism? — remains **unanswered**. 自閉症の原因は何かという重要な問題には答えがないままである.

anticipated

[接頭] (un) **unanticipated** *adj*

❶予期しない ▸ This is difficult to do if **unanticipated** relationships develop between the model and the analytical data. モデルと分析データの間に予期しない関連性が発生した場合，これを実行するのは難しい.

❷予測できない ▸ previously unforeseen and **unanticipated** questions 前もって予測することができない思いがけない問題 ▸ No social purpose would be served by encouraging everyone who suffers an investment loss because of an **unanticipated** change in market conditions to sue. 市場状況が予測できなかったために投資で損失を出したすべての人を勇気づけるのが社会目的にかなうとはいえない. ▶ The previous fear-fest came about because Lehman's bankruptcy disrupted financial markets in **unanticipated** ways. 先の不安が生じたのは, リーマンの破産が予測できなかった形で金融市場を混乱させたためであった.

apologetic

接頭 (un) **unapologetic** *adj*

❶申し訳なさそうでない ▶ Ward is **unapologetic**. ウォード氏は, 申し訳なさそうな様子はない.

❷謝罪する気がない ▶ If a Japanese smiles while apologizing, an American may think the Japanese is not only **unapologetic** but mocking him. 日本人が微笑を浮かべながら謝罪すると, 本気で謝罪する気がないどころか, 相手をばかにしているとアメリカ人は受け取るかもしれません.

appealable

接頭 (un) **unappealable** *adj* 訴えられない

appear

接頭 (dis) **disappear** *v*

❶消える, 消えてなくなる ▶ One reason that aged bourbon is so expensive is that it **disappears** over time. 年代もののバーボンが非常に高価な理由の一つは, 時が過ぎると共にそれが少なくなることである. ▶ While digital transmission is becoming more and more popular, it will be decades before analog transmission **disappears**. デジタル送信がますます広く使用されるようになる一方で, ここ何十年かのうちにアナログ送信は姿を消すであろう.

❷消失する ▶ Since the contents of RAM **disappear** when you shut off the computer, . . . コンピューターを切ったときRAMの内容は消失するので, …

appearance

接頭 (dis) **disappearance** *n*

❶ 消失, 紛失 ► They eagerly unearthed fossils of now-extinct plants, insects, and small animals and pondered their **disappearance** from the earth. 彼らは現在は絶滅した植物, 昆虫, 小動物の化石を熱心に掘り起こし, 地球から消滅した謎について熟考した.

❷ 失踪

接頭 (non) **nonappearance** *n* 不出頭, 不出廷 ► The principals' **nonappearance** concluded the hearing. 当事者の不出頭により聴聞会は終結した.

appetizing

接頭 (un) **unappetizing** *adj* 食欲をそそらない ► The fact is that everything is becoming increasingly **unappetizing**. 事実, 何もかも食べたいと思えなくなってきている.

applicable

接頭 (in) **inapplicable** *adj* 適用できない ► The rule is **inapplicable** to this case. この規則はこの場合には適用しない.

appreciable

接頭 (in) **inappreciable** *adj* 感知できないくらいの, ごくわずかの ► **inappreciable** temperature fluctuations 温度のごくわずかな変動

appreciably

接頭 (in) **inappreciably** *ad* 取るに足らないように

appreciated

接頭 (un) **unappreciated** *adj* 感謝されない ► Such achievements always seem to be **unappreciated**. この種の業績はいつも高く評価されないように見える. ► He is an **unappreciated** genius. 彼は世に認められない天才だ.

appreciative

接頭 (in) **inappreciative** *adj* 鑑賞する目がない ► He is **inappreciative** of her efforts. 彼は彼女の努力を理解しない.

apprehensible

接頭 (in) **inapprehensible** *adj* 理解できない

apprehension

接頭 (in) **inapprehension** *n* 理解(力)のないこと

apprehensive

接頭 (in) **inapprehensive** *adj* 理解力のない

approachable

接頭 (un) **unapproachable** *adj* 近寄りがたい ► The crippled reactor was **unapproachable**. 活動を停止した原子炉には近づくことができなかった. ► Even top executives say she was virtually **unapproachable**, preferring to communicate by e-mail and quarterly videocast. 重役も彼女には近寄りがたいので, 電子メールや四半期に一度のビデオ会議で連絡をしていると言っている.

appropriate

接頭 (in) **inappropriate** *adj* 不適当な, 不似合いな, 不適切な, まずい ► **Inappropriate** use of the PC usually involves tasks that are too trivial to use a computer for. PC のまずい使い方の多くは, コンピューターで行うまでもない仕事をしようとするといったものだ.

appropriated

接頭 (un) **unappropriated** *adj* 特定の目的に当てられていない

appropriately

接頭 (in) **inappropriately** *ad* 不適当に, 不適切に ► **inappropriately** change the subject of a conversation 会話の主題を不適切にすり替える

appropriateness

接頭 (in) **inappropriateness** *n* 不適当な行為 ► It was a comment of astounding **inappropriateness**. それは, 驚愕する不適切なコメントであった.

approval

接頭 (dis) **disapproval** *n* 不承知，不認可，不賛成 ▶ The chorus of **disapproval** also extends to such organizations as British Telecom and Sweden's Televerket. ブリティッシュ・テレコムやスウェーデンのテレフェルケットなどの管理体制に対して，非難の声が，また一斉に広がっている.

approve

接頭 (dis) **disapprove** *v* 否認する，承知しない ▶ The head mistress **disapproved** of her behavior. 女性校長は，彼女の行動を良しとしなかった.

apt

接頭 (in) **inapt** *adj*

❶ 不適切な

❷ 未熟な ▶ be **inapt** at dancing 踊りが下手である

aptitude

接頭 (in) **inaptitude** *n* 不向き，不適当

aqueous

接頭 (non) **nonaqueous** *adj* 水を含まない ▶ Various other processes are under development which use **nonaqueous** solvents to reduce the volume of nonfuel material handled. 水を含まない溶剤を使用するその他のさまざまな方法が，処理する非燃料材料の容積を減らすために開発されてきた.

arcing

接頭 (non) **nonarcing** *adj* アークの出ない ▶ Sparking may be reduced by using mercury switches and **nonarcing** relays. 火花の発生は，水銀スイッチおよび無電弧[アークの出ない]リレーを用いて，減少させることができる.

arguable

接頭 (in) **inarguable** *adj* 議論の余地のない ▶ It is **inarguable** that his theory is true. 彼の理論が真実であることは議論の余地がない.

接頭 (un) **unarguable** *adj* 議論の余地のない ▶ Breakthroughs

in communication are always brought about by saying **unarguable** things and never by blaming. コミュニケーションのブレークスルーは，非難することではなく，議論の余地のないことを言うことで常にもたらされます.

arguably

接頭 (in) **inarguably** *ad* 議論の余地なく ▸ His theory is **inarguably** true. 彼の理論は議論の余地がなく正しい.

argued

接頭 (ill) **ill-argued** *adj* 十分に検討されていない

arm

接尾 (less) **armless** *adj*

❶腕のない ▸ He is an **armless** musician. 彼は腕のない音楽家です.

❷無防備な

接頭 (dis) **disarm** *v*

❶無力化する ▸ further **disarm** the virus by removing part of another gene 他の遺伝子の一部を取り除くことでそのウイルスをさらに無力化する

❷武装解除する

接頭 (dis) **disarming** *adj* 敵意を除く

接頭 (dis) **disarmingly** *ad* 敵意を除くように ▸ One additional problem with the superficial pattern of agreement is that it makes the Japanese seem **disarmingly** polite. 表面的な同意のパターンにさらに加わる問題点の一つは，それによって相手が敵意を除くほど日本人が丁重に見えることである.

armament

接頭 (dis) **disarmament** *n* 武装解除，軍備縮小 ▸ Arms control and **disarmament** are our ideals. 軍備制限と軍縮は，われわれの理想である. ▸ Both the Belgian and the Dutch cabinets have said progress in **disarmament** negotiations between the U.S. and the Soviet Union would affect their decisions on missile deployment. ベルギーとオランダの両内閣は，米ソ両

国の軍縮交渉の進展がミサイル配備に関する自分たちの決定に影響するのだと言った.

armed

接頭 (un) **unarmed** *adj* 非武装の, 武装しないで ▶ It takes courage to go **unarmed**. 武装せずに行くことは勇気のいることです. ▶ This is my firm belief as someone who has worked **unarmed** in some very dangerous places for the last 20 years. これは, 非常に危険な場所で20年も武装せず働いてきた者としての私の確固たる信念です.

arrange

接頭 (dis) **disarrange** *v* 混乱させる

arranged

接頭 (ill) **ill-arranged** *adj* 並びの悪い

array

接頭 (dis) **disarray** *n* 乱雑, 混乱 ▶ On January 10, something happened that amplified the growing sense of **disarray** at ABC Co. 1月10日, ABC社において増大しつつあった混乱感をさらに拡げる何かが生起した.

art

接尾 (less) **artless** *adj*

❶無技巧の, 未熟な, 下手な

❷自然な, ありのままの ▶ She is an **artless** girl. あの娘はわざとらしいところがない.

articulate

接頭 (in) **inarticulate** *adj*

❶はっきり言えない ▶ He becomes **inarticulate** when he is angry. 彼は怒ると (興奮して) 口がきけなくなる.

❷言葉にならない ▶ utter a loud **inarticulate** cry as of pain or excitement 痛みや興奮を表す大きくて意味不明の叫びを上げる

articulately

接頭 (in) **inarticulately** *ad* 言葉 [発音] が不明瞭に ▶ He

mumbled **inarticulately** about the accident that had just taken his wife's life. 彼は妻の命を奪ったばかりの事故に関して不明瞭な声でつぶやいた.

articulateness

接頭 (in) **inarticulateness** *n* 言葉[発音]が不明瞭なこと ▶ He was confused, painfully conscious of his **inarticulateness**. 彼は混乱していて, 言葉が不明瞭なことを痛々しいほど意識していた.

artificial

接頭 (in) **inartificial** *adj* 非芸術的な, 拙劣な, 自然な

artistic

接頭 (in) **inartistic** *adj* 非芸術的な, 芸術のわからない ▶ Every step took him nearer to London and further from his sober **inartistic** life. 一歩一歩, 彼はロンドンに近づき, それとともに, 落ち着いた非芸術的な生活から遠ざかっていった.

artistically

接頭 (in) **inartistically** *ad* 非芸術的に, 無趣味に

ashamed

接頭 (un) **unashamed** *adj* 恥を知らない, あからさまな

ashamedly

接頭 (un) **unashamedly** *ad* 恥ずかしくもなく ▶ He **unashamedly** abandoned the project when he realized he would not gain from it. 彼は, 得るものが何もないと分かったとき, 平気でそのプロジェクトを放棄した.

asked

接頭 (un) **unasked** *adj* 質問されていない ▶ You've probably learned that this question is best left **unasked**, particularly of people you don't know very well. 多分, あなたはこの件は, 特によく知らない人には質問しないのが最善であることを学んだでしょう.

asked-for

接頭 (un) **unasked-for** *adj* 求められていない

assailable

接頭 (un) **unassailable** *adj* 攻撃できない，論破できない ► a hereditary religious leader whose position had been considered **unassailable**. その地位は不滅だと思われていた世襲の宗教指導者

assemble

接頭 (dis) **disassemble** *v*

❶ 分解する ► Periodically **disassemble** the cylinder for cleaning, inspection, and lubrication. シリンダーは定期的に分解し，洗浄，検査，および潤滑を行ってください．

❷〈コンピューター言語などを〉変換する

assembly

接頭 (dis) **disassembly** *n* 分解 ► Most modern dairy equipment is designed to be cleaned in place, without **disassembly**. ほとんどの近代的酪農機器は，分解しないでそのまま清掃できるように設計されている．

assertive

接頭 (non) **nonassertive** *adj* 非断定的な ► She was quiet and **nonassertive** as she took control. 支配権を握ったとき，彼女は静かで，独断的ではなかった．

接頭 (un) **unassertive** *adj* 自己主張しない

assign

接頭 (un) **unassign** *v* 割り当てない ► Thirty-five permutations were assigned to control characters, and the remainder were **unassigned**. 35の順列が文字制御に割り当てられたが，その残りは割り当てられなかった．

assisted

接頭 (un) **unassisted** *adj* 助けを受けない ► He is unable to walk **unassisted**. 彼は，助けなしでは歩けない．

associate

接頭 (dis) **dissociate** *v* 関係を絶つ，分離する ► The proteins from large and small subunits of organelle and cytoplasmic ribosomes have been **dissociated** and separated by weight and charge. 細胞器官の大小副組織および細胞質のリボゾームで生成されるタンパク質は，重量（垂直軸）と電荷（横軸）によって分離されてきた．

association

接頭（dis） **dissociation** *n* 分離，解離 ► The **dissociation** of the transport of signaling and information exchanged between users favors the construction of a specific signaling network. ユーザー間で交換される信号と情報の伝達を分離すれば特殊信号ネットワークの構成に好都合である．

assorted

接頭（ill） **ill-assorted** *adj*

❶ 選別されていない，寄せ集めの ► It was an **ill-assorted** crew on the ship. それは，寄せ集めの船上乗組員であった．

❷ 不釣り合いな ► They are an **ill-assorted** couple. 彼らは釣り合わないカップルだ．

assuming

接頭（un） **unassuming** *adj*

❶ 気取らない

❷ 目立たない ► The revolution began with an **unassuming** element known as iridium. その大変革は，あまり目立たないイリジウムという元素を使って始まった．

atomize

接頭（un） **unatomize** *v* 噴霧しない ► Delivering liquid at a rate in excess of a nozzle's maximum capacity results in some or all of the liquid's being ejected **unatomized**. ノズルの最大能力を超える速度で射出する液体は，霧状になっていない［噴霧しない］まま射出されることもある．

attached

接頭（un） **unattached** *adj*

❶ 取りつけない ► It may be desirable to leave the actuating pins and lower disk **unattached** to each other. 作動ピンと下部

ディスクは，おそらくお互いに連結させないままにしておくほうが望ましい．
❷無所属の

attainable

接頭 (un) **unattainable** *adj* 〈目標などが〉 達成できない ► The reliability routinely exercised by the computer is **unattainable** by man. コンピューターがあたりまえのように果たしている信頼性は，人間には達成できない．

attendance

接頭 (non) **nonattendance** *n* 不参加， 欠席 ► The school district worked on ways to lower the rate of **nonattendance** among its students. その学区では，生徒の欠席率を低下させる方法に取り組んだ．

attended

接頭 (ill) **ill-attended** *adj* 参加者が少ない
接頭 (un) **unattended** *adj* 付き添われていない，放置された ► Do not leave equipment operating **unattended**. 作動中の機器を無人のまま放置しないこと． ► In auto-answer mode, the modem will automatically answer an incoming call, allowing you to leave it **unattended**. モデムは，自動応答モードに設定されていると入ってくる呼び出しに自動的に応答し，モデムを放置しておくことが可能になる． ► The stored speed associated with the user profiles is only significant when operating in **unattended** auto-answer mode. 無人の自動応答モードで使用する場合には，ユーザープロファイルに関連づけられて保存された速度のみが意味を持つことになる．

attention

接頭 (in) **inattention** *n* 不注意，油断 ► **inattention** to one's own person 自分の人柄に気を配らないこと ► Slight **inattention** can cause a great disaster. ちょっとした油断が，大惨事につながる恐れがある．

attentive

[接頭] (in) **inattentive** *adj* 不注意な，怠慢な ► She's **inattentive** to her guests. 彼女は，客に対して怠慢な態度を示した.

attentively

[接頭] (in) **inattentively** *ad* ぼんやりして，気を取られている態度で ► do something **inattentively** 何かをうわの空で行う

attentiveness

[接頭] (in) **inattentiveness** *n* 思慮のないこと ► Her **inattentiveness** caused an accident. 彼女は不注意で事故を起こした.

attractive

[接頭] (un) **unattractive** *adj* 魅力のない ► the technique of using color to emphasize the good features and to minimize the **unattractive** ones 特徴の部分は強調し，人目を引かない[魅力のない]部分を最小限に抑える色使いの技法 ► If interest rates remain unchanged, your return will be about 2% a year; if interest rates go up, this is an **unattractive** investment. 利率が変わらなければ，年間2％の利益が得られますが，逆に，利率が上がると魅力がないのは明らかです.

attributed

[接頭] (un) **unattributed** *adj* 作者不明の

audibility

[接頭] (in) **inaudibility** *n* 聴き取れないこと

audible

[接頭] (in) **inaudible** *adj*

❶ 聴き取れない ► The noise was so loud that his words were almost **inaudible**. 騒音で彼の言葉がよく聞き取れなかった.

❷ はっきりしない ► not necessarily **inaudible** but not heard 必ずしもはっきりしないわけではないが，聞こえない

audibleness

[接頭] (in) **inaudibleness** *adj* 耳によって知覚できない性質

audibly

[接頭] (in) **inaudibly** *ad* 聞こえないように ► She spoke in an

inaudibly low voice. 彼女は聞き取れないように低い声で話した.

auspicious

接頭 (in) **inauspicious** *adj* 縁起の悪い, 不運な, 不吉な ► an **inauspicious** dream 不吉な夢

auspiciously

接頭 (in) **inauspiciously** *ad* 不吉な方法で ► The New Year begins **inauspiciously**. 新年早々悪いことがある.

auspiciousness

接頭 (in) **inauspiciousness** *n* 悪い結果を暗示する特質

authorized

接頭 (un) **unauthorized** *adj*

❶ 認可されていない ► water that leaks from **unauthorized** connections 認められていない接続部からの漏水 ► The system alerts the IT department if workers miss an important update or start using their devices in an **unauthorized** way. もし作業者が自分の機器のスタートやアップデートを認められていない方法で行って失敗した場合は, システムはIT部門に警告を送ります.

❷ 資格のない ► A security feature prevents **unauthorized** personnel from changing the program. プログラム機密保護機能は, 資格のない人間がプログラムを変更するのを防ぐ.

automatic

接頭 (non) **nonautomatic** *adj* 非自動の ► They may be **non-automatic**, with the caller requesting a number through the switchboard operator, or automatic, with the caller dialing a number. それらは, 呼び出し側が交換手を経由して番号を要求する非自動式または呼び出し側が番号をダイアルする自動式である.

availability

接頭 (un) **unavailability** *n* 入手不可能 ► the **unavailability** of certain supplementary services ある種の補足的サービスの利

用不可能性

available

[接頭] (un) **unavailable** *adj*

❶ 利用できない ► More work than necessary might be performed if pruning information obtained from one processor is **unavailable** to the other processor. あるプロセッサーから得た選定データが他のプロセッサーに利用できない場合，必要以上の作業がなされる場合がある．

❷ 使用できない ► . . . where conventional sources of electrical energy are either **unavailable** or too expensive 電気エネルギーの在来の発生装置が使用不能かまたは高価につきすぎる場合，…

❸ 入手できない ► Dried, frozen, or unsweetened tinned fruit may be acceptable alternatives to fresh fruit if that is **unavailable**. 生の果物が入手できない場合，乾燥，冷凍，あるいは甘みを付けていない缶詰の果物を，それらの代替品として受け入れてもよい．

availing

[接頭] (un) **unavailing** *adj* 効果のない ► an **unavailing** attempt 無駄な試み

avoidable

[接頭] (un) **unavoidable** *adj* 不可避の ► The aerodynamic penalties imposed by such a canopy are regarded as **unavoidable** if the pilot is to be able to perform his air superiority mission effectively. そのようなキャノピによって生じる空気力学上の不利益は，パイロットが自分の制空任務を効果的に実施できるようにするには不可避と見なされる．

avoidably

[接頭] (un) **unavoidably** *ad* やむを得ず ► Carbon steel is an iron-carbon alloy with small amounts of other elements (either intentionally added or **unavoidably** present). 炭素鋼は，他の微量物質（故意に追加されたかまたは不可避的に［やむを得ず］

存在する）が含まれた鉄と炭素の合金である.

aware

接頭 (un) **unaware** *adj* 気が付かない ► As it turned out, the design team was **unaware** of some serious quality control problems. 結局, 設計班は品質管理に関するいくつかの重要な問題に気づかなかった. ► You cannot count the rate accurately unless the patient is **unaware** of what you are doing. 回数を正確に計測するには, 患者はあなたが行っていることに気が付いてはいけません.

B

back

[接尾] (less) **backless** *adj* 背中のない ▸ a **backless** dress 背が大きく開いたドレス

backed

[接頭] (un) **unbacked** *adj* 支持[支援]されていない ▸ an **unbacked** dielectric layer portion 誘電体層の裏打ちされていない部分

balance

[接頭] (im) **imbalance** *n* 不均衡, アンバランス ▸ The higher the level of the signals and the degree of transitory conditions or degree of **imbalance** is, the larger is the perturbing effect. 信号のレベルと, 一時的条件の程度または不均衡の程度が高いほど, 摂動効果も大きい. ▸ The trade **imbalances** with the emerging countries are growing larger. 新興国との貿易不均衡は, 大きく開きつつある.

[接頭] (un) **unbalance** *v* …の均衡[バランス]を失わせる ▸ A little tilt would **unbalance** the load. わずかな傾きも, 荷重のバランスを失わせる.

—— *n* 不均衡

balanced

[接頭] (ill) **ill-balanced** *adj* バランスの悪い

[接頭] (im) **imbalanced** *adj* アンバランスな ▸ an **imbalanced** gait アンバランスな歩行

[接頭] (un) **unbalanced** *adj* 釣り合いのとれていない ▸ The **unbalanced** load caused a severe accident. 荷重が不釣り合いなために大きな事故が発生した. ▸ This is equivalent to an **unbalanced** two-phase motor, and the resultant rotating field causes the motor to start. これは, 釣り合いのとれていない2相モーターと同じであり, それによって生じる回転磁界に

よってモーターは始動する.

ban

接頭 (un) **unban** *v* 〈規制などを〉撤廃する

band

接頭 (dis) **disband** *v* 解散する, 解体する ▸ Dell's independently managed communications group **disbanded** last year after its smartphone flopped. デルの下で独立して管理されていた通信グループは, そのスマートフォン事業に失敗した後の昨年に解散した.

接頭 (dis) **disbandment** *n* 解散, 解体 ▸ He also said that he would hold an extraordinary party congress today to seek approval for the **disbandment** of the party. 彼は, 今日, 臨時党大会を開催し, 党解散の承認を求めるつもりであると述べた.

bank

接頭 (non) **nonbank** *n* ノンバンク ▸ a **nonbank** financial company ノンバンクの金融会社

bar

接頭 (dis) **disbar** *v* 〈資格などを〉剥奪する

接頭 (un) **unbar** *v* (戸などの) かんぬきを外す

base

接頭 (a) **abase** *v* 〈地位や評判などを〉落とす, 下げる ▸ He was willing to **abase** himself before the paramount British power. 彼は, 強大な英国の権力を前にして, 自らの地位を下げたかった.

接頭 (de) **debase** *v* 〈価値などを〉低下させる ▸ You must not **debase** yourself by such behavior. そのような行動をして品位を落としてはいけない.

接尾 (less) **baseless** *adj*

❶ 根拠のない ▸ This is a **baseless** rumor. これは根拠のない噂である.

❷ 基礎のない

basement

接頭 (a) **abasement** *n* 〈地位や評判などを〉落とすこと, 失墜すること

接頭 (de) **debasement** *n* 〈価値などの〉低下 ▶ I think it will continue to benefit from the global **debasement** of currencies. それは, この全世界規模での通貨切り下げの利点であり続けると私は考える.

bearable

接頭 (un) **unbearable** *adj* 耐えられない ▶ When the neurosis develops to its fullest extent, the patient harbors an **unbearable** dislike for himself. 神経症が行きつくところまで行くと, 患者はもはや自分自身にも耐え難い嫌悪感を抱くことになるだろう.

bearably

接頭 (un) **unbearably** *ad* 耐えられないほど ▶ Actually passing messages between processes by copying them would be **unbearably** slow. コピーすることによってプロセス間でメッセージを実際に通過させるのは耐えられないほど遅いであろう.

beard

接尾 (less) **beardless** *adj*

❶ひげのない ▶ **beardless** barley のぎのない麦

❷青二才の ▶ a **beardless** youth 青二才の若者

beatable

接頭 (un) **unbeatable** *adj*

❶打ち負かすことのできない ▶ an **unbeatable** ball team 無敵の野球チーム

❷ (何にも負けない) 強力な ▶ Microsoft will be buying a fast-growing, well-positioned global asset with an **unbeatable** brand. マイクロソフトは強力なブランド名を持ち急成長していて有利な地位にある世界的資産を購入しようとしている.

❸ (何にも負けない) 決定的な ▶ Use fruit or vegetable kabobs for an **unbeatable** flavor addition to your brunch or dinner menu. あなたのブランチまたはディナーメニューに決定的な趣向を付け加えるには，果物または野菜のケバブを使用することだ.

beaten

接頭 (un) **unbeaten** *adj* 負けたことのない

beautiful

接頭 (un) **unbeautiful** *adj* 美しくない ► Making teen-agers wear those totally **unbeautiful** and stuffy uniforms can only be called violence. ティーンエージャーにむさ苦しい[美しくない]だけの制服を着せるなんて，暴力以外の何物でもない.

becoming

接頭 (un) **unbecoming** *adj* 似合わない

behaved

接頭 (ill) **ill-behaved** *adj* 行儀の悪い ► an **ill-behaved** student 品行の悪い学生 ► But now you know him, and you know, too, how **ill-behaved** he is! しかし今では，君は彼を知っていて，おまけに彼がどんなに行儀が悪いかも知っている.

behavior

接頭 (mis) **misbehavior** *n* 不正行為 ► So widespread and grave was the **misbehavior** that the FDA barred the company from importing 30 different drug products into the U.S. 不正行為が非常に広汎で重大であったので，FDA はその薬剤を米国に輸入する30の各種製剤から除外した.

belief

接頭 (dis) **disbelief** *n* 不信，疑惑 ► Confronting the unthinkable, Smith went gradually from **disbelief** to doubt to desperation. とても考えられそうもないことに出くわして，スミス氏は不信から疑惑，絶望へとだんだん考えを変えていった.

believable

接頭 (un) **unbelievable** *adj* 信じられない ► **Unbelievable** as it may seem, people have been known to immerse plugged-in electric coffee pots in water for washing. 信じられないようなことだが，プラグイン・タイプの電気コーヒーポットを洗おうとして流しに浸す人がいる.

believably

接頭 (un) **unbelievably** *ad* 信じられないほど ▶ The program's requirements are **unbelievably** minimal. このプログラムには信じられないくらい要求事項が少ない.

believe

接頭 (dis) **disbelieve** *v* 信用しない ▶ It is better to believe than to **disbelieve**. 信じないよりも信じるほうがよい.

believer

接頭 (non) **nonbeliever** *n* 無信心な人，非信者

接頭 (un) **unbeliever** *n* 信じない人，無信仰の人 ▶ Though most Japanese are **unbelievers**, they are fond of festivals and enjoy giving and receiving presents. 大体，日本人は無信仰であるが，お祭り好きなうえに贈り物が好きである.

believing

接頭 (non) **nonbelieving** *adj* 無信心な

接頭 (un) **unbelieving** *adj* 信じない，信じようとしない ▶ Even **unbelieving** people will appreciate his preaching. 不信心な人でも彼の説教の素晴らしさを認めるでしょう.

belt

接頭 (un) **unbelt** *v* ベルトを外す ▶ **Unbelt** your trousers. ズボンのベルトを外しなさい.

bend

接頭 (un) **unbend** *v* 〈曲がったものを〉 真っ直ぐにする ▶ **unbend** the bar 棒を伸ばす

bending

接頭 (un) **unbending** *adj* 曲がらない ▶ He took an **unbending** attitude. 彼は確固とした態度をとった.

bias(s)ed

接頭 (un) **unbias(s)ed** *adj*

❶片寄らない ▸ The proposal should always appear to be presenting an **unbiased** assessment of the company's skill and ability. 提案は，いつもその会社の技術および能力についての正直な[片寄らない]姿を表しているように見えなければならない．

❷偏見のない ▸ Television commercials can hardly be considered a source of **unbiased** information. テレビコマーシャルは偏見のない情報の源とはどうしても考えられない．

bidden

接頭 (un) **unbidden** *adj* 招かれない，不意の ▸ an **unbidden** guest 招かれざる客

bind

接頭 (un) **unbind** *adj* 〈結ばれたものを〉解く，ほぐす

binding

接頭 (non) **nonbinding** *adj* 拘束力のない ▸ a **nonbinding** goal 努力目標

blame

接尾 (less) **blameless** *adj* 責められることのない ▸ On the other hand, this doesn't mean that the young people are entirely **blameless**. その一方で，これは若者がまったく非難に値しないことを意味するのではない．

blemished

接頭 (un) **unblemished** *adj* 傷のない，汚点のない ▸ He has an **unblemished** employment record. 彼の職歴には汚点がない．

blinking

接頭 (un) **unblinking** *adj* 瞬きしない ▸ He stood **unblinking** and accepted a sentence of a year. 彼は瞬きもせずに立ちすくみ，1年の判決を受け入れた．

block

接頭 (un) **unblock** *v* 妨げない ▸ They try to think through the pluses and minuses of **unblocking** the full show. 一方で彼らは，

番組全体をブロックしない[妨げない]利点と欠点を十分に考えようとしている.

blood

[接尾] (less) **bloodless** *adj*

❶無血の ► a **bloodless** victory 無血の勝利

❷血の気のない, 青白い ► He tried to speak with **bloodless** lips. 彼は血の気のない唇で話そうとした.

❸冷淡な ► He may have struck some as a **bloodless** technocrat. 彼は冷淡なテクノクラートであるという印象を誰かに与えたかもしれない.

blushing

[接頭] (un) **unblushing** *adj* 恥を知らない ► an **unblushing** apologist for fascism ファシズムに対する恥知らずな擁護者

bode

[接頭] (ill) **ill-boding** *adj* 不吉な

body

[接尾] (less) **bodiless** *adj*

❶胴体のない

❷実体のない ► **bodiless** ghosts 実体のない幽霊

bolt

[接頭] (un) **unbolt** *v* ボルトを緩める ► **Unbolt** the ladder that allows the pirates to climb on to your ship before you set sail. 出航する前に, 海賊が乗船できる梯子のボルトを緩めておけば, 更に安全です.

border

[接尾] (less) **borderless** *adj* 境界のない ► It is necessary to make the width of an ink absorber narrower when performing a **borderless** recording with an ink-jet recorder インクジェット記録装置において, 縁なし記録をする場合, インク吸収体の幅を小さくする必要がある.

born

[接頭] (un) **unborn** *adj* まだ生まれていない ► an **unborn** child

胎児

bottom

接尾 (less) **bottomless** *adj*

❶底がない

❷底なしの, 不可解な ► a **bottomless** mystery 計り知れない神秘

❸根拠のない

bound

接尾 (less) **boundless** *adj* 際限のない, 果てしない ► The **boundless** expanse of clouds was a new spectacle. 果てしなく広がる雲海は, 新たな壮観であった.

接頭 (un) **unbound** *adj*

❶無限である ► The complexity of configurations or shapes that can be treated is essentially **unbound**. 形態または形状の組合せは本質的に無限である.

❷縛られていない ► The doodling seemed to free his thinking so that he was **unbound** by mere logic. その落書きによって彼の思考は自由になり, 単なる論理から解放された[縛られていない]ように見えた.

bounded

接頭 (un) **unbounded** *adj* 拘束されない; 限界のない ► One of the most outstanding characteristics of all these settlers was their **unbounded** optimism. ここのすべての定住者の最も際だっている特徴の一つは, 限りない楽観主義であった.

bowed

接頭 (un) **unbowed** *adj*

❶曲がっていない ► He stood defiantly with **unbowed** back. 彼は背中を曲げずに反抗的に立っていた.

❷屈しない ► He fought on, broken-bladed but **unbowed**. 彼は刀は壊れているが, 屈しないで戦い続けた.

brain

接尾 (less) **brainless** *adj* 馬鹿な, 愚かしい ► She is beautiful

but **brainless**. 彼女は美人だが頭が悪い.

branded

接頭 (non) **nonbranded** *adj* ブランド品でない, 非ブランドの ▶ You'd think that in this era of generic-drug dominance, making the transition to a **nonbranded** version would be smooth. ジェネリック医薬品優位のこの時代には, ブランドでない製品への移行は円滑であると思うであろう.

branding

接頭 (mis) **misbranding** *n* 不当表示 ▶ Each of the three pleaded guilty to a misdemeanor count of **misbranding**. 3人はそれぞれ, 不当表示の軽罪の訴因について罪を認めた.

breakable

接頭 (un) **unbreakable** *adj* 壊すことのできない, 壊れにくい ▶ anything that makes a noise, and is lightweight and **unbreakable** ノイズを出し, 軽くて壊れにくいものであれば何でも.

breath

接尾 (less) **breathless** *adj*

❶息を切らした, 呼吸困難の ▶ The doctor will probably ask you to observe several specific things about the **breathless** patient. おそらく, 医師は呼吸困難の患者についていくつかの具体的な点を観察するよう要求するであろう.

❷緊迫した

接尾 (less) **breathlessness** *n* 呼吸困難, 呼吸不能 ▶ Various conditions cause **breathlessness**, which may be chronic or intermittent. 呼吸困難はさまざまな条件によって発症し, 慢性の場合と周期性の場合がある.

breed

接頭 (ill) **ill-bred** *v* 育ちの悪い, 粗野な ▶ He is **ill-bred**. 彼は行儀が悪い.

breeding

接頭 (ill) **ill-breeding** *n* 無作法, 粗野なこと, 育ちの悪さ

bridgeable

接頭 (un) **unbridgeable** *adj* 〈溝などが〉埋められない

bridle

接頭 (un) **unbridle** *v* 解放する

bridled

接頭 (un) **unbridled** *adj* 抑制のきかない ▶ He has an **unbridled** tongue. 彼は言いたいことを言う.

brim

接尾 (less) **brimless** *adj* つばのない ▶ a **brimless** hat 縁のない帽子

broken

接頭 (un) **unbroken** *adj*

❶壊れていない

❷途切れない，つながっている ▶ **unbroken** fine weather 連日の好天 ▶ The old Constitution stated that "the Empire of Japan shall be reigned over and governed by a line of Emperors **unbroken** for ages eternal." 旧憲法の条項では「大日本帝国は，万世一系の天皇これを統治す」となっている.

brush

接尾 (less) **brushless** *adj* 刷毛のない，ブラシレス ▶ Synchronized waveforms are used to power steppers, multiphase ac, or **brushless** dc motors. 同期波形は，パワーステッパー，多相交流，またはブラシレス直流モーターに使われる.

buckle

接頭 (un) **unbuckle** *v* バックルを外す ▶ **Unbuckle** your seat belt. シートベルトの留め金を外してください.

budgeted

接頭 (un) **unbudgeted** *adj* 予算に計上されていない ▶ They left $68.8 million of the $200 million **unbudgeted**. 2億ドルのうちの6880万ドルの財源を予算に計上しないでおいた.

burden

接頭 (dis) **disburden** *v* 〈負担などを〉取り除く

接頭 (un) **unburden** *v*

❶荷を下ろす ▶ **unburden** a horse 馬の荷を下ろす ▶ Many patients are able to **unburden** themselves of their misery simply by talking to a sympathetic listener. 耳を傾けてくれる人に話をするだけでも，自分たちの深い苦しみの荷を下ろし心を安らかにすることができる患者も多い.

❷負担をなくす ▶ **unburden** one's troubles 悩み事を打ち明ける

❸〈負担などを〉取り除く

burned

接頭 (un) **unburned** *adj* 燃焼していない ▶ In either event, large amounts of **unburned** fuel were sprayed into the jetpipe, creating a momentary build-up of fuel. どちらの事象においても，大量の燃焼していない燃料がジェットパイプに噴出されて瞬間的に燃料が集中する.

business

接頭 (non) **nonbusiness** *n* ビジネス以外 ▶ Follow-up comments and questions, directed at the topic or even at **nonbusiness** topics, might lead to further elaboration. そのトピックやビジネス以外のトピックに向けられた追加のコメントと質問があれば，結果としてさらに仕上げの完成度が高まるかもしれない.

button

接頭 (un) **unbutton** *v* ボタンを外す ▶ **Unbutton** the shirt. シャツのボタンを外してください.

buttoned

接頭 (un) **unbuttoned** *adj* ボタンが外れた ▶ If someone is walking along with her blouse **unbuttoned**, a friend can save her embarrassment by quietly saying, . . . 誰かがブラウスのボタンを閉め忘れて歩いていたら，友人の場合は……と静かな声で教えてあげれば相手は恥ずかしい思いをしないですむでしょう.

C

caffeinated

[接頭] (de) **decaffeinated** *adj* カフェインを取り除いた ▸ **decaffeinated** coffee カフェイン抜きのコーヒー

calculability

[接頭] (in) **incalculability** *n* 無数, 数え切れないこと

calculable

[接頭] (in) **incalculable** *adj*

❶ 数え切れない ▸ an **incalculable** loss 計り知れない損失

❷ 予想[予測]できない

❸ 不安定な

calibrated

[接頭] (un) **uncalibrated** *adj* 校正されていない ▸ It is seen that the standard deviation for the calibrated data is significantly smaller than that for the **uncalibrated** measurements. 校正データに対する標準偏差は, 未校正[校正されていない]測定値のものより著しく小さいことがわかった.

canny

[接頭] (un) **uncanny** *adj*

❶ 気味の悪い ▸ Stung by the petition and aware of Rifkin's **uncanny** success in obtaining court injunctions to back his demands, the USDA beat a hasty retreat. 訴訟に苦しめられ, またリフキン氏の要求を支持する裁判所の強制命令を得ることに成功するという異常な[気味の悪い]出来事を知って, USDA は慌てて撤退した.

❷ 信じられないほどの ▸ In the office she shows an **uncanny** ability to identify a winning plan and then pursue it doggedly. 事務所では, 信じられないほどの能力を発揮して勝てる計画を決め, それを根気強く追及している.

cap

接頭 (un) **uncap** *v* キャップを外す ▸ **uncap** a bottle of beer ビールの栓を開ける

capable

接頭 (in) **incapable** *adj*

❶ 能力がない, (〜が)できない ▸ The flux must be nonhygroscopic, that is, **incapable** of absorbing water. フラックスは非吸湿性, すなわち水分を吸わない性質でなければならない. ▸ **incapable** of being justified or explained 正当化できないか, 説明できない

❷ 無資格の, 無能の

capacitate

接頭 (in) **incapacitate** *v* (人から)〈能力や資格などを〉奪う ▸ disqualify a man from teaching — **incapacitate** a teacher 教員の資格を取り上げる

capacitation

接頭 (in) **incapacitation** *n* (人から)〈能力や資格などを〉奪うこと

capacity

接頭 (in) **incapacity** *n*

❶ 不適格, 〔法〕就労不能 ▸ **incapacity** for one's position 地位に不適任であること

❷ 無能 (力) ▸ It is the appearance of industrial **incapacity** that is to be avoided. それは避けるべき産業の無能力という状況を呈するまでになる.

capsulate

接頭 (non) **noncapsulated** *adj*

❶ カプセルになっていない[入っていない]

❷ 莢膜のない ▸ **Noncapsulated** mutant cells occasionally arise. 莢膜のない変種の細胞がときおり発生する.

carbonated

接頭 (non) **noncarbonated** *adj* 炭酸が入っていない ▸ Bottles of **noncarbonated** beverages can contain tap water added by unscrupulous vendors. 炭酸が入っていない飲料瓶には悪徳販売業者が水道水を混ぜていることがある.

carbonize

接頭 (de) **decarbonize** *v* 炭素を除去する

card

接頭 (dis) **discard** *v* 捨てる, 放棄する ► When you return to the shell, the information loaded in memory by BREAK will be **discarded**. シェルに戻った場合, BREAK によってメモリーにロードされた情報は捨てられる.

care

接尾 (less) **careless** *adj*

❶不注意な, 無頓着な ► The installation also faces a huge cleanup bill for its **careless** handling of waste in the past. その施設は, 過去に行なってきた廃棄物の無頓着な処理に対する巨額の浄化の請求書もつきつけられている.

❷無関心な ► a **careless** attitude 無関心な態度

❸心配事がない ► He is a **careless** bachelor. 彼は気楽な独身者だ.

接尾 (less) **carelessly** *ad*

❶ぞんざいに, 大雑把に ► Good paints will eventually dry no matter how **carelessly** they have been applied. 良い塗料はどんなにぞんざいに塗られたとしても結局は乾いてしまう. ► In the U.K., the British just slosh it **carelessly** into mugs and slurp it down. 英国では, 英国人はそれを無頓着にマグに注ぎ込んで音に構わずに飲み干す.

❷不注意に ► act or speak **carelessly** 不注意に言動する

接頭 (un) **uncared-for** *adj* 手入れされていない ► The garden is **uncared-for**. その庭は手入れしないままになっている.

cash

接尾 (less) **cashless** *adj* 現金が要らない ► Most of the current transition to a **cashless** society is being done voluntarily.

キャッシュレス社会への現在の移行の大部分は，自発的に起きている．

catalyze

[接頭]（un）**uncatalyze** *v*〈化学反応を〉触媒作用で促進させない

catalyzed

[接頭]（un）**uncatalyzed** *adj*〈化学反応を〉触媒作用で促進されない ▶ Since the rate of the **uncatalyzed** steam-carbon reaction for gasification of bituminous coals is prohibitively slow, the process is not competitive for the gasification of these types of coals. 軟炭をガス化するために行う，触媒作用を引き起こさない蒸気炭素反応の速度が極端に遅いので，このプロセスは，この種の石炭のガス化には競争力がない．

cause

[接尾]（less）**causeless** *adj* 理由のない，根拠のない ▶ **Causeless** consequences are impossible. 原因なき結果は不可能である．

cautious

[接頭]（in）**incautious** *adj* 軽率な，無謀な，不注意な ▶ An **incautious** step sent her headlong down the stairs. 足元を注意しなかったために彼女は階段をまっさかさまに落ちた．

[接頭]（un）**uncautious** *adj* 注意深くない，不用心な ▶ This is my **uncautious** prediction. これは私の慎重さを欠いた予測だ．

cautiously

[接頭]（in）**incautiously** *ad* 軽率に，浅い考えで ▶ One of the members of the committee **incautiously** admitted this. 委員の一人は，これを軽率にも認めた．

cautiousness

[接頭]（in）**incautiousness** *n* 軽率さ ▶ the **incautiousness** of character inherited from her father 父親から受け継がれる性格の軽率さ

ceasing

接頭 (un) **unceasing** *adj* 止まることのない ▸ Continuous action is **unceasing** action. 連続動作とは間断のない[止まることのない]動作のことである.

ceasingly

接頭 (un) **unceasingly** *ad* 止まることなく ▸ He has to practice his art **unceasingly**. 彼は, 絶えず技術を実践しなければならない.

cellular

接頭 (non) **noncellular** *adj* 非細胞の ▸ The ancestors of modern viruses were free-living **noncellular** predecessors of cellular organisms. 現在のウイルスの祖先は, 細胞生物の前身である自由生活性の非細胞生物であった.

centralization

接頭 (de) **decentralization** *n* 分権, 分散 ▸ Large urban areas may have more than one subsidiary long-distance office because of the physical limitations at a single office or to ensure service continuity with **decentralization**. 広い都市区域では, 単一の事業所での物理的な限界や分散化によってサービスの継続性を確保することが必要になった場合に, 複数の遠隔事業所が存在することがある.

centralize

接頭 (de) **decentralize** *v* 分権する, 分散する ▸ a **decentralized** school administration 分権化された学校経営

centralized

接頭 (de) **decentralized** *adj*

❶ 分権された ▸ The company is **decentralized**, so the product organizations have the facilities to conduct their own specialized activities. その会社は製品別組織に特有の活動を実施するための設備を持たせる目的で, 分権を基本原理として組織されている.

❷ 分散された ▸ The token bus protocol goes to considerable

lengths to do ring maintenance in a fully **decentralized** way. トークンパスプロトコルは，リング整備を完全な分散方式で実施するため，かなりの長さに及ぶことがある.

ceremonious

接頭 (un) **unceremonious** *adj*

❶ 儀式ばらない ▸ in an **unceremonious** manner 儀式ばらない方法で

❷ 無遠慮な，不意の ▸ **unceremonious** dismissal from office 役職からの突然の免職

❸ 無作法な

ceremoniously

接頭 (un) **unceremoniously** *ad* 無作法に，ぞんざいに ▸ I was thrown **unceremoniously** to the ground. 私はドサッと［無作法に］地面に放り投げられた.

certain

接頭 (un) **uncertain** *adj*

❶ 確信のない ▸ What about dealing with employees who are **uncertain** about their future and **uncertain** about you because they do not know you? あなたを知らないために，自分たちの将来も，またあなたに対しても確信がないような従業員をどのように扱ったらいいでしょう.

❷ 不確かな，不確実な ▸ However, the **uncertain** heat transfer rates mitigate the use of these sources. しかしながら，その伝熱率が不確実なので，これらの熱源を使用することは少ない. ▸ He sees big gains ahead even amid an **uncertain** economy. 彼は，不確かな経済状態の真っただ中ではあるが，大きな利益が目の前にあると考えている. ▸ This is very **uncertain** because it depends, to a large extent, on local topography, although certain types of storms produce vertical wind components. このことは，ある種類のストームによって風の垂直方向成分が発生するとはいえ，局地的な地形に大きく依存するため，非常に不確実である. ▸ Tarhouni remains **un-**

certain about what role he'll play in the new government. タルフーニ氏は，この新しい政府でどのような役割を担うのか不確かなままでいる．

certainly

接頭 (un) **uncertainly** *ad* 不確かに ► "Don't move," he said **uncertainly**.「動くな」と彼はあやふやな口調で言った．

certainty

接頭 (un) **uncertainty** *n*

❶ 不確実性 ► the **uncertainty** principle 不確定性原理 ► The difference is small compared with the other **uncertainties** and may be merely the result of experimental error. その他の不確実性と比較すると差異が小さく，実験誤差の結果にすぎないかもしれない． ► Because of the obvious **uncertainties** it is difficult to predict the wind forces on a given bridge section. 明らかな不確実性のため，橋のあるセクションに加わる風の力を予測するのは困難である．

❷ 不確実さ ► So, they all had some **uncertainty** about their positions. したがって，誰もが自分の地位にある程度の不確実さを持っていた． ► One day Moore bluntly asked him to resolve this financial **uncertainty**. ある日，ムーアはこの財政的な不確実さを明らかにするように彼にぶっきら棒に頼んだ．

chain

接頭 (un) **unchain** *v* 鎖から解放する ► **unchain** a dog 犬の鎖を外す

chained

接頭 (un) **unchained** *adj* 鎖を解かれた ► Users cannot choose and move an **unchained** circle but must individually move each vector in that circle. ユーザーは連鎖されていない円を選んだり移動したりすることはできず，その円の中で各ベクトルを個別に動かさなければならない．

challenged

接頭 (un) **unchallenged** *adj* 問題にされない, 尋問されない, 反対されない ► This is in sharp contrast with long-**unchallenged** conceptions of cognition and language development hypothesized by Piaget. これは, 長年検討されずにいたピアジェが唱えた認識と言語の発達の概念とは明らかに異なる.

change

接尾 (less) **changeless** *adj* 変化のない ► She showered her children with **changeless** love. 彼女は子供たちに変わらない愛情を注いだ.

changeable

接頭 (un) **unchangeable** *adj* 変えられない ► Because these instructions are permanent and **unchangeable**, they are often referred to as firmware. これらの命令は, 恒久的で変更できないものであるため, ファームウェアとしばしば呼ばれる.

changed

接頭 (un) **unchanged** *adj* 変わっていない ► The dielectric constant is essentially **unchanged**. 誘電率は本質的には不変である. ► Left **unchanged**, the current pattern of greenhouse gas emissions will result in higher global temperatures and rising sea levels. 温暖化ガス排出の現在のパターンが変わらずに放置されたら, 世界の温度は上がり, 海面の上昇が起きる. ► Scientists are scrutinizing the AIDS virus for any sections of its outer coat that remain **unchanged** during its rapid mutations. 科学者たちは, 急速な突然変異時に外胞子殻のどこかの部分に変化しないままのものがないか AIDS ウイルスを調べている.

changing

接頭 (un) **unchanging** *adj* 変わらない

chaperon

接頭 (un) **unchaperon** *v* 付き添わない ► It goes against the Philippine tradition for a young lady like you to be traveling

unchaperoned. あなたのような若い女性がお付きなしで旅行することはフィリピンの伝統に反します.

characteristic

接頭 (un) **uncharacteristic** *adj* 特徴のない ► a book **uncharacteristic** of its author 作者の特徴が出ていない本

characteristically

接頭 (un) **uncharacteristically** *ad* いつになく, 珍しく ► Durban and Andreessen are **uncharacteristically** mum when it comes to the juicy details of the negotiations. ダーバン氏とアンドリーセン氏は, 交渉の核心部分に来るといつになく寡黙である. ► Just two days earlier, he had faced an **uncharacteristically** hostile Spanish press corps. ほんの2日前に, 彼はいつになく敵意に満ちたスペインの報道陣を相手にしたところであった.

charge

接頭 (dis) **discharge** *v*

❶〈電気などを〉放出する, 放電する ► Touch the computer's power case to **discharge** any static electricity on your person or clothing. コンピューターの中の電源ケースに触れて, 身体や衣服が帯びているかもしれない静電気を放電させなさい.

❷〈液体や気体などを〉放出する ► When the contacts part, a blast valve is opened to **discharge** the high-pressure air. 接点が離れると, 送風弁が開き高圧空気を放出する.

❸〈病院などを〉退院する ► Patients are being **discharged** from hospital earlier, some to the care of the community nursing service but many to the care of their families. 患者は病院から早めに退院させられつつあり, 人によっては地域共同体による看護サービスの世話を受けるが, 多くはその家族の世話を受ける. ► While a patient with appendicitis was formerly hospitalized for ten days or two weeks, he is now **discharged** in a few days. かつては虫垂炎の患者は10日間ないし2週間入院させられたのに対して, 今では2, 3日で退院させられる.

❹〈人などを〉釈放する，解放する

❺解雇する ▸ **discharge** an employee from one's service 従業員を解雇する

charged

[接頭]（dis） **discharged** *adj* 放出された ▸ **Discharged** air does not become turbulent when it hits a wall. 放出された空気は壁に当たっても乱流にはならない．

[接頭]（un） **uncharged** *adj*

❶帯電していない ▸ **Uncharged** droplets continue to the receiving surface. 荷電していない小滴が印刷面にとどまっている．

❷告訴されていない

charging

[接頭]（dis） **discharging** *adj*

❶放電する ▸ The operating speed of MOS circuits is limited somewhat by capacitance charging and **discharging** times. MOS 回路の作動速度は，静電容量の充放電時間により若干制限される．

❷排出する ▸ Automatic charging and **discharging** equipment controlled by microprocessors provides tight quality control in the heating and forging operations. マイクロプロセッサー制御による自動装填および排出装置が，加熱および鍛造工程における高度の品質管理を行う．

charitable

[接頭]（un） **uncharitable** *adj* 思いやりのない ▸ an **uncharitable** and unsympathizing attitude 無慈悲で非同情的な態度

charted

[接頭]（un） **uncharted** *adj* 地図に載っていない，未踏の ▸ **uncharted** seas 地図に載っていない海

check

[接頭]（un） **uncheck** *v*

❶抑制しない

❷チェックしない，チェック（マーク）を外す ▶ **Uncheck** all checkboxes. すべてのチェックボックスのチェックを外してください.

checked

[接頭]（un） **unchecked** *adj*

❶チェックされていない，検査を受けていない ▶ We came through customs **unchecked**. 私たちは税関をフリーパスだった.

❷抑制されない ▶ Left **unchecked**, the onslaught would eventually kill cells. 抑制されないままに放置しておくと，猛攻撃によって細胞はついには殺されてしまう.

cheer

[接尾]（less） **cheerless** *adj* 元気のない，覇気のない，陰気な ▶ He looks **cheerless**. 彼はつまらなそうな顔をしている.

[接尾]（less） **cheerlessly** *ad* 元気なく ▶ He **cheerlessly** set out to do the task. 彼は元気なく仕事に着手した.

child

[接尾]（less） **childless** *adj* 子供のいない ▶ He is **childless**. 彼は子供がいない.

chin

[接尾]（less） **chinless** *adj* あごのない ▶ **chinless** faces and great eyes 顎のない顔と巨大な目

Christian

[接頭]（non） **non-Christian** *adj* 非キリスト教徒 ▶ a person who performs religious duties and ceremonies in a **non-Christian** religion 非キリスト教の宗教で宗教的義務と式典を行う人

christian

[接頭]（un） **unchristian** *adj* キリスト教徒にふさわしくない

citizen

[接頭]（non） **non-citizen** *n* 外国人 ▶ The **non-citizen** population of the city is growing larger every year. その都市の外国人

の人口は年々増加している.

civil

接頭 (un) **uncivil** *adj* 礼儀をわきまえない, 無作法な ► He is **uncivil** to his colleagues. 彼は同僚に対して無礼なことをする[言う].

civility

接頭 (in) **incivility** *n* 無作法, 無礼 ► I will not forgive his **incivility**. 私は彼の無礼を許さない.

civilized

接頭 (un) **uncivilized** *adj* 文明化されていない ► Many Caucasians see me as an **uncivilized** Asian girl because of my looks. 外見から私を文明化されていないアジアの少女とみている白人は多い.

civism

接頭 (in) **incivism** *n* 愛国心の欠如

clad

接頭 (un) **unclad** *adj* 外装を施していない, 裸の

claim

接頭 (dis) **disclaim** *v*

❶否定する, 否認する

❷権利を放棄する ► Patentee may **disclaim** anything included in patent by mistake. 特許権者は, 錯誤により特許に含まれた事柄を部分放棄することができる.

接頭 (dis) **disclaimer** *n*

❶否認, 拒否 ► make a **disclaimer** about . . . …について否認する

❷否認者 ► Behind these essentially marginal matters lay the fact that the railroads were then the largest and most powerful corporations in the nation and, their **disclaimers** notwithstanding, were really the arbiters of economic life. 当時鉄道は国家の最大かつ最強の組織であり, またそうではないと否認する者はいたけれど, 実際に経済生活を支配する存在であったとい

う事実が，これら本質的には重要度の低い事象の背後に存在していた.

❸免責条項，権利放棄書

接頭 (un) **unclaimed** *adj* 要求されていない，請求者がいない ▸ **unclaimed** baggage 持ち主不明の［引き取り手がいない］荷物

clasp

接頭 (un) **unclasp** *v* 留め金を外す ▸ **unclasp** a pocket-book 財布の留め金を外す

class

接尾 (less) **classless** *adj* 階級のない ▸ a **classless** society 階級差別のない社会

classified

接頭 (non) **nonclassified** *adj* 秘密扱いでない ▸ It was **nonclassified**. それは機密扱いになっていませんでした.

接頭 (un) **unclassified** *adj*

❶分類されていない ▸ the **unclassified** division 無差別級

❷〈情報などが〉機密扱いでない ▸ Each such report shall be submitted in **unclassified** form with a classified annex if necessary. 各報告書は，機密扱いとしない書式で，また添付書類は必要な場合は機密扱いとして提出することとする.

classify

接頭 (de) **declassify** *v* 機密を解除する ▸ He **declassified** documents damaging to him. 彼は自分に不利な機密文書を公開した.

clean

接頭 (un) **unclean** *adj* 不潔な，汚れた ▸ **unclean** meat 不浄の肉

cleanly

接頭 (un) **uncleanly** *adj* 不潔に，汚く

clear

接頭 (un) **unclear** *adj*

❶ 不明瞭な，曖昧な ▶ The specialist reading an article in a professional journal may puzzle out **unclear** writing because of the basic importance of the subject matter. 専門分野の定期刊行物の記事を読んでいる専門家は，題材が基本的に重要なものであるため，不明瞭に書かれたものについて解読することができる． ▶ Schmidt himself actively campaigned for Barack Obama, although it is **unclear** what will happen after he transitions from CEO to executive chairman in April. シュミット氏は，4月にCEOから会長に就任した後にどうなるか判らないが，バラク・オバマ氏のために精力的に選挙運動を行った．
❷ 不鮮明な ▶ The radiograph examination film is **unclear** and indiscernible. 放射線試験のフィルムは，不鮮明であり，識別できない．

clement

接頭 (in) **inclement** *n* 厳しい，無情な，冷酷な ▶ The weather is **inclement**. 天候は不良である．

clench

接頭 (un) **unclench** *v* 緩める ▶ I'm trying to **unclench** my teeth. 私は歯のくいしばりを緩めようと気を付けている．

cloak

接頭 (un) **uncloak** *v* 暴露する

clog

接頭 (un) **unclog** *v* 〈詰まったものなどを〉 除去する ▶ A broom straw can be used to **unclog** the fluid tip. ほうきのわらを使って流体の先端部の障害を除くことができる．

close

接頭 (dis) **disclose** *v*

❶ 明らかにする ▶ However, if such testing should **disclose** an attempt to defraud or gross nonconformance to this code, repair work shall be done at the contractor's expense. しかしながら，このような試験を実施した結果，欺瞞行為またはこのコードへの著しい不適合が明らかになった場合は，修理作

業は契約業者の費用負担によって行われるものとする. ► Tests for digestion of protein, starch, fats, cellulose, pectin, and many other insoluble materials **disclose** other physiological characteristics useful in classification. タンパク質, デンプン, 脂肪, 繊維素, ペクチンおよびその他の不溶性物質の消化諸試験により, 分類に役立つ生理学的特質が明らかになる.

❷〈秘密などを〉暴露する ► Last week Manglapus **disclosed** that he had initially asked for even more. 先週, マングラプス氏は, 彼が当初はさらに多くの金額を要求したことを暴露した.

接頭 (un) **unclose** *v*

❶〈窓やふたなどを〉開ける

❷明らかにする

closure

接頭 (dis) **disclosure** *n* 暴露, 公開, 明示, 発表 ► Each limited **disclosure** about Chernobyl was followed by a shrill TASS account of nuclear problems in the U.S. and Europe. タス通信社は, チェルノブイリについてささやかな事実を公開するたびに, 米国及びヨーロッパにおける核関連の問題についての辛らつな記事を付け加えた.

clothe

接頭 (un) **unclothe** *v*〈衣服などを〉脱がす, 裸にする ► **Unclothe** your heart of envy. あなたの嫉妬心を打ち明けなさい.

clothed

接頭 (un) **unclothed** *adj*〈衣服などが〉脱がされた ► a figure whose upper body is **unclothed** 上半身の衣服を脱いだ姿

cloud

接尾 (less) **cloudless** *adj* 晴れた, 雲のない ► a **cloudless** sky 晴れ渡った空

clouded

接頭 (un) **unclouded** *adj* 曇りのない ► A Buddhist patient may not wish to have analgesics, as Buddhists regard **unclouded** consciousness as crucial to the finest death. 仏教徒ははっきりと意識があることが素晴らしい死を迎えるには重要であると考えているので，仏教を信じている患者は鎮痛剤を望まない場合もある．

clue

接尾 (less) **clueless** *adj* 頭の悪い，無知な，愚かな ► They were oblivious to those facts and, at first, were also **clueless** about the import of what was going on. 彼らはそれらの事実について何も知らず，初めのころは進められていることの意味についても無知であった． ► "Those guys at Microsoft," he said. "What a bunch of **clueless** losers."「マイクロソフトの奴ら，揃いも揃ってなんという世間知らずの駄目な奴らなんだ」と彼は言った．

cluttered

接頭 (un) **uncluttered** *adj*

❶ 整然とした ► Here are some general guidelines for designing with fonts that will help you produce an **uncluttered**, easy-to-read publication. ここに示したのは，整然としていて読みやすい出版物を製作するのを支援するフォントによってデザインするためのいくつかの一般的な指針である．

❷ 混乱するようなところがない ► instruments with **uncluttered** and easily interpreted displays 不要[混乱するような]反射像がなく，容易に理解できる表示装置が付いている計器

coated

接頭 (un) **uncoated** *adj* 被覆されていない ► **Uncoated** tablets may be divided into smaller pieces with a knife or crushed between two spoons. 被覆されていない錠剤は，ナイフで小片に分けてもよいし，また二つのスプーンの間で砕いてもよい．

code

接頭 (de) **decode** *v* 暗号を解く，解読する ► Researchers have **decoded** the content of people's dreams using brain scanning technology. 研究者は，脳スキャニング技術を使用して，人の

夢の内容を解読した.

cognizance

接頭 (in) **incognizance** *n* 知識［認識］の不足 ▶ He demonstrates an **incognizance** of the dangers. 彼は，危険性の認識欠如を示している.

cognizant

接頭 (in) **incognizant** *adj* 認識しない ▶ They were unconscious or **incognizant** or something like that. 彼らは意識不明だったか，気付かないか，そのようだった.

coherence

接頭 (in) **incoherence** *n* 論理が一貫していないこと，支離滅裂 ▶ drink oneself into **incoherence** 飲んで支離滅裂になる

coherency

接頭 (in) **incoherency** *n* 非干渉性 ▶ improve **incoherency** 非干渉性を向上する

coherent

接頭 (in) **incoherent** *adj* 論理が一貫しない ▶ He is **incoherent**. 彼の言うことは筋が立たぬ.

接頭 (non) **noncoherent** *adj* 非干渉性の ▶ One approach that will not reduce the fixturing costs is the use of coherent and **noncoherent** fiber optics. 取付け費用を軽減するための一方法として，干渉性および非干渉性の光ファイバーを使用する方法がある.

coherently

接頭 (in) **incoherently** *ad* 支離滅裂に，めちゃくちゃに，矛盾して ▶ He talked **incoherently** when he drank too much. 飲み過ぎて，彼はつじつまの合わないことを言った.

coil

接頭 (un) **uncoil** *v* 〈巻かれたものなどを〉 解く ▶ **uncoil** a wire 巻き線を延ばす

collectable

接頭 (un) **uncollectable** *adj* 回収不可能な ▶ The money I

lent him became **uncollectable**. 彼に貸したお金が焦げ付いた.

collected

接頭（un） **uncollected** *adj* 回収されていない ► Callers will be able to send in photos to report crimes and complain about other problems, such as **uncollected** garbage. 写真を送って犯罪を報告したり，ゴミの未回収のような問題を報告することができます.

collectible

接頭（un） **uncollectible** *adj* 回収不可能な ► an **uncollectible** debt 不良債権

collegiate

接頭（non） **noncollegiate** *adj* 学寮制でない

collision

接頭（non） **noncollision** *n* 非衝突 ► This **noncollision** path is called the mean free path of the molecule. この非衝突行程は分子の平均自由行程と呼ばれている.

colonize

接頭（de） **decolonize** *v* 植民地状態を解く，独立させる

color

接尾（less） **colorless** *adj*

❶ 無色の ► Crystals are usually snow-white but may be **colorless** and more rarely brownish, reddish, or even black. 結晶は通常雪のように白いけれども，無色であったり，さらに珍しいこととして，茶色がかった色，赤茶色，または，黒色が混ざったりしていることがある.

❷ 生彩のない ► a **colorless** negative personality 生気のない消極的な性格

❸ 偏見のない，中立の

接頭（dis） **discolor** *v*

❶ 退色する ► Another problem is that some materials may **discolor** or turn cloudy during cobalt sterilization. 材料の中に

は，コバルト滅菌中に退色したり濁ったりするものもあるという問題もある．

❷変色する ► The tape withstands temperatures from − 40°F to +150°F and will not curl nor **discolor** with age. そのテープは − 40°F から + 150°F の温度に影響されず，時間がたってもねじれたり，変色したりすることはない．

coloration

接頭 (dis) **discoloration** *n* 変色，退色 ► an abnormal yellow **discoloration** of the skin 皮膚の異常な黄色の変色

colored

接頭 (dis) **discolored** *adj* 変色した ► When a mild flux is used, the foil pattern should be buffed if it has become **discolored** from aging. 柔らかいフラックスを使用するときは，フォイルパターンが時間の経過と共に変色してしまうならそれは磨かなければならない．

接頭 (un) **uncolored** *adj* 無着色の ► an **uncolored** description ありのままの記述

coloring

接頭 (dis) **discoloring** *n* 変色，退色 ► Peel and slice potatoes and put them into water to prevent **discoloring**. ジャガイモの皮をむいて薄切りにしたら，変色させないために水に浸ける．

combat

接頭 (non) **noncombat** *adj* 非戦闘の ► If he cannot tell the difference, how can he say he is only sending the Self-Defense Forces to **noncombat** zones? 彼にその違いがわからない場合，自衛隊を非戦闘地域にしか送っていないと言えるであろうか．

combatant

接頭 (non) **noncombatant** *n* 非戦闘員

combined

接頭 (un) **uncombined** *adj* 結合されない ► Oxygen-deficient

explosives also may yield **uncombined** hydrogen and carbon. 酸素が欠乏している爆薬によっても，非結合状態の水素と炭素が生じることがある.

combustibility

接頭 (in) **incombustibility** *n* 不燃性 ▸ Not only is it easily available, it also possesses such features as pliability, **incombustibility**, and durability. それは，簡単に手に入るだけでなく，柔軟性，不燃性，耐久性などの特徴を備えている.

combustible

接頭 (in) **incombustible** *adj* 不燃性の ▸ Tuesday is the day they collect **incombustible** garbage. 不燃ごみの回収は毎週火曜日です.

接頭 (non) **noncombustible** *adj* 非燃焼性の，不燃性の ▸ The detonation velocity is a characteristic constant for a combustible gas, not unlike the velocity of sound for a **noncombustible** gas. 爆ごう速度は，可燃性ガスの特性定数であり，不燃性ガスについては音速と異なるわけではない.

comfort

接頭 (dis) **discomfort** *n*

❶苦痛 ▸ Sit the patient up if the **discomfort** is severe. 苦痛が強い場合は患者の上体を起こす. ▸ Hull vibration can cause any of a number of problems for a ship, ranging from major crew **discomfort** to costly structural or machinery damage. 船体の震動は，乗組員に大きな苦痛を与えることを始めとして，船体や機関に費用のかかる損傷を与えるなど多くの問題の原因となる.

❷不快 ▸ **Discomfort** is rare: most patients need only a nonnarcotic analgesic, if anything. 不快なことはまれである．つまり患者は大抵，もしなにかあれば，非中毒性鎮痛薬がありさえすればよい.

comfortable

接頭 (un) **uncomfortable** *adj*

❶ 不快な，不快感を持つ ▸ The coming changes will be **uncomfortable** for some. これから起きる変化を不快に思う人もいる． ▸ He says he is **uncomfortable** exposing investors to “another 2008.” 彼は，「2008年の再来」に投資家を巻き込むことに不快感を感じると言っている． ▸ It was **uncomfortable** and I thought it looked kind of stupid, but I fit in better. それは，不快であったし，何かばかばかしくも思えたが，少しなじんでいた．

❷ 不快な，不快感を与える ▸ It is been many years since any female engineers asked her how to handle potentially **uncomfortable** gender-related situations. あやゆる女性技術者が彼女に性が関係する潜在的にやっかいな状況に対処する方法を尋ねてから何年も経っている．

❸ 賛成できない ▸ If you are **uncomfortable** with this idea as a mark of professional gravitas, I urge you to vote against him. 職業的な厳粛さの指標としてこの考え方に賛成できない場合は，彼に反対票を投じるよう要求する．

commensurability

接頭 (in) **incommensurability** *n* 非整合性 ▸ He pointed out the theories' **incommensurability**. 彼はそれらの理論の非整合性を指摘した．

commensurable

接頭 (in) **incommensurable** *adj* 同じ基準で測れない ▸ Heat and electricity are **incommensurable**. 熱と電気は単位を異にする．

commensurably

接頭 (in) **incommensurably** *ad* 比較できないほどに ▸ Those observations denote **incommensurably** higher mercury exposure than what is reported here. それらの観察結果は，ここでの報告とは比較できないほどに高い水銀露出時間を意味する．

commensurate

接頭 (in) **incommensurate** *adj* 不釣り合いな ▶ a reward **incommensurate** with his effort 彼の努力には不十分な報酬

commensurately

接頭 (in) **incommensurately** *ad* 不釣り合いな状態で，不相応な状態で ▶ There are values which are, almost **incommensurately,** more valuable than economic affluence. ほとんど不相応なほど，経済的豊かさよりも価値があるものがある．

commercial

接頭 (non) **noncommercial** *adj* 非営利の ▶ a **noncommercial** library, often supported with public funds, intended for use by the general public 多くの場合に公的資金により維持されており，一般市民による使用を目的とする非営利の図書館

接頭 (un) **uncommercial** *adj*

❶商業に関係のない

❷商道徳に反する ▶ A transaction is treated as **uncommercial** if a reasonable person in the company's position would not have entered into the transaction. 取引は，もしその会社の立場で適切な人物がその取引に含まれていなかった場合は，非商業道徳的取引とされる．

❸非営業的な

commission

接頭 (de) **decommission** *v* 使用を廃止する ▶ We should look at the country's most vulnerable, riskiest plants and set them on a rapid timeline for being **decommissioned**. 私たちは国内で最も脆弱かつ危険度の高い工場を調べ，操業を中止させるための緊急スケジュール表にその工場を設定する必要がある．

commissioned

接頭 (non) **noncommissioned** *adj* 委任状のない，任命されていない ▶ a **noncommissioned** officer who instructs recruits in military marching and discipline 新兵の軍隊行進と訓練を

指導する下士官

committal

接頭 (non) **noncommittal** *adj* 言質を与えない，曖昧な ▶ But in other areas he has remained **noncommittal**. しかし，その他の分野では，彼は漠然として曖昧なままだった.

committed

接頭 (un) **uncommitted** *adj*

❶〈特定の行事や行動などに〉拘束されない，自分の立場を決めていない ▶ remain **uncommitted** 中立的な立場を維持する

❷〈犯罪などが〉行われていない ▶ an **uncommitted** crime 未遂罪

commodious

接頭 (in) **incommodious** *adj* 狭苦しい，不便な，不都合な ▶ This is an **incommodious** house. これは使いにくい不便な家だ.

commodiousness

接頭 (in) **incommodiousness** *n* 不便で不快なこと ▶ He was proud of its **incommodiousness**. 彼は，その不便さを誇りに思った.

common

接頭 (un) **uncommon** *adj* 普通でない，　珍しい ▶ Overgrowths of dodecahedrons are not **uncommon**. 十二面体の過形成は珍しいことではない. ▶ It's not **uncommon** for them to confuse their humble opinions with arrogance. 彼らがその粗末な意見を横柄さと混同するのは珍しいことではない. ▶ Nausea is not **uncommon** and the patient is often reluctant to eat. 吐き気は珍しいことではなく，患者は食欲がない場合が多い.

commonly

接頭 (un) **uncommonly** *ad* まれに，非常に，目立って ▶ Not **uncommonly** in these circumstances they cling to a particular nurse or volunteer, insisting that she is their daughter, niece, or long-lost friend. これらの環境で，彼らが特定の看護師やボランティアに固執して，彼女が自分の娘，姪あるいは長年行方のわからなかった友人であると主張することもまれではない．

communicability

接頭 (in) **incommunicability** *n* 伝達できない状態

communicable

接頭 (in) **incommunicable** *adj* 伝達できない，口の重い ▸ Whatever we had missed, we possessed together the precious, the **incommunicable** past. たとえ何を逸していたとしても，我々は貴重な，言葉では言い表せない過去を共有した．

接頭 (non) **noncommunicable** *adj* 非伝染性の ▸ Today the top causes of death are **noncommunicable** diseases that result mostly from the way we live. 今日，上位を占める死亡原因の大部分はわれわれの生活様式に起因する非伝染性の疾病である．

communication

接頭 (mis) **miscommunication** *n* 誤った伝達，伝達不良 ▸ These anecdotes can occasionally lead to **miscommunication** and misunderstanding. これらの逸話は，ときに誤った伝達と誤解をもたらすことがある．

communicative

接頭 (in) **incommunicative** *adj* 無口な，口の重い ▸ He is a shy, **incommunicative** boy. 彼は恥ずかしがりで口数の少ない少年だ．

接頭 (un) **uncommunicative** *adj* 打ち解けない ▸ He is **uncommunicative**. 彼は打ち解けない人だ．

commutable

接頭 (in) **incommutable** *adj* 交換できない，不変の ▸ a rare **incommutable** skill 交換できないまれな技術

commutation

接頭 (in) **incommutation** *n* 逆方向通勤

commuter

接頭 (in) **incommuter** *n* 逆方向通勤者

compact

接頭 (in) **incompact** *adj* 締まりのない，散漫な

comparability

接頭 (in) **incomparability** *n* 無比，無類，比較できないこと

comparable

接頭 (in) **incomparable** *adj* 無類の，比較にならない，けた違いの，ずば抜けた ▶ That spectacle proved absolutely **incomparable** and overwhelming in its vastness of scale. その景観はスケールの大きさからして断然比べようのない，圧倒的なものだった.

comparably

接頭 (in) **incomparably** *ad* 比較にならないくらい，圧倒的に ▶ These skills are **incomparably** more important. これらの技能は圧倒的に重要である.

compatibility

接頭 (in) **incompatibility** *n*

❶ 不一致，不適合 ▶ More and more couples are getting divorced on grounds of **incompatibility**. 性格の不一致が理由で離婚する夫婦が増えている.

❷ 両立しがたいこと，両立不能性，非互換性 ▶ Such **incompatibility** would be inconvenient for users. この非互換性はユーザーにとっては不便である.

compatible

接頭 (in) **incompatible** *adj*

❶ 一致しない，矛盾した ▶ a theory **incompatible** with the facts 事実と矛盾する理論

❷ 互換性がない ▶ Furthermore, in some layers, multiple, **incompatible** standard protocols also exist. さらに，いくつかの

層では，多重で互換性のない標準プロトコルもある．

❸両立しない，相容れない

compensate

[接頭] (de) **decompensate** *v* 補償作用がはたらかなくなる

compensated

[接頭] (un) **uncompensated** *adj* 補償されていない

compete

[接頭] (non) **noncompete** *adj* 無競争［競合］の，競争しない，競業避止の，競争禁止の ▶ Some states, including California, have declared that **noncompete** clauses are unenforceable. カリフォルニア州などいくつかの州では，競業禁止条項は強制力をもたないと宣言している． ▶ Customer relationships and the **noncompete** agreement are being amortized over their estimated useful lives. 顧客関係及び競業避止義務は予想耐用期間にわたって償却される．

competence

[接頭] (in) **incompetence** *n* 無能 ▶ People attribute his failure to his **incompetence**. 世間では彼の失敗は無能のためだと言っている．

competency

[接頭] (in) **incompetency** *n* 不適格 ▶ Seen in that light, it was simple **incompetency**. この観点から考えると，これは単純な不適格の事例である．

competent

[接頭] (in) **incompetent** *adj*

❶不適格な ▶ an **incompetent** person 不適格者

❷無能な ▶ He was discharged from office as **incompetent**. 彼は無能として免職になった． ▶ The present mayor is an **incompetent** administrator. 現在の市長は行政的手腕に欠けている．

competitive

[接頭] (non) **noncompetitive** *adj*

❶競争のない，非競合の ▸ A **noncompetitive** inhibitor can bind to an enzyme with or without a substrate at different places at the same time. 非競合阻害剤は，基質の有無にかかわらず同時にさまざまな場所で酵素と結合することができる.

❷競争力のない ▸ Many U.S. companies are very poorly run and **noncompetitive** because corporate governance in the U.S. is, to a large extent, dysfunctional. 米国の企業統治が，大部分は機能不全であるので，多くの米国企業はあまり十分に運営されておらず，競争力がない.

接頭 (un) **uncompetitive** *adj* 競争力のない ▸ The Greeks borrowed and consumed recklessly, and got totally **uncompetitive** at making things and providing services like tourism. ギリシャ人は，無謀なほど借金をし消費した，その結果，製造業や観光のようなサービス産業で競争力を完全になくしてしまった. ▸ That made the use of carbon fiber **uncompetitive** until Toray came up with a breakthrough technology that slashed the time needed to mold parts. 東レが技術革新を起こし部品成型に必要な時間を短縮するまで，炭素繊維を使用すると競争力はなかった.

complaining

接頭 (un) **uncomplaining** *adj* 不平を言わない ▸ **uncomplaining** courage 不平を言わない勇気

complete

接頭 (in) **incomplete** *adj* 不完全な，不十分な，未完成の ▸ When examined, the welds revealed **incomplete** fusion defects at the outer interfaces. 調べてみたら，外側の界面の溶接に不完全な融解による欠陥が見つかった. ▸ an **incomplete** (intransitive [transitive]) verb 不完全(自［他］)動詞.

接頭 (un) **uncompleted** *adj* 未完成の ▸ An operation is said to be pending if it is left **uncompleted** while the calculator performs another operation having a higher priority. 計算機が優先順位が高い別な操作を実施している間，ある演算が完了しな

い状態で放置されていると，演算は保留状態にあると呼ばれる．

completely

接頭 (in) **incompletely** *ad* 不完全に ▶ words **incompletely** understood きちんと理解されていない言葉

completeness

接頭 (in) **incompleteness** *n*

❶ 〔数学〕 不完全性 ▶ The impact of the **incompleteness** theorem was not restricted to mathematics. 不完全性定理のインパクトは，数学の分野にとどまらない．

❷ 不完全さ，不備 ▶ The study was criticized for **incompleteness** of data, but it stimulated further research. 研究はデータの不備を批判されたが，更なる研究を刺激した．

compliance

接頭 (non) **noncompliance** *n* 不承諾 ▶ **noncompliance** with the United Nations resolutions 国連決議への不承諾

complicated

接頭 (un) **uncomplicated** *adj* 複雑でない ▶ I found the problem **uncomplicated**. 私は，その問題は複雑でないとわかった．

complimentary

接頭 (un) **uncomplimentary** *adj* 無礼な，礼を失した ▶ an **uncomplimentary** dress 礼儀を欠いている服

compose

接頭 (de) **decompose** *v*

❶ 分解する ▶ These particles begin to **decompose** and harmful bacteria flourish and multiply. これらの小片は分解し始め，有害なバクテリアが繁殖して倍増する． ▶ Kevlar, which **decomposes** only above 500℃, provides a fiber material which is as strong as steel at one-fifth its weight. ケブラーは，500℃を超える温度においてのみ分解し，鋼鉄の1/5の重量でありながらそれと同じ強度を持つ繊維材料である．

❷ 腐敗する ► some special methods to prevent the body from **decomposing** 死体が腐敗するのを防ぐための特別な方法

composition

接頭 (de) **decomposition** *n* 分解 ► In thermal cracking, free radicals are reaction intermediates, and the products are determined by their specific **decomposition** patterns. 熱分解においては，遊離基は反応中間体であり，その生成物は遊離基の特殊分解パターンによって決まる.

comprehending

接頭 (un) **uncomprehending** *adj* 理解力のない ► I tried to explain to her **uncomprehending** husband. 私は，彼女のものわかりの悪い夫に説明しようとした.

comprehensibility

接頭 (in) **incomprehensibility** *n* 不可解なこと ► **incomprehensibility** as a result of being much too technical 非常に技術的なので理解できないこと

comprehensible

接頭 (in) **incomprehensible** *adj*

❶ 理解できない ► They answered your question in **incomprehensible** gobbledygook. 彼らはわけのわからない言葉で，貴方の質問に答えた.

❷ わからない ► for some **incomprehensible** reason ある理解できない理由で

❸ 不可解な ► an **incomprehensible** talk 不可解な話

comprehensibly

接頭 (in) **incomprehensibly** *ad* 不可解なことに ► **Incomprehensibly**, the enemy stopped their attack. 不可解なことだが，敵は攻撃をやめた.

comprehension

接頭 (in) **incomprehension** *n* 理解できないこと，理解不能 ► his **incomprehension** of the consequences その結果についての彼の無理解

comprehensive

接頭 (in) **incomprehensive** *adj* 包括的でない，非包括的な，理解力のない

compress

接頭 (de) **decompress** *v*

❶減圧する，圧力を下げる ▶ **decompress** inside of the water storage tank 貯水タンク内を減圧する

❷圧縮データをもとに戻す ▶ **Decompress** data. データを展開［解凍］する

compressed

接頭 (un) **uncompressed** *adj* 圧縮されていない ▶ Figure 2 shows diagrammatically how the **uncompressed** code could be mapped on to a compressed code for both polarities of signal. これは図2のとおりで，信号の両方の極性について非圧縮コードをどのように圧縮コード上にマップできるかを図式的に示している．

compressibility

接頭 (in) **incompressibility** *n* 非圧縮性 ▶ **incompressibility** condition 非圧縮性条件

compressible

接頭 (in) **incompressible** *adj*

❶圧縮できない，非圧縮性の ▶ All liquids are relatively **incompressible.** 液体はすべて相対的に非圧縮性である．

❷圧縮できない ▶ the property of being **incompressible** 圧縮できない特性

compression

接頭 (de) **decompression** *n*

❶減圧 ▶ **decompression** zone geometry 減圧ゾーン形状部

❷圧縮解除 ▶ the reverse **decompression** operation 逆の圧縮解除する作業

compromise

接頭 (un) **uncompromised** *adj* 危険にさらされていない ▶

The U.S. military-defense system remains largely **uncompromised.** 米国の軍事防衛システムは，ほとんどまだ危険にさらされていない.

compromising

接頭 (un) **uncompromising** *adj*

❶強硬な，厳しい ▸ any political theory favoring immoderate and **uncompromising** policies 過度に強硬な政策を支持する政治理論

❷妥協しない ▸ Apple's devices are examples of **uncompromising** industrial design. アップル社の製品は，妥協しない工業製品の例である. ▸ While Gerstner gained a reputation for his quick temper, Palmisano honed a measured but **uncompromising** leadership style. ガースナー氏は短気で有名であったが，パルミサーノ氏は慎重ではあるが，妥協しないリーダーシップのスタイルを貫いていた.

computerized

接頭 (non) **noncomputerized** *adj* コンピューター化していない，自動化されていない ▸ An important hidden benefit is the greatly increased lead time a computerized manufacturer gains over a **noncomputerized** competitor. 隠れた重要な利点は，準備期間が大幅に延長されることであり，コンピューター化した製造業者は，コンピューター化していない競合相手をこの点で引き離している.

conceivable

接頭 (in) **inconceivable** *adj*

❶想像できない，想像もつかない ▸ an **inconceivable** occurrence 想像もできないような出来事

❷信じられない ▸ It's **inconceivable** that she should do something like that. 彼女がそんなことをするなんて信じられない.

conceivably

接頭 (in) **inconceivably** *ad* 想像もつかないほど，思いもよら

ぬほど ► **inconceivably** small 想像もつかないほど小さい

conceived

接頭 (ill) **ill-conceived** *adj*

❶〈準備・用意・計画などが〉不十分な ► an **ill-conceived** design 準備不足の計画 ► At first he had ascribed this failure to his **ill-conceived** attempt. 彼は，最初は，この失敗を自分の準備不足な試みのせいにした.

❷まずい発想の

conception

接頭 (mis) **misconception** *n* 誤った考え，誤解，思い違い ► Why should these **misconceptions** of China arise? 中国はなぜこう誤解されるのか.

concern

接頭 (un) **unconcern** *n* 無関心，無頓着 ► assume an attitude of **unconcern** 無関心を装う

concerned

接頭 (un) **unconcerned** *adj*

❶無関心な ► Yet for all his talk about connections and ties he sounds surprisingly **unconcerned** about wooing executives. 彼は縁故や人との結びつきについてよく話す割に会社の上層部の支持を得ることには至って無関心のようであった.

❷無関係な ► They were completely **unconcerned** about the meaning of Halloween. 彼らにとっては，ハロウィンがどういうものなのかまったく関係なかった.

concert

接頭 (dis) **disconcert** *v* 狼狽させる，　びっくりする ► I opened the book and was **disconcerted** to find from the numerous notes that I had already read it. 私は本を開き，すでに読んでいたことを示す多数のメモを見つけてびっくりした.

concinnity

接頭 (in) **inconcinnity** *n* 不一致，不調和

conclusive

接頭 (in) **inconclusive** *adj*

❶ 決定的でない ▶ **inconclusive** evidence 決定的でない証拠.

❷ 結論に達しない ▶ a trial that is invalid or **inconclusive** 無効あるいは結論の出ない裁判

conclusively

接頭 (in) **inconclusively** *ad* 結論に達しないで，物別れに終わって ▶ The long dispute ended **inconclusively**. 議論は水かけ論で終わった.

concordance

接頭 (dis) **discordance** *n* 不一致， 不調和 ▶ I believe the "beauty of **discordance**" is one of the bases of democracy. 私は，「不調和の美」は民主主義の根本原理の一つであると信じている.

concordant

接頭 (dis) **discordant** *adj*

❶ 一致しない

❷ 耳障りな，不和の

condensable

接頭 (in) **incondensable** *adj* 凝縮できない ▶ **incondensable** gas 不凝縮ガス

condense

接頭 (un) **uncondensed** *adj* 凝縮されていない ▶ The attenuation even from moderate rain far exceeds that from **uncondensed** water vapor or oxygen. 普通の雨から生じる減衰でさえ，凝縮されていない水蒸気または酸素から生じる減衰をはるかに上回る. ▶ Tropospheric attenuation can be attributed to two causes, molecular absorption by resonant excitation of **uncondensed** gases and ... 対流圏減衰は，二つの要因，すなわち，非凝縮ガスの共振励起による分子レベル吸収と，……によると考えられる.

condensible

[接頭] (in) **incondensible** *adj* 凝縮できない

condition

[接頭] (de) **decondition** *v*

❶体力を減退させる

❷条件反応を消去する

conditional

[接頭] (un) **unconditional** *adj* 無条件の ▶ **unconditional** surrender 無条件降伏

conditionally

[接頭] (un) **unconditionally** *ad* 無条件に ▶ But for a man to beat up a woman is **unconditionally** prohibited. しかし，男が女を殴ることは無条件に許されない． ▶ If the original is fed and copied **unconditionally,** the copy of the top original will be copied on the back of the paper when there is an odd number of originals. もとの原稿が供給され，無条件に複写されるなら，原稿の枚数が奇数の場合，最初の原稿はコピーされる紙の裏側に複写される． ▶ There is no way the old Constitution's claim that . . . could be maintained when Japan had surrendered **unconditionally**. 旧憲法の条項にある……を維持することは，日本が無条件降伏をした以上あり得ないことであった．

conditioned

[接頭] (ill) **ill-conditioned** *adj* 悪い状態の，たち［体調］の悪い

[接頭] (un) **unconditioned** *adj* 無条件の ▶ an **unconditioned** reflex 無条件反射

conducive

[接頭] (in) **inconducive** *adj* 役に立たない

conduct

[接頭] (mis) **misconduct** *n* 違反［不法］行為，非行 ▶ The company has denied **misconduct** and asserted that it has cooperated fully with the government. 同社は不法行為を否定しており，政府には十分に協力したと主張した．

conducting

[接頭] (non) **nonconducting** *adj* 導通していない，伝導しない，非伝導の ▸ With no signal voltage applied, the driver transistor is at zero gate voltage and is **nonconducting**. 信号電圧をかけない場合，ドライバートランジスターはゲート電圧がゼロになり，伝導しない． ▸ T2 becomes **nonconducting** and its collector voltage goes positive to full supply voltage. T2は非伝導になり，そのコレクター電圧は正の全供給電圧になる．

conductive

[接頭] (non) **nonconductive** *adj* 導通していない， 非電導の ▸ In approximately the middle of the sawtooth period, the damper tube becomes **nonconductive**. 鋸歯状パターン期間の中央付近でダンパーチューブが非導通状態になる． ▸ Most insoluble contaminants can be removed from hydraulic fluids, lubricating oils, and other **nonconductive** liquids. ほとんどの不溶性汚染物質は，油圧油，潤滑油，その他の非電導液から除去できる．

conductor

[接頭] (non) **nonconductor** *n* 不導体，絶縁体 ▸ All except a few diamonds are **nonconductors** of electricity. 数種のダイヤモンド以外はすべて，電気の不導体である． ▸ Diamond is a **nonconductor** and retains the induced charge, while the gangue minerals lose their charge to the grounded cylinders. ダイヤモンドは絶縁体で誘導電荷を保持するのに対して，脈石鉱物は接地されたシリンダーに電荷を放電する． ▸ The insulative value of these materials lies in the fact that the basic material is a **nonconductor**. これらの鉱物の絶縁値は，基本的材料が絶縁体であるという事実に基づく．

confidence

[接頭] (non) **nonconfidence** *n* 不信任 ▸ a **nonconfidence** area 非信頼領域 ▸ a vote of **nonconfidence** 不信任投票

confined

接頭 (un) **unconfined** *adj* 縛られていない, 無制限の ▶ a place where the air is **unconfined** 空気が閉ざされていない場所

confirm

接頭 (dis) **disconfirm** *v* 確認しない, 無効にする, 否定する ▶ We can neither confirm nor **disconfirm** whether there were lawyers involved. その件に弁護士が関係していたかどうか, 私たちは肯定も否定もできない.

confirmed

接頭 (un) **unconfirmed** *adj* 未確認の ▶ In an **unconfirmed** service, there is just a request and an indication. 未確認サービスでは, 要求と表示のみが存在する. ▶ This dramatic but **unconfirmed** account was seized on by the media. この劇的ではあるが未確認の報告はメディアによって入手された.

conformable

接頭 (un) **unconformable** *adj* 不整合の

conformance

接頭 (non) **nonconformance** *n* 違反 ▶ Should such testing disclose an attempt to defraud or gross **nonconformance** to this code, repair work shall be done at the contractor's expense. そのようなテストで詐欺行為やこの規約への大きな違反が明らかになった場合, 修理は契約者が自費で行うものとする.

conformity

接頭 (in) **inconformity** *n* 不同形, 不適合

接頭 (non) **nonconformity** *n* 不一致, 不調和, 矛盾, 非同調 ▶ the practice of **nonconformity** 不一致の習慣

接頭 (un) **unconformity** *n* 〈地層の〉不整合 (面)

congenial

接頭 (un) **uncongenial** *adj*

❶ 相性が合わない

❷ 適合しない, 好みに合わない ▶ **uncongenial** work いやな

仕事

congruence

[接頭] (in) **incongruence** *n* 不一致，不調和 ▶ This particular **incongruence** doomed an entire industrial culture. まさしくこの不調和が産業文化全体をだめにした．

congruent

[接頭] (in) **incongruent** *adj* 一致しない，調和しない ▶ This place is **incongruent** with our needs. この物件は私たちの求めるものと一致しない．

congruently

[接頭] (in) **incongruently** *ad* 調和しないで，一致しないで ▶ It may be repeated in essentially the same way **incongruently**. それは本質的に調和せず同様に繰り返されるかもしれない．

congruity

[接頭] (in) **incongruity** *n* 不適切，不一致，不適合 ▶ **incongruity** between what might be expected and what actually occurs 予想されることと実際に起こることとの間にある不適合

congruous

[接頭] (in) **incongruous** *adj* 釣り合わない，場違いの ▶ a joke that was **incongruous** in polite conversation 礼儀正しい会話と釣り合わない冗談

congruously

[接頭] (in) **incongruously** *ad* おかしなことに，一致しないで ▶ **Incongruously**, he spends several days a week at the library even though he doesn't like to read. おかしなことに，彼は読書が好きでないのに，週の何日かを図書館で過ごす．

conjunct

[接頭] (dis) **disjunct** *adj* 分離した

conjunction

[接頭] (dis) **disjunction** *n* 分離，分裂 ▶ I have been deeply concerned about the growing **disjunction** between legal education and the legal profession. 私は，法律教育と法律家との間で拡

大する乖離について深く憂慮してきた.

conjunctive

接頭 (dis) **disjunctive** *adj* 分離させる

connect

接頭 (dis) **disconnect** *v*

❶〈接続などを〉切る ▶ These locking connectors prevent the cables from being accidentally **disconnected**. これらのロッキングコネクターは, ケーブルが誤って接続を切られることを防いでいる.

❷〈電源などを〉切り離す ▶ The SCR energizes the solenoid, releasing the switch, and **disconnects** the appliance from the power source. SCR がソレノイドに電流を流してスイッチを開放し, 機器を電源から切り離す.

❸〈電源などを〉切る ▶ **Disconnect** the power cord, or shut off power at the fuse or circuit breaker panel. 電源コードを抜くか, またはフューズかサーキットブレーカーパネルで電源を切る.

connected

接頭 (dis) **disconnected** *adj*

❶〈接続や電源などが〉切られた ▶ The telephone is **disconnected**. 電話がつながらない.

❷一貫性のない

接頭 (un) **unconnected** *adj*

❶接続されていない ▶ With the second transistor **unconnected**, the first-stage output voltage at B swings from VCE up to Vcc. 2番目のトランジスターを接続しないままにしておくと, B の1段の出力は, VCE から Vcc まで振れる. ▶ It is essential you put a plug into an empty socket, even if it is **unconnected** to any equipment, or cover it with a specially designed safety socket cover. コンセントが器具に接続されていなくてもプラグを空のコンセントにつないでおくか, あるいは特別にデザインされた安全コンセントカバーを付けておく

ことは重要です.

❷ 無関係の ▸ If the hole is drilled too deep, it may break the core into two **unconnected** pieces. ドリルで穴を深く開け過ぎると，コアが割れてつながっていない二つの破片になることがある.

connection

接尾 (less) **connectionless** *adj* 無接続の ▸ Administration is minimal with **connectionless** service but more complex with connection-oriented service. 管理業務は，接続がないサービスでは最小限であるが，接続を重視したサービスでは複雑さが増す.

接頭 (dis) **disconnection** *n* 切断，分離 ▸ They initiate **disconnection** of the trouble area with circuit breakers. 彼らはまず遮断器で故障部分を分離することから始める.

conquerable

接頭 (un) **unconquerable** *adj* 征服できない，不屈の

conscionable

接頭 (un) **unconscionable** *adj* 非良心的な ▸ The court also rejected the plaintiff's contention that there was anything **unconscionable** about requiring the arbitration to take place in Guernsey. 法廷はまた，調停をガーンジー島で行うことを要求するということには非良心性があるという原告の主張を却下した.

conscious

接頭 (un) **unconscious** *adj*

❶ 無意識の ▸ Suitable organization of the keyboard allows a very high speed of operation owing to the development of **unconscious** automatics structures by the user. ユーザーが気づかない自動構造が開発されたのでキーボードが適切に配列してあると非常に速く操作することができる. ▸ As soon as I get this **unconscious** impulse to clap, I drop my hands in confusion. 思わず[無意識に]手を叩きたくなって，あわててひっ

こめることがある.

❷意識を失った ► An **unconscious** patient loses the swallowing reflex. 患者の意識がない場合, 嚥下反射は失われている.

❸意識していない, 気づいていない

consciously

接頭 (un) **unconsciously** *ad* 無意識のうちに ► Patients file the information away **unconsciously**. 患者は情報を無意識のうちに保管しておく. ► Sometimes the eulogy is so moving that one **unconsciously** feels like applauding it. 時として弔辞がとても感動的で, 思わず[無意識に]拍手をしたくなることもある.

consciousness

接頭 (un) **unconsciousness** *n* 意識がないこと ► If weakness, paralysis, or **unconsciousness** makes movement impossible, the pressure may be enough to cut off the blood supply to the underlying tissues. 力が入らなかったり, 痺れたり, 意識がなくなることで動けなくなった場合, 圧力は下になっている組織に送る血液を止めるほどになっている可能性があります.

consequent

接頭 (in) **inconsequent** *adj* 取るに足らない ► Your argument is illogical, inconsistent, and **inconsequent**. 君の言っていることは, 非論理的で, つじつまが合わず, かつ取るに足らない.

consequential

接頭 (in) **inconsequential** *adj* 重要でない, 不合理な, 論理的でない ► His work seems trivial and **inconsequential**. 彼の仕事は些細なことで重要ではないようだ.

consequentiality

接頭 (in) **inconsequentiality** *n* 取るに足らないこと

consequentialness

接頭 (in) **inconsequentialness** *n* 重要でないこと

consequently

[接頭] (in) **inconsequently** *ad* 結果を欠いて, 見当違いに ▶ She chattered ceaselessly and **inconsequently** until they reached the Green Gables Lane. 彼らがグリーンゲーブルス通りに着くまで, 彼女は絶え間なく, 見当違いにしゃべりまくった.

considerable

[接頭] (in) **inconsiderable** *adj* わずかな, 小さな, 取るに足らない ▶ His contribution to the project was not **inconsiderable**. その計画への彼の貢献は相当大きかった.

considerably

[接頭] (in) **inconsiderably** *ad* わずかに ▶ Football shirts for fans are **inconsiderably** expensive. ファン向けのフットボール・シャツの値段はあまり高くない.

considerate

[接頭] (in) **inconsiderate** *adj*

❶ 身勝手な, 軽率な ▶ We cannot have such **inconsiderate** behavior here. ここではそんな身勝手な行動は許されない.

❷ 思いやりのない, 不親切な ▶ He is **inconsiderate**. 彼は思いやりがない.

❸ 察しのない, 礼儀作法を心得ない ▶ a state of being stupid and **inconsiderate**. 愚かで礼儀作法を心得ないこと

considerately

[接頭] (in) **inconsiderately** *ad* 無分別に, 無神経に ▶ an unpleasant person who grabs things **inconsiderately** 無分別に物を手に入れる不快な人

considerateness

[接頭] (in) **inconsiderateness** *n* 無分別, 軽率さ, 思いやりのなさ ▶ a high degree of **inconsiderateness** 並外れた軽率さ

considered

[接頭] (ill) **ill-considered** *adj* 無分別な ▶ **ill-considered** remarks 無分別な発言

[接頭] (un) **unconsidered** *adj* 考慮されない, 取るに足らない,

軽率な，不用意な

consistency

接頭 (in) **inconsistency** *n* 食い違い，矛盾，つじつまの合わないこと ► Inspectors found **inconsistencies** in enforcement of agency policies. 調査官らは機関の方針の執行に食い違いを見つけた.

consistent

接頭 (in) **inconsistent** *adj*

❶ 両立しない，矛盾した ► Those methods often yield **inconsistent** results. これらの方法はしばしば矛盾する結果をもたらす.

❷ 一貫性がない ► The argument is **inconsistent**. 議論は終始一貫していない.

consistently

接頭 (in) **inconsistently** *ad* 両立しないで，一貫性がなく ► He acted **inconsistently** when he bought these stocks. 彼はこれらの株を買うとき，一貫性なく行動していた.

consolable

接頭 (in) **inconsolable** *adj* 慰められない ► Her father's grief was **inconsolable**. 彼女の父親の悲しみは慰めようもないほどだった.

接頭 (in) **inconsolably** *ad* 慰めようもなく，やるせなく ► She cried **inconsolably**. 彼女は慰めようもないほど泣いた.

consonance

接頭 (in) **inconsonance** *n* 不調和 ► Researchers have used a variety of approaches; this variety, in turn, has led to an **inconsonance** in the overall findings. 研究者は，さまざまなアプローチを用いたが，そのことが結果として全体的な研究成果の不一致につながった.

consonant

接頭 (in) **inconsonant** *adj* 調和しない，一致しない ► People have **inconsonant** views on this just as individuals have different tastes in clothes and food. 人によって衣服や食べ物の好みが違うように，このことについて個人の見解は一致しない．

conspicuous

接頭 (in) **inconspicuous** *adj* 目立たない，注意を引かない ▶ You should wear clothes that are subdued in color and **inconspicuous**. 君は色が地味で目立たない洋服を着るべきだ．

conspicuously

接頭 (in) **inconspicuously** *ad* 目立たないように，注意を引かないように

constancy

接頭 (in) **inconstancy** *n* 変わりやすいこと，〈友情，愛情などの〉移り気，浮気 ▶ We are all bewildered by her **inconstancy**. 彼女の移り気にはみんな当惑している．

constant

接頭 (in) **inconstant** *adj* 不安定な，変わりやすい，気まぐれな，浮気な，移り気な ▶ a woman whose words or deeds are **inconstant** and unsettled. 言動がうわついて定まらない女性

constantly

接頭 (in) **inconstantly** *ad* 変わりやすく ▶ In practice the personal responsibility system is functioning **inconstantly** in different parts of the country. 実際には，自己責任システムは国のさまざまな地域で機能しているが変動しやすい．

constitutional

接頭 (un) **unconstitutional** *adj* 憲法違反の，違憲の ▶ Visits by the Prime Minister and other public officials to Yasukuni Shrine are **unconstitutional**. 総理大臣や他の公務にある者が靖国神社を参拝することは憲法違反である． ▶ This law is a potential infringement of the right to privacy and other inherent rights, and suspicions are strong that it is **unconstitutional**. この法律は，プライバシー権やその他の固有の権利を侵害する恐れがあり，憲法違反の疑いが高い． ▶ Debate within the party came to focus on whether the SDF should be seen as constitutional or **unconstitutional**. 党内の議論は, 自衛隊を合憲と見るか違憲と見るかに焦点が当てられている. ► The government has just decided on the potentially **unconstitutional** course of sending the SDF to Iraq. 政府は憲法違反に当たる可能性のある自衛隊のイラクへの派遣を決めたばかりである.

constitutionality

接頭 (un) **unconstitutionality** *v* 違憲

constrained

接頭 (un) **unconstrained** *adj*

❶ 拘束されない ► features which may be optimum for a ship in an **unconstrained** system 拘束されていないシステムでの船舶には最適の機能

❷ 強制されない, 自発的な

constricted

接頭 (non) **nonconstricted** *adj* 収縮させていない, 非収縮の

► Gas tungsten-arc cutting with a **nonconstricted** arc can be used to sever nonferrous metals and stainless steel up to 1/2 in. thick. 非収縮アークを使用するガスタングステンアーク切断は, 厚さ1/2インチまでの非鉄金属およびステンレススチールを切断するのに使用できる.

construct

接頭 (de) **deconstruct** *v* 分解する, 解体する

constructed

接頭 (ill) **ill-constructed** *adj* 作りの悪い

接頭 (un) **unconstructed** *adj* 〈服が〉詰め物をしていない

consumable

接頭 (in) **inconsumable** *adj* 焼き尽くされない

接頭 (non) **nonconsumable** *adj*

❶ 無消費の, 非消耗性の ► Arc welding with consumable electrodes is more widely practiced than welding with **nonconsumable** electrodes. 消耗電極を使用するアーク溶接は, 非消耗性電極による溶接よりも広く実施されている. ► Desiccant dryers use **nonconsumable** chemicals to remove moisture from the air. 乾燥剤は空気中の湿気をとる非消耗性化学薬品である.

❷ 非溶性の ▶ **Nonconsumable** arc welding electrodes are not deposited as part of the weld metal. 非溶性のアーク溶接電極は溶接金属の一部として析出しない.

consumed

接頭 (un) **unconsumed** *adj* 消費されていない ▶ The rate of gas production is roughly proportional to the product of the surface area of the **unconsumed** propellant. ガス生成率は, 消費されていない噴射剤の表面積の積に比例する.

contact

接頭 (non) **noncontact** *n* 非接触(性)の ▶ The **noncontact** nature of the process is a clear advantage in coding small, fragile electronic components. 非接触性のこの方法は, 小さく, こわれやすい電子部品のコード化に明らかに有利である.

contacting

接頭 (non) **noncontacting** *adj* 非接触の ▶ These encoders consist of a glass scale and a **noncontacting** scanning head. これらのエンコーダーはガラスのスケールおよび非接触走査ヘッドからなる.

contaminate

接頭 (de) **decontaminate** *v* 汚染物質[毒ガスなど]を除去する ▶ The final separated fuel material must be very completely **decontaminated**. 最終的に分離された燃料物質は, まさしく完全に汚染物質を除去しておかなければならない.

contaminated

接頭 (un) **uncontaminated** *adj* 汚染されていない ▶ The discoloration sometimes observed with bright copper has been shown to be due to dissolved oxygen in **uncontaminated** dielectric coolants. 明るい色の銅で時々観察される変色は, 汚染されていない誘電冷却剤中に溶解した酸素によることが示さ

れた.

contamination

接頭 (de) **decontamination** *n* 汚染物質[毒ガスなど]の除去 ▶ Various other processes have been under development which use nonaqueous solvents to reduce the volume of nonfuel material handled and to achieve higher **decontamination** in fewer stages. 処理を要する非燃料物質を減少させ，より少ない工程で高度の汚染物質除去を行うために，非水ソルベントを使用するさまざまな別の処理方法が開発されつつある.

content

接頭 (dis) **discontent** *n* 不平，不満 ▶ I don't want them all trying to make the same thing because such breeds **discontent**. 彼らすべてが同じものを作ろうとするとそれが不満の種になるので，私はそれを望んではいない.

contented

接頭 (dis) **discontented** *adj* 不満のある

contentious

接頭 (non) **noncontentious** *adj* 争いを好まない

contestable

接頭 (in) **incontestable** *adj* (証拠などについて)議論の[疑う]余地のない，否定できない ▶ That is an **incontestable** truth. それは議論の余地のない真実だ.

接頭 (in) **incontestability** *n* 不可抗争，不可争性 ▶ He reviews case law in such fields as infringement of trademark **incontestability**. 彼は，商標不可争性の侵害のような領域の判例法を見直している.

contestably

接頭 (in) **incontestably** *ad* (証拠などについて)議論の[疑う]余地なく ▶ It was **incontestably** necessary to bring his children up in the same family. 彼の子供たちを同じ家族の中で育てることが，疑いなく必要だった.

contested

接頭 (un) **uncontested** *adj* 異論のない，競争のない ► an **uncontested** divorce 争いのない離婚

contiguous

接頭 (non) **noncontiguous** *adj* 非連続の ► Although there is no harm in **noncontiguous** files, a large number of widely scattered files can noticeably slow your computer's performance. ファイルが非連続であっても有害ではないが，ファイルが広い範囲に大量に散在していると使用するコンピューターの速度が大幅に低下する．

continence

接頭 (in) **incontinence** *n* 自制不可能なこと，失禁 ► **incontinence** of speech (tongue) 多弁

continent

接頭 (in) **incontinent** *adj* 自制心のない，失禁の ► If the patient becomes **incontinent**, his skin should be washed and dried carefully and a protective cream applied. 患者が失禁するようになったら，注意深く皮膚を洗浄して乾かし保護クリームを塗らなければなりません．

接頭 (in) **incontinently** *ad* 自制心を失って，失禁して ► pass water **incontinently** 尿を失禁する

continue

接頭 (dis) **discontinue** *v* 中止する，中断する ► That model of personal computer has been **discontinued**. あのモデルのパソコンは製造中止になっている． ► Although the reactor resumed operation in 1970, the project was **discontinued** in 1972, primarily for economic considerations. 原子炉の運転は1970年に再開されたが，そのプロジェクトは1972年に，主として経済的な理由から中止することになった．

continuity

接頭 (dis) **discontinuity** *n*

❶中止，中断

❷ 不連続性 ► A line of **discontinuity** existed in the northern Pacific Ocean. 不連続線は北部太平洋にあった. ► Unlike a conventional wing, it has no **discontinuity** from spoilers, flaps, or fairings to disturb the air flow over the wing. 従来型の翼と異なり, その翼はスポイラー, フラップ, フェアリングに翼の上の気流をかき乱す不連続性がない.

continuous

接頭 (dis) **discontinuous** *adj*

❶ 不連続の ► Visible increments of fatigue crack growth may be correlated with each load cycle or by **discontinuous** jumps after a certain number of cycles. 疲労亀裂成長の可視増分は, 各負荷周期, または, 一定回数の周期のあとの不連続跳びなどと関係があるという. ► Large-displacement analyses are often nonlinear. They include many **discontinuous** effects, making the mathematics extremely complicated. 大型変位分析は非線形であることが多い. それらには多くの不連続効果があり, その結果, 計算を極端に複雑にしている.

❷ 一貫性のない

continuously

接頭 (dis) **discontinuously** *ad* 不連続的に, 断続的に ► The feature is particularly valuable when examining the position of servodrive systems that move **discontinuously**. 断続的に作動するサーボドライブ装置の位置を調整するとき, この特長はとりわけ役に立つ.

contrastive

接頭 (non) **noncontrastive** *adj* 対照的でない ► The topic (initial position) can be contrastive or **noncontrastive**. トピック[初期位置]は, 対照的であっても, 対照的でなくてもよい.

contributory

接頭 (non) **noncontributory** *adj* 寄与しない, 無拠出の ► a **noncontributory** defined benefit pension plan 従業員無拠出[雇用者全額負担]の確定給付年金制度

control

[接頭] (de) **decontrol** *v* 統制を解除する

controllable

[接頭] (in) **incontrollable** *adj* 抑制できない，絶対の

[接頭] (un) **uncontrollable** *adj* 抑制［制御］できない ▶ The time range compensates for the **uncontrollable** differences in food shapes, starting temperatures, and regional preferences. 時間範囲は食品の形状，初期温度，場所の違いなどの制御できない違いを補正する．

controlled

[接頭] (un) **uncontrolled** *adj* 抑制されていない ▶ Fusion energy has already been tapped in an **uncontrolled** manner in the form of the hydrogen bomb. 核融合エネルギーは，すでに水素爆弾という形の抑制されていない方法で利用されている． ▶ **Uncontrolled** temperature changes can cause cracking. 制御されていない温度変化は，ひび割れの原因になることがある．

controversial

[接頭] (non) **noncontroversial** *adj* 論争の余地のない

[接頭] (un) **uncontroversial** *adj* 議論を引き起こさない ▶ Some tactics, like promotions on Google.com, are effective and **uncontroversial**. グーグルのサイト上での販売促進のような戦略は効果的であり議論を引き起こすことはない．

controvertible

[接頭] (in) **incontrovertible** *adj* 議論の余地のない ▶ **incontrovertible** proof of the defendant's innocence 被告の潔白性を証明する議論の余地がない証拠

controvertibly

[接頭] (in) **incontrovertibly** *ad* 明白で，証明が可能な ▶ **Incontrovertibly** material evidence is necessary to verify his testimony. 彼の証言を立証するには，証明可能な物的証拠が必要である．

convenience

接頭 (in) **inconvenience** *n*

❶ 不便(さ), 不都合 ▶ More than an **inconvenience,** flicker can cause serious problems for operators, including eye strain and headaches. 不便という以上に, ちらつきは眼精疲労や頭痛などオペレーターにとって深刻な問題を起こすことがある. ▶ There would be no end to it if I were to start listing all the **inconveniences** I suffer. 私がこうむっている不都合を, すべて数えだしたらきりがない.

❷ 迷惑 ▶ His absence put us to great **inconvenience**. 彼が欠席して非常に迷惑をこうむった.

—— *v* 不便を感じる, 迷惑をかける ▶ He was **inconvenienced** by this schedule. 彼はこのスケジュールでは都合が悪い.

convenient

接頭 (in) **inconvenient** *adj*

❶ 不便な ▶ Supercomputers are usually available only through time-sharing, which is expensive and **inconvenient**. スーパーコンピューターは, 高価で不便なタイムシェアリングでしか利用できないのが普通だ.

❷ 不都合な ▶ The person is not apologizing but is making the unfortunate or **inconvenient** information easier for the hearer to accept. その人は謝っているわけではなく, むしろ, 好ましくないあるいは不都合な情報を聞き手が受け入れやすいようにしている.

conveniently

接頭 (in) **inconveniently** *ad* 不便なことに ▶ **inconveniently** located [situated] 不便な場所にある

conventional

接頭 (non) **nonconventional** *adj* 非伝統的な ▶ While such processes have been called **nonconventional** or nontraditional, . . . そのような方法は, 非在来的もしくは非伝統的であると言われてきたが, ….

接頭 (un) **unconventional** *adj*

❶従来のものではない ▸ a decidedly **unconventional** second marriage 明らかに従来にはなかった再婚 ▸ a simple fail-safe system which requires no pitch locks, and yet uses no **unconventional** components. ピッチロックは必要としないが，従来のものではない部品も使っていない単純なフェールセーフシステム

❷慣習にとらわれない ▸ Its **unconventional** approaches have won accolades from insiders. その慣習にとらわれないやり方は部内者から賞賛をかち得ていた．

converted

接頭 (un) **unconverted** *adj* 未変換の ▸ The cells starve, and the **unconverted** sugar builds up in the bloodstream. 細胞が飢餓状態となり，変換されていない糖が血流内に増大する．

convertible

接頭 (in) **inconvertible** *adj* 交換できない ▸ Banks are allowed to issue **inconvertible** notes. 銀行は，不換紙幣の発行を認められる．

接頭 (non) **nonconvertible** *adj* 両替できない

convinced

接頭 (un) **unconvinced** *adj* 納得[確信]していない ▸ Some politicians and many citizens remain **unconvinced** that the $1.8 billion needed for the first segment will be money well spent. 何人かの政治家と多くの市民は，最初のセグメントに必要とされる18億ドルが有効に使用されるとはまだ納得[確信]していない．

convincing

接頭 (un) **unconvincing** *adj* 説得力のない ▸ We recently saw a television talk show about war and felt that the young people's comments were **unconvincing** and seemed unreal. 最近，テレビのトーク番組を見たが，若者のコメントは説得力がなく非現実的であるように感じた．

cooked

接頭 (un) **uncooked** *adj* (熱を使って) 調理していない ▸ Bacterial contamination of water is not serious unless severely contaminated water is used on crops which are eaten **uncooked**. バクテリアによる水の汚染は, 調理しないで食べる農作物に非常に汚れた水を使わない限り, 深刻なものではない.

cool

接頭 (un) **uncool** *adj* 野暮な, 時代遅れの

cooperation

接頭 (non) **noncooperation** *n* 非協力

cooperative

接頭 (un) **uncooperative** *adj* 非協力的な

coordinated

接頭 (in) **incoordinated** *adj* 失調性の ▸ **incoordinated** reflex 失調性反射

接頭 (un) **uncoordinated** *adj* うまく調整されていない, まとまりのない

coordination

接頭 (in) **incoordination** *n* 不均衡

cord

接尾 (less) **cordless** *adj* コードの付いていない, コードレスの ▸ For example, **cordless** mice have two infrared bulbs and a recharger cord socket rather than a cord. 例えば, コードレスマウスには赤外線電球2個と, コードの代わりの充電器コードソケット1個がついている.

cork

接頭 (un) **uncork** *v* 栓を抜く ▸ They wouldn't **uncork** the wine until they took control of the House. 彼らは, 議会の主導権を取るまではワインのコルクは抜かない.

corporate

接頭 (non) **noncorporate** *adj* 企業形態でない, 個人の ▸ Your **noncorporate** e-mail is up in the cloud already. あなた個

人の電子メールも，すでにクラウドの中にあるのです．

corporeal

[接頭] (in) **incorporeal** *adj* 実体のない，霊的な，無形の，無体の ► an **incorporeal** property called an intellectual property right 知的財産権という無体財産権

corporeity

[接頭] (in) **incorporeity** *n* 実体のないこと，無形

correct

[接頭] (in) **incorrect** *adj* 不正確な ► This terminology is **incorrect**. この用語の使い方は不正確だ．

correctable

[接頭] (un) **uncorrectable** *adj* 直すことのできない，絶望的な ► For example, if a new **uncorrectable** sector is found on your hard disk, you will be notified. 例えば，もしハードディスクに新しい修正できない[直すことのできない]セクターが見つかれば，警告が出されます．

corrected

[接頭] (un) **uncorrected** *adj* 訂正されていない

correctly

[接頭] (in) **incorrectly** *ad* 不正確に，間違って ► spell a word **incorrectly** 綴りを間違える

correlation

[接頭] (non) **noncorrelation** *n* 非相関性 ► The device only functions because of the **noncorrelation** of the echo and the remote signal. この装置は，エコーと遠隔信号に相関がないために機能するにすぎない． ► Taking the various assumptions of signal **noncorrelation** into consideration, ... 信号の非相関性に関するさまざまな仮定を考慮に入れると，….

corrigible

[接頭] (in) **incorrigible** *adj* 手に負えない，矯正できない ► He is an **incorrigible** fool to have begun dabbling in stocks again. 彼は，手に負えない馬鹿者で，また株に手を出している．

corroborated

接頭 (un) **uncorroborated** *adj* 確証されていない

corrosive

接頭 (non) **noncorrosive** *adj* 非腐食性 ▸ Methyl chloride, CH_3Cl, is a colorless, **noncorrosive**, liquefiable gas which condenses to a colorless liquid. 塩化メチル (CH_3Cl) は, 無色, 非腐食性の液化可能ガスで, 濃縮すると無色の液体になる. ▸ In soldering components there is a positive need for a flux which is **noncorrosive**. 部品のはんだ付けには非腐食性のフラックスが絶対的に必要である.

corrupted

接頭 (un) **uncorrupted** *adj* 冒されていない ▸ The preservation of the countryside is proof that beautiful emotions still exist **uncorrupted** by money-worship. 美しい田園が保たれていることは, 金銭至上主義に冒されていない証拠である.

corruptible

接頭 (in) **incorruptible** *adj*

❶ 堕落することのない, 清廉潔白な ▸ an **incorruptible** public official 清廉潔白な公務員

❷ 腐食しない, 溶解しない ▸ Gold is **incorruptible**. 金は腐食しない.

corruption

接頭 (in) **incorruption** *n* 清廉潔白

count

接尾 (less) **countless** *adj* 無数の ▸ The same can be said for **countless** others. その他の無数といえるほど多くのものについて同じことが言える.

接頭 (dis) **discount** *v* 値引きする

―― *n* 値引き, 割引 ▸ The proliferation of route awards, new airlines, and unrealistic fare **discounts** has contributed to the current financial crisis in the airline industry. 航路認定の急増, 航空会社の新規参入, 非現実的な料金割引が, 今日の航空業

界の財務危機を招いた.

countable

[接頭] (un) **uncountable** *adj* 数えられない

counted

[接頭] (un) **uncounted** *adj* 無数の; 数えられていない

couple

[接頭] (de) **decouple** *v* 結合を解く, 切り離す; 減結合する

[接頭] (un) **uncouple** *v* 切り離す, 連結を解く ► As entire trains are moved continuously over the hump, the cars are **uncoupled** at the crest. 列車全体がハンプ上を間断なく移動するとき, 各車両は頂上で切り離される.

coupling

[接頭] (de) **decoupling** *n* 減結合 ► Correct **decoupling** is obtained over at most 500 m. 正しい減結合は, せいぜい500メートルの範囲で得られる.

courage

[接頭] (dis) **discourage** *v*

❶ やる気をなくさせる ► Complex commands and bulky manuals will only **discourage** a manager's occasional involvement. 複雑な指令や膨大な手引書で監督者はたまたまのやる気が阻まれるだけだろう.

❷ 遅らせる, 抑止する ► **discourage** surface growth on cheese チーズの表面生成を抑制する

[接頭] (dis) **discouragement** *n* 落胆させること

[接頭] (dis) **discouraging** *adj* 落胆する, やる気をなくさせる ► However, the company does not want to be too **discouraging**. だからといって, 会社はやる気をなくさせ過ぎるのを望んではいない. ► Although this may be very **discouraging** to novice negotiators, a number of tactics can be tried. これはまだ新参の交渉者に対してはやる気を非常になくさせるかもしれないが, さまざまな手法を試してみることができる.

courteous

[接頭] (dis) **discourteous** *adj* 無礼な ▸ Meaningless presents given for no reason whatsoever are burdensome to the recipient and are **discourteous** rather than pleasing. 意味もなく贈るプレゼントは受け取る側にとって重荷になり，喜ばせるよりもむしろ失礼にあたる.

[接頭] (un) **uncourteous** *adj* 無作法な，失礼な，粗野な

courtesy

[接頭] (dis) **discourtesy** *n* 無礼，無作法

couth

[接頭] (un) **uncouth** *adj* 無礼な，粗野な

cover

[接頭] (un) **uncover** *v*

❶ カバーを外す ▸ The cylinder may have a single port **uncovered** by the main piston. シリンダーには，メインピストンによって開口する［カバーを外す］出入口が一つ付いていることがある. ▸ He **uncovered** it, washed it off, and put the cover back on. 彼は，そのカバーを外し，洗い流し，そしてカバーをもとに戻した. ▸ the time elapsing between the instant when the first observer **uncovered** his lantern and when he observed the light from the second 最初の観察者が彼のランタンのカバーを外した瞬間から2番目の観測者からの光を観察した時までに経過した時間

❷ 明らかにする ▸ A survey of the power transmission industry **uncovered** a variety of innovations aimed at meeting these goals. 送電業界を調査したところ，これらの目標に適合させるためのさまざまな改革がなされていることが明らかになった.

❸ 予測する ▸ It is devilishly difficult to predict the next category-creating product, much less **uncover** the next Google. 次のカテゴリーを創り出す商品を予測することは，グーグルの次に来るのは何かを予想するのと同じぐらい非常に難しい

ことである.

coverable

接頭 (un) **uncoverable** *adj* 明らかな

covered

接頭 (un) **uncovered** *adj*

❶ふたがとられた ▶ Place the **uncovered** foil pan on the cooking grill; cook for one hour or until done. ふたをしないフォイルパンを料理用グリルに載せ, 1時間またはできあがるまで熱を加える.

❷衣服を着ていない ▶ If a baby is kicking vigorously, especially at night, with the result that he is cold and **uncovered**, a sleeping-bag outfit is very practical. 赤ちゃんが特に夜によく足を動かし, 体がむき出しになって冷える場合は, 寝袋タイプの洋服が非常に便利です.

credibility

接頭 (in) **incredibility** *n* 信じられないこと

credible

接頭 (in) **incredible** *adj*

❶すごい, 驚くべき, とてつもない ▶ The **incredible** proliferation of wires made the development of more suitable cables necessary. 電線の驚くべき激増から, もっと適当なケーブルの開発が必要となった.

❷信じられない ▶ an **incredible** story 信じられない話

credibly

接頭 (in) **incredibly** *ad* 信じられないほど, 途方もなく ▶ While each phosphor dot is **incredibly** bright for its size, the overall display is relatively dim. 一つ一つのリン光体ドットは大きさのわりには信じられないくらいに明るいが, ディスプレー全体となると暗めだ.

credit

接頭 (dis) **discredit** *v* 信用を傷つける ▶ Ultimately his efforts to **discredit** his opponents failed. 結局, 競争相手の信用を傷つ

けようとする彼の努力は失敗に終わった.

接頭 (non) **noncredit** *adj* 履修単位にならない

creditable

接頭 (dis) **discreditable** *adj* 信用を傷つけるような

credulity

接頭 (in) **incredulity** *n* 不信感 ► He expressed **incredulity** at the government's plans. 彼は政府の計画に不信感を表明した.

credulous

接頭 (in) **incredulous** *adj* 容易に信じない, 疑い深い ► Affected by the solemnity of the scene, there was a wondering gaze of **incredulous** curiosity in his countenance. 情景の厳粛さに影響され, 疑い深い好奇心に満ちた驚嘆の表情が彼の顔に浮かんだ.

credulously

接頭 (in) **incredulously** *ad* 疑うような目つきで ► Steve looked at us **incredulously** and muttered something. スティーブは疑うような目つきで私たちを見て, 何かぼそぼそと呟いた.

crescent

接頭 (de) **decrescent** *adj* 漸減する

criminalize

接頭 (de) **decriminalize** *v*

❶解禁する

❷処罰の対象から外す

critical

接頭 (a) **acritical** *adj*

❶批判的でない

❷危険のない

接頭 (un) **uncritical** *adj* 批判的でない, 批判力のない

cross

接頭 (un) **uncross** *v* 〈クロスされたものなどを〉もとに戻す

crossed

[接頭] (un) **uncrossed** *adj* 〈小切手が〉線引きできない

crowded

[接頭] (un) **uncrowded** *adj* 混雑していない ► In an **uncrowded** train the passengers sit in a well-balanced posture so as to avoid contact with each other. すいている[混んでいない]電車では，乗客は互いに相手を避けてバランス良く座る．

crowned

[接頭] (un) **uncrowned** *adj* 戴冠式を済ませていない，無冠の

crushable

[接頭] (un) **uncrushable** *adj*

❶しわにならない

❷打ち砕かれない，不屈の

crystalline

[接頭] (non) **noncrystalline** *adj*

❶透明な，澄んだ

❷非結晶，非晶形 ► The terms "disordered" and "amorphous" have misleading connotations for **noncrystalline** materials. 非晶形物質に用いる不規則および無定形という用語には，誤解を与える意味合いがある．

crystallized

[接頭] (non) **noncrystallized** *adj* 非結晶の ► A **noncrystallized** (amorphous) area is more flexible and has higher impact strength. 非結晶(無定形)域はより弾力があり，衝撃強度も高い．

[接頭] (un) **uncrystallized** *adj*

❶結晶化していない

❷明確に定まっていない

cultivated

[接頭] (un) **uncultivated** *adj*

❶耕されていない ► Around the world, grazing by livestock has probably been more important than any other factor in reducing the productive capacity of **uncultivated** land. 世界中でまだ耕作されていない土地の生産力を減少させる最も重大な要因となっているのは，おそらく放牧であろう．

❷教養のない

cultured

接頭 (un) **uncultured** *adj* 教養のない，洗練されていない ► If you're **uncultured**, you do none of those things. あなたに教養がなければ，これらのどれもしないはずだ．

curability

接頭 (in) **incurability** *n* 不治，矯正不能

curable

接頭 (in) **incurable** *adj* 救いがたい，不治の，治らない ► Recovery from an **incurable** disease has given him a new lease on life. 彼は難病が治って若返った． ► The majority are cured quite quickly; some take longer, but only a few are **incurable**. 多くの人はきわめて早く治癒するが，治癒に時間が掛かる人もいれば，また数は少ないが治らない人もいる．

curably

接頭 (in) **incurably** *ad* 治らない，どうしようもない ► Her manner was **incurably** gentle. 彼女の態度は，どうしようもないほど穏やかだった．

cure

接尾 (less) **cureless** *adj* 救済できない，不治の ► He sought the help of society to fight this **cureless** disease. 彼はこの不治の病と闘うために，社会の助けを求めた．

cured

接頭 (un) **uncured** *adj*

❶〈傷などが〉治っていない

❷硬化していない ► The invention relates to cleaning solutions for removing **uncured** polyester resin systems from processing equipment surfaces. 本発明は，未硬化ポリエステル樹脂を処理装置の表面から取り除くためのクリーニング方法に

関するものである.

curiosity

[接頭] (in) **incuriosity** *n* 無関心 ► No sane man can affect indifference or **incuriosity**. 正気の男性は, 無頓着または無関心を装うことができない.

curious

[接頭] (in) **incurious** *adj* 無関心な, 好奇心のない ► be strangely **incurious** about the cause of the political upheaval 政治動乱の原因に関して妙に無関心である

curl

[接頭] (un) **uncurl** *v* 真っ直ぐにする[なる]

custodial

[接頭] (non) **noncustodial** *adj*

❶留置しない, 非拘禁の

❷監護権のない

cut

[接頭] (ill) **ill-cut** *adj* 仕立ての悪い ► **ill-cut** hair 変な髪形

[接頭] (un) **uncut** *adj* 切られていない

D

dairy

接頭 (non) **nondairy** *adj* 牛乳[乳製品など]を含まない

damaged

接頭 (un) **undamaged** *adj* 傷が付いていない，損傷を受けていない，無傷の，完全な ▶ This consists of directing at the affected part of the body special X-rays that destroy unwanted scar tissue while leaving the surrounding tissue **undamaged**. これは，周囲の組織を損傷させずに不要な瘢痕組織を破壊する特殊なX線が，身体の患部に向けられるように構成されている．

damped

接頭 (un) **undamped** *adj*

❶不減衰の ▶ The additional flexibility of the structure will result in increased displacement during resonance, caused by the presence of the **undamped** structure. 不減衰の構造がもたらす付加された柔軟性によって，共振中の変位が増大する．

❷湿っていない

date

接尾 (less) **dateless** *adj* 日付のない ▶ This **dateless** letter has been assigned a tentative date based upon the content. この日付のない手紙は，その内容から仮の日付を割り当てられた．

dated

接頭 (un) **undated** *adj*

❶日付の付いていない，年代不詳の ▶ These **undated** handout images provided by NASA show the extent of surface melt over Greenland's ice sheet. NASAが提供したこれらの日付がない画像サンプルは，グリーンランド氷床表面の融解の広がりを示す．

❷期限の定めのない

daunt

接尾 (less) **dauntless** *adj* 恐れを知らない，勇敢な

daunted

接頭 (un) **undaunted** *adj* 〈危険などを〉恐れない ▶ The old gentleman, who appeared to be a friend of long standing just like the speaker, continued clapping with tears in his eyes, quite **undaunted** and unabashed. その話し手と同様に古くからの友人と見受けられるその老紳士は，涙を流しながら，少しも臆することなく堂々と手を叩き続けた.

death

接尾 (less) **deathless** *adj* 不死の，不滅の

deceive

接頭 (un) **undeceive** *v* 〈誤りなどを〉悟らせる

decency

接頭 (in) **indecency** *n* 無作法，無礼，見苦しいこと ▶ He had intended no rudeness or **indecency** thereby. 彼は，それによって無礼または下品さを示そうとするつもりはなかった.

decent

接頭 (in) **indecent** *adj* 無作法な，見苦しい，みだらな，下品な ▶ The talk grew **indecent**. 話が落ちてきた.

decided

接頭 (un) **undecided** *adj*

❶決めていない ▶ Our position on this bill is still **undecided**. この法案に対する我々の立場はまだ未決定である.

❷未解決の

decipherable

接頭 (in) **indecipherable** *adj* 判読できない ▶ The signboard was dark and **indecipherable**. 看板は暗くて，判読できなかった.

decision

接頭 (in) **indecision** *n* 優柔不断 ▶ I was irritated by his **indecision**. 私は彼の優柔不断さにいらいらした.

decisive

接頭 (in) **indecisive** *adj*

❶決定的でない，決着のつかない，どっちつかずの

❷優柔不断な ► He is an **indecisive** character. 彼は，うじうじして煮え切らない男だ.

decisively

接頭 (in) **indecisively** *ad* どっちつかずに，煮え切らないで ► The battle ended **indecisively**; neither side had clearly won but neither side admitted defeat. 戦いは決着がつかずに終わった. すなわち，どちらの側も確実に勝ったわけではなく，どちらの側も敗北を認めたわけでもなかった.

decisiveness

接頭 (in) **indecisiveness** *adj* 優柔不断 ► I grew impatient with his **indecisiveness**. 私は，彼の煮え切らない態度にはいらいらした.

declared

接頭 (un) **undeclared** *adj* 宣言していない，申告されていない ► The majority of first year students in the School of Business enter as **undeclared** business majors. そのビジネススクールの一年生の大半は，未申告のビジネス専攻として入学する.

declinable

接頭 (in) **indeclinable** *adj* 語尾変化をしない，不変化の ► **Indeclinable** words were used as an exclamation. 不変化語が，感嘆詞として使われた.

接頭 (un) **undeclinable** *adj*

❶拒絶できない

❷＝indeclinable

decomposed

接頭 (un) **undecomposed** *adj* 分解されていない，腐敗していない ► The cathode compartment contains the sodium hydroxide produced as a solution in **undecomposed** brine and hydrogen gas. 陰極の区画には，分解されていない塩水と水素

ガス中の溶液として生成される水酸化ナトリウムが含まれる.

decorous

接頭 (in) **indecorous** *adj* 無作法な ▶ **indecorous** behavior 無作法な振舞い

decorously

接頭 (in) **indecorously** *ad* 無作法に ▶ The audience behaved **indecorously**, as if the concert were an informal dress rehearsal. 聴衆は, まるでコンサートが平服でのリハーサルであるかのように無作法に振る舞った.

decorum

接頭 (in) **indecorum** *n* 無作法, 下品, 無礼 ▶ There is no **indecorum** in the proposal. 提案に関し無礼はない.

deductible

接頭 (non) **nondeductible** *adj* 控除できない, 非控除の

defeasible

接頭 (in) **indefeasible** *adj* 破棄できない, 無効にできない ▶ an **indefeasible** claim to the title そのタイトルへの絶対的な権利

defeated

接頭 (un) **undefeated** *adj* 負けたことのない, 無敗の

defend

接頭 (un) **undefended** *adj*

❶ 無防備な ▶ The laws of war stipulate that **undefended** places should not be attacked. 戦時国際法は, 無防備な場所を攻撃してはならないと明記している.

❷ 弁護されていない, 弁護人のいない

defense

接尾 (less) **defenseless** *adj* 無防備な ▶ In such a case, both sides have to honor the social contact under which the people agree to go unarmed and **defenseless** and the state agrees to provide them all necessary protection. そのような場合, 両者

は，人々が非武装かつ無防備で行くことに合意した社会契約を遵守しなければならず，国家は彼らに必要なすべての防護を提供することに合意している.

defensible

接頭 (in) **indefensible** *adj* 弁解の余地のない，許せない，防御不可能な ▸ a chess move constituting an inescapable and **indefensible** attack on the opponent's king 相手のキングが逃げられず，防御不可能な攻撃となるチェスの一手

defensively

接頭 (in) **indefensively** *ad* 弁解の余地もないほど ▸ The following is **indefensively** stupid. 以下は，弁解の余地もないほど馬鹿げている.

definable

接頭 (in) **indefinable** *adj* 定義できない，説明できない，漠然とした ▸ He has an **indefinable** charm about him. 彼には何とも言えない愛嬌がある.

definably

接頭 (in) **indefinably** *ad* なんとなく，言いようのない状態で ▸ **indefinably** white なんとなく白い

defined

接頭 (ill) **ill-defined** *adj* 定かでない ▸ In certain **ill-defined** and perhaps unknown quantities, radiation in the air, soil, and water can, of course, be deadly. 範囲の定かでない，おそらく量もわからない放射能が空気，土，水の中にあるなら，当然命にかかわることもあり得る.

接頭 (un) **undefined** *adj* 定義されていない ▸ The concept opens up a wide variety of as yet **undefined** applications. そのコンセプトによって，まだ定義されていない多種多様なアプリケーションの開発が広がる.

definite

接頭 (in) **indefinite** *adj*

❶明確でない，はっきりしない ▸ Approximations or **indefi-**

nite measurements should be written out. 近似または正確でない測定は全部書き出さなければならない.

❷ 不定の ▸ Viral DNA is reproduced with the chromosome for an **indefinite** number of generations. ウイルスのDNAは染色体によって不定数の世代にわたって複製される.

definitely

接頭 (in) **indefinitely** *ad*

❶ 無期限に ▸ The President's state visit to Japan was postponed **indefinitely**. 大統領の日本への公式訪問は無期延期となった.

❷ 漠然と, 曖昧に ▸ The fluids are thermally stable **indefinitely** at 150℃ in air. この液体は大気中では150℃のあたりで熱的に安定する.

delicacy

接頭 (in) **indelicacy** *n* 粗野, 無作法, 下品 ▸ behavior or language bordering on **indelicacy** 下品な言動

delicate

接頭 (in) **indelicate** *adj* 無神経な, 粗野な, 下品な ▸ It is **indelicate** to give money uncovered. 金をむき出しで渡すのは失礼だ.

deliverable

接頭 (un) **undeliverable** *adj* 送信不能な ▸ This message was **undeliverable** for the following reason: このメッセージは, 以下の理由により送信できませんでした.

demeanor

接頭 (mis) **misdemeanor** *n* 軽罪, 不品行 ▸ That's why they were charged with only a strict liability **misdemeanor**. そういうわけで, 彼らは無過失責任の軽罪のみで起訴された.

democratic

接頭 (un) **undemocratic** *adj* 非民主的な ▸ South Africa's current labour relations system is fundamentally **undemocratic**. 南アフリカの現在の労使関係制度は, 基本的に非民主的であ

る.

demonstrate

接頭 (un) **undemonstrated** *adj* 論証されていない

demonstrative

接頭 (un) **undemonstrative** *adj* 内気な, 控えめな

deniable

接頭 (un) **undeniable** *adj*

❶否定できない ▶ Underlying this professional maxim is an **undeniable** truth: PC software isn't cheap.「PCのソフトウェアは安価に手に入るものではない」という専門分野に関するこの定説は否定できない真実である.

❷不可避の ▶ The pressure for policy revision may be **undeniable**. 政策の修正に向けた圧力が掛かることは避けがたい.

❸申し分のない

denominational

接頭 (non) **nondenominational** *adj* 特定の宗派に限定されない

接頭 (un) **undenominational** *adj* 非宗派的な

dependable

接頭 (un) **undependable** *adj* 当てにならない ▶ The computers are too **undependable** for routine police work. それらのコンピューターは警察の日常業務にはとても堪えられないものだ.

dependence

接頭 (in) **independence** *n* 独立(心), 自主, 自活, 主体性, 非依存性 ▶ The Declaration of **Independence** of The United States of America 米国独立宣言書

dependent

接頭 (in) **independent** *adj* 他の支配を受けない ▶ These consequences or outcomes are determined by two types of **independent** factors. これらの結果や成果は2種類の互いに無関係な要因によって決まる.

dependently

接頭 (in) **independently** *ad*

❶ 独立して, 独自に, 無関係に ▸ A separate channel transports the messages between the user and the network completely **independently** of the information channels. 特定のチャネルが, 情報チャネルとはまったく独立して, ユーザーとネットワークの間でメッセージを運ぶ.

❷ 自主的に, 自立して ▸ a society in which young people can play their roles **independently** 青少年が主体的に役割を果たしていける社会

describable

接頭 (in) **indescribable** *adj* 言葉では言い表せない, 言語に絶する ▸ The human memory encompasses an **indescribable** universe of types and kinds, far beyond the range of a computer. 人間の記憶は, コンピューターの限界を超え, 言葉では言い表せない様式や種類の世界にも及ぶ.

describably

接頭 (in) **indescribably** *ad* 言葉では言い表せないくらい, たとえようもなく ▸ The taste of burnt rice and soy sauce blended well together, and I found this **indescribably** fragrant taste irresistible. 焦げたご飯と醤油の味がうまく混じり合い, なんとも香ばしい味が, 私はたまらなく好きだった. ▸ The greenery in the rainy season is **indescribably** beautiful. 梅雨時の緑は, たとえようもなく美しい.

designed

接頭 (ill) **ill-designed** *adj* 設計の悪い

desirability

接頭 (un) **undesirability** *n* 迷惑, 好ましくないこと

desirable

接頭 (un) **undesirable** *adj* 好ましくない, 有害な ▸ The oxygen no longer has an **undesirable** effect on the product. 酸素はもはや製品に好ましくない効果を及ぼすことはない. ▸

The echo suppressors have several properties that are **undesirable** for data communication. エコー減衰器には，データ通信にとって好ましくない特性がいくつかある．▶ Where it is **undesirable** to receive a result code, the Quiet Enable (Q) command can be used to prevent the modem from sending result codes. リザルトコードを受信したくない場合に，Quiet Enable (Q) コマンドを使用するとモデムがリザルトコードを送るのを防止できる．

desirably

接頭 (un) **undesirably** *ad* 好ましくなく，不快に ▶ Also, **undesirably** high pipe separation loads are produced. また，好ましくないことに，配管分離の高い負荷が生じる．

desired

接頭 (un) **undesired** *adj*

❶不良… ▶ **undesired** products 不良品

❷望まれていない ▶ whether magnetic objects represent desired or **undesired** objects 磁気を帯びた物質が望まれた物であるか望まれていない物であるかどうか

destructible

接頭 (in) **indestructible** *adj* 破壊できない ▶ With their sweet sound, easy operation, and virtually **indestructible** disks, they represent a technological leap beyond records and tapes. 音が良く，操作が簡単で，ほとんど壊れることのないディスクを使っているという点で，レコードやテープと比べて技術的な飛躍がある．

destructive

接頭 (non) **nondestructive** *adj* 非破壊的な ▶ An amorphous memory array also has a fast read speed, since in either state the memory can be considered simply as a resistor and readout is **nondestructive**. どちらの状態でもメモリーは単にレジスターであり，読み出しは非破壊的であると考えられるので，非結晶記憶配列もまた読み取り速度が速い．

detectable

接頭 (un) **undetectable** *adj* 検出不能な ► Once it has embedded itself within a program, a virus is virtually **undetectable**. ウイルスがプログラム内に入り込むと実質上検出できない.

detected

接頭 (un) **undetected** *adj* 検出されていない ► Because of the checking procedures built into the scanner coding system, there were no **undetected** errors made with the magnetic device. スキャナーのコーディングシステムに組み込まれたチェック手順によれば, 磁気装置に生じる検出されないエラーはなかった.

determinable

接頭 (in) **indeterminable** *adj* 決着のできない ► an unpredictable (or **indeterminable**) future 予測できない(または判定できない)未来

determinacy

接頭 (in) **indeterminacy** *n* 不確定性 ► the **indeterminacy** principle 不確定性原理

determinate

接頭 (in) **indeterminate** *adj*

❶はっきりと決められない, 不確定の ► **indeterminate** work that falls under no occupational classification 職業分類でどの項にもあてはまらない職業

❷不定の

determination

接頭 (in) **indetermination** *n*

❶不確定, 未確定, 曖昧さ ► There seems to be no difference, in your view, between underdetermination and **indetermination**. 未決定性と不確定性の間で, あなたの意見では違いがないようだ.

❷不決断, 優柔不断

determined

接頭 (un) **undetermined** *adj* 未決定の

determinism

接頭 (in) **indeterminism** *n* 非決定論，自由意志論 ► the doctrine of denying determinism, called **indeterminism** 非決定論という，決定論を否定する学説

determinist

接頭 (in) **indeterminist** *n* 非決定論者 ► But for an **indeterminist**, more than one outcome is possible at some moments. しかし，非決定論者にとって，複数の結果は，ある瞬間，可能である．

deterministic

接頭 (in) **indeterministic** *adj* 非決定論的 ► an **indeterministic** world 非決定論的世界

developed

接頭 (un) **undeveloped** *adj* 未開発の ► an **undeveloped** region 未開発地帯

difference

接頭 (in) **indifference** *n*

❶ 無関心 ► The introduction of 1982 models this fall collided with a wall of **indifference** from potential auto buyers. 今秋の1982年型モデルカーの発表では，見込み客の無関心という壁に突き当たった． ► Tolerance is another name for **indifference**. 寛容とは無関心の別称である．

❷ 重要でないこと

different

接頭 (in) **indifferent** *adj*

❶ 無頓着な，無関心な ► I am quite **indifferent** to such criticism. 私は，そんな批評は痛くもかゆくもない． ► I am **indifferent** to politics. 僕は政治には無関心だ．

❷ 重要でない

❸ 平凡な

❹公平な，中立の

digested

接頭 (in) **indigested** *adj* 不消化の

接頭 (un) **undigested** *adj* 未消化の ▶ **Undigested** food in stool generally isn't a problem unless it's accompanied by other symptoms. 排せつ物の中に未消化の食物があっても，それが他の症状を伴わない限り，一般的に問題はない．

digestible

接頭 (in) **indigestible** *adj*

❶〈飲食物が〉消化できない，消化が悪い ▶ You ought to abstain from **indigestible** food. 君は，消化の悪い食物を食べないほうがよい．

❷〈物事が〉容易に理解できない

digestion

接頭 (in) **indigestion** *n* 消化不良 ▶ an **indigestion** remedy 消化不良の治療 ▶ Heartburn and **indigestion** are two very common problems causing large amounts of discomfort. 胸やけと消化不良は大きな不快感をもたらすきわめてよくみられる二つの問題である．

digestive

接頭 (in) **indigestive** *adj* 消化不良の[になった] ▶ I am glad to be disturbed from an **indigestive** after-dinner sleep. 私は，消化不良の食後の睡眠から起こされてうれしい．

dignified

接頭 (un) **undignified** *adj* 不体裁な

dignity

接頭 (in) **indignity** *n* 侮辱，冷遇 ▶ The politician suffered the **indignity** of arrest for suspected bribery. その政治家は収賄罪の容疑で逮捕されるという屈辱を味わった．

diluted

接頭 (un) **undiluted** *adj* 希釈していない ▶ Essential oils should never be used on the skin **undiluted**. 希釈していない

エッセンシャルオイルを皮膚に塗ってはいけない.

dimension

接尾 (less) **dimensionless** *adj* 無次元の ▸ It is convenient to use **dimensionless** coefficients to define the magnitude of the forces. 力の大きさを定義するために無次元係数を用いると便利である.

dimensional

接頭 (non) **nondimensional** *adj* 無次元の ▸ Using **nondimensional** analysis, the residual stresses on the weldment were determined. 無次元解析を用いて, 溶接部の残留応力を決定した.

diminished

接頭 (un) **undiminished** *adj* 低減していない ▸ On the Moon, **undiminished** solar energy can be soaked up by solar cells. 月では, 低減していない太陽エネルギーを太陽電池で吸収することができる.

diplomatic

接頭 (un) **undiplomatic** *adj* 非外交的な, 機転のきかない, 無神経な ▸ Mitt Romney made some **undiplomatic** criticism of London's preparations for the Olympic Games on Wednesday. ミット・ロムニー氏は, 水曜日に, ロンドンでのオリンピックの準備に対して, 無神経な批判をした.

direct

接頭 (in) **indirect** *adj* 間接の, 素直でない, 真っ直ぐでない ▸ a political system called **indirect** democracy 間接民主主義という政治体制

directed

接頭 (ill) **ill-directed** *adj* 的外れの

接頭 (un) **undirected** *adj* 方向性のない ▸ A Hamiltonian cycle in an **undirected** graph is a simple cycle. 無向グラフにおけるハミルトンサイクルは, 単純サイクルである.

direction

接頭 (in) **indirection** *n* 回り道, 無目的, 不正な手段 ► His presidential campaign got mired in **indirection**. 彼の大統領選挙戦は回り道に陥った.

directional

接頭 (non) **nondirectional** *adj* 非方向性の ► The series motor has the disadvantage of being a **nondirectional** device. 直列モーターは非方向性の装置であるという不利点がある.

directly

接頭 (in) **indirectly** *ad* 間接的に, 側面から ► I am indebted to him in many ways, directly and **indirectly**. あの人には直接的にも間接的にもさまざまな恩恵を受けている.

discernible

接頭 (in) **indiscernible** *adj* 見分けにくい, 聞きとりにくい ► The transition was almost **indiscernible**. 遷移は, ほとんど識別できなかった.

discharged

接頭 (un) **undischarged** *adj* 〈負債などが〉支払われていない

discipline

接頭 (in) **indiscipline** *n* 〈集団・組織などにおける行動の〉無規律 ► **indiscipline** with regard to sensuous pleasures 感覚的な喜びに関しての無規律

disciplined

接頭 (in) **indisciplined** *adj* 無規律の, 訓練されていない ► an **indisciplined** soldier 訓練されていない兵士

disclosed

接頭 (un) **undisclosed** *adj* 明かされていない, 公開されていない ► an **undisclosed** bank account 非公開の銀行口座

disclosure

接頭 (non) **nondisclosure** *n* 不開示, 開示[発表, 暴露]しないこと, 非開示 ► The harm of **nondisclosure** is greater than the harm of disclosure. 非開示の害は開示の害を上回る. ►

Because of this, it is sometimes referred to as a **nondisclosure** clause. このために，これはしばしば不開示条項と呼ばれる．

discovered

接頭 (un) **undiscovered** *adj* 発見されていない ► The spacecraft detected previously **undiscovered** moons. その宇宙船は，これまで発見されていなかった衛星を発見した．

discreet

接頭 (in) **indiscreet** *adj* 無分別な，軽率な ► Young people will be **indiscreet**. 若者は無分別である． ► I am one of the most **indiscreet** men alive. 私は，最も軽率な男の一人だ．

discreetly

接頭 (in) **indiscreetly** *ad* 無分別に，軽率に ► He sometimes acts **indiscreetly**. 彼は，時々，無分別［軽率］に行動することがある． ► She inquired **indiscreetly** after the state of his health 彼女は軽率に彼の健康状態を尋ねた．

discreetness

接頭 (in) **indiscreetness** *n* 軽率さ ► His **indiscreetness** led to the fall of the Hojo clan. 彼の軽率さが，北条氏の滅亡のきっかけとなった．

discretion

接頭 (in) **indiscretion** *n* 無分別，軽率 ► I reproved her for her **indiscretion**. 彼女の無分別をたしなめた．

discretionary

接頭 (non) **nondiscretionary** *adj* 自由裁量でない，任意でない ► We are seeing . . . because people still have the need for **nondiscretionary** expenditures. 人々が依然として任意に決定できない額を出費する必要があるために，…と理解している．

discriminate

接頭 (in) **indiscriminate** *adj* 見境のない，でたらめな ► My brother is an **indiscriminate** stamp collector. 弟は切手収集に見境がない．

discriminately

接頭 (in) **indiscriminately** *ad*

❶ 無差別に, 見境なく ► Some physicians may be using them **indiscriminately** in response to patient demand. 医師の中には, 患者の要求にこたえて見境なくそれを使っている人もいるかもしれない. ► The idea is **indiscriminately** everywhere in the world. その考えは, 世界中至るところに無差別に存在する.

❷ やたらに, 無節操に ► You must not admit people so **indiscriminately**. そうやたらに人を入れるべきでない.

discriminating

接頭 (in) **indiscriminating** *adj* 識別力のない, 敏感でない ► A casual and **indiscriminating** observer, in passing, might not cast a second glance upon the figure. 通りがかりの無頓着で識別力がない観察者は, 外観に二度と目を留めることはないだろう.

接頭 (in) **indiscriminatingly** *ad* 無差別に, 選別せずに

接頭 (un) **undiscriminating** *adj* 識別できない ► The list is a come-on designed to attract an **undiscriminating** audience. そのリストは, 識別力のない顧客を引きつけるように意図されている.

discriminatory

接頭 (non) **nondiscriminatory** *adj*

❶ 差別(待遇)をしない, 無差別(的)な ► To achieve **nondiscriminatory** long-term financing, official export credit agencies may need to neutralize the cost differential caused by use of off-shore funds. 無差別的長期融資を得るために, 公的輸出信用調査機関は在外投資信託を用いることにより生ずる経費の格差をなくす必要がある.

❷ 識別できない, 特徴的でない

disguised

接頭 (un) **undisguised** *adj* 隠されていない

disk

接尾 (less) **diskless** *adj* ディスクのない

dispensable

接頭 (in) **indispensable** *adj* 必須の，不可欠な ► There are some jobs for which a database program is almost **indispensable**. 仕事の中には，データベースプログラムがほぼ必須であるものもある． ► Practice is **indispensable** to language study. 練習は，語学の勉強に不可欠だ．

dispersed

接頭 (un) **undispersed** *adj* 分散されていない ► These include **undispersed** carbon black aggregates and even "pellets." これらは，分散していないカーボンブラックの集合体またはペレットを含む．

disposed

接頭 (ill) **ill-disposed** *adj* 悪意をもった，たちの悪い

接頭 (in) **indisposed** *adj*

❶ やる気をなくさせる ► someone **indisposed** toward work 働く気をなくした人間

❷ 気分がすぐれない ► The patient was merely temporarily **indisposed**. その患者は単に一時的に気分が悪くなっただけだ．

disposition

接頭 (in) **indisposition** *n* 気が進まないこと，いや気 ► She has fully recovered from her recent **indisposition**. 彼女は最近の（軽い）病気からすっかり回復した．

disputable

接頭 (in) **indisputable** *adj* 議論の余地のない，明白な ► It is an **indisputable** fact that examinations provide an impetus to study. 試験が勉強の刺激となることは議論の余地のない事実である．

disputably

接頭 (in) **indisputably** *ad* 議論の余地なく，確実に ► It is **in-**

disputably a leading company in the industry. それは，誰もが認める業界一の企業だ.

disputed

接頭 (un) **undisputed** *adj* 異論のない ► The steam locomotive was **undisputed** king of the rails. 蒸気機関車は，異論なく鉄道の王だった.

dissociable

接頭 (in) **indissociable** *adj* 分離できない

dissoluble

接頭 (in) **indissoluble** *adj*

❶ 永続的な，不変の ► We were childhood friends, and there is a sort of **indissoluble** tie between us. 僕と彼とは幼馴染みで，切っても切れない縁を感じる.

❷ 分解［分離］できない ► Our cannon must be **indissoluble** by the corrosive action of acids. 我々の大砲は，酸の腐食作用によって分解できないはずである.

distinct

接頭 (in) **indistinct** *adj* 不明瞭な，ぼやけている，はっきりしない ► If the light source has a finite width, increasing D causes these fringes to become **indistinct** and eventually to disappear. 光源の幅が有限なら，D を増すとこれらの縞は不明瞭になっていき，最後には消えてしまう.

distinctive

接頭 (in) **indistinctive** *adj* 目立たない，区別できない，特色のない ► He absolutely was the most **indistinctive** of them all. 彼は絶対に，皆の中で最も目立たなかった.

distinctly

接頭 (in) **indistinctly** *ad* 不明瞭に ► a person who speaks softly and **indistinctly**. 静かに不明瞭に話す人

distinctness

接頭 (in) **indistinctness** *n* 不明瞭

distinguishable

接頭 (in) **indistinguishable** *adj* 区別できない(ほど似ている)

▶ Different phenomena may cause similar, and even **indistinguishable**, external effects. 異なる現象が類似の，それどころか区別できないような表面上の効果を呈するかもしれない．

接頭 (un) **undistinguishable** *adj* 識別不能な ▶ Particles are considered to be **undistinguishable** if their wave packets overlap significantly. 粒子は，その波束が大幅に重なり合っている場合，識別不能であると考えられている．

distinguished

接頭 (un) **undistinguished** *adj* 識別されていない ▶ Mr. Obama's record in office was also **undistinguished**. オバマ氏の在職時の実績も，特に目立たなかった．

distressed

接頭 (non) **nondistressed** *adj* 困窮していない，貧乏でない

▶ But in the **nondistressed** cities, the existing home inventory is lower, closer to seven months on average. しかし，困窮していない都市では，現行の住宅の在庫は少なく，平均で約7か月分である．

distributable

接頭 (in) **indistributable** *adj* 分配できない

disturbed

接頭 (un) **undisturbed** *adj*

❶ 邪魔されない ▶ geologic formations that have been **undisturbed** for millions of years 何百万年もの間邪魔されなかった地質形成

❷ 乱されない ▶ The contents of the original two registers are left **undisturbed**. 二つの基本レジスターのデータは，乱されていないままだ． ▶ Much farther from the surface, the effect of the surface vanishes and the flow is **undisturbed**. 表面から遠く離れると表面の影響が消えて流れに乱れがなくなる．

divided

接頭 (un) **undivided** *adj*

❶〈注意などが〉分散されない，集中した ▸ Sit quietly, give the patient your **undivided** attention, and you may find that you only need to smile or nod and he will be encouraged to continue. 静かに座り，気を散らさずに患者に注目すれば，ただほほえんだり，うなずいたりするだけで十分に患者に治療を続けさせられることに気付くかもしれない．

❷分割されない

dividing

接頭 (non) **nondividing** *adj* 分割しない，不分割の，非分裂の ▸ Under most circumstances this sex factor can replicate within an **nondividing** cell. ほぼ，どんな状況においても，この性因子は非分裂細胞内で複製される．

do

接頭 (un) **undo** *v*

❶もとに戻す ▸ Type style changes (such as italic or bold) are permanent overrides and remain until you specifically **undo** them. 字体変更（イタリックや太字など）は永久的なオーバーライドであり，その変更を特にもとに戻すまではそのままである．

❷〈結び目などを〉解く

docile

接頭 (in) **indocile** *adj* 素直でない，御し難い，言うことを聞かない ▸ She was ignorant, **indocile**, careless, and irrational. 彼女は，無知で，言うことを聞かず，不注意で，分別が無かった．

docility

接頭 (in) **indocility** *n* 教えにくいこと，不従順

dock

接頭 (un) **undock** *v*

❶〈宇宙船を〉切り離す ▸ The European Space Agency says the **undocking** of its cargo craft from the International Space

Station has been postponed. 欧州宇宙機関(ESA)によると，国際宇宙ステーションからの貨物船の切り離しは延期になったと伝えられている.

❷〈船を〉ドックから出す

documented

接頭 (ill) **ill-documented** *adj* 適切に文書化されていない

接頭 (un) **undocumented** *adj* 書類で立証されていない

doing

接頭 (un) **undoing** *n*

❶破滅の原因 ► A new book by Terry Moe argues that it's technology, not politics, that will be their **undoing**. テリー・モエは新しい本の中で，政治ではなく技術が彼らの破滅の原因であると主張している.

❷取り消し

done

接頭 (un) **undone** *adj* 完成していない

doped

接頭 (un) **undoped** *adj* ドープ処理されていない ► In previous lessons, discussion has centered around the elemental semiconductors, those containing only one element in the **undoped** state. 前のレッスンでは，ドープ処理されていない状態で一元素しか持っていない元素半導体に議論の中心が置かれた.

doubt

接尾 (less) **doubtless** *adj* 間違いのない，疑いのない ► They are **doubtless** from China. 彼らは間違いなく中国人だ.

接尾 (less) **doubtlessly** *ad* 疑いなく ► You **doubtlessly** mean to say something, but hide your thoughts for fear. あなたは疑いなく何かを言うつもりだが，怖くて本心を隠すだろう.

接尾 (less) **doubtlessness** *n* 疑いのないこと

doubted

接頭 (un) **undoubted** *adj* 疑いのない

接頭 (un) **undoubtedly** *ad* 疑いなく，確実に ► **Undoubtedly**

one of the most frustrating things about using personal computer software is printing. パソコンソフトを使用するに当たり最もいらいらすることの一つが印刷であることは疑いない. ► These processes will be emphasized in this lesson, with greater attention given to the planar process, **undoubtedly** the most important process in semiconductor technology. この課ではこれらのプロセスについて重点が置かれるが，半導体技術で疑問の余地なく最も重要なプロセスであるプレーナープロセスの方をより重視していく.

dream

接尾 (less) **dreamless** *adj*

❶夢のない ► One dark night in midsummer a man waking from a **dreamless** sleep in a forest lifted his head from the earth. ある真夏の闇夜に，男は森の中で夢のない眠りからさめ，地面から頭をもたげた.

❷夢を見ない(睡眠)

dreamed-of

接頭 (un) **undreamed-of** *adj* 考えてもみない

dress

接頭 (un) **undress** *v*

❶衣服を脱がせる ► Close the door and draw the curtains when **undressing** the patient. 患者の衣服を脱がせるときは，ドアを閉めて，カーテンを引いてください.

❷〈飾りなどを〉取り外す

dressed

接頭 (un) **undressed** *adj* 衣服を脱がされた

dressing

接頭 (un) **undressing** *grd* 脱衣 ► Dressing and **undressing** may be time-consuming processes if he is blind, stiff, weak from old age, arthritic, has lost a limb, or is paralyzed. もし患者が盲目，硬直，老いによる衰え，関節炎，手足の欠損，麻痺などを患っていると，着衣や脱衣に時間がかかるかもしれない.

drinkable

接頭 (un) **undrinkable** *adj* 飲むことができない

due

接頭 (un) **undue** *adj* 過度の ► The metal support ring should not exert **undue** pressure on . . . 金属保持リングは…に過度の圧力を加えないようにする必要がある.

duly

接頭 (un) **unduly** *ad*

❶ 過度に ► The carbon content of steel must not be raised **unduly**. 鋼の炭素含有量を過度に多くしてはならない. ► Therefore, these equipment trailers are painted aluminum so that the interior of the trailer is not **unduly** heated by the sun's radiant energy. それゆえ, これらの機材トレーラーは, 内部が太陽の放射エネルギーを吸収して過度に熱せられないように, アルミが塗られている.

❷ 不当に, 不法に

dust

接尾 (less) **dustless** *adj* 埃のない ► He ran to an exclusive residential district of **dustless** roads. 彼は, 塵一つない高級住宅地区に着いた.

dying

接頭 (un) **undying** *adj* 絶えることのない

E

earned

接頭 (un) **unearned** *adj* 労働によって得たものでない

earth

接頭 (un) **unearth** *v* 〈埋もれたものなどを〉掘り出す ► **unearth** a hidden treasure box 隠された宝の箱を掘り出す ► Thus far only some of the hull's planking and part of the vessel's keel have been **unearthed** from the sediment. これまでのところ，船体の厚板の一部と縦材による船の竜骨のみが堆積土から発掘されている．

earthly

接頭 (un) **unearthly** *adj* 超自然的な，不気味な

ease

接頭 (un) **unease** *n* 心配，不安 ► Relaxation is indeed vital considering the degree of **unease** mammography patients can develop. マンモグラフィー検査を受ける患者が抱く不安の程度を考慮すると，緊張を緩和することは非常に重要である．

easily

接頭 (un) **uneasily** *ad* 不安そうに，心配そうに ► Patients and advocates are watching **uneasily** as the state moves at a leisurely pace toward implementation. 患者と擁護団体は，実施へ向けた国ののんびりとした動きを不安そうに見ている．

easiness

接頭 (un) **uneasiness** *n* 心配，不安

easy

接頭 (un) **uneasy** *adj* 不安な，心配な ► New eating disorder research highlights the nation's **uneasy** relationship with food. 摂食障害の新たな研究では，国民と食物との深刻な関係を浮き彫りにする．

eatable

接頭 (un) **uneatable** *adj* 食べられない，食用に適さない ► The United States forbid the presence of **uneatable** products in confectioneries. 米国は，菓子類が食用でない物を含有することを禁止している．

economic

接頭 (non) **noneconomic** *adj* 経済的でない

接頭 (un) **uneconomic** *adj* 非経済的な，採算が取れない ► The replacement could result in a weight savings but only minor gains in performance and the cost of new tooling and recertifying make the proposal **uneconomic**. その交換は軽量化につながる可能性があるが，パフォーマンスの改善はわずかで，新規のツールと再認証のコストは，その計画の採算を合わなくする．

economical

接頭 (un) **uneconomical** *adj* 不経済な，経済的でない ► Heat pumps are **uneconomical** if used for the sole purpose of comfort heating. ヒートポンプを，ただ暖を取るためにのみ使用するのは経済的ではない． ► Electronic technology enhances specialization that would otherwise be **uneconomical** and encourages new forms of interactive argument. 電子技術によって，それ以外の手段では不経済となるであろう専門化をいっそう進めるとともに，双方向の議論という新しい形を促進している．

edible

接頭 (in) **inedible** *adj* 食べられない，食用に適さない ► These are produced under federal inspection and are classified as edible or **inedible** depending upon the source of fatty tissue. これらは連邦の検査のもとで生産され，脂肪組織の出所に応じて食用に適すものと適さないものに分類される．

edifying

接頭 (un) **unedifying** *adj* 啓発しない，教化しない

educated

[接頭] (ill) **ill-educated** *adj* 教育不足の

[接頭] (un) **uneducated** *adj* 教育を受けていない ▸ Schultz's father was an **uneducated** veteran of World War II. シュルツ氏の父親は第二次世界大戦に従軍した無学の退役軍人であった.

effable

[接頭] (in) **ineffable** *adj*

❶ 言語に絶する, 筆舌に尽くしがたい ▸ **ineffable** anger toward the wrongdoers 犯罪者に対する言いようのない怒り

❷ 言いようのない, えも言われぬ ▸ The sight filled me with **ineffable** emotions. 私はこれを見て感慨無量だった.

effaceable

[接頭] (in) **ineffaceable** *adj* 消すことのできない ▸ I have covered myself with **ineffaceable** shame. 私は消すことのできない恥をかいた.

effective

[接頭] (in) **ineffective** *adj* 効果のない, 無力な, 役に立たない, 無能な ▸ The technical ladder may serve as a dumping ground for **ineffective** managers. 無能な管理職にとっては, この技術職の地位はごみ置き場のようなものだ.

[接頭] (non) **noneffective** *adj* 効力のない

effectiveness

[接頭] (in) **ineffectiveness** *n* 効果のなさ ▸ **ineffectiveness** of drug therapy 薬物治療の無効性

effectual

[接頭] (in) **ineffectual** *adj* 効果の上がらない, 無駄な, 無力な ▸ Doctor after doctor gave her the same **ineffectual** advice. どの医者も彼女に同じ無意味なアドバイスを与えた.

effectuality

[接頭] (in) **ineffectuality** *n* 無力さ ▸ There was a strange air of **ineffectuality** about the three men. 3人の男たちは, 異様な無

力感に取り巻かれていた.

effectually

接頭 (in) **ineffectually** *ad* 効果なく, 無駄に, 無力にも ► She tried **ineffectually** to light the stove, and Thomas came to help her. 彼女は, 無力にも, ストーブを点けようとし, トーマスに助けられた.

efficacious

接頭 (in) **inefficacious** *adj* 〈薬剤などの〉 効き目のない ► laws that are **inefficacious** in stopping crime 犯罪阻止の効力がない法律

efficiency

接頭 (in) **inefficiency** *n*

❶ 無効果, 効率の悪さ, 不手際, 手落ち ► Considerable labor is involved in operating an irrigation system, and some of the **inefficiencies** of irrigation result from inadequate attention to such operations. 潅漑システムの運用にはかなりの労働力が必要となるが, 潅漑の効率の悪さには, そのような運用への配慮のなさが原因となるものもある.

❷ 非能率(性) ► Our company should eliminate **inefficiency** in our production system. わが社は, 製造態勢の非能率性[ムダ]を取り除かなければならない.

efficient

接頭 (in) **inefficient** *adj*

❶ 効果のない, 能率的でない, 役に立たない, もたもたしている ► An **inefficient** filing system cannot be made more efficient simply by transferring information from paper to PC memory. 単に情報を紙からPCメモリーに移しただけでは, 役に立たないファイリングシステムをもっと能率的にすることはできない.

❷ 非能率的な ► He criticized the hopelessly **inefficient** tax system. 彼は, どうにもならないほど非能率的な税制を非難した.

❸効率の悪い ► And since democracy is **inefficient**, we won't need it either. そして民主主義は効率が悪いので，我々はそれも必要としないであろう．

efficiently

接頭 (in) **inefficiently** *ad* 非能率的に，のらりくらりと ► He dealt **inefficiently** with the crisis. 彼は，非効率的に危機に対処した．

effort

接尾 (less) **effortless** *adj* 努力を必要としない，難しくない ► comparatively **effortless** editing 比較的楽な［難しくない］編集作業

接尾 (less) **effortlessly** *ad* 苦もなく，努力することなく ► He was way down the trail in front of them, gliding **effortlessly** over the ground in true wolf fashion. 彼は，本物の狼のように苦もなく地面をスッと通り越して，彼らの前で道を外れた．

接尾 (less) **effortlessness** *n* 努力を必要としないこと ► Such **effortlessness** is achieved only after hours of practice. このような無用な努力は，何時間か練習しさえすれば回避できる．

ejection

接頭 (non) **non-ejection** *n* 非駆出性 ► a single **non-ejection** systolic click 単純非駆出性収縮期クリック音

elastic

接頭 (in) **inelastic** *adj*

❶弾力性のない，非弾性的な，非弾性の ► Economists speak of an **inelastic** price structure. 経済学者は非弾力的な価格構造について話している．

❷適応性のない，順応性のない

electable

接頭 (un) **unelectable** *adj* 当選困難な

electoral

接頭 (non) **non-electoral** *adj* 非選挙の ► As a result, I am in favor of letting localities with too few candidates choose a **non-**

electoral means of selecting assembly members. その結果，候補のほとんどいない地域では議員の選出に選挙以外の手段を選択させることに私は賛成である.

electro

接尾 (less) **electroless** *adj* 無電解の ▶ **electroless** metal deposition 無電解金属めっき ▶ This led to a general belief that the problem was caused by excessive or uncontrolled phosphorus co-deposition during **electroless** nickel plating. このことが，その問題が無電解ニッケルめっき中に過度のあるいは無制御のリンの共析出により生じるという一般認識を招く.

electrolytic

接頭 (non) **nonelectrolytic** *adj* 非電子的 ▶ Chlorine production for 1967 in the United States was about 69.8% in diaphragm cells . . . and the remainder in fused-salt electrolysis and **nonelectrolytic** cells. 米国における1967年の塩素の生産は，69.8 %が隔膜電解槽法であり，…，残りは溶融塩電解槽法および非電解槽法で行った.

elegance

接頭 (in) **inelegance** *n* 優雅でないこと，不粋

elegant

接頭 (in) **inelegant** *adj* 優雅でない，洗練されていない ▶ Both these methods are considered **inelegant** and imprecise by experts. これらの方法は，どちらも，専門家からは，洗練されておらず，不正確だとみなされている.

eligibility

接頭 (in) **ineligibility** *n* 不適格，無資格

eligible

接頭 (in) **ineligible** *adj* 資格のない，不適格な，不適当な ▶ On examination, half the goods were found to be **ineligible**. 検査の結果，物品の半数は不合格であった.

eloquent

接頭 (in) **ineloquent** *adj* 口下手の

elucidated

接頭 (un) **unelucidated** *adj* 解明不可能な ▶ During cell division, these units are duplicated and a complete set is distributed to each new cell by an orderly but as yet **unelucidated** mechanism. 細胞分裂の間，これらのユニットは複製され，完全なセットが，まだ解明不可能であるが規則正しい機構によって，それぞれの新しい細胞に配られる．

embarrass

接頭 (dis) **disembarrass** *v* 〈心配や困難から〉 解放する ▶ She was able to **disembarrass** herself from all the busy complications of life. 彼女は，生きていく上でのあらゆる煩雑さから自分自身を解放することができた．

emotion

接尾 (less) **emotionless** *adj*

❶感情を表さない ▶ He kept his **emotionless** objectivity and faith in the cause he served. 自分の主義として彼は感情的にならない客観性と誠実さを保った．

❷無表情の ▶ Her face was set and **emotionless** and I knew that she did not recognize me. 彼女の顔がこわばり無表情だったので，私のことも見覚えがないということが分かった．

emotional

接頭 (un) **unemotional** *adj* 感情を表さない

emphasis

接頭 (de) **de-emphasis** *n* 重点を置かないこと ▶ One significant trend has been a **de-emphasis** on value-of-service pricing. 一つの特徴ある傾向は，サービス価格についてはこれまでほど強調しないことであった．

emphasize

接頭 (de) **de-emphasize** *v* 重点を置かない ▶ Scientists and engineers use it to **de-emphasize** the actor and place the emphasis on the action. 科学者や技術者らは動作主にあまり重きをおかず，動作を重視する．

employable

接頭 (un) **unemployable** *adj* 雇用に適さない

employed

接頭 (un) **unemployed** *adj* 失業中の ► He's been **unemployed** for two years. 彼は2年間失業している.

employment

接頭 (un) **unemployment** *n* 失業 ► the temporary **unemployment** created by the mechanization of hand work 手作業の機械化による一時的失業者数

encapsulated

接頭 (un) **unencapsulated** *adj*

❶ カプセルに包まれていない ► Encapsulated strains of a given bacteria species are more likely to cause disease than **unencapsulated** strains. バクテリアのある種は, 莢膜を形成しない菌株よりも莢膜を形成する菌株のほうが病気を引き起こしがちだ.

❷ 保護されていない

enchant

接頭 (dis) **disenchant** *v* 迷いを覚ます ► They are not necessarily **disenchanted** with engineering. 彼らは, 工学技術に関して必ずしも幻滅を感じているわけではない.

enchantment

接頭 (dis) **disenchantment** *n* 幻滅 ► The terms of this enactment, as well as of later statutes during the New Deal of the 1930s revealed a **disenchantment** with interrailroad competition and . . . 1930年代のニューディール政策施行時代の後半の情勢と同様, この法律の言葉は, 国内鉄道の競争に幻滅を見たり, …

end

接尾 (less) **endless** *adj*

❶ 無限の ► In addition to having an almost **endless** source of fuel in deuterium which is quite easily separable from . . . …か

ら極めて簡単に分離できる重水素中には，ほとんど無限の燃料源があるのに加えて，…

❷ 無数の ▸ Modern books include **endless** varieties and styles. 現代の書籍には，無数の種類と様式がある.

❸ 循環の，継ぎ目なしの ▸ An **endless** belt carrying the dry concentrates passes into a tank where . . . 乾燥した精鉱を運ぶ継ぎ目なしのベルトはタンク内に入り，….

❹ 果てしない ▸ The executives began what seemed like an **endless** string of discussions about Kindler's complex vision. 重役たちは，キンドラーの複雑な構想について果てしなく続くようにみえる議論を始めた.

接尾 (less) **endlessly** *ad*

❶ 際限なく，止めどなく，延々と ▸ We laughed, cried, and talked **endlessly** into the night. 私たちは夜まで延々と，笑い，泣き，話し合った.

❷ 果てしなく続く ▸ It is a sort of steady, **endlessly** driving downpour. それは，果てしなく降りつける，一種の継続的な土砂降りである.

接尾 (less) **endlessness** *n* 果てしなさ，終わりがないこと

ending

接頭 (un) **unending** *adj* 終わることのない ▸ Inside the body, a trillion highly specialized cells, honed by hundreds of millions of years of evolution, launch an **unending** battle against the alien organisms. 体の内部で，数億年の進化で磨かれることによって高度に特殊化した何兆もの細胞は，異質の有機体との終わることのない戦いを始める.

endurable

接頭 (un) **unendurable** *adj* 耐えられない ▸ Sometimes **unendurable** boredom leads one to form friendships and fall in love. 耐えられない倦怠感が友情や恋愛を導くこともある.

energize

接頭 (de) **de-energize** *v*

❶活気を弱める

❷〈電気や接続を〉遮断する ► A circuit breaker serves in the course of normal system operation to energize or **de-energize** loads. ブレーカーは，通常のシステム作動の過程において，負荷を加えたり，遮断したりする働きをする．

energized

接頭 (de) **de-energized** *adj* 非通電にされた ► A portion of the output signal is fed to an output stage which keeps the relay **de-energized** as long as no object breaks the ultrasonic beam. 出力信号の一部は，物体が超音波ビームを遮断しないかぎりリレーを非通電状態に保持する出力ステージに供給される．

engage

接頭 (dis) **disengage** *v* 解放する，離す，自由にする ► Depress and **disengage** the receiver pin lock and remove it from the receiver pin. 受信機ピンロックを押し下げて離し，受信機ピンから取り外してください．

engaged

接頭 (dis) **disengaged** *adj* 解放された

English

接頭 (un) **un-English** *adj* 英国(人)らしくない ► The purple shutters on her house had a decidedly **un-English** look. 彼女の家の紫色のシャッターは，明らかに英国らしくない．

enlightened

接頭 (un) **unenlightened** *adj* 知らされていない

entangle

接頭 (dis) **disentangle** *v* 解き放つ

enthrall

接頭 (dis) **disenthrall** *v* 束縛を解く

entity

接頭 (non) **nonentity** *n* 実在しないこと

entomb

接頭 (dis) **disentomb** *v* 〈墓などから〉掘り出す

enviable

接頭 (un) **unenviable** *adj* 好ましくない，やりたくない ► Adobe runs the risk of becoming of the standard bearer of a commodity industry — an **unenviable** position for a company that once owned the market for printer graphics. アドビ社は，かつてプリンターグラフィックスの市場を保有した会社にとってはあまり羨ましがられることのない地位である，汎用品産業界の旗頭となるリスクをあえて冒そうとしている．

equable

接頭 (in) **inequable** *adj* 均一でない

equal

接頭 (un) **unequal** *adj* 同等でない ► However, cracking in extrusions of unsymmetrical shape may occur because of **unequal** flow in different sections. しかしながら，異種断面で同等ではない流れが生じるために，非対称形状の押し出し材にクラッキングが発生する可能性がある．

equaled

接頭 (un) **unequaled** *adj* 匹敵するものがない，無比の ► Railroads assembled supplies at forward depots and shifted thousands of troops with **unequaled** dispatch from one theater of war to another. 鉄道は，前線基地に補給を行い，ある戦域から別の戦域へと無比の手早さで数千の軍隊を移動させる．

equality

接頭 (in) **inequality** *n*

❶ 不平等 ► a movement to do away with **inequality** 不平等をなくす運動．

❷ 不等 ► a mathematical sign, called the sign of **inequality** 不等号という数学記号

equation

接頭 (in) **inequation** *n* 不等式

equilateral

接頭 (in) **inequilateral** *adj* 不等辺の ► an **inequilateral** triangle 不等辺三角形

equilibrium

[接頭]（dis）**disequilibrium** *n* 不均衡 ▶ Despite the impact of global economic **disequilibrium** and surging oil prices, the world economy has performed well beyond expectations. 世界的な経済不均衡と高騰している石油価格の影響にもかかわらず，世界経済は予想以上に良くなっている．

equipped

[接頭]（ill）**ill-equipped** *adj* 設備の不十分な，準備不足の ▶ **ill-equipped** for the many challenges and hardships 多くの難題や苦難に対する心構えができていない

equitable

[接頭]（in）**inequitable** *adj* 不公平な ▶ an **inequitable** tax system 不公平税制

equitably

[接頭]（in）**inequitably** *ad* 不公平に

equity

[接頭]（in）**inequity** *n* 不公平

equivocal

[接頭]（un）**unequivocal** *adj* 曖昧でない，絶対的な

equivocally

[接頭]（un）**unequivocally** *ad* 曖昧でなく，絶対的に ▶ "Much the same question existed for IDL until this decade, when it was **unequivocally** shown that lowering IDL decreases the risk," says Levy.「IDL の低減はリスクを削減するということがはっきりと示されるこの年代まで，IDL に関してほとんど同じ疑問が存在していた」と，レビー氏は述べている．

erasable

[接頭]（in）**inerasable** *adj* 消すことのできない

errancy

[接頭]（in）**inerrancy** *n* 間違いのないこと

errant

接頭 (in) **inerrant** *adj* 誤りのない

erring

接頭 (un) **unerring** *adj* 誤りを犯さない

erringly

接頭 (un) **unerringly** *ad* 誤ることなく ▶ It can store binary numbers of 36 digits and recall them **unerringly** at microsecond speeds. それは，36桁のバイナリー数値を格納でき，マイクロ秒の速度で誤ることなくそれらを呼び出すことができる．

escapable

接頭 (in) **inescapable** *adj* 逃げられない，不可避の ▶ But sad to say, the increase of three kilograms was an **inescapable** fact. しかし悲しいかな，3キロの増加は紛れもない事実だった．

接頭 (un) **unescapable** *adj* 逃げることのできない，必然の

接頭 (in) **inescapably** *ad* 不可避的に，必然的に，いや応なく ▶ **inescapably** tied to ～とは切っても切れない関係である

essential

接頭 (in) **inessential** *adj* 不必要な，本質的でない ▶ characterized by the absence of **inessential** features 不必要な機能の欠如によって特徴づけられる

接頭 (non) **nonessential** *adj* 重要でない，基本的でない ▶ Episomes are usually **nonessential** to the individual cell. エピソームは，個々の細胞においては一般に重要ではない．

接頭 (un) **unessential** *adj* 本質的でない ▶ It's time to remove everything **unessential** in your life. あなたの人生で本質的でないすべてのものを取り除く時が来た．

establish

接頭 (dis) **disestablish** *v* 〈体制などを〉廃止する

established

接頭 (un) **unestablished** *adj* 設定されていない

estimable

接頭 (in) **inestimable** *adj* 計り知れない（ほど貴重な），評価

しがたい，無数の ▶ The extent of the damage is **inestimable**. 損失の程度は計り知れない．

ethical

接頭 (un) **unethical** *adj* 非倫理的な ▶ While the idea predates insider trading, it has never been considered illegal or **unethical**. その考えは，インサイダー取引に先行する一方，不当とも非倫理的とも思われなかった．

even

接頭 (un) **uneven** *adj*

❶ 不均質な，不均一な ▶ A variation in sheet thickness causes a nonuniform sheet temperature distribution resulting in **uneven** pulling and possible tearing of the sheet. シート厚の変動によってシートの温度分布が不斉一になり，引っ張りが不均一になってシートが裂ける可能性がある．

❷ むらがある ▶ It is usually wasteful of water, and unless the land is naturally smooth, the resulting irrigation will be quite **uneven**. それは通常は水の浪費であり，土地が自然な状態でも平坦でない限り，それによって形成される潅漑に大きなむらができる．

❸ 一様でない ▶ **Uneven** brush wear causes apparent brush-axis shaft. ブラシの摩耗が一様でないと，ブラシ軸は目でわかるほど変化する．

❹ でこぼこな ▶ The wheels bumped and jolted over the **uneven** surface. 車輪はでこぼこな路面をがたがた揺れて通った．

evenness

接頭 (un) **unevenness** *n*

❶ 不均質 ▶ Machine-planed surfaces are given slight hollows, to simulate the **unevenness** of early lumber processing methods, by local sanding with a disk sander. 機械によって平面加工した表面には，初期の材木加工方法の不均質さを模倣するために，ディスクサンダーを使用した局部的な研磨加工によっ

てくぼみが少し作られている.

❷凹凸 ▸ **unevenness** of the crack surface 破面の凹凸

event

接頭 (non) **nonevent** *n* 期待はずれの行事

eventful

接頭 (un) **uneventful** *adj* 何事もない

evitable

接頭 (in) **inevitable** *adj*

❶ついてくる, (〜に) つきものの ▸ The signal becomes weaker with distance, dropping nearer to the **inevitable** noise in the medium. 信号は距離が増すとともに弱まり, 媒体につきもののノイズに近いレベルまで落ちる.

❷避けられない, 不可避の ▸ However, this situation is not **inevitable**. だが, この状況は避けられないことではない. ▸ Though adults criticize children for becoming absorbed in computer games and cartoons, this phenomenon is the **inevitable** product of the present-day environment. 大人は子どもたちがコンピューターゲーム機や漫画に没頭することを非難するが, この現象は現在の環境が生み出した避けられない産物である.

❸避けられない, 当然の ▸ It is **inevitable** that people are concerned about their own interests. 人が, 自身の利害得失にこだわるのは当然である.

接頭 (in) **inevitability** *n*

❶必然性 ▸ An examination of the Edo period shows that Japan's astonishing modernization during the Meiji period was an **inevitability**. 江戸時代を見れば, 明治以降の目の覚めるような近代化は必然だった.

❷不可避性 ▸ the **inevitability** of the decision 決定が避けがたいこと

接頭 (in) **inevitably** *ad*

❶必然的に, 不可避的に ▸ Who is going to help the large

number of weaker and less successful people that such a system **inevitably** spawns? このようなシステムが不可避的に生み出す大量の弱者や敗者を，誰が救済するのか．

❷ 間違いなく，いや応なく ► When these components are finally put together, new bugs **inevitably** turn up. これらの構成要素を最終的に組み立てると，新しいバグが間違いなく現れてくる．

exact

接頭 (in) **inexact** *adj*

❶ 不完全な ► **inexact** differential 不完全微分

❷ 不正確な ► If you have been **inexact** in any point, you had better correct it. もし少しでも不正確な点があれば，訂正した方が良い．

exactitude

接頭 (in) **inexactitude** *n* 不正確

exactly

接頭 (in) **inexactly** *ad* 不正確に

exactness

接頭 (in) **inexactness** *n* 不正確，厳密でないこと

exampled

接頭 (un) **unexampled** *adj* 例を見ない ► The country is in a condition of profound peace as well as of **unexampled** prosperity. 同国は，例を見ないほどの繁栄と完全な平和状態にある．

exceptionable

接頭 (un) **unexceptionable** *adj* 申し分のない

exceptional

接頭 (un) **unexceptional** *adj* 例外でない

excitable

接頭 (in) **inexcitable** *adj* すぐに興奮しない，冷静な ► an **inexcitable** cell 非興奮性細胞

excited

接頭 (non) **nonexcited** *adj* 非励起の ► **Nonexcited** motors

are made in reluctance and hysteresis designs. 非励起モーターは，磁気抵抗およびヒステリシス形である．

excusable

接頭 (in) **inexcusable** *adj* 弁解できない，けしからん ► Your late arrival at the meeting is **inexcusable.** 会議に遅れるとはけしからん．

excusableness

接頭 (in) **inexcusableness** *n* 許しがたいこと，弁解の余地のないこと

executive

接頭 (non) **nonexecutive** *adj* 非常勤の，管理職でない ► The **nonexecutive** chairman founded the New York office. その非常勤の会長がニューヨークオフィスを設立した．

exhaustible

接頭 (in) **inexhaustible** *adj*

❶尽きることのない，無尽蔵の ► An almost **inexhaustible** energy source becomes possible with breeder reactors. 増殖炉により，ほとんど無尽蔵のエネルギー源が実現する．

❷疲れを知らない

接頭 (in) **inexhaustibleness** *n*

❶無尽蔵

❷疲れを知らないこと

接頭 (in) **inexhaustibly** *adj*

❶尽きることなく

❷疲れを知らないように

exhaustive

接頭 (in) **inexhaustive** *adj* すべてを網羅していない，徹底的でない

接頭 (non) **nonexhaustive** *adj* 徹底していない，不徹底の ► An examination of this **nonexhaustive** list of supplementary services shows that several are not fundamentally new. 追加サービスの不完全な［不徹底な］リストによる検査では，そのいく

つかのサービスは基本的に新しいものではないことを示している.

exhaustively

接頭 (in) **inexhaustively** *ad* すべてを網羅せずに, 徹底的でなく

existence

接頭 (non) **nonexistence** *n* 存在しないもの, 非実在

existent

接頭 (in) **inexistent** *adj* 存在しない

接頭 (non) **nonexistent** *adj* 存在しない ► It is **nonexistent** in nature, although it is believed that ... それは自然界には存在しないが, …と考えられている. ► To pass over the style of technical writing as **nonexistent** is to miss the basic ingredient of the craft. テクニカルライティングのスタイルを存在しないとして片付けてしまうと, その技法の基本的な要素をとらえそこなうことになる. ► Back then, America was as good as **nonexistent** on the stage of world history. その当時は, アメリカは世界史の舞台に存在しないに等しかった. ► Tritium is almost **nonexistent** in nature, although it is believed that cosmic rays may produce some of it in the earth's upper atmosphere. トリチウムは, 宇宙線により地球の大気の上層部で一部生じると思われているが, 自然界にはほとんど存在しない.

exorable

接頭 (in) **inexorable** *adj*

❶ 不変の, 不動の ► the **inexorable** passage of the seasons 人の力では動かしがたい季節の移り変わり

❷ 断固とした ► one's **inexorable** resolution 断固とした決意

❸ 容赦ない, 無慈悲な ► North American gas production was in **inexorable** decline. 北米のガス生産量は容赦なく下がった.

接頭 (in) **inexorably** *ad* 容赦なく ► Time moves on **inexorably**. 時は容赦なく過ぎてゆく.

expectant

[接頭] (in) **inexpectant** *adj* 期待していない

expected

[接頭] (un) **unexpected** *adj*

❶ 予期しなかった ▸ Animals wearing assist pumps developed blood clots in **unexpected** places, such as kidneys and lungs. 補助ポンプを装着した動物では，腎臓や肺など予想外の場所に凝血塊ができた.

❷ 期待していなかった ▸ If you get **unexpected** results — if the application behaves strangely — these are indications that you probably need to update the system software. 結果が予想外の場合—アプリケーションの挙動が奇妙な場合—これらはシステムソフトウェアのアップデートが必要であることを示している可能性がある.

❸ 思いがけない ▸ It was **unexpected** news. それは，思いがけないニュースだった. ▸ **unexpected** changes in water pressures 水圧の思いがけない変化

❹ 意外な ▸ an **unexpected** trend 一つの意外な傾向

expectedly

[接頭] (un) **unexpectedly** *ad* 予期せずに，突然に ▸ **Unexpectedly,** researchers found that . . . 調査員たちは，突然，…ということに気づいた. ▸ After being moistened inside the lab, it suddenly released an **unexpectedly** high burst of oxygen, setting off a flurry of speculation among scientists on earth. それは，ラボ内で湿らされた後，予想に反して一気に酸素を放出し，地上の科学者の間に憶測による混乱を引き起こした.

expedience

[接頭] (in) **inexpedience** *n* (目的達成を阻害する)不都合，不便

expedient

[接頭] (in) **inexpedient** *adj* 不便な，不得策な ▸ Why resort to such **inexpedient** means? なぜそんな不便な方法を取るのか.

expedienly

[接頭] (in) **inexpediently** *ad* 〈目的などに〉不適当に

expendable

[接頭] (un) **unexpendable** *adj* 欠くことのできない

expensive

[接頭] (in) **inexpensive** *adj* 安価な, 費用のかからない ► Public-domain programs and shareware provide an **inexpensive** alternative to costly commercial software. パブリック・ドメイン・プログラムやシェアウエアは, 高価な市販のソフトに替わり, 安価に提供される.

[接頭] (less) **less-expensive** *adj* 高価でない, 安価な ► Pre-cooling reduces the load on the chiller so that smaller, **less-expensive** heat exchangers and compressors can be used. 予冷却によって, より小型で低価格の熱交換器とコンプレッサーを使用できるように, チラーに加わる負荷を低下させる.

expensively

[接頭] (in) **inexpensively** *ad* 安価に, 安い費用で ► Hydrogen can be made **inexpensively** by passing steam over hot carbon. 熱した炭素にスチームをかけると水素を安上がりに作ることができる.

experienced

[接頭] (in) **inexperienced** *adj* 経験不足の, 未熟な, ふつつか者で ► My daughter is too **inexperienced** and innocent to know that. うちの娘は未熟であり純真なため, そんなことを知らない.

[接頭] (un) **unexperienced** *adj* 経験のない

expert

[接頭] (in) **inexpert** *adj* 未熟な, 上手でない ► Balance sheets can be made to look all right to the **inexpert** eye. 貸借対照表というものは, 素人の眼にはすべて問題ないように見せかけることができるものだ.

[接頭] (non) **nonexpert** *n* 非専門家 ► In this lesson, the "classic" families of integrated logic circuits will be described to help the **nonexpert** engineer become more familiar with their operation. この課では，総合論理回路の「古典的」ファミリーについて説明し，非専門技術者がもっとこの操作に慣れるようにする．

expertly

接頭 (in) **inexpertly** *ad* 素人っぽく，不器用に

expertness

接頭 (in) **inexpertness** *n* 素人っぽさ，不器用さ

expiable

接頭 (in) **inexpiable** *adj* 償いようのない ▶ **inexpiable** guilt 罪深い過ち

expiated

接頭 (in) **inexpiate** *adj* 〈罪が〉償われていない

explainable

接頭 (in) **inexplainable** *adj* 説明できない，不可解な

explained

接頭 (un) **unexplained** *adj* 説明されることなく ▶ The shape of Type II is almost independent of RF power but depends on the magnetic field modulation, which remains **unexplained** at the present stage. タイプ II の形状は，RF パワーにおおよそ依存はしないが，現段階ではまだ説明されていない磁界変調に依存する．

explicable

接頭 (in) **inexplicable** *adj*

❶ 説明できない，理解できない ▶ They pieced together the almost more fantastical story of the dinosaurs and their **inexplicable** demise. 彼らは，恐竜とそれらの説明のつかない絶滅について，ほとんど空想的な物語をつなぎ合わせた．

❷ 不可解な ▶ a completely **inexplicable** phenomenon まったく不可解な現象

接頭 (in) **inexplicably** *ad* 不可解に(も)，説明できないほどに ▶ **Inexplicably**, Mary said she wouldn't go. 不可解なことだが，

メアリーはどうしても行かないと言った.

explicit

接頭 (in) **inexplicit** *adj* はっきり言わない, 言葉の曖昧な ► It is **inexplicit** on the subject. それは, そのことについてはっきりしていない.

exploited

接頭 (un) **unexploited** *adj* 〈資源などが〉開発されていない

explosive

接頭 (in) **inexplosive** *adj* 不爆発 (性) の

expressed

接頭 (un) **unexpressed** *adj* 表現されない

expressible

接頭 (in) **inexpressible** *adj*

❶ 説明できない ► something **inexpressible** in words 言葉では説明できないあること

❷ 言葉で表せない ► For an instant they gazed upon each other with **inexpressible** tenderness. 一瞬, 彼らは言い表せない優しさでお互い見つめあった.

expression

接尾 (less) **expressionless** *adj* 表情なく, 無表情な, のっぺり ► **expressionless** white face 無表情で青白い顔 ► Monty's hand was limp and cold, his eyes were glazed and **expressionless**. モンティの手は, だらんとして冷たく, 目はどんよりして, 無表情だった.

接尾 (less) **expressionlessly** *ad* 無表情に, 表情に乏しく ► She reads **expressionlessly**, her sweep of shiny hair hiding her face, but the content is fascinating. 彼女は無表情に朗読し, 豊かな艶のある髪の毛が顔を隠していたが, 話の内容は魅惑的であった.

接尾 (less) **expressionlessness** *n* 無表情な状態

expressive

接頭 (in) **inexpressive** *adj* 無表情の ► an **inexpressive** face

無表情な顔

接頭 (un) **unexpressive** *adj* 表現が乏しい ► You can never get a date if you are always shy and **unexpressive** of your feeling. あなたが常に内気で，感情表現に乏しければ，決してデートに成功できない．

expugnable

接頭 (in) **inexpugnable** *adj* 難攻不落の，論破できない ► build oneself a castle in an **inexpugnable** position 難攻不落の場所に城を構える

expurgated

接頭 (un) **unexpurgated** *adj* 〈書物などの不適切な部分などが〉削除されていない

extensible

接頭 (in) **inextensible** *adj*

❶ 伸びない ► A simple pendulum is defined as a particle suspended from a fixed point by a weightless **inextensible** string. 単振子は，重量がなく伸びない糸で，固定点から吊るされる小片であると定義される．

❷ 延期できない ► within an **inextensible** term of 15 days as from respective notifications 各々の通知から起算して延期できない15日以内に

extension

接頭 (in) **inextension** *n* 不拡張

extensional

接頭 (in) **inextensional** *adj* 伸びない ► **inextensional** deformation 伸びなし変形

extinguishable

接頭 (in) **inextinguishable** *adj* 消すことのできない，抑え切れない ► **inextinguishable** ardor 抑え切れない情熱 ► At first my efforts met with stares of surprise or **inextinguishable** laughter. 最初のうち，私の努力は驚きの凝視か，とめどない笑いをもって迎えられた．

extricable

接頭 (in) **inextricable** *adj*

❶ほどけない ► an **inextricable** knot ほどけない結び目

❷切り離せない ► That message is **inextricable** from Peter's biography. あのメッセージは，ピーターの経歴から切り離せない．

❸問題が解決できない ► a state of **inextricable** confusion 手がつけられないほど物事が混乱している状態

eye

接尾 (less) **eyeless** *adj* 目のない，盲目の ► I held out my hand, and the horrible, soft-spoken, **eyeless** creature gripped it in a moment like a vise. 手を出すと，恐ろしい，穏やかな声を出す，目のない生き物が，あっという間に万力のように手をしっかりとつかんだ．

接尾 (less) **eyelessly** *ad* 盲目の状態で

接尾 (less) **eyelessness** *n* 盲目

F

face

［接尾］(less) **faceless** *adj*

❶ 個性のない ► Heisei is still nebulous, something **faceless** and intangible.「平成」はまだあやふやで，個性がなくつかみどころがない．

❷ 匿名の ► the **faceless** accusers of the police state 警察国家の匿名の告発者

❸ のっぺりした ► the **faceless** monster of Japanese legend, called 'nopperabo' 日本の言い伝えで,「のっぺらぼう」という化け物

［接尾］(less) **facelessness** *n*

❶顔のないこと

❷個性のないこと，特徴のないこと

fade

［接尾］(less) **fadeless** *adj* 色あせない

failing

［接頭］(un) **unfailing** *adj* 間違いのない，信頼できる

failingly

［接頭］(un) **unfailingly** *ad* 間違いなしに ► He is **unfailingly** polite, greeting all the staff and many of the customers by name. 彼は確かに礼儀正しく，すべてのスタッフと多くの顧客に名前を呼びながら挨拶をする．

fair

［接頭］(un) **unfair** *adj* 不公平な ► The question of **unfair** subsidization can be simply overcome. 不公平な助成金支給の問題は簡単に解決できる． ► This should not be construed as an **unfair** trade subsidy since its only purpose would be to rectify market imperfections. その唯一の目的は市場の欠陥を是正することであるから，これは不公平な貿易助成金として解釈さ

れるべきではない.

fairly

接頭 (un) **unfairly** *ad* 不公平に ► These engineers feel it would be difficult for them to continue working for a company they know to be dealing **unfairly** with customers. これらのエンジニアは, 顧客と不公正な取引をしている会社と認めて働き続けることは困難であると感じるであろう.

fairness

接頭 (un) **unfairness** *n* 不公平, 不当

faith

接尾 (less) **faithless** *adj*

❶ 信仰心のない ► Jesus answered, "**Faithless** and perverse generation! How long will I be with you? How long will I bear with you? イエスは彼らに言った,「信仰のないねじ曲がった世代よ! いつまで私はあなた方と一緒にいようか. いつまであなた方のことを我慢しようか」

❷ 不誠実な, 不忠実な, 不実な

接尾 (less) **faithlessly** *ad* 不誠実に ► Not since The Day After Tomorrow has New York City itself been so **faithlessly** rendered on the big screen. ニューヨーク市自体が大スクリーンで非常に不誠実に描かれてきたのは映画「ザ・デイ・アフター・トゥモロー」に始まったことではない.

接尾 (less) **faithlessness** *n* 不誠実 ► Now you shall receive your due for your **faithlessness**. 今こそ君は自分の不誠実さの報いを受けるべきだ.

faithful

接頭 (un) **unfaithful** *adj* 誠実でない, 忠実でない ► Commonly quoted statistics suggest that more men are **unfaithful** to their partners than women. 一般的な統計は, 女性よりも男性のほうが多く浮気をしていることを示唆している.

fallibility

接頭 (in) **infallibility** *n* 絶対確実性 ► All silencing of discussion is an assumption of **infallibility**. 議論を黙らせることはすべて，無謬性を仮定することになります.

fallible

接頭 (in) **infallible** *adj*

❶ 絶対間違いのない，絶対確実な ▶ There is no **infallible** method of curing hiccups. しゃっくりを治す絶対確実な方法はない.

❷ 間違いのないこと ▶ an **infallible** watch 狂いのない時計

接頭 (in) **infallibleness** *n* 完璧さ

fallibly

接頭 (in) **infallibly** *ad* 完璧に ▶ I know that it leads **infallibly** to me. 私が割り出されるのは分かりきっています.

faltering

接頭 (un) **unfaltering** *adj* (足取りなどが) よろよろしない

famed

接頭 (ill) **ill-famed** *adj* 評判の悪い

familiar

接頭 (un) **unfamiliar** *adj*

❶ 不慣れな，精通していない ▶ Technical writing abounds in new terms and concepts that may be **unfamiliar** to the reader. テクニカルライターの仕事は，読者が精通していない新しい用語や概念にあふれている. ▶ It is certain that he is **unfamiliar** with the technical ramifications. 彼が，技術的な派生問題には精通していないことは間違いない.

❷ (人との) 親交がない

familiarity

接頭 (un) **unfamiliarity** *n* 不慣れ，精通していないこと ▶ If **unfamiliarity** of surroundings is keeping the patient awake, all you can do is try and leave the rest of his routine as unchanged as possible. 周辺環境に対する不慣れが原因で患者が眠れない場合にできることは，患者のすべての日課を可能な限り変えないように努めることである.

famous

接頭 (in) **infamous** *adj*

❶ 評判の悪い ► The PC industry is **infamous** for a lack of standards. PC 業界は規格がないことで悪評を買う.

❷ 不名誉な ► **infamous** names 不名誉な名前 ► The companies in the most **infamous** scandals of the past several years were in widely different industries but shared one trait. 過去数年間で最も不名誉なスキャンダルを起こした企業は, 広くさまざまな業界に存在したが, ある特徴を共有していた.

famously

接頭 (in) **infamously** *ad* 不名誉にも ► His team suffered an **infamously** crushing defeat in the game. 不名誉なことに彼のチームはその試合で大敗してしまった.

fashionable

接頭 (un) **unfashionable** *adj* 流行遅れの, 人気のない

fasten

接頭 (un) **unfasten** *adj* 〈ベルトやねじなどを〉緩める ► Finally I was able to **unfasten** my seatbelt. やっとシートベルトを緩めることができた.

fat

接尾 (less) **fatless** *adj* 脂肪分のない ► a **fatless** girl 脂肪のない女の子

接頭 (non) **nonfat** *adj* 脂肪分のない, 脱脂の ► High-test sweet cream, **nonfat** dry milk solids, and water may be added to produce a cheese. 高度スイートクリーム, 脱脂粉乳固形物, および水を加えてチーズを作ることができる.

fated

接頭 (ill) **ill-fated** *adj* 不運な ► an **ill-fated** battle 不運な戦い

father

接尾 (less) **fatherless** *adj* 父親のいない, 父が亡くなった ► For some reason, he grew up in a **fatherless** family. 彼は, ある事情から父親のいない家庭で育った. ► a **fatherless** daughter

父親のいない娘

fathomable

接頭 (un) **unfathomable** *adj* 計り知れない

fault

接尾 (less) **faultless** *adj* 欠点のない，無傷の，非の打ちどころのない

接尾 (less) **faultlessly** *ad* 非の打ちどころなく ► He solved all the problems **faultlessly**. 彼はすべての問題を完全に解決した.

接尾 (less) **faultlessness** *n* 無傷，非の打ちどころのないこと ► It is the chill **faultlessness** of the man which is so depressing. それはその男の冷たい完全無欠さで，非常に気がめいるものである.

favor

接頭 (dis) **disfavor** *n* 冷遇，嫌悪

favorable

接頭 (un) **unfavorable** *adj* 好ましくない，不都合な ► These conditions are **unfavorable** to the experiment. これらの条件で実験を行うのは好ましくない. ► For a further check on the probability of this **unfavorable** occurrence, vibratory forces can be measured on the model using the techniques of Kuo. この不都合なことが発生する確率についてさらにチェックするため，そのモデルの起振力をクオの技術を使用して測定する.

favored

接頭 (ill) **ill-favored** *adj* 容姿が悪い，いやな感じの ► the room which he had rented from his **ill-favored** hostess 彼がいやな感じの女主人から借りていた部屋

faze

接頭 (un) **unfaze** *v* 煩わせない，動じない ► Ordinarily the agency, long hailed by intimidated taxpayers as a model of efficiency, is **unfazed** by the awesome bureaucratic burden. 脅威におびえる納税者によって，効率的モデルとして長い間支持さ

れたその機関は，すさまじい官僚主義の重荷にも動じないのが普通である．

fazed

接頭 (un) **unfazed** *adj* 煩わされた

fear

接尾 (less) **fearless** *adj* 恐れ知らずの，勇敢な，神経が太い ▶ He is a clever and **fearless** player. 彼は，賢くて，怖いもの知らずのプレーヤーである．

接尾 (less) **fearlessly** *ad* 恐れず（に） ▶ In the meantime, all we can do is to work patiently, **fearlessly**, and unselfishly to an end that we think is right. しばらくの間，我々のできることは，正しいと思うことを終わりまで，根気よく，恐れずに，寛大に取り組むことである．

接尾 (less) **fearlessness** *n* 恐怖心のなさ ▶ an editor who was always vaunting the purity, enterprise, and **fearlessness** of his paper いつも自らの新聞の純粋さ，進取の気象，大胆さを自慢している編集長

feasibility

接頭 (in) **infeasibility** *n* 実行できないこと

feasible

接頭 (in) **infeasible** *adj*

❶ 実行不可能な ▶ This is, of course, technologically **infeasible** for large problems. これは，いうまでもなく，大きな問題に対しては技術的に実行不可能である．

❷ 実際にはできない ▶ **infeasible** in spite of eagerness 熱望はするが実際には出来ないさま

接頭 (un) **unfeasible** *adj* 実行困難な ▶ This additional radiation loss can be very serious in the care of a reactor and may make some schemes which have been proposed **unfeasible** energy-wise. このさらなる放射損失は，原子炉の保護に非常に深刻なものとなり，提案された計画をエネルギー的に実行困難なものにする．

feasibleness

接頭 (in) **infeasibleness** *n* 実行できないこと

feather

接尾 (less) **featherless** *adj* 羽根のない ▶ Two **featherless** beings appeared, uninvited, at the door of the summer-house and surveyed the creepers. 夏の別荘のドアに，招かれざる2匹の羽のない生き物が現れ，そのつる植物を見回した.

接尾 (less) **featherlessness** *n* 羽根のない状態

feature

接尾 (less) **featureless** *adj* 特徴［特色］のない ▶ The spacecraft detected a tenth ring and other surface features on five large moons that until now had been seen only as **featureless** spots of light. 宇宙船は，今まではなんら特徴のない光の点にしか見えなかった5つの大きな衛星の上に，10番目の環と，その他の表面兆候を認めた.

接尾 (less) **featurelessly** *ad* 特徴のないように

接尾 (less) **featurelessness** *n* 特徴のない状態

feck

接尾 (less) **feckless** *adj*

❶ 無気力な，無関心な ▶ Perhaps this lad's mother also was a **feckless** old woman devoid of character? 多分，この若者の母親も無気力な老婦人で，品性に欠けていたか.

❷ 無駄な ▶ **feckless** attempts to repair the plumbing 配管を修理する無駄な試み

fed

接頭 (ill) **ill-fed** *adj* 栄養不良の

feeling

接頭 (un) **unfeeling** *adj* 感覚のない

feigned

接頭 (un) **unfeigned** *adj* 偽りのない

felicitous

接頭 (in) **infelicitous** *adj* 不適切な，不幸な

ferrous

接頭 (non) **nonferrous** *adj* 非鉄の ▸ **Nonferrous** metals are generally softer and easier to polish than hardened steel. 非鉄金属は一般的に硬化鋼よりも軟らかく，研磨しやすい． ▸ It is convenient to discuss separately the procedures used with ferrous and **nonferrous** metals. 鉄金属と非鉄金属で用いられる手順を別々に分けて論議すると便利である．

fertile

接頭 (in) **infertile** *adj* 繁殖［生殖］力のない，不妊の ▸ In a study of 102 previously **infertile** patients, he found that 60.7% were able to conceive within two years of videolaseroscopy treatment. 過去に不妊であった患者102名を調べたところ，60.7 %の患者はビデオレーザースコープ治療で2年以内に妊娠できたことを彼は見出した．

fertility

接頭 (in) **infertility** *n* 不妊 ▸ Endometriosis is a major cause of **infertility**. 子宮内膜症は不妊症の主要な原因である．

fertilized

接頭 (un) **unfertilized** *adj* 受精されない ▸ The males are rendered sterile by radiation, and all of the eggs produced by the female, who mates only once, remain **unfertilized** and fail to hatch. 雄は放射線によって無精子症になり，一度だけ交尾した雌が生んだすべての卵は受精せず，孵化に失敗する．

fettered

接頭 (un) **unfettered** *adj* 拘束されない ▸ **Unfettered** competition is a wonderful thing, and the state should neither regulate nor interfere, instead leaving everything to the market. 国が規制したり干渉したりすることなく，市場にすべて任せるという拘束されない競争こそがすばらしい．

fiction

接頭 (non) **nonfiction** *n* ノンフィクション

fidelity

接頭 (in) **infidelity** *n* 不貞，不信心

figure

接頭 (dis) **disfigure** *v* 美観を損なう ▸ The surface is **disfigured** by superficial dust and dirt. その外面は，表面のちりとほこりによって美観を損ねている．

filial

接頭 (un) **unfilial** *adj* 親不孝な

fill

接頭 (un) **unfilled** *adj* 埋められていない ▸ All of the cage slots should be **unfilled**. ケージスロットはいずれも埋められてはならない．

filter

接頭 (un) **unfiltered** *adj* 濾過されていない ▸ It is an **unfiltered**, extra virgin oil that contains more antioxidants than filtered oil. それが濾過されていないエキストラバージンオイルであり，濾過されたオイルよりも抗酸化物質を多く含む．

finished

接頭 (un) **unfinished** *adj*

❶ 終わっていない ▸ Pressing ON/C while the calculator is on clears the number in the display and any **unfinished** calculations. 計算機の電源が入っているときに ON/C を押すと表示部の数字と終わっていない計算がすべて消える．

❷ やりかけの ▸ undertake the **unfinished** construction やりかけの工事を引き受ける

finite

接頭 (in) **infinite** *adj* 無限の，無尽蔵の ▸ one quarter wavelength away from a short circuit, the input impedance is **infinite**. 短絡から波長の1/4ほど離れると，入力インピーダンスは無限になる．

接頭 (non) **nonfinite** *adj* 限定しない

finitely

接頭 (in) **infinitely** *ad*

❶ 無限に，無尽蔵に ► These clutches offer advantages over ratchet devices in that they are smooth and reliable and provide **infinitely** variable angular increments. これらのクラッチは，円滑で信頼性があり，角度の増しかたを無限に変えられるという点でラチェット装置に優る．

❷ 無段に ► Speed is **infinitely** variable, with a maximum ratio of 20:1. 速度は，最高20:1の比率で無段変速する．

finitude

接頭 (in) **infinitude** *n* 無限，　無数 ► It is one speck in the **infinitude** of the universe, a momentary flash in the absolute darkness. それは無限の宇宙の1点，絶対的な暗闇の中の瞬間的な閃光である．

fire

接尾 (less) **fireless** *adj* 火の気のない ► All night long the boy and the dog sat by the **fireless** hearth in the darkness. 一晩中，少年と犬は暗闇の中で火の気のない暖炉のそばに座っていました．

firm

接頭 (in) **infirm** *adj*

❶ 〈身体などが〉弱い ► It's also careful to offer a personal touch when sending out specially qualified drivers to help aged and **infirm** passengers. さらには，高齢や身体の弱い乗客を介助するために特別に資格のあるドライバーを派遣する場合にも人間的に接触するように心がけている．

❷ 〈物などが〉頑丈でない

fissionable

接頭 (non) **nonfissionable** *adj* 非核分裂性の ► The plutonium isotope 239Pu is produced in chain-reacting nuclear reactors by capture of excess neutrons in **nonfissionable** U-239. プルトニウム同位体239Puは，連鎖反応原子炉で非核分裂性の

U-239の過剰中性子を捕獲する連鎖反応で生み出される.

fit

接頭 (un) **unfit** *adj* 適していない ▶ The degraded water was **unfit** for further use. 質の低下したその水はそれ以上の使用には適していなかった.

fitted

接頭 (ill) **ill-fitted** *adj* 不適切な ▶ An **ill-fitted** construction member will possibly result in serious damage. 構造部材の建付けが悪いと，重大な損傷を招く可能性がある.

fitting

接頭 (ill) **ill-fitting** *adj*

❶〈靴などが〉合わない ▶ an **ill-fitting** shoe 足に合わない靴

❷ 似合わない ▶ He wore a ridiculously **ill-fitting** suit. 彼は滑稽なほど似合わないスーツを着ていた.

fix

接頭 (un) **unfix** *v* 取り外す

fixed

接頭 (un) **unfixed** *adj* 未定の ▶ the **unfixed** values of input resistance 未定の入力抵抗値

flagging

接頭 (un) **unflagging** *adj* 疲れを知らない，たゆまぬ ▶ an **unflagging** curiosity about the way things are done 物事が執り行われる方法に対するたゆまぬ好奇心

flammability

接頭 (non) **non-flammability** *n* 不燃性 ▶ In addition, the Dielectric Coolants have the important advantages of **non-flammability**, low toxicity, and excellent compatibility. さらに，絶縁性クーラントは，非可燃性で，毒性が低く，併用性が優れているという重要な利点を備えている.

flammable

接頭 (non) **nonflammable** *adj* 不燃性の ▶ Chloroform is a colorless, **nonflammable**, volatile liquid. クロロフォルムは，

無色で不燃性の揮発性液体である. ► Nomex has a melting point of about 365 ℃ and is virtually **nonflammable**. ノメックスは融点が約365℃で, 実質的には不燃性である. ► The gases are combustible, but **nonflammable** components such as carbon dioxide, nitrogen, and helium are often present. そのガスは可燃性であるが, 二酸化炭素や窒素, ヘリウムなどの不燃成分も多くの場合に含まれている.

flappable

接頭 (un) **unflappable** *adj* 動揺しない ► She is also, say her fans, nearly **unflappable**. 彼女はまた, ほとんど動揺しないと彼女のファンは言っている.

flattering

接頭 (un) **unflattering** *adj* 好意的でない, マイナスとなる ► He wished to strip posting and voting rights from members who make **unflattering** comments about candidates. 彼は, 候補者について好意的ではない意見を述べるメンバーの投稿や投票権を剥奪したいと望んでいた. ► Manufacturers naturally avoid specifying information that is not only very difficult to measure and define but **unflattering** to their products. 製造会社は, 自社製品を測定し明示することが困難な情報だけでなく, 自社製品にとってマイナスとなる情報も詳細に述べることを当然避ける.

flavor

接尾 (less) **flavorless** *adj*

❶ 薄味の ► a large plate of **flavorless** mabo-nasu (eggplant in mabo sauce) 薄味のマーボ茄子 [マーボソース味の茄子] の大きな皿

❷ 素っ気ない, 風味のない ► The reporters had no alternative but to write their stories on the basis of the **flavorless**, dry Buckingham Palace announcements. 記者団は, バッキンガム宮殿当局の味も素っ気もない発表で記事を書くよりほかはなかった.

flaw

接尾 (less) **flawless** *adj*

❶傷のない ▶ Large **flawless** crystals of quartz are employed in the manufacture of quartz oscillators plates. 大型の傷のない水晶振動子が，水晶発振器の製造に用いられる.

❷非の打ちどころのない，そつのない ▶ Bob speaks **flawless** Japanese. ボブは非の打ちどころのない日本語を話す.

接尾 (less) **flawlessly** *ad* 器用に，そつなく ▶ I know companies are looking for work carried out **flawlessly**. 仕事をそつなくこなすことを会社は求めていることはわかります.

fledged

接頭 (un) **unfledged** *adj* 未熟な，未経験の

flexible

接頭 (in) **inflexible** *adj*

❶融通性がない ▶ However, this approach is **inflexible**, because the parameters of the control strategies are problem dependent. しかしながら，制御戦略のパラメーターが問題によって決まることから，この解決法には融通性がない.

❷柔軟性がない ▶ This basic problem exists with any internal combustion engine due to its **inflexible** power-RPM (constant torque) relationship. この基本的問題は，出力-RPM（一定トルク）関係に柔軟性がないために，どの内燃機関にも存在する. ▶ The weaker European governments need belatedly, but definitively, to undertake wide reforms to liberalize their **inflexible** economies. 弱体化したヨーロッパの政府は，遅ればせながらではあるが決定的に，柔軟性のない経済を自由化する広範囲の改革を行う必要がある.

❸曲がらない

flight

接尾 (less) **flightless** *adj* 飛べない ▶ a **flightless** bird called an ostrich 駝鳥という飛べない鳥

flinching

[接頭] (un) **unflinching** *adj* ひるまない

flower

[接尾] (less) **flowerless** *adj* 花の咲かない，花のない ▸ tiny leafy-stemmed **flowerless** plants 葉状の茎を持つ無花植物

fluctuating

[接頭] (non) **nonfluctuating** *adj* 変動しない ▸ As we will see, a **nonfluctuating** asset can be laden with risk. すぐに分かるように，変動しない資産にはリスクが課せられることがある．

fly

[接頭] (no) **no-fly** *n* 飛行禁止 ▸ Or that a volcanic-ash cloud could turn much of Northern Europe into a **no-fly** zone, disrupting air travel and impairing economic activity? あるいは，火山灰雲が北ヨーロッパの多くを飛行禁止区域に変え，飛行機での移動を不可能にし，経済活動を減じるだろうか．

focused

[接頭] (un) **unfocused** *adj* 焦点の合っていない ▸ In the split-image range finder, the **unfocused** image appears unaligned, or split. スプリットイメージ式距離計では，焦点が合っていない像は整合しないか，または分割される．

fog

[接頭] (de) **defog** *v* 曇りを取る

fold

[接頭] (un) **unfold** *v* 〈折り畳まれているものなどを〉開く ▸ Interactive computations can be **unfolded** into parallel computation. 数台の対話型コンピューターを展開して，演算を並行して行うことができる．

foliate

[接頭] (de) **defoliate** *v* 葉を落とす

food

[接頭] (non) **nonfood** *n* 非食料品

foot

接尾 (less) **footless** *adj* 足のない ▶ naturally **footless** snakes 生まれつき足のないヘビ

接尾 (less) **footlessness** *n* 足のない状態 ▶ leglessness or **footlessness** 足がないという属性

forced

接頭 (un) **unforced** *adj* 強制的でない

foreseen

接頭 (un) **unforeseen** *adj* 予期しない, 予測しない ▶ Some **unforeseen** accident occurred. 予期しない事故が発生した. ▶ The event was entirely **unforeseen**. その事件はまったく予見できなかった.

forestation

接頭 (de) **deforestation** *n* 〈森林などの〉 伐採 ▶ They have figured out a novel way to put a dent in **deforestation**—by harvesting trees not on land but underwater. 彼らは, 樹木を陸上ではなく水中で採取することによって, 伐採を減らす素晴らしい方法を考え出していた.

forested

接頭 (un) **unforested** *adj* 植林されていない ▶ The influences of the forest on the site result in a characteristic pattern of streamflow differing from that on **unforested** land. その土地における樹木の影響によって, 樹木がない土地上のそれとは異なった特徴がある流水のパターンができる.

forgettable

接頭 (un) **unforgettable** *adj* 忘れがたい ▶ For Google's employees in China, the day was **unforgettable**. 中国のグーグル社員にとって, その日は忘れがたかった.

forgivable

接頭 (un) **unforgivable** *adj* 許せない ▶ That the country said nothing is **unforgivable**. 国が何も言わなかったことは, 許せないことだ. ▶ Yet despite some almost **unforgivable** deficiencies, Ventura still excels in several key areas. ほとんど許容できない欠陥が少しあるにもかかわらず，ヴェンチュラはなおいくつかの主要な分野で卓越している．

forgivably

接頭 (un) **unforgivably** *ad* 容赦できないほどに ► As I read more about the HIV-tainted blood products, I came increasingly to feel that the government and the pharmaceutical companies had acted **unforgivably**. 私は HIV に汚染された血液製剤について読み進むと，政府と製薬会社の行動をますます容赦できなくなった．

forgiving

接頭 (un) **unforgiving** *adj* 寛大でない ► Despite the **unforgiving** conditions of the High Arctic, Mech and Brandenburg discovered that the Ellesmere wolves are secure, unlike their brethren elsewhere. 高緯度北極の厳しい条件にもかかわらず，エルズミア島のオオカミが他の場所の彼らの仲間たちとは違い安全であることをメカとブランデンブルクは発見した．

form

接頭 (de) **deform** *v* 変形させる ► In the drawing process the material to be shaped is gripped, heated, and **deformed** to the desired shape. 引抜きの過程において，被成形物は，しっかりつかまれ，加熱され，希望の形に変形される．

接尾 (less) **formless** *adj* 形のない，実体のない ► the **formless** and disordered state of matter before the creation of the cosmos 宇宙が創造される前の物質の形と秩序がない状態

接尾 (less) **formlessly** *ad*

❶形なく ► The dress hung **formlessly** on her body. そのドレスは彼女の身体に不格好に垂れ下がっていた．

❷雑然と ► My clothes hung **formlessly** on my shrunken limbs. すると手足では服がだらんとぶらさがった．

接尾 (less) **formlessness** *n* 形のないこと，無定形，秩序立っていないこと ► The world of **formlessness** of Mushikikai (the realm of non-form). 無色界の四空処天のこと

formal

接頭 (in) **informal** *adj* 形式ばらない，非公式の ▶ an **informal** party 非公式の［気楽な］パーティ

formality

接頭 (in) **informality** *n* 非公式 ▶ In the negotiations, an attempt at **informality** through the use of first names is rejected by the Japanese. 交渉において，ファーストネームを使用する非公式の試みは，日本人によって拒絶される．

formally

接頭 (in) **informally** *ad* 非公式に ▶ an **informally** appointed worker 採用内定者 ▶ The man has since joined me in asking **informally**, and she says he'll submit a formal request soon. その男性はすでに非公式に依頼して私を入会させているので，彼がすぐにも正式な要請を提出すると彼女は言う．

formation

接頭 (de) **deformation** *n* 変形，変形したもの ▶ Large **deformations** and strains must be taken into account when analyzing superplastic forming. 超塑性成形を解析するときには，大きな変形やひずみを考慮に入れなければならない．

formatted

接頭 (non) **nonformatted** *adj* フォーマットされていない ▶ AppleWorks does not recognize **nonformatted** disks or disks that were formatted with operating systems other than ProDOS. アップルワークスは，フォーマットされていないディスクまたは ProDOS 以外の OS によってフォーマットされたディスクを認識しない．

接頭 (un) **unformatted** *adj* フォーマットされていない ▶ The calculator stores calculated results in an **unformatted** form with up to twelve digits. その計算機はフォーマットのない様式で12桁までの計算結果を記憶する． ▶ One of the most effective uses of these commands is in quickly transforming **unformat-**

ted text into a formatted publication. これらのコマンドの最も効果的な用途の一つは，フォーマットされていないテキストをフォーマットされた刊行物に迅速に変換することである．

formed

接頭 (de) **deformed** *adj* 変形した ▶ a **deformed** body 変形した本体

接頭 (ill) **ill-formed** *adj* 形の悪い，不適格な ▶ syntactically **ill-formed** 構文的には不適格な

接頭 (ill) **ill-formedness** *n* 不適格性 ▶ a word with one ill-formed structure and a word with multiple instances of **ill-formedness** 一つの不適格構造を持つ言葉と，複数の不適格性事例を持つ言葉

接頭 (un) **unformed** *adj* 型ができていない，発達途上の ▶ Instead of **unformed** scribbling he now makes up and down strokes with a crayon. 型ができていない殴り書きの代わりに，彼は現在，クレヨンで上下の筆運びができる．

fortunate

接頭 (un) **unfortunate** *adj* 不幸な ▶ Fishing boats with low freeboards have an **unfortunate** history. 乾舷の低い漁船には，遭難者が多いという不幸ないわれがある． ▶ We have an **unfortunate** tendency in this country to treat people as either heroes or villains. この国には人を英雄か悪役のどちらかとして取り扱う残念な傾向がある． ▶ Intuitive decisions have all too frequently dominated the most important aspects of basic design, sometimes with **unfortunate** consequences. 直観的な決断は，基本的なデザインの最も重要な側面をしばしば支配し過ぎてしまい，時には不幸な結果をもたらしたこともある．

fortunately

接頭 (un) **unfortunately** *ad* 不幸にも ▶ **Unfortunately**, this is not the case. 運が悪いことに，それはこの事例に当てはまらない． ▶ **Unfortunately**, this process seldom results in the best choice. 不幸にも，この方法が最良の選択となることはめった

になかった.

founded

接頭 (ill) **ill-founded** *adj* 根拠の弱い，正当な理由のない ▶ an **ill-founded** argument 根拠の貧弱な議論 ▶ Their plan is **ill-founded**. 彼らのプランは，なんら根拠がない.

接頭 (un) **unfounded** *adj* 根拠のない ▶ Even when such relationships are kept on a professional level, there is no guarantee that **unfounded** rumors will not damage the careers of both parties. このような関係がプロのレベルに保たれている場合でも，根拠のない噂が双方のキャリアを損なわないことを保証するものではない.

franchise

接頭 (dis) **disfranchise** *v* 〈選挙権や権利を〉奪う

freeze

接頭 (un) **unfreeze** *v* 解凍する ▶ To **unfreeze** the titles, press OS-T again and choose None. タイトルを解凍するには，もう一度 OS-T を押して None を選択する.

frequent

接頭 (in) **infrequent** *adj*

❶ 頻繁でない，まれな ▶ Nuclear is more in Black Swan territory, where you have **infrequent** but big events. 原子力はさらにブラックスワン的領域であり，まれではあるが起きれば衝撃が大きい事象がありうる. ▶ An **infrequent** but often overlooked problem results from a parasitic voltage induced in the shafts of large inverter-powered motors. 大型のインバーター駆動モーターのシャフトに誘導された寄生電圧によって，まれだがしばしば見のがされる問題が生じる.

❷ 頻度が低い ▶ no matter how often or how **infrequently** samples are taken サンプル採取の頻度が高かろうと低かろうと

frequented

接頭 (un) **unfrequented** *adj* 人通りがない

frequently

接頭 (in) **infrequently** *ad* まれに ▶ In some cases, but **infrequently**, it could reflect on the contractor's bidding practices. 場合によっては，しかしまれであるが，それは契約業者の入札習慣に影響を及ぼすことができた． ▶ The most **infrequently** used controls should be placed behind the front panel or in other locations available only to the technician. 最もまれにしか使わない調節つまみは，フロントパネルの裏か，専門技術者にしか手が届かないどこかほかの場所に配置するべきだ． ▶ When the relative costs are plotted, it becomes clear that consultants are most cost-effective if used **infrequently**. 相対費用をプロットしてみると，コンサルタントをあまり使わなければ費用効果が最もあがることが明らかになる．

接頭 (un) **unfrequently** *ad* 人通りが少なく

friend

接尾 (less) **friendless** *adj* 友達のいない ▶ Soon you will find yourself **friendless**. 友人がいなくなるよ．

接尾 (less) **friendlessly** *ad* 友なしで，友人がいない様子で

接尾 (less) **friendlessness** *n* 友人がいないこと ▶ Nello, in his innocence and his **friendlessness**, had no strength to stem the popular tide. ネロは無実でしたが友達もありませんでしたので，人々の気持ちがネロから離れていくのをせき止める力はありませんでした．

friendly

接頭 (un) **unfriendly** *adj*

❶ 親切でない ▶ The work environment she first entered was decidedly **unfriendly**. 彼女が最初に入った職場環境としては明らかに親切ではなかった．

❷ わかりやすくない

frost

接頭 (de) **defrost** *v* 霜を取り除く ▶ When it is necessary to use coils for temperatures below 35°F, as in cold-storage rooms, two coils are used so one can be **defrosted** while the other is in operation. 冷蔵室におけるように，35°F 以下の温度に対してコイルの使用が必要なとき，2つのコイルはどちらも使われ，一つが運転中の場合はもう一つが除霜中である．

frosted

接頭 (un) **unfrosted** *adj* 砂糖をまぶしていない ▶ Use artificial sweeteners, unsweetened fruit juices, low calorie drinks, and "**unfrosted**" cereals. 人工甘味料，無糖のフルーツジュース，低カロリー飲料，そして，「砂糖をまぶしていない」シリアルを使用する．

frosting

接頭 (de) **defrosting** *adj* 除霜の ▶ Automatic **defrosting** systems, when air is the heat source, are essential for best performance, with the defrost cycle occurring twice a day 自動霜取システムは，空気が熱源のとき，最良の作動には，霜取サイクルは1日2回が大切である．

frozen

接頭 (un) **unfrozen** *adj* 凍結していない ▶ There would not be the moderating influence on climate that large under-the-ice bodies of **unfrozen** H_2O now exert. 現在，氷の下の凍っていない H_2O の大きな塊が気候を緩和する影響はないであろう．

fruit

接尾 (less) **fruitless** *adj*

❶ 無駄な，意味のない ▶ Let's stop this **fruitless** argument. 無駄な議論はやめよう．

❷ 成果のない，効果のない ▶ All my efforts have proved **fruitless** せっかくの骨折りも徒労に帰した．

接尾 (less) **fruitlessly** *ad* 実りなく，効果なく，無駄に，無益に ▶ The negotiations ended **fruitlessly**. 交渉は実りなく終わった．

接尾 (less) **fruitlessness** *n* 無駄，無益 ▶ **fruitlessness** of efforts 努力しても甲斐のないこと

fruitful

接頭 (un) **unfruitful** *adj*

❶無益の ► After several frustrating, **unfruitful** trips taken on temperamental mules, the Fosters found an almost untouched forest full of many old growth palms. フォスター一家は気難しいロバに乗り，うんざりするような実りのない旅の後，年月を経て成長したヤシでいっぱいのほとんど自然のままの森を発見した.

❷実がなっていない

fulfilled

接頭 (un) **unfulfilled** *adj* 履行されていない

furl

接頭 (un) **unfurl** *adj* 〈巻いたものなどを〉開く

furnished

接頭 (un) **unfurnished** *adj* 家具が取り付けられていない ► Some friends recently found an **unfurnished** flat. 最近家具付きでないアパートを見つけた友人もいる.

fusible

接頭 (in) **infusible** *adj* 溶けない，不溶解性の ► **infusible** powder 不溶融性粉末 ► Thermosets undergo a permanent set, i.e., become essentially insoluble and **infusible**, under the action of heat. 熱硬化材料は永久的に固まる．すなわち，熱の作用によって基本的に不溶解性で融解しなくなる. ► Thermosetting plastics are thereby converted to **infusible** masses which cannot be softened by subsequent heating. 熱硬化性プラスチックは，それによって，その後に加熱しても軟化できない不溶解性の物質に変えられる.

future

接尾 (less) **futureless** *adj* 将来性のない，見込みのない ► a **futureless** area 将来性のない地域

接尾 (less) **futurelessness** *n* 将来性のないこと

G

gainly

接頭 (un) **ungainly** *adj* 不格好な

garnished

接頭 (un) **ungarnished** *adj* 装飾されていない

gasketed

接頭 (un) **ungasketed** *adj* ガスケットが付いていない ▶ **Ungasketed** shaft openings which have a length-of-path not less than 1/2 inch shall not be tested. 1/2インチより短い長さのパスのガスケットが付いていない軸開口はテストしないこととする.

gauss

接頭 (de) **degauss** *n* 消磁, 減磁 ▶ The **degauss** switch corrects small patches of color distortion that can occur on your screen. その消磁スイッチは, スクリーン上に起こりうる色のひずみによる小斑点を修正する.

generate

接頭 (de) **degenerate** *v* 悪化する, 退廃する ▶ "Reform" can **degenerate** into political payback by the reformers. 改革主義者によると,「改革」は政治的な仕返しに落ちる. ▶ I might also add that questions about this organization get so few replies because discussion of the organization often **degenerates** into a flame war of some sort. 私は, この組織に関する質問は, その組織について討議すると何らかの形の熱い闘争に悪化することがあるので, 回答が非常に少ないことも付け加えておく.

generated

接頭 (de) **degenerated** *adj* 縮退した ▶ The manipulator has lost a degree of freedom, which is called a **degenerated** condition. マニピュレーターが自由度を失ったが, これを縮退状態という.

[接頭] (de) **degeneration** *n*

❶退化, 変質 ► prevent **degeneration** in meat 肉が変質しないようにする

❷退廃, 非生産 ► This theory represents a combination of massive waste of human and natural resources, inequitable economic disparities, and the **degeneration** of the human spirit. この理論は, 人材および天然資源の膨大な浪費, 不公平な経済的不均衡, および人間精神の退廃の組み合わせを表している.

generative

[接頭] (de) **degenerative** *adj* 衰退しやすい, 退化しやすい ► This is a fast-moving, **degenerative** brain disease, with no treatment and no cure. これは高速で進行して頭脳が退化する病気で, 処置も治療法もない.

generous

[接頭] (un) **ungenerous** *adj* 寛大でない, 気前のよくない

gentlemanly

[接頭] (un) **ungentlemanly** *adj* 紳士らしくない ► It is dishonorable or **ungentlemanly** for a man to pry into another's private life. 男性が他人の私生活を詮索することは, 不道徳で紳士らしくない.

germinated

[接頭] (un) **ungerminated** *adj* 発芽していない ► **Ungerminated** spores may eventually germinate. 発芽しない種子もいずれは発芽することがある. ► The survival of **ungerminated** spores reduces the effectiveness of this method and it has been supplanted by other methods. 発芽していない種子の活着によって, この方法の有効性が低下し, そして他の方法に取って代わられている.

getatable

[接頭] (un) **ungetatable** *adj* 近づきにくい

giving

接頭 (un) **ungiving** *adj* つまらない

glamorous

接頭 (un) **unglamorous** *adj* 魅力のない ► He squeezed working capital, an **unglamorous** tactic that pays handsomely. 彼は，運転資金，すなわち金遣いが荒く魅力のない施策を絞った.

glaze

接頭 (de) **deglaze** *v* うわ薬を除去する

glazed

接頭 (un) **unglazed** *adj* うわ薬をかけていない ► **unglazed** pottery うわ薬をかけていない[素焼きの]壺

glued

接頭 (un) **unglued** *adj* 引き剥がされた

glyceride

接頭 (non) **nonglyceride** *n* 非グリセリド ► **Nonglyceride** components are not saponified by alkali. 非グリセリド成分は，アルカリで鹸(けん)化されない.

god

接尾 (less) **godless** *adj* 神を認めない ► **godless** doings 神を恐れぬ所業

接尾 (less) **godlessly** *ad* 神の存在を否定して，不敬に

接尾 (less) **godlessness** *n* 神を認めないこと ► Religious people tend to associate **godlessness** with nihilism and crime. 信心深い人々は，無神論を虚無主義や犯罪に結びつけがちである.

godly

接頭 (un) **ungodly** *adj* 不信心な

gorge

接頭 (dis) **disgorge** *v* 放出する，吐き出す

gotten

接頭 (ill) **ill-gotten** *adj* 不当な方法で得た ► **Ill-gotten** wealth seldom descends to the third generation. 不正の富は三代続かぬ.

governable

接頭 (un) **ungovernable** *adj* 制御できない

governmental

接頭 (non) **nongovernmental** *adj* 非政府の, 民間の

grace

接頭 (dis) **disgrace** *n* 不名誉, 恥辱 ▶ The Democrat resigned in **disgrace** two years ago. その民主党員は, 2年前, 面目を失い辞任した.

—— *v* 名を汚す, 名誉を傷つける ▶ Manners are learned by making mistakes and **disgracing** oneself. マナーは, 間違いを冒し自分が恥をかくことによって学ぶものである.

接頭 (dis) **disgraced** *adj* 不名誉な ▶ Mr. and Mrs. A left their home after the speech to begin rural exile, a traditional way for **disgraced** leaders to show repentance. A夫妻は地方放浪生活を始めるという言葉を残して家を去ったが, これは不名誉な指導者が遺憾の意を表明する伝統的な形である.

接尾 (less) **graceless** *adj*

❶無作法な ▶ in a **graceless** manner 品のない態度で

❷野暮な ▶ It is a **graceless** figure. 殺風景な姿だ.

接尾 (less) **gracelessly** *ad* 無作法に ▶ She moves rather **gracelessly**. 彼女はやや粗野に体を動かす.

接尾 (less) **gracelessness** *n* 無作法なこと, 動作に上品さのないこと ▶ Scientists in Spain are trying to find a way to tackle **gracelessness** in robots. スペインの科学者は, ロボットの無作法さに取り組む方法を見つけようとしている.

graceful

接頭 (dis) **disgraceful** *adj*

❶けしからん ▶ People often say it is **disgraceful** that Japan should be a “drunkards’ heaven.” 日本が「酔っぱらい天国」に違いないというのはけしからんという人たちがいる.

❷不名誉な，恥をかく

gracious

接頭 (un) **ungracious** *adj* 無礼な

gradation

接頭 (de) **degradation** *n*

❶〈地位などの〉降格，左遷

❷〈質などの〉低下，〈環境などの〉悪化 ▶ It calls for the company to create new business opportunities by responding to environmental **degradation**, energy shortages, and aging populations. それは，会社に対して，環境悪化，エネルギー不足，および人口高齢化に対応することによって新しいビジネスチャンスを作り出すことを求めている．

grade

接頭 (de) **degrade** *v*

❶地位を下げる，降格させる

❷〈質などを〉下げる ▶ Geologists have long assumed that when living organisms die, heat, light, and bacteria begin to **degrade** the constituent compounds. 地質学者たちは，生物が死ぬと，熱や光やバクテリアが構成する化合物を分解し始めると，長い間簡単に考えてきた．

graded

接頭 (un) **ungraded** *adj* 平坦でない ▶ The mountain roads — **ungraded** and often without guardrails — are perilous. 平坦でなく，しばしばガードレールもない山道は危険である．

grammatical

接頭 (un) **ungrammatical** *adj* 非文法的な

grateful

接頭 (un) **ungrateful** *adj* 感謝の気持ちのない ▶ I don't think all people are **ungrateful**. 私は，すべての人々が恩知らずであるとは思わない．

gratitude

接頭 (in) **ingratitude** *n* 恩知らず ▶ He repaid me only with

ingratitude. 彼は私にただ忘恩という返報をくれただけだった.

green

接頭 (un) **ungreen** *adj* 環境に対する配慮がない

ground

接尾 (less) **groundless** *adj* 根拠のない, 事実無根の, いわれのない, 根も葉もない ► The rumor proved to be unfounded—**groundless**. 風説は事実無根と判明した.

接尾 (less) **groundlessly** *ad* 根拠なく ► **groundlessly** imagine something 根拠のない想像をする

接尾 (less) **groundlessness** *n* 事実無根 ► The **groundlessness** of their report was quickly recognized. 彼らの報告の根拠のなさは, すぐにわかった.

接頭 (un) **unground** *adj* 挽かれていない ► Where heavy loads or high speeds are involved, the heavy-duty fitting practice should be used, regardless of whether the cone seats are ground or **unground**. 大きな荷重または高速度が関連する場合は, コーンシートが研磨されているかいないかにかかわらず, 高荷重装着手順を使用する必要がある.

grounded

接頭 (un) **ungrounded** *adj*

❶ 接地されていない ► exposed **ungrounded** metal parts 露出した接地されていない金属部品

❷ 根拠のない

growing

接頭 (non) **nongrowing** *adj* 成長しない, 非成長の ► Precipitation during the **nongrowing** season will help to leach salts from the soil. 非生長期の降水は, 塩分が土壌から滲出するのを助ける.

gruntled

接頭 (dis) **disgruntled** *adj* 不機嫌な, 不満な ► A better approach is for the manager to talk to **disgruntled** employees individually and have them express their points of view. 不満をもつ従業員に個々に面接し，彼らの考え方を表明させることは，責任者にとって良い方法である．

guarded

接頭 (ill) **ill-guarded** *adj* しっかりと守られていない

接頭 (un) **unguarded** *adj* 無防備な

guess

接頭 (un) **unguessed-at** *adj* 予想さえできない

guide

接尾 (less) **guideless** *adj* ガイドのない，案内人がいない ▶ **guideless** street 案内のない道

guided

接頭 (un) **unguided** *adj* 無誘導の ▶ There are two primary categories of modern missiles; **unguided** and guided. 現代のミサイルには二つの主要なカテゴリーがあり，それは無誘導および誘導ミサイルである．

guile

接尾 (less) **guileless** *adj* 悪意のない，実直な，誠実な ▶ She looked at me with a **guileless** smile. 彼女は無邪気な笑顔で私を見た．

接尾 (less) **guilelessly** *ad* 無邪気に，はばかることなく ▶ My classmates and I **guilelessly** heckled Waseda with shrill shouts. クラスメートと私は誰はばかることなく，黄色い声をはりあげて，早稲田をヤジった．

接尾 (less) **guilelessness** *n* ずるさがないこと，正直さ

guilt

接尾 (less) **guiltless** *adj*

❶ 覚えがない ▶ I'm **guiltless** of any intent to offend him. 私は，彼の感情を害そうとした覚えはない．

❷ 罪のない，無実の

接尾 (less) **guiltlessness** *n* 罪のないこと ▶ The woman wasn't even given a chance to prove her **guiltlessness**. その女性

は，自分の無罪を証明する機会さえも与えられなかった．

guise

[接頭]（dis） **disguise** *v*

❶ 変装させる ▶ This type of virus can sneak into your system **disguised** as a relatively innocuous program. この種のウイルスは，比較的害のないプログラムに変装してあなたのシステムに忍び込むことができる．

❷ 偽る，だます ▶ If the child dislikes the taste of his medicine, you can **disguise** it by mixing the medicine with a spoonful of jam or honey. 子供が飲む薬の味をいやがる場合は，その薬品を一匙のジャムか蜂蜜に混ぜて騙すことができる．

gust

[接頭]（dis） **disgust** *n* 嫌悪，反感

―― *v* いや気を持たせる ▶ A former Republican, he describes himself as a "fiscal conservative but social moderate" who has grown **disgusted** with both parties. 元共和党員である彼は，両方の党にいや気を感じることになった自分のことを「財政的には保守主義者で社会福祉的には中道派」であると表現した．

gusting

[接頭]（dis） **disgusting** *adj* 嫌悪感を抱かせる ▶ It is **disgusting** to see them making an unseemly spectacle of themselves by singing drunkenly in the street at the top of their voices. 彼らが酔っぱらって街頭で声を張り上げて歌ってみっともない光景を呈しているのを見ると嫌悪感が湧いてくる．

gut

[接尾]（less） **gutless** *adj*

❶ 意気地のない ▶ a **gutless** wonder 臆病者

❷ 〈機器が〉力強くない，パワー不足の ▶ a **gutless** car 馬力不足の車

[接尾]（less） **gutlessly** *ad* 意気地なく

H

hair

接尾 (less) **hairless** *adj* 無毛の ▶ any of an old breed of small nearly **hairless** Mexican dogs メキシコ産の小型でほとんど無毛の古い犬種の総称

接尾 (less) **hairlessness** *n* 無毛

接頭 (un) **unhair** *v* 毛を抜く

hallowed

接頭 (un) **unhallowed** *adj* 神にささげていない, 無信心な

hand

接尾 (less) **handless** *adj*

❶手のない ▶ a **handless** war veteran 手がない退役軍人

❷不器用な

接頭 (un) **unhand** *v* 手を離す

handling

接頭 (mis) **mishandling** *grd* 誤った処置 ▶ He must weigh these issues while fending off his critics who accuse him of **mishandling** the emergency response. 緊急状態応答の処置を誤ったとして非難する評論家をかわしながら, 彼はこれらの問題を検討しなければならない.

handsome

接頭 (un) **unhandsome** *adj* ハンサムでない, 美しくない ▶ Worn and **unhandsome** as he had become, it was plain that she did not discern the least fault in his appearance. 彼は疲れ切って醜くなったのだが, 彼女が彼の外見上の欠点を全く認識しなかったことは明らかだった.

handy

接頭 (un) **unhandy** *adj* 扱いにくい, 不便な ▶ This computer is **unhandy** to carry about. このコンピューターは携帯するのに不便だ.

hap

接尾 (less) **hapless** *adj* 不幸な，哀れな ▶ a **hapless** victim 不運な犠牲者

接尾 (less) **haplessly** *ad* 不幸にも，不運にも ▶ He is **haplessly** in love with her. 彼は哀れにも彼女に恋をしています.

接尾 (less) **haplessness** *n* 不運，不幸，哀れ ▶ At one time it was the norm for his biographers to make ironic comments about their subject's **haplessness** as a colonial businessman in Africa. かつては伝記作家が，その伝記の対象のアフリカ植民地における実業家としての不運について皮肉なコメントを書くことは，普通のことでした.

happily

接頭 (un) **unhappily** *ad* 不幸にも

happiness

接頭 (un) **unhappiness** *n* 不幸，不運 ▶ Read's growing **unhappiness** was no secret to members of Pfizer's board. リード氏のますます大きくなる不運は，ファイザーの取締役会のメンバーには隠されていなかった.

happy

接頭 (un) **unhappy** *adj*

❶不幸な ▶ The Japanese smile can be cover for confused, ambiguous, embarrassing, and even **unhappy** situations. 日本人のほほえみは，混迷，不確実，狼狽，さらには不幸な状況を隠すものである可能性がある.

❷不満足な ▶ A few engineers are **unhappy** with their present lot in life. エンジニアの中には，自分たちの人生における現在の巡り合わせに不満足な者も多少いる.

hardenable

接頭 (non) **nonhardenable** *adj* 硬化しない ▶ The carbon steels used range from the low-carbon group, which are **nonhardenable**, to the high-carbon grades which attain high surface hardness. 使用されている炭素鋼は，硬化しない低炭素鋼

グループから，表面が非常に硬くなる高炭素鋼まで広範囲にわたっている．

harm

接尾 (less) **harmless** *adj*

❶無害な，安全な ▶ The drug is **harmless** as long as it is used properly. その薬物は適切に使用する限り害はない．

❷罪のない ▶ He is a **harmless** fellow. 彼は悪気のない男だ．

接尾 (less) **harmlessly** *ad* 害を及ぼさない形で，無害に ▶ This is a **harmlessly** childish game. これは無害な子供のゲームだ．

接尾 (less) **harmlessness** *n* 無害 ▶ It will not do to say that the heretic may be allowed to maintain the utility or **harmlessness** of his opinion, though forbidden to maintain its truth. 異端者にはその意見が真実だと言い張ることは禁じているのに，彼らがその意見が有用だとか無害だとか言い続けるのは許されているとは，言うべきではないでしょう．

harmed

接頭 (un) **unharmed** *adj* 傷を受けていない，無傷の ▶ The bacteria can pass **unharmed** through a fine porcelain filter. バクテリアは，目の細かな磁器フィルターを無傷で通過することができる．

harmonious

接頭 (dis) **disharmonious** *adj* 不調和な

接頭 (in) **inharmonious** *adj*

❶調和のとれない，不調和の

❷仲のよくない

harmony

接頭 (dis) **disharmony** *n* 不調和，不協和 ▶ The **inharmony** of agricultural modernization and regional economic development is an important reason for the imbalance. 農業近代化と地域経済の成長との不調和は，アンバランスを引き起こす重大な理由である．

harness

接頭 (un) **unharness** *v* 馬具を取り外す

hat

接尾 (less) **hatlessly** *ad* 帽子がない状態で

healthy

接頭 (un) **unhealthy** *adj*

❶ 健康的でない，不健全な ▶ Managers believe that any real or imagined wrong done in distributing extra income will engender jealousies, secretiveness, and **unhealthy** competition. 臨時収入の配分にあたっての実際または想像上の不適切な行為は，嫉妬，隠し立て，および不健全な競争を引き起こすと管理者は信じている．

❷ 健康に良くない ▶ Many children may have been exposed to **unhealthy** levels of radioactive iodine. 多くの子供たちが，健康に良くないレベルの放射性ヨウ素の汚染にさらされたかもしれない．

hear

接頭 (un) **unheard** *adj*

❶ 聞こえない ▶ But the people's faces have vanished; their voices are **unheard**. しかし，人々の顔が見えなくなった．それ故，彼らの声も聞かれなくなった．

❷ 聞いたことのない，前代未聞の ▶ The maglev can attain speeds **unheard** of in conventional land travel. 磁気浮上式高速鉄道は，従来の陸上移動では前代未聞の速度に達することができる．

接頭 (un) **unheard-of** *adj* 聞いたことのない，前代未聞の ▶ It includes an ongoing program that guarantees acceptable quality levels; it involves **unheard-of** commitments to research and development. それは，許容品質レベルを保証する継続的なプログラムを含み，研究開発に関する前代未聞の約束を含む．

heart

接尾 (less) **heartless** *adj* 無情な，つれない ► It is **heartless** of you to do such a thing. こんなことをするとは君もあんまりだ.

接尾 (less) **heartlessly** *ad* 薄情に，　冷酷に ► She behaves rather **heartlessly** toward her admirers. 彼女は自分のファンに対してかなり無情にふるまう.

接尾 (less) **heartlessness** *n* 薄情 ► one's degree of **heartlessness** toward others 相手に対する思いやりのなさの程度

hearten

接頭 (dis) **dishearten** *v* 落胆させること ► At such times, I feel really **disheartened**. そのような時，私は本当にがっかりする.

heed

接尾 (less) **heedless** *adj* 不注意な，無頓着な，ぼんやりする ► He is so **heedless** that he often forgets his hat. あの人はそそっかしいから，しばしば帽子を忘れて行く.

接尾 (less) **heedlessly** *ad* 無頓着に ► He spent the money **heedlessly** on his hobby. 彼は金を気遣いなしに趣味に使った.

接尾 (less) **heedlessness** *n* 無頓着 ► the state of regretting one's **heedlessness** 気づかないことに後悔する状態

heeded

接頭 (un) **unheeded** *adj* 注目されない

help

接尾 (less) **helpless** *adj*

❶ 無力な ► As the weekend progressed, Maloney felt **helpless**. 週末が進むにつれ，マロニーは無力感に襲われた.

❷ 体が不自由な ► I am old and **helpless**. 私は年をとって身体が利かない.

接尾 (less) **helplessly** *ad* どうしようもなく，頼るものもなく ► The crowd watched him **helplessly**. 群衆はなすすべもなく彼を見ていた.

接尾 (less) **helplessness** *n* どうすることもできないこと，無力 ▶ We will have to get over the feeling of **helplessness**. 我々は無力感を克服しなければならないであろう．

hero

接頭 (non) **nonhero** *n* 反英雄

hesitating

接頭 (un) **unhesitating** *adj* 躊躇しない

hesitatingly

接頭 (un) **unhesitatingly** *ad* 躊躇なく ▶ Reviewers will **unhesitatingly** recommend it as required reading in the schools. 査読者は，学校の必読書として躊躇なくそれを推薦する．

hierarchical

接頭 (non) **non-hierarchical** *adj* 非階層式の ▶ A variety of progressive build-up features are allowed for, including hierarchical and **non-hierarchical** coding, bit slicing, and spectrum selection. さまざまな漸進式ビルドアップ機能で，階層式および非階層式コーディング，ビットスライシングを含め，スペクトル選択ができる．

hindered

接頭 (un) **unhindered** *adj*

❶ 邪魔されない ▶ The maglev is **unhindered** by any friction except wind resistance. 磁気浮上式高速鉄道は，風の抵抗以外の摩擦に邪魔されない．

❷ 遅らされない ▶ In a gas, the thermal motion consists of substantially **unhindered** movement of the individual particles with different velocities. 気体の中では，速度の異なる個々の粒子の本質的には何ら遅らされることのない動きが熱運動を構成している．

hinge

接頭 (un) **unhinge** *v* ヒンジを外す

historical

接頭 (a) **ahistorical** *adj* 歴史と無関係な，歴史的視点を欠いた

接頭 (un) **unhistorical** *adj* 歴史的でない，史実と異なる ▸ Obviously, the character identified as their eight-year-old son named Lucius Verus in the movie is **unhistorical**. その映画に出てくるルキウス・ウェルスという彼らの8歳の息子の役柄は明らかに歴史に合わない.

historically

接頭 (un) **unhistorically** *ad* 史実に合わずに

hitch

接頭 (un) **unhitch** *v* 〈馬やものなどを〉放す

holy

接頭 (un) **unholy** *adj* 神聖でない，不浄な

home

接尾 (less) **homeless** *adj* 家のない， ホームレスの ▸ The **homeless** children were placed in my charge. そのホームレスの子供たちは私に預けられた. ▸ a **homeless** cat 野良猫

接尾 (less) **homelessness** *n* (住む) 家のないこと ▸ The government cannot avoid the issue of **homelessness** any longer. 政府はもはやホームレスの問題を避けて通るわけにはいかない.

homogeneous

接頭 (in) **inhomogeneous** *adj*

❶異質の，不等質な ▸ . . . an overall factor which accounts for the flow stress, friction, and **inhomogeneous** deformation …流れによる応力，摩擦，および不均等な変形の原因となる全体的要因

❷不均一な ▸ . . . which is consistent with the observed asymmetric line-shapes of that component due to **inhomogeneous** broadening. …，この成分の不均一な広がりのせいで非対称に観測された線形と一致する. ▸ Because of the **inhomogeneous** deformation in the direct extrusion of the billet, the center of the billet moves faster than the periphery. ビレットの直接押出しでは，不均一な変形があるため，ビレットの中心

部の方が周辺部より速く移動する.

❸ 不均質な ► Numerical results are presented and compared with extract solutions for homogeneous and **inhomogeneous** circular cylinders. 数値結果を示し, 均質および不均質の円筒の抽出解と比較する.

homogeneously

接頭 (in) **inhomogeneously** *ad* 不均一に ► This is **inhomogeneously** in the bulk. これは不均一に固まって存在している.

honest

接頭 (dis) **dishonest** *adj* 不正直な

honestly

接頭 (dis) **dishonestly** *ad* 不正直に, 不正に

honor

接頭 (dis) **dishonor** *n* 不名誉

honorable

接頭 (dis) **dishonorable** *adj* 不名誉な, 恥知らずの ► The philosophy of the samurai would regard this logic as base or **dishonorable**. 武士の哲学では, この論理を卑劣または不名誉と見なすであろう.

hook

接頭 (un) **unhook** *v*

❶ 〈留め金などを〉外す

❷ 〈受話器などを〉取る ► A dial tone obtained almost instantaneously on **unhooking** is the only enhancement provided to the user by electronic switching at present. 受話器を取るとほとんどすぐに聞こえる通話音は, 電子交換によってユーザーへ提供される現時点で唯一の長所である.

hope

接尾 (less) **hopeless** *adj*

❶ 見込みのない ► **hopeless** love かなわぬ恋

❷ 絶望的な ► With a **hopeless** sigh he sat down. 絶望的な溜

息をついて彼は座った.

❸どうしようもない ► I am **hopeless** when it comes to money. 僕は金に縁がない.

接尾 (less) **hopelessly** *ad*

❶救いようがなく, どうしようもないほど ► Politicians today are **hopelessly** corrupt. 今の政治家は腐敗しきっている.

❷あきれるほど ► The BlackBerry, contrariwise, is **hopelessly** lame as a media tool. 逆に, ブラックベリーは, 媒体手段としてあきれるほど時代遅れだ.

接尾 (less) **hopelessness** *n* 絶望 ► the voicelessness of those who live in situations of **hopelessness** 希望のない状況で生きる人に発言権のないこと

hoped-for

接頭 (un) **unhoped-for** *adj* 期待していない, 予期していない

horse

接頭 (un) **unhorse** *v*

❶落馬させる

❷失脚させる

hospitable

接頭 (in) **inhospitable** *adj*

❶納まりの悪い, 住みにくい ► Oscillations in atmospheric temperature could then be so great that what is now called the geographic temperate zone could become quite **inhospitable**. 大気温度の変動が大きくなり, 今でいう地理学的温帯がまるで居住に適さなく[住みにくく]なり得る可能性があった.

❷もてなしの悪い, 無愛想な

接頭 (in) **inhospitability** *n* もてなしのよくないこと

house

接頭 (un) **unhouse** *v* 〈家から〉追い出す

human

接頭 (in) **inhuman** *adj* 不人情な, 非人間的な ► An increasingly **inhuman** load is being dumped on the shoulders of the workers. ますます非人間的な負荷が労働者の肩にかかりつつある.

接頭 (non) **nonhuman** *adj* 人間でない, 人間以外の

humane

接頭 (in) **inhumane** *adj* 不人情な, 非人間的な, 非人道的な

humanity

接頭 (in) **inhumanity** *n* 非人道的行為

humanize

接頭 (de) **dehumanize** *v* 非人間的にする

humidification

接頭 (de) **dehumidification** *n* 除湿, 脱湿 ► No **dehumidification** is obtained during the reactivation cycle. 再開サイクル中は除湿は得られない.

humidified

接頭 (de) **dehumidified** *adj* 除湿された ► The dual-bed machine is larger than the single-bed unit in capacity and has the advantage of providing a continuous supply of **dehumidified** air. ダブルベッド式機械は, 容量の点ではシングルベッド式より大きく, 除湿された空気を連続供給することができるという利点がある.

humidify

接頭 (de) **dehumidify** *v* 除湿する ► In this way, air can be **dehumidified** simply by cooling the air below the temperature where it is saturated. このようにして, 空気は, その飽和温度以下に冷却すれば, 簡単に除湿することができる. ► While one bed is **dehumidifying**, the other bed is reactivating. 一つの床[層]が除湿中のときは, もう一つの床[層]は再開中である.

humidifying

接頭 (de) **dehumidifying** *adj* 除湿している

humor

接尾 (less) **humorless** *adj* ユーモアの (センスの) ない ►

None of this is to say he's **humorless**. これは，彼にはユーモアのセンスがないというのではない．

接尾 (less) **humorlessly** *ad* ユーモアを解さないで ▸ He reacted rather **humorlessly** to these rumors. 彼は，どちらかというとユーモアもなしにこれらの噂に反応した．

接尾 (less) **humorlessness** *n* ユーモアを解さないこと ▸ The interview was conducted before the recent spate of **humorlessness**. インタビューは，最近大勢のユーモアを解さない人々の面前で行われた．

humored

接頭 (ill) **ill-humored** *adj* 不機嫌な ▸ At first no one could say anything **ill-humored** of her. 最初は，彼女の不機嫌さに誰も何も言えなかった．

hurried

接頭 (un) **unhurried** *adj* 急がない ▸ I am writing this blog to encourage my church family and others to spend **unhurried** time with God daily. 私は，教会の信者やその他の仲間が，急ぐことのない日々の時間を神と共に過ごすことを奨励するために，このブログを書いている．

hurt

接頭 (un) **unhurt** *adj* 無傷の

hydrate

接頭 (de) **dehydrate** *v* 脱水する ▸ Most oxy acids can be **dehydrated** by heat to give oxides. 大抵のオキシ酸は，熱で脱水されて酸化物を出す．

hydration

接頭 (de) **dehydration** *n* 脱水，脱水状態 ▸ Diarrhea is particularly serious in a baby as **dehydration** occurs very rapidly and the baby can die in a matter of hours. 下痢は，脱水状態が非常に急速に発生して赤ん坊は数時間以内に死亡することがあるので，赤ん坊にとって特に深刻である．

hygroscopic

接頭 (non) **non-hygroscopic** *adj* 非吸湿性の ► The flux must be **non-hygroscopic**, that is, incapable of absorbing water. フラックスは非吸湿性，すなわち水分を吸わない性質でなければならない.

hysteretic

接頭 (non) **nonhysteretic** *adj* 非ヒステリシスの，非履歴現象の ► This is true only for **nonhysteretic** elastomers; however, alternative fracture mechanics models have been proposed that include hysteresis effects. しかしながら，これは，非ヒステリシスエラストマについてのみ通用し，ヒステリシスの影響を含めた代替の破断メカニズムモデルが提案されている.

I

ice

接頭 (de) **deice** *v* 氷を取り除く

ideal

接頭 (non) **nonideal** *adj* 非理想的 ► An ideal detonation is in accord with the C-J theory, and a **nonideal** detonation, because the reaction is slow, does not accord with theory. 理想デトネーションは, C-J 理論と一致するが, 非理想デトネーションは反応が遅いので, この理論に一致しない.

identified

接頭 (un) **unidentified** *adj*

❶〈物質などが〉確認できない ► The large amount of oxygen had probably been produced by a simple chemical reaction between water vapor and some **unidentified** oxygen-rich compound. 多量の酸素が, おそらく水蒸気と正体が確認されていないある種の酸素の豊富な化合物との間の単純な化学反応によって生成されていた.

❷〈身元や国籍などが〉確認できない

illusion

接頭 (dis) **disillusion** *n* 幻惑を覚ますこと

—— *v* 幻滅させる ► I was **disillusioned** by the scandals I kept reading about. 私は読み続けていたスキャンダルによって幻滅させられていた.

接頭 (dis) **disillusioned** *adj* 幻滅を感じた

接頭 (dis) **disillusionment** *n* 幻滅感 ► After the panic of 1873, **disillusionment** with government aid set in and this policy fell away. 1873年の大恐慌の後, 政府援助に関して幻滅感が起こり, この政策は消えた.

image

接頭 (non) **nonimage** *n* 非画像 ► Both image and **nonimage**

areas are dampened, but the image area rejects the water solution. 画像域と非画像域のいずれも湿らせるが，画像域は水溶液をはじく．

imaginable

接頭 (un) **unimaginable** *adj* 想像できない ▶ It calls for courage and resolution **unimaginable** to Japanese for Romeo and Juliet to arrange to meet in an underground burial chamber. 地下の墓地で会おうとするロミオとジュリエットには，日本人が想像できないほどの勇気と覚悟が必要である．

imaginably

接頭 (un) **unimaginably** *ad* 想像できないほどに ▶ That makes the catastrophe **unimaginably** worse than the 1979 partial meltdown at Three Mile Island. それは，その大災害を，1979年のスリーマイル島の部分的なメルトダウン以上に，想像ができないほど悪化させる．

imaginative

接頭 (un) **unimaginative** *adj* 想像力のない ▶ The writings of such people, though they may be logically correct, are very **unimaginative** in their use of words. そういう人の文章は，論理的な筋は通っていても，言葉に関しては全く想像力が欠けている．

imitability

接頭 (in) **inimitability** *n* 独自性 ▶ Understanding the **inimitability** of Chinese culture is essential to the mission. 中国文化の独自性を理解することは，その任務には必須である．

imitable

接頭 (in) **inimitable** *adj* 独特の ▶ His **inimitable** fantastic world is highly praised. 彼の比類のない空想の世界は高い評価を得ている．

impair

接頭 (un) **unimpair** *v* 損なわれない ▶ In vitamin C-deficient guinea pigs the number of macrophages is lowered and their migration is reduced; but their phagocytosis is **unimpaired**. ビタミンCの欠乏したモルモットではマクロファージの数が低下し，移動が抑制されるが，それらの食作用が損なわれることはない．

impeachable

[接頭]（un） **unimpeachable** *adj* 疑いの余地がない ▸ As he told New York Times columnist Maureen Dowd at the time, he wanted someone "of rather **unimpeachable** integrity, very kind, very calm." 彼は当時ニューヨークタイムズのコラムニスト，モーリーン・ダウドに言ったように,「非常に親切で，非常に穏やかな，誠実さに疑いの余地がないような」人物を望んだ．

[接頭]（un） **unimpeachably** *ad* 疑いの余地なく

impeded

[接頭]（un） **unimpeded** *adj* 障害のない

importance

[接頭]（un） **unimportance** *n* 重要でないこと ▸ He recognized the **unimportance** of the events developing in Krugerville. 彼は，クルガービル周辺で行われているイベントが重要でないことを認めた．

important

[接頭]（un） **unimportant** *adj* 重要でない ▸ In these cases, high production rates are **unimportant**. このような場合，生産速度が高いことは重要ではない． ▸ Series motors are ideal for fans, where speed is relatively **unimportant**. 速度が比較的重要ではないファンには，直列モーターが理想的である． ▸ The passive may be necessary and effective in technical documents where there is no actor or agent or when the actor is **unimportant**. 技術文書では，行為者または作用者がいないかまたは行為者が重要ではない場合には受動態が必要で効果的と考えられる．

impressive

[接頭]（un） **unimpressive** *adj* 印象的でない ▸ Walter Lord,

author of *A Night to Remember*, pored over the old damage claims and found that the Titanic's cargo was insured for an **unimpressive** $420,000.『タイタニック号の最期』の著者ウォルター・ロードは，古い損害請求を詳しく調べ，タイタニック号の積荷は，たかだか42万ドルの保険にしか入っていなかったことがわかった.

improved

接頭 (un) **unimproved** *adj*

❶改良[改善]されていない ▶ The flood situation in Chiang Rai remains **unimproved**. チェンライの洪水の状況は改善されないままである.

❷利用されていない ▶ The **unimproved** land value of each block is assessed by examining the sales records for similar properties. 各ブロックの利用されていない土地の価値は，類似不動産の売却実績を調べることにより評価される.

incentive

接頭 (dis) **disincentive** *adj* 向上意欲をそぐ

inclination

接頭 (dis) **disinclination** *n* いや気 ▶ Your **disinclination** to travel or refusal of a visa application is not a reason for cancelling. 旅行に気が進まないことやビザ申請の許可が下りないことをキャンセルの理由にすることはできない.

inclined

接頭 (dis) **disinclined** *adj* 気が進まない

incorporated

接頭 (un) **unincorporated** *adj*

❶法人化されていない ▶ The following is a partial list of named, but **unincorporated**, communities in the state of North Carolina. 以下に示すのは，ノースカロライナ州の非法人のコミュニティで，名前を付けられた部分的なリストである.

❷合体されていない

infect

接頭 (dis) **disinfect** *v* 消毒する ► For this purpose, Lister decided to use carbolic acid which had served previously to **disinfect** sewage. この目的のために，リスターは，これまで汚水を消毒するのに有効であった石炭酸を使用することにした．

infectant

接頭 (dis) **disinfectant** *adj*

❶ 消毒用の ► Dip a fine tooth comb into a **disinfectant** solution. 目が細かい「くし」を消毒用の溶液に浸ける． ► Spores of many species can survive long periods of drying, and they can even withstand treatment with strong **disinfectant** solutions. 多くの種の胞子は，長期の乾燥を生き抜くことができ，また強力な消毒液の処置に耐えることさえもできる．

❷ 殺菌性のある ► On the premise that sunshine is the best **disinfectant**, my preference is for the debate to be as open and public as possible. 太陽光が最良の殺菌剤であるという前提に立って，その議論ができるかぎり広く公開の場で行われるのが私の意向である．

infected

接頭 (un) **uninfected** *adj*

❶ 〈ウイルスなどに〉感染していない ► The interferon acts as a messenger from infected cells to **uninfected** cells. インターフェロンは，感染した細胞から感染していない細胞へのメッセンジャーとして作用する． ► Whenever the infected computer comes in contact with an **uninfected** piece of software, a fresh copy of the virus passes into the new program. ウイルスに感染したコンピューターが感染していないソフトウェアと接触すると，ウイルスの新しいコピーが必ずその新しいプログラムに送り込まれる．

❷ 影響を受けていない

infection

接頭 (dis) **disinfection** *n* 殺菌，消毒 ► This is a highly oxidizing gas (O_3) used as a deodorizer, and also for **disinfection** of air and water. これは，消臭剤，そして，空気，水の消毒用に利用される酸化能力の高いガス (O_3) である．

infest

接頭 (dis) **disinfest** *v* 〈害虫などを〉駆除する

inflation

接頭 (dis) **disinflation** *n* ディスインフレーション ► **Disinflation** occurs when the rate of inflation declines. インフレ率が低下するときに，ディスインフレーションが生じる．

inflected

接頭 (un) **uninflected** *adj*

❶ 屈曲のない

❷ 抑揚のない

❸ 語尾変化をしない，屈折しない ► an **uninflected** word 語尾変化しない語

information

接頭 (dis) **disinformation** *n* 偽情報

informed

接頭 (ill) **ill-informed** *adj* 大事[大切]なことを(よく)知らない，不案内な ► It boils down to this: we were **ill-informed** as to American affairs. せんじ詰めれば，我々がアメリカの事情に，はなはだうとかったということになる．

接頭 (mis) **misinformed** *adj* 誤解される， 誤って知らされる ► Such indictments are **misinformed**, says Union Pacific's Young. そのような非難は誤解されるとユニオン・パシフィックのヤング氏は言う．

接頭 (un) **uninformed** *adj* 知らされていない

ingenuous

接頭 (dis) **disingenuous** *adj* 不誠実な

inhabitable

接頭 (un) **uninhabitable** *adj* 住居に適していない ► If left unchanged, the current pattern of greenhouse gas emissions will result in rising global temperatures and sea levels, rendering some cities **uninhabitable**. 温室効果ガス排出の現在の行動が変わらなければ, 地球の気温と海面は上昇し, いくつかの都市には, 人々が住めなくなってしまう.

inhabited

接頭 (un) **uninhabited** *adj* 無人の

inherit

接頭 (dis) **disinherit** *v* 相続権を奪う ► Without some planning, you could unwittingly **disinherit** intended beneficiaries. 何らかの計画を持っていないと, 意図した利権を不注意によって相続できなくなる可能性がある.

inhibited

接頭 (un) **uninhibited** *adj* 〈言動などが〉抑制されていない ► an **uninhibited** proprietary mixture 制約されていない専売特許の混合物 ► The **uninhibited** program swapping that made the early days of the computer revolution so exciting may be gone forever. コンピューター革命の初期の段階を非常に刺激した制約されていないプログラム交換は永久に失われる可能性がある.

initiated

接頭 (un) **uninitiated** *adj* 経験のない

injured

接頭 (un) **uninjured** *adj* 怪我をしていない, 損傷を受けていない ► Arkansas quarterback Tyler Wilson was involved in a two-vehicle accident Tuesday morning on Interstate 540 but was **uninjured**, officials said. 当局によると, アーカンソー大学のクォーターバック, タイラー・ウィルソンは火曜日の朝, 州間高速道路540号線で2台の車両事故に巻き込まれたが, 怪我はなかったとのことである.

ink

接頭 (de) **deink** *v* インクを消す

inking

接頭 (de) **deinking** *n* インクを消すこと, インク抜き ▶ Repulping of wastepaper includes a process for **deinking**. 古紙の再パルプ化にはインク抜きの工程が含まれている.

inspired

接頭 (un) **uninspired** *adj* 独創性のない, 刺激のない

inspiring

接頭 (un) **uninspiring** *adj* 〈人を〉退屈させる ▶ This makes us dreary and **uninspiring**. これにより, われわれは憂鬱になったり, 退屈になったりする.

instructed

接頭 (un) **uninstructed** *adj* 指示を受けていない

insulated

接頭 (un) **uninsulated** *adj* 絶縁されていない ▶ At the beginning of the century, **uninsulated** wires spaced 25 cm apart on telephone poles were common. 世紀の初頭においては電柱上で25センチ間隔の非絶縁ワイヤがよく使用されていた.

insured

接頭 (un) **uninsured** *adj* 保険が掛けられていない ▶ It soon became evident that 30% to 35% of the trauma victims were **uninsured** and unable to pay their bills. 精神的傷害を受けた被害者の30％ないし35％は保険が掛けられておらず治療費を払えなかったことがすぐに明らかとなった.

integrate

接頭 (dis) **disintegrate** *v*

❶ 崩壊する ▶ The rocks were **disintegrated** by rain. 岩石は雨のため崩壊した.

❷ ばらばらにする [なる] ▶ I struck a log time and time again until it gradually began to **disintegrate** into wood chips and shavings. 私はその棒がやがてばらばらになり始めて, 小さな木片と削りくずになるまで何度も叩き付けた. ▶ In the production of semichemical pulp, wood chips are first subjected to a mild chemical treatment and then mechanically **disintegrated** in rotating-disk refiners. セミケミカルパルプの生産において，木材チップは最初に弱い化学処理を受ける．そして次に，回転円盤型叩解機に入れられて機械的に砕かれる．

❸やる気を失う

integration

接頭 (dis) **disintegration** *n*

❶崩壊，分解 ▸ **disintegration** of the family 家庭崩壊 ▸ Figure 1 shows the **disintegration** of the isotope produced in the reactor. 図1は，原子炉で形成されたアイソトープの崩壊を示したものである．

❷気力喪失

intelligent

接頭 (un) **unintelligent** *adj* 知能［知性］のない ▸ Rubisco is not an example of **unintelligent** design. ルビスコは，知性のないデザインの例ではない．

intelligible

接頭 (non) **nonintelligible** *adj* 不明瞭な ▸ **Nonintelligible** crosstalk cannot be understood regardless of its received volume. 不明瞭な漏話は，受信音量に関係なく理解できない．

接頭 (un) **unintelligible** *adj*

❶不明瞭な ▸ Abbreviations save space and typing time, but if overused they make a report **unintelligible**. 略語は，スペースとタイピングの時間を節約するが，使い過ぎた場合，報告書が不明瞭なものになってしまう．

❷わかりにくい ▸ output data that would be virtually **unintelligible** in tabular form 表形式ではほとんど理解できない出力データ

intelligibly

接頭 (un) **unintelligibly** *ad* 不明瞭に

intended

接頭 (un) **unintended** *adj* 意図的でない ▸ The emergency

stop mechanism shall be protected against **unintended** use. 非常停止機能は，意図せず誤って使用されないようにしなければならない．

intentional

[接頭] (un) **unintentional** *adj* 故意でない ► **Unintentional** contrasts of ideas should be avoided. アイデアを意図なしに対比するのは避けるべきである． ► prevent **unintentional** contact 意図せざる接触を避ける

intentionally

[接頭] (un) **unintentionally** *ad* 故意でなく，偶然に ► So there is no confusion, the penalty for revealing Apple secrets, intentionally or **unintentionally**, is clear. したがって混乱は何もなく，故意か偶然かを問わず，アップル社の秘密を漏らす行為に対する処罰は明確である．

intentioned

[接頭] (ill) **ill-intentioned** *adj* 悪意のある ► **ill-intentioned** criticism 悪意ある批判

interconnecting

[接頭] (non) **noninterconnecting** *adj* 相互連結していない ► Millions of tiny **noninterconnecting** air cells effectively resist the passage of heat and water vapor. 何百万もの極小の相互連結していない気嚢は，熱や水蒸気の通過阻止に効果がある．

interest

[接頭] (dis) **disinterest** *n* 興味のないこと，無関心 ► Sexual **disinterest** in women stems from primordial times. 女性の性的無関心さは原始時代に端を発する．

interested

[接頭] (dis) **disinterested** *adj* 興味がない，無関心である

[接頭] (un) **uninterested** *adj*

❶ 関心のない ► For years, Steve Jobs was **uninterested** in the human resources department. 何年もの間，スティーブ・ジョブズは人事部門に関心がなかった．

❷ 興味がない ▸ He was **uninterested** in discussing money. 彼は金銭についての話し合いには興味がなかった.

interesting

接頭 (un) **uninteresting** *adj*

❶ 興味のない ▸ Just as a technically accurate report may be incomprehensible, a report written in perfect grammar can be dull, **uninteresting**, and difficult to understand. 技術的に正確なレポートが理解しにくいことがあるのと同様に, 完璧な文法によって書かれたレポートは退屈で関心を呼ばず, 理解しにくいことがある.

❷ つまらない ▸ If a room is perfectly square and **uninteresting** in shape . . . もし部屋が完全に真四角で, つまらない作りなら, ….

interference

接頭 (non) **noninterference** *n* 不干渉

interpret

接頭 (mis) **misinterpret** *v* 誤解する ▸ However, if he had intended, with no devious thoughts, to be merely more hospitable by using the other's language, his strategy was **misinterpreted** and it backfired. けれども, 彼が邪な考えなしで, 他の言語を用いて単により温かくもてなすつもりだったとしたら, 彼の計画は誤解され, 逆効果となっていた.

interpretation

接頭 (mis) **misinterpretation** *n* 誤解 ▸ I am solely responsible for any mistakes or **misinterpretation** of their views. 彼らの見解の何らかの間違いや誤解についてはもっぱら私に責任がある. ▸ Cognitive theories of panic disorder suggest that the catastrophic **misinterpretation** of bodily sensations is the trigger for a panic attack. パニック障害の認識理論は, 体感の破局的な誤解が不安発作の誘因であることを示唆する.

interrupted

接頭 (un) **uninterrupted** *adj* 不断の, 連続的な ▸ The satellite

in this orbit was suitable for relaying telecommunication signals for **uninterrupted** service. この軌道の衛星は，連続的なサービスを提供するための電話通信信号を中継することに適していた． ▶ By the time World War II began, an **uninterrupted** 24-hr radar watch was maintained over the principal air and sea approaches to Britain. 第二次世界大戦が始まるまで，英国への主要な空と海の進入路に対する24時間不断のレーダー監視が維持された．

intervention

接頭 (non) **nonintervention** *n*

❶不干渉

❷非介入 ▶ This study is limited by the self selection of patients and the lack of a **nonintervention** comparison group. 患者の自己選択が入り，また非介入対照群が欠如していることから，この研究には限界がある．

invasive

接頭 (non) **noninvasive** *adj* 非侵入式 ［非侵襲性］ の ▶ a handheld device that uses **noninvasive** computer imaging to help doctors spot melanomas 非侵襲性コンピューター画像を使用して，医師が黒色腫を発見するのに役に立つ携帯用デバイス ▶ Errors are detected by both concurrent on-line hardware checkers and periodic, **noninvasive** on-line diagnostic tests. 並行処理オンラインハードウェアチェッカーと非侵入式定期オンライン診断テストの両方でエラーが検出される． ▶ Digital radiography has become increasingly important in the development of **noninvasive** diagnostic and treatment techniques. デジタル放射線写真術は非侵襲性の診断と治療の方法の開発において，ますます重要になってきた．

invest

接頭 (dis) **disinvest** *v* 投資をやめる［減らす］，～から資本を引き揚げる，負の投資を行う

invited

接頭 (dis) **disinvite** *v* 招待しない

接頭 (un) **uninvited** *adj*

❶招待されていない ▶ Like a biological vaccination, a vaccine program is a preventive measure — an attempt to protect an uninfected disk from invasion by an **uninvited** program. 生物学的なワクチン接種と同様に，ワクチンプログラムは，感染していないディスクを招かれざるプログラムの侵入から保護するための予防策である．

❷余計な

inviting

接頭 (un) **uninviting** *adj* 魅力のない ▶ Seeing that **uninviting** mess, it's easy to understand that last year the company spent $1.2 billion on a stunning 590 promotions. やる気をなくさせるほどの混乱を見ていると，会社が昨年に590という驚くべき数の販売促進策に12億ドルを使ったことが容易に理解できる．

ionic

接頭 (non) **nonionic** *adj* 非イオン(性)の ▶ Humates are ionic and dissolved, whereas tannins are **nonionic** and undissolved. フミン酸塩はイオン性および溶解性であるが，一方タンニンは非イオン性および非溶解性である．

ionization

接頭 (de) **deionization** *n* 脱イオン，消イオン ▶ Without **deionization**, current flows across the same point between electrode and workpiece, and causes excessive heating. 消イオン化していないと，電流は電極と工作物間の同じ位置を通って流れ，過度の加熱状態を生ずる．

ionize

接頭 (de) **deionize** *v* イオンを除去する ▶ In the absence of the transmitter pulse, the gas is **deionized** and the impedance across the tube is essentially infinite. 送信機パルスがないとき

は，そのガス体のイオンは除去され，電子管全体のインピーダンスは本質的に無限大となる．

ionized

接頭 (de) **deionized** *adj* 消イオンの ▸ Surface damage left by the lapping is removed by etching with an acid mixture and washing with **deionized** water. ラップ仕上げでつけられた表面の損傷は，酸性混合物でエッチングし，脱イオン水で洗浄すれば取り除くことができる．

接頭 (un) **unionized** *adj* イオン化していない

iron

接頭 (non) **noniron** *adj* アイロンがけの要らない ▸ a drip-dry **noniron** shirt 絞らずにそのまま干し，アイロンがけの要らないシャツ

J

job

接尾 (less) **jobless** *adj* 失業中の ▸ The newspaper warned that further automation would increase the **jobless** rate. ある新聞は，さらに自動化が進むと，失業率を上げることになりかねないと警告している． ▸ Five **jobless** survivors of the war got together and translated the text into Japanese. 職にありつけない［失業中の］戦争の生き残りの仲間が5人集まって，そのテキストを日本語に訳した．

接尾 (less) **joblessness** *n*

❶ 仕事のない状態 ▸ Changing Libya — its poverty, its **joblessness**, and its lack of economic growth — will require more than magic. リビアの変革，すなわちその貧困，仕事のない状態，経済成長の不足を変えるには魔法以上の力が必要である．

❷ 失業 ▸ Long term **joblessness** is especially sinister. 長期失業は特に不吉である．

joint

接頭 (dis) **disjoint** *v*

❶〈関節などを〉外す

❷ 支離滅裂にする

接頭 (un) **unjoint** *v*〈接続部などを〉切り離す

接尾 (less) **jointless** *adj* 関節のない

jointed

接頭 (dis) **disjointed** *adj*

❶ ばらばらにされた ▸ Dark cabinet sides reduce shadows between cabinets and make multiple units appear unified rather than **disjointed**. キャビネットの両側の暗さがキャビネットの間の影を弱め，複数のユニットをばらばらに見せるのではなく一体になったように見せる．

❷支離滅裂の

joy

接尾 (less) **joyless** *adj* 楽しくない ► To be more precise, it's a hateful, **joyless** look. より正確にいえば，それは見た目では憎しみに満ちており，楽しくない様子である．

judged

接頭 (ill) **ill-judged** *adj* 判断を誤った，思慮のない ► an **ill-judged** attempt 無分別な試み

judgmental

接頭 (non) **nonjudgmental** *adj* 間違った判断をしない

juror

接頭 (non) **nonjuror** *n* 宣誓を拒否する人

just

接頭 (un) **unjust** *adj* 不平な，不公平な ► The war waged in Iraq was **unjust**. イラクでの戦争は，不公平なものだった．

justice

接頭 (in) **injustice** *n* 不正，不正行為 ► But they belie a fierce ambition and an obsession to root out **injustice** on Wall Street and beyond. しかし，それらは米国金融市場とその背後の不正を根絶やしにしようという熱心な意欲や強迫観念と一致しない．

justifiable

接頭 (un) **unjustifiable** *adj* 正当化できない ► Granting that it can't be helped if luxury goods cost several times the overseas prices, this discrepancy seems **unjustifiable** in the case of daily necessities. 高級品の値段が外国の何倍かするのは仕方がないとしても，生活必需品の場合，この相違は正当化できないように思われる．

justified

接頭 (ill) **ill-justified** *adj* 正当化できない

justly

接頭 (un) **unjustly** *ad* 不当に，不法に ► Likewise, he believes

his CEO was **unjustly** convicted of making false criminal accusations against clients. 同様に，彼は自社のCEOが顧客に対して間違った刑事告発を行ったかどで不法に有罪宣告を受けたと信じている．

K

kempt

接頭 (un) **unkempt** *adj* 〈髪や服装などが〉だらしない ▶ Cannas looked like a forest in the **unkempt** garden. カンナは，だらしなく荒れた庭の森のように見えた.

kept

接頭 (ill) **ill-kept** *adj* 手入れされていない，がさつな

key

接尾 (less) **keyless** *adj* 鍵のない

kind

接尾 (less) **kindless** *adj* 不親切な

接頭 (un) **unkind** *adj* 不親切な ▶ I have said some **unkind** things about the United States, but the situation is not much different here in Japan. アメリカの不親切なところをいくらか述べたが，ここ日本だって状況は似たようなものである.

kindly

接頭 (un) **unkindly** *adj* 不親切に

knit

接頭 (un) **unknit** *v* 〈結び目などを〉ほどく

knot

接尾 (less) **knotless** *adj* 結び目のない，無結節の ▶ a **knotless** net making machine 無結節網製造機

knowable

接頭 (un) **unknowable** *adj* 知ることができない ▶ I am interested in the unknown and the **unknowable**. 私は，知られていないものと知ることのできないものに興味を持っている.

knowing

接頭 (un) **unknowing** *adj* 知らない，気が付かない

knowingly

接頭 (un) **unknowingly** *ad* 知らずに，気が付かずに

known

接頭 (un) **unknown** *adj*

❶ 知られていない ▸ The reproduction and other details of viral biology remained totally **unknown**. ウイルス生物学のうち生殖などの細部はまったく未解明のままだった.

❷ 原因不明の ▸ There was a fever of **unknown** etiology. 原因不明の発熱があった.

L

labored

接頭 (un) **unlabored** *adj* 労せずして得た

lace

接頭 (un) **unlace** *v* 〈靴などの〉ひもを解く ► **unlace** the shoes 靴のひもをほどく

laminar

接頭 (non) **nonlaminar** *adj* 非層状の ► If the possibility of **nonlaminar** flow can be ruled out and the fluid is known to be time-independent, then ... 非層流の可能性を除外できて，液体が時間非依存であることが判明しているならば，…

land

接尾 (less) **landless** *adj* 土地を持っていない

laser

接頭 (non) **nonlaser** *adj* 非レーザーの ► **Nonlaser** processes, including electro-discharged machining (EDM), produced clean, straight, accurate holes. 放電加工 (EDM) などの非レーザー法により，きれいでまっすぐで正確な穴が作られた．

latch

接頭 (un) **unlatch** *adj* 〈かけ金具などを〉外す ► An electromechanical actuation system **unlatches** and deploys the radiators. 電気と機械による作動システムがラジエーターの取り外しと作動を行う．

law

接尾 (less) **lawless** *adj* 無法の，不法な ► In the rest of the park, which is utterly **lawless**, we can only conclude there has been an uncontrolled massacre. 残りの地区は，全く無法の状態であり，大虐殺を抑えられなかったと結論するしかない．

lawful

接頭 (un) **unlawful** *adj* 非合法の，違法の ► commit an **unlaw-**

ful act 違法行為をする

lawfulness

接頭 (un) **unlawfulness** *n* 非合法, 違法 ▶ an act of **unlawfulness** 違法行為

leaded

接頭 (un) **unleaded** *adj* 無鉛の, 鉛を含んでいない ▶ The same reasoning holds for the fact that premium **unleaded** is recommended for the SFI engine. 同じ理由により無鉛化プレミアムがSFIエンジンに推奨されているという事実がある.

leader

接尾 (less) **leaderless** *adj* リーダーのいない

leading

接頭 (mis) **misleading** *adj* 誤解を招く ▶ Similarly, the U.S. executive cannot erase the repertoire of euphemistic and potentially **misleading** idioms from the lexicon of negotiation. 同様に, 米国側の幹部は, 婉曲的および潜在的に誤解を招く慣用語のレパートリーを交渉の際の語彙から排除することができない.

leaf

接尾 (less) **leafless** *adj* 葉のない ▶ Many deciduous plants flower during the period when they are **leafless**, as this increases the effectiveness of pollination. 多くの落葉植物は葉のない期間に花が咲くが, それが授粉の効果を増大する.

learn

接頭 (un) **unlearn** *v* 〈知識などを〉捨てる, 忘れる

learned

接頭 (un) **unlearned** *adj* 教育のない, 学問のない

leash

接頭 (un) **unleash** *v* 解放する ▶ It **unleashed** $800 million to purchase its shares, which were dancing near an all-time high of $80. それは, 史上最高の80ドル近くに高騰していた株式を購入するため, 8億ドルを放出した.

leg

[接尾] (less) **legless** *adj* 脚のない

legal

[接頭] (il) **illegal** *adj* 違法の, 非合法の, ルール違反の, 反則の ▸ In just about every country in the world, stringing private transmission lines across public property is also **illegal**. おおむね世界中のどの国でも, 公共施設を横切って個人の送電線を張るのも違法である. ▸ While the idea predates insider trading, it has never been considered **illegal** or unethical. その考え方は, インサイダー取引以前のものであるが, 違法または倫理にもとると見なされたことはなかった. ▸ Insider trading is now **illegal** in the United States. インサイダー取引は米国では今や非合法である.

legally

[接頭] (il) **illegally** *ad* 不法に, 違法に ▸ He is **illegally** selling narcotic drugs. 彼は麻薬を非合法に販売[密売]している.

legible

[接頭] (il) **illegible** *adj* 読みにくい, 判読できない ▸ If any of your nameplates are missing or **illegible**, check the appliance's requirements in the chart below. 自分のネームプレートを紛失した場合や, 判読しにくい場合には, 下の図表にある装置の要件をチェックすること. ▸ A few pencil marks followed; but they were **illegible**. 2, 3の鉛筆の跡が続いていたが, 判読できなかった.

legitimacy

[接頭] (il) **illegitimacy** *n* 違法, 不法, 非合法 ▸ Who could approach them with the disclosure of their own **illegitimacy**? 彼ら自身の非合法を暴露するために近づくような者はいるか.

legitimate

[接頭] (il) **illegitimate** *adj*

❶違法な, 非合法の ▸ The idea of renewable energy as slightly **illegitimate** is pervasive here. やや非合法な再生可能エネル

ギーのアイデアは，ここでは広がりつつある．

❷ 正統性がない ▶ That's an **illegitimate** question. それは，筋の通らない質問だ．

❸ 非嫡出の，私生の ▶ The divorced mother would have her own **illegitimate** family. 離婚した母親は，自身の私生家族を持つことになる．

leisure

接尾 (less) **leisureless** *adj* 暇のない

lettered

接頭 (un) **unlettered** *adj* 教養のない，無学の

liberal

接頭 (il) **illiberal** *adj* 狭量な，粗野な，下品な

liberalism

接頭 (il) **illiberalism** *n* 反[非]自由主義 ▶ They increase **illiberalism** in these associations. 彼らは，これらの団体の反自由主義を増大させる．

licensed

接頭 (un) **unlicensed** *adj* 無免許の

licit

接頭 (il) **illicit** *adj*

❶ 道徳的，倫理的に認められない[是認されない] ▶ **illicit** love 道ならぬ恋

❷ 法的に認められない，不法な ▶ **illicit** trade 違法な取引

lid

接尾 (less) **lidless** *adj* ふたのない

life

接尾 (less) **lifeless** *adj* 命のない ▶ Some patients report that they are unable to experience usual emotions and feel that the world has become colorless and **lifeless**. 一部の患者は，普通の感情を経験することができず，世界が色褪せ，命がなくなってしまうように感じると報告する．

like

接頭 (dis) **dislike** *v*

❶ 嫌う，　好きでない ► Longer response time decreased throughput, increased procedural errors, and were generally **disliked** by users. 長い応答時間は処理量を減少し，手続き上の誤りを増加し，一般的にユーザーに嫌われていた．

❷ 嫌悪感 ► When neurosis develops to its full extent, the patient comes to harbor an unbearable **dislike** of even herself. 神経症の症状が最高度に達すると，患者は自分自身に対してさえも堪えがたい嫌悪感を抱くようになる．

接頭 (un) **unlike** *ad* ～と違って ► The walls of Archaebacteria are **unlike** those of . . . 始原細菌の細胞壁は…のそれとは異なる．

liked

接頭 (dis) **disliked** *adj* 嫌われた，好ましくない ► Scanning data with the magnetic slot reader was the most preferred method of entry, while keying long digit entries was the most **disliked**. 磁気スロット読取装置でデータをスキャンするのは最も好まれていた方法であったが，一方，長い数字をキー入力することは最も好ましからざるものであった．

likely

接頭 (un) **unlikely** *adj*

❶ ありそうもない ► Small particles of carbon black filler would be an **unlikely** cause. カーボンブラック充填材の微粒子が原因ということはありそうもない．

❷ 見込みのない ► Because of the fundamental characteristics of radioactive wastes, the development of other methods seems **unlikely**. 放射性廃棄物の根元的な性質のために，他の方法の開発は見込みがないようだ．

limb

接尾 (less) **limbless** *adj* 肢［腕，脚］のない

limit

接尾 (less) **limitless** *adj* 無制限の, 無限の ▶ If it is only a matter of logic, then there is a **limitless** number of reasons on both sides of the question. それが論理だけの問題ならば, 良い理由も悪い理由も無限にある. ▶ Mixing different cheese varieties provides an almost **limitless** number of blends. 各種のチーズを調合すると, 無限に近い数のブレンドができる. ▶ The versatility of this process suits it to an almost **limitless** number of applications. この方法には融通性があるので, それを無限といってよいくらいの用途に適合させることができる. ▶ We feel that as long as we stay true to who we are — quality, good-tasting products that are priced fairly and honestly positioned — our growth potential is **limitless**. 我々が, 適正な価格の正当な手段で販売される, 品質の高い優れた味の製品を正直に生産し続ける限り, 無限に成長すると感じる.

limitable

接頭 (il) **illimitable** *adj* 無限の, 際限のない ▶ the **illimitable** desert, extending the whole breadth of Africa アフリカ全土に広がる広大な砂漠

limited

接頭 (un) **unlimited** *adj* 無制限の ▶ These deposits are mainly of sodium chloride, the supply of which is **unlimited** for practical purposes. この埋蔵物はおもに塩化ナトリウムであり, 実用化する場合にはその供給に制限はない. ▶ Notwithstanding the present contribution and **unlimited** promise of the computer to the design process, one must, however, recognize certain limitations. 設計工程に対しコンピューターは現在のように貢献し無限の将来性を備えているが, その反面でなんらかの限界があることを認識しなければならない.

linear

接頭 (non) **nonlinear** *adj*

❶ 非線形の ▶ The signal must not be subjected to any **non-**

linear operation, such as envelope or phase detection, or passage through a **nonlinear** amplifier. この信号には，包絡線や位相検出または非直線増幅器通過などの非線形処理が実施されてはならない． ▸ There is a need for a mixed-mode (linear and **nonlinear**) circuit analysis program. 混合モード（線形および非線形）の回路分析プログラムが必要である． ▸ Optimization analyses, given a model of the design and using linear and **nonlinear** programming, determines the best values of the parameters. 最適化分析とは，設計のモデルを与えられ線形および非線形プログラムを使用し，諸要因の最適値を決定することである．

❷ 非直線の ▸ The water molecule is **nonlinear**, with the H-O-H angle equal to 104.5°. 水の分子は非直線でH-O-Hの角度が104.5°になっている．

linearity

接頭 (non) **nonlinearity** *n* 非線形性，非直線性 ▸ The **nonlinearity** suppresses the natural polarization rotation phenomenon of the second-order modes. その非線形性のため，二次モードの固有偏波回転現象は抑制される．

link

接頭 (un) **unlink** *v* リンクを外す

lint

接尾 (less) **lintless** *adj* 綿ぼこり[糸くず]の付いていない ▸ For those who would like to closely approximate the effect of this type of polish with a simpler method, a wad of soft, **lintless** cloth can be used to apply the shellac. この種のつや出し剤の効果をより簡単な方法でできるだけ完全に発揮させたいならば，やわらかい，綿ぼこりの付いていない布を束にして，セラックを塗布してもよい．

liquid

接頭 (il) **illiquid** *adj* 非流動性の，〈資産が〉現金化しにくい，現金不足の ▸ an **illiquid** asset 非流動資産

list

[接尾] (less) **listless** *adj* 元気のない ▶ He spent hours in a **listless** funk. 彼は元気がなく憂鬱な気分で何時間も過ごした.

listed

[接頭] (un) **unlisted** *adj* リストに載っていない ▶ An **unlisted** country is any country not listed in the list of EU or non-EU countries. リストに載っていない国とは, EU 加盟国や EU 非加盟国のリストに記載されていない国のことである.

lit

[接頭] (ill) **ill-lit** *adj* 暗い, 薄明かりの

[接頭] (un) **unlit** *adj* 〈火や電気などが〉消えた ▶ The controller also can reverse black and white so that screen images, which have a background of black, **unlit** pixels, can be printed without that background. コントローラーはまた, 画素が発光していない黒い背景を持つ画像を, 背景なしでプリントできるように, 黒と白を反転することができる.

literacy

[接頭] (il) **illiteracy** *n* 読み書きのできないこと ▶ the condition of **illiteracy** 教育を受けていないこと

literate

[接頭] (il) **illiterate** *adj*

❶ 無学の, 教養のない ▶ He is **illiterate**. 彼は, 教養がない.

❷ 読み書きのできない人 ▶ They are absolutely **illiterate**—grossly ignorant. 彼らはいろはのいの字も知らない.

livable

[接頭] (un) **unlivable** *adj* 住むことのできない

living

[接頭] (non) **nonliving** *n* 無生物 ▶ Sometime during the evolution of the universe, life was derived from the **nonliving**. 宇宙の進化の過程のある時期に, 無生物から生命が生まれ出た.

load

[接頭] (un) **unload** *v*

❶〈積み荷などを〉降ろす ▸ The product may be used directly as it is **unloaded**. 製品は，荷揚げされたままの状態で，直接使用されることがある．

❷〈接触などを〉外す ▸ Generally the Belleville toggle type mechanism will not **unload** the contacts at actuation and thereby insures reliable switch ratings. 一般的に，ベルビルトグルタイプメカニズムは作動しても接点の負荷を解放せず，それによってスイッチ定格を信頼できるものにしている．

loading

接頭 (un) **unloading** *adj*〈積み荷などを〉降ろす ▸ As a result, many new loading and **unloading** facilities have been designed and constructed at railroad terminal points. その結果，多くの新しい積み込みと荷下ろし施設が設計され，鉄道のターミナルに建設された．

locate

接頭 (dis) **dislocate** *v*

❶位置を変えさせる，移す

❷混乱させる

location

接頭 (dis) **dislocation** *n* 転位，転置 ▸ It is important to restrict **dislocation** to the interfacial region between the two materials. 二つの材料の連接領域への転位を制限することが重要である． ▸ These defects may be vacancy sites, **dislocations**, grain boundaries, and phase boundaries. これらの欠陥は，空格子の位置，転位，粒界，面界などである．

lock

接尾 (less) **lockless** *adj*

❶鍵のない ▸ a **lockless** cabin 鍵のない小屋

❷水門のない ▸ a long **lockless** stretch of water 水門のないどこまでも続く川

接頭 (un) **unlock** *v* ロックを外す ▸ A key can be used to **unlock** an application, which can be used on any network computer. アプリケーションのロックを外すキーを使用することができ，それはどのネットワークコンピューター上でも使用することができる．

locked

接頭 (un) **unlocked** *adj* ロックが外された ▸ Never place a ladder against a window sash, or in front of an **unlocked** door. はしごは窓サッシにかけたり，ロックが外されたドアの前には置かないでください．

locking

接頭 (non) **nonlocking** *adj* ロックされていない，非ロック式の ▸ The Apple Desktop Bus ports can accept either locking or **nonlocking** cable connectors. アップルデスクトップバスのポートには，ロック式または非ロック式ケーブルコネクターを使用できる．

接頭 (un) **unlocking** *adj* ロックを外す

lodge

接頭 (dis) **dislodge** *v*

❶もとの場所から移動させる ▸ It was possible, he said, that if the partition had cracked in flight, the air rushing from the cabin could have had enough force to **dislodge** the hollow tail fin. もし隔壁が飛行中に裂けたとしたら，キャビンから押し寄せる空気は，空洞の尾翼を動かすのに十分な力があったと思われると彼は言った．

❷追い出す，駆逐する ▸ In hydraulic mining, as now practiced, a stream of water is directed against the coal face with sufficient pressure to **dislodge** the coal. 現在行われている水力式採鉱では，石炭を移動させるのに十分な圧力となるように水の流れを石炭の表面に当てる．

logical

接頭 (il) **illogical** *adj* 非論理的な，筋の通らない，ばかげた，不合理な ▸ Your argument is **illogical**. 君の論は非論理的だ．

look for

接頭 (un) **unlooked-for** *adj* 予期しない，意外な

looking

接頭 (ill) **ill-looking** *adj* 醜い

loose

接頭 (un) **unloose** *v* 〈結び目などを〉緩める

loss

接尾 (less) **lossless** *adj* 損(失)のない ► Their scheme incorporates **lossless** current sensing. 彼らの計画は，ロスのない電流感知を織り込んでいる． ► Some, for example entropy coding with variable length codes, achieve data reduction in a **lossless** way. たとえば，可変長コードによるエントロピーコーディングのように，いくつかは，損失がない方法でデータ整理を達成する．

love

接尾 (less) **loveless** *adj* 愛のない

loved

接頭 (ill) **ill-loved** *adj* 歓迎されない，好まれない

接頭 (un) **unloved** *adj* 愛されていない ► Many problems of childhood arise from a lack of security if the child feels **unloved** and unwanted. 子供の頃の多くの問題は，子供が，愛されていないのではないか，望まれていないのではないかと感じる，安心の欠如から生じる．

lovely

接頭 (un) **unlovely** *adj* 可愛らしくない ► She became beautiful onstage despite her **unlovely** face and figure. 彼女は，愛らしくない容姿にもかかわらず舞台上で美しくなった．

loyal

接頭 (dis) **disloyal** *adj* 忠実でない

loyalty

接頭 (dis) **disloyalty** *n* 不忠実，不誠実 ► Veteran directors never got over what they viewed as an act of **disloyalty** that fateful week in December. ベテランの監督者たちは，あの12月の重大な週に背信行為と映ったものをけっして忘れることができなかった.

lubricated

接頭 (non) **nonlubricated** *adj* 潤滑されていない ▶ A **nonlubricated** plug valve may use a tapered plug with a mechanical lifting device that . . . 非潤滑式プラグバルブでは，…の機械式持ち上げ装置付きのテーパー付きプラグを使用できる.

luck

接尾 (less) **luckless** *adj* 不運な

luckily

接頭 (un) **unluckily** *ad* 不幸にも，不運にも

lucky

接頭 (un) **unlucky** *adj* 不幸な，不運な ▶ Lest you think that I am just particularly **unlucky**, let me share the story of another woman. 私が不運だったに過ぎないとあなたが考えることがないように，別の女性のことについてお話ししたい.

M

maculate

接頭 (im) **immaculate** *adj*

❶ 汚れのない ► The cars and platforms are **immaculate**. 車両もプラットフォームも汚れ一つなくきれいだ.

❷ 一点の曇りもない ► The bride wore an **immaculate** white gown. 花嫁は純白のドレスを着ていた.

made

接頭 (un) **unmade** *adj* 用意ができていない

magnetic

接頭 (non) **nonmagnetic** *adj* 非磁性の ► The **nonmagnetic** property of magnesium alloys makes it valuable for instrument cases and parts. マグネシウム合金は非磁性であるから, 計器のケースや部品に役に立つ.

magnetizable

接頭 (un) **unmagnetizable** *adj* 消磁できる

magnetization

接頭 (de) **demagnetization** *n* 消磁 ► Most brushless dc motor controllers require current limiting to prevent **demagnetization** of the PM rotor during starting and fast reversals. ほとんどのブラシレス直流モーター制御器は, 始動および高速反転中, PM ローターの消磁を妨げるような電流制限を必要とする.

magnetize

接頭 (de) **demagnetize** *v* 消磁する ► In this case, a magnetized electronic or nuclear paramagnetic substance is thermally isolated and then **demagnetized**. この場合, 磁気を帯びた電子あるいは核常磁性物質が熱的に隔離され, そして磁気が除かれる.

magnetized

接頭 (un) **unmagnetized** *adj* 消磁された ► When one of them passes over an **unmagnetized** donut, a current is induced in the coil. その一つが，磁化されていないドーナツ状のコイルの上を通過するとき，コイルに電流が誘導される．

magnetizing

接頭 (de) **demagnetizing** *adj* 消磁状態の，無磁界の ► Possible broadening mechanisms prevailing in the Si-H system are, in general, 1H-1H dipole-dipole interaction, chemical shift dispersion, chemical shift anisotropy and **demagnetizing** field originated by bulk magnetic susceptibility. Si-H システムにおいて支配的な広がりが起きる有力なメカニズムは，一般的に，1H-1H 双極子－双極子相互作用，化学シフト分散，化学シフト異方性およびバルク磁化率により起こされた無磁界である．

maintained

接頭 (ill) **ill-maintained** *adj* 手入れが行き届いていない

make

接頭 (un) **unmake** *v* もとの状態に戻す

manageable

接頭 (un) **unmanageable** *adj* (取り)扱いにくい ► Manned flight is enormously expensive and **unmanageable**. 有人飛行は法外な費用がかかり御しがたい． ► Such conglomerates are now seen as **unmanageable** at best. そのような複合企業体は，今日ではせいぜい厄介ものと見られている．

manly

接頭 (un) **unmanly** *ad* 男らしく

manned

接頭 (un) **unmanned** *adj* 無人の ► Solar cells are the primary power supply for **unmanned** spacecraft. 太陽電池は無人宇宙船の主要動力源である． ► During the last few years, space probes, or **unmanned** spacecraft, have acquired a vast amount of information. 過去数年間に，宇宙探査ロケットまたは無人宇宙船が膨大な量の情報を収集してきた.

manner

接尾 (less) **mannerless** *adj* 無作法な ► The best way to avoid **mannerless** gaffes at work is to pay attention. 仕事において無作法な失態を避ける最良の方法は，注意を払うことである.

mannered

接頭 (ill) **ill-mannered** *adj* 行儀の悪い，無作法な ► It is **ill-mannered** of him to leave without giving notice. 黙って去るとは彼は無作法だ.

接頭 (un) **unmannered** *adj* 無作法な ► Developmental works will gain nothing in an **unmannered** society. 無作法な社会では，発展的な仕事でも成果は得られないだろう.

mannerly

接頭 (un) **unmannerly** *adj* 無作法な，下品な

mantle

接頭 (dis) **dismantle** *v*

❶ 取り外す，撤去する ► This means **dismantling** the computer room and letting engineers, office managers, and factory people become the operators. これはつまり，コンピュータールームを撤去し，技師，責任者，工員たちをオペレーターにすることである.

❷ 分解する ► She knew that she wanted to be an engineer as a sophomore in high school, because she preferred **dismantling** the sewing machine to threading it. 彼女は，ミシンで裁縫するより分解するほうが好きだったから，高校2年生にして将来は技師になることを望んでいることを自覚した.

❸ 潰す，解体する ► To crush the elite, the Americans immediately **dismantled** the old-style middle and high schools. エリート層を壊滅させるために，米国人たちは旧制の中等学校と高等学校をすぐに解体した.

mapped

接頭 (un) **unmapped** *adj* 地図に載っていない, 未踏の

marked

接頭 (un) **unmarked** *adj* 印の付いていない, 無印の ▶ In a modest **unmarked** storefront near Dupont Circle in downtown D.C., ShopHouse Southeast Asian Kitchen is finalizing the menu and training the staff. DC 繁華街にあるデュポンサークル近くの標示のない上品な店頭で, ショップハウス・サウスイースト・エイジアン・キッチンは, メニューを最終的に決定し, スタッフをトレーニングしている.

marred

接頭 (un) **unmarred** *adj* 欠点のない

marriageable

接頭 (un) **unmarriageable** *adj* 結婚に適さない

married

接頭 (un) **unmarried** *adj* 未婚の ▶ High school and college students, and you **unmarried** readers, you mustn't miss it because it's about something that concerns you too! 高校生, 大学生, それから未婚の読者のあなた, それはあなた方が関わっていることでもあるから見逃してはいけない.

mask

接頭 (un) **unmask** *adj* 仮面をはぐ, 正体を暴く

match

接尾 (less) **matchless** *adj* 比べものにならない ▶ His sister was a girl of **matchless** beauty. 彼の妹は比べものにならないほど美しかった.

接頭 (mis) **mismatch** *n* 不釣り合い, 食い違い ▶ **Mismatch** of expectations on either side could lead to dissatisfaction. いずれの側の予想の食い違いも, 不満をもたらす可能性があった.

matchable

接頭 (un) **unmatchable** *adj* 匹敵しがたい

matched

接頭 (ill) **ill-matched** *adj* 不釣り合いな ► an **ill-matched** couple 不釣り合いな夫婦

接頭 (un) **unmatched** *adj* 無比の，無類の ► Pen plotters were once preferred for most graphics applications because their high-quality color printing was **unmatched**. ペンプロッターは，高品質のカラー印刷が他に類を見なかったので，かつてほとんどのグラフィックスアプリケーションに好まれていた.

material

接頭 (im) **immaterial** *adj* 重要でない ► The price was **immaterial**. 価格は重要ではなかった.

materialism

接頭 (im) **immaterialism** *n* 非物質論

materiality

接頭 (im) **immateriality** *n* 非物質性，重要でないこと

materialize

接頭 (de) **dematerialize** *v* 物質的性質をなくす，非物質化する

接頭 (im) **immaterialize** *v* 無形にする

materially

接頭 (im) **immaterially** *ad*

❶無関係に，関連なく

❷重要でなく

mature

接頭 (im) **immature** *adj*

❶未完成の ► The technology used here is still relatively **immature**. ここで使用されている技術は，相対的にまだ未完成である.

❷幼稚な ► an **immature** understanding of life 人生についての幼稚な理解

❸未成熟の ► His art is **immature**. 彼は芸が幼い. ► The

people are eternally **immature**. その国民は永久に未成熟である.

meaning

接尾 (less) **meaningless** *adj* 意味のない, 無意味な ► Many workpieces in the real world make positioning error analysis look **meaningless**. 実世界における機械加工の仕掛品には, 位置誤差分析を無意味と思わせるものがたくさんある. ► Unfortunately, the values indicated by the clip gauges were **meaningless**. 残念ながら, そのクリップゲージに示される値は意味がなかった. ► In these small display areas, the useful measure of sensitivity, volts per centimeter, becomes **meaningless**. これらの小さな表示範囲では, 有効な感度の計測値(ボルト/センチメートル)は意味がなくなる. ► It is **meaningless** to give presents reluctantly or grudgingly, from a sense of obligation, or out of regard for custom. 義理やしきたりで, しかたなくまたはいやいや贈り物をするのは無意味である.

接尾 (less) **meaninglessness** *n* 無意味さ ► People who merely do and say the same things as others will eventually be thrown into despair by the **meaninglessness** of their lives. 皆と同じことを言い, 同じことをするだけの人は, そのうちに人生の無意味さに失望することになる.

接頭 (un) **unmeaning** *adj* 無意味な, 要領を得ない ► Silence is better than **unmeaning** words. 沈黙は無意味な言葉よりも優れている.

measurable

接頭 (im) **immeasurable** *adj*

❶ 測定できない ► an **immeasurable** length or weight 測定不可能な長さまたは重さ

❷ 計り知れない ► This is an **immeasurable** sense of accomplishment. これは計り知れない達成感である.

measure

接尾 (less) **measureless** *adj* 計り知れない

measured

接頭 (un) **unmeasured** *adj* 測定されていない ▸ If you do not have a meter fitted, you will be charged for water on an **unmeasured** basis. もし適合したメーターがない場合は，測定できないときの基準にもとづき水道料金を請求させていただく．

meat

接尾 (less) **meatless** *adj* 肉のない

mediacy

接頭 (im) **immediacy** *n* 即時性，緊急性 ▸ Letters don't have the same **immediacy** as e-mail. 手紙は，イーメイルと同じような即時性はない．

medicable

接頭 (im) **immedicable** *adj* 取り返しのつかない ▸ **immedicable** result of a momentary impulse by despondency 落胆の末の一時の衝動による取り返しのつかない結果

member

接頭 (non) **nonmember** *n* 非会員

memorial

接頭 (im) **immemorial** *adj* (人の記憶・記録にないほど)遠い昔の ▸ from time **immemorial** 太古の時代から

mentionable

接頭 (un) **unmentionable** *adj* 口に出して言えない

merciful

接頭 (un) **unmerciful** *adj* 非情な

mercy

接尾 (less) **mercilessly** *ad* 無慈悲に ▸ Moreover, its logical starting point is the doctrine of predestination, which **mercilessly** and cruelly writes off perhaps 90 percent of all humanity. しかも，世界中の人間のおそらく9割以上の人を無意味なものと見なすあまりにも無慈悲かつ冷酷な予定説に，論理の出発点があるのです．

merit

接頭 (de) **demerit** *n* 短所, 欠点 ► the merits and **demerits** of the plan 計画の長所と短所

metal

接頭 (non) **nonmetal** *n* 非金属 ► Intermediate-viscosity fluids are utilized in **nonmetal** to metal lubrication. 非金属と金属間の潤滑には, 中粘度の流体が利用される.

metallic

接頭 (non) **nonmetallic** *adj* 非金属の ► If the wiring is of **nonmetallic** cable ... 配線が非金属外装ケーブルの場合は….
► Organic coatings are **nonmetallic** and are used in a variety of ways to prevent steel corrosion. 有機塗料は非金属であり, 鋼鉄の腐食防止用にさまざまに用いられている.

met

接頭 (un) **unmet** *adj*

❶〈要求などが〉満たされていない

❷〈目標などが〉達成されていない

militarize

接頭 (de) **demilitarize** *v* 非武装化する

mind

接尾 (less) **mindless** *adj*

❶思慮のない

❷気をつけない, 不注意な

mindful

接頭 (un) **unmindful** *adj* 心にとどめない

mine

接頭 (de) **demine** *v* 地雷を除去する

mirth

接尾 (less) **mirthless** *adj* 面白みがない

miscible

接頭 (im) **immiscible** *adj*〈液体などが〉混ざらない ► Oil and water are **immiscible**. 水と油は混ざらない.

mistakable

接頭 (un) **unmistakable** *adj* 間違えようもない ► What excited scientists the most was the **unmistakable** traces of dry riverbeds and . . . 最も科学者を興奮させたものは，間違えようがない干上がった川床の跡や…だった． ► Even if we ignore the subject matter, the difference in impact between this and the Hemingway passage is **unmistakable**. 私たちは主題をないがしろにしているとしても，これとヘミングウェイの一節の間の影響力の違いは間違えようもなかった．

mistakably

接頭 (un) **unmistakably** *ad* まぎれもなく ► **Unmistakably** smoking has bad effect on health. タバコはまぎれもなく身体に悪い．

mitigated

接頭 (un) **unmitigated** *adj* 〈痛みなどを〉和らげられない ► Their English was an **unmitigated** catastrophe. 彼らの英語はとにかくひどいものであった．

mixed

接頭 (un) **unmixed** *adj* 混ざりもののない

mobile

接頭 (im) **immobile** *adj*

❶ 動かせない，固定した ► Specialized capital is **immobile** for technical reasons. 特定資本は技術的な理由から動かしがたい．

❷ 動けない ► A bed bath will be necessary if the patient is to ill or **immobile** to make the journey to the bathroom. もし病人が，病状がひどくて動けない場合は，ベッドの上で病人を洗うことは不可欠である．

mobility

接頭 (im) **immobility** *n* 不動性 ► Intellectual **immobility** was the result. 知的な停滞がその結果として残った．

mobilization

[接頭] (de) **demobilization** *n*

❶ (軍隊などの) 動員解除

❷ 復員, 除隊

mobilize

[接頭] (de) **demobilize** *v* 除隊させる, 解体する ► At the end of the Second World War all of Japan's military forces were **demobilized** as one of the conditions of surrender. 第2次世界大戦の終了時, 降伏条件の一つとして日本の軍隊がすべて解散させられた.

[接頭] (im) **immobilize** *v*

❶ 固定する ► An enzyme called glucose oxidase is **immobilized** on a platinum electrode. グルコースオキシダーゼという酵素がプラチナの電極に固定されている.

❷ 動かなくする ► an orthopedic mechanical device used to **immobilize** and protect a part of the body (as a broken leg) 身体の一部分 (折れた足のような) を固定し守るための整形外科の用具

❸ 止める ► **immobilize** a piece 部品を固定する

moderate

[接頭] (im) **immoderate** *adj*

❶ 節度のない ► any act of **immoderate** indulgence 節度のない道楽のあらゆる行為

❷ 過度の

moderately

[接頭] (im) **immoderately** *ad* むやみに, 節度なく ► He is **immoderately** — inordinately — fond of his children. 彼は子どもをみやみに可愛がる.

modest

[接頭] (im) **immodest** *adj* 慎みのない, 無遠慮な, 無作法な ► At the risk of being **immodest**, my record proves this point. うぬぼれを承知でいうが, 私の記録は自分の正しさを証明する

ものである.

modified

接頭 (un) **unmodified** *adj* 修正していない, 無修正の ▶ We run the **unmodified** device driver, with its original operating system, in a virtual machine. 私たちは, 仮想マシンの中で, もとのオペレーティングシステムを使用しながら無修正のデバイスドライバーを実行させている.

modulate

接頭 (de) **demodulate** *v* 復調する ▶ This voltage is amplified in a standard ac amplifier and is then **demodulated** by the other chopper contact. この電圧は, 基準的交流増幅器の中で増幅され, ついで, 接触断続器のもう一つの接触により復調される.

接頭 (un) **unmodulated** *adj* 調整されていない, 非変調の ▶ These are short samples of **unmodulated** subcarrier transmitted during the horizontal blanking periods after the horizontal sync pulses. これらは, 水平同期パルス後の水平帰線消去時に送信された非変調の短い副搬送波のサンプルである.

modulation

接頭 (de) **demodulation** *n* 復調 ▶ The process of shifting the input signal to the assigned frequency slot is called modulation, and the inverse process at the receiving end is called **demodulation**. 入力信号を割当周波数スロットに変えていく過程を変調と呼び, 受信側でのその反対の過程を復調と呼んでいる.

molested

接頭 (un) **unmolested** *adj* 悩まされない

moon

接尾 (less) **moonless** *adj* 月の出ていない

moored

接頭 (un) **unmoor** *v* ともづなを解く, 錨を上げる

接頭 (un) **unmoored** *adj* ともづなを解かれた ▶ **Unmoored** vessels are a danger during storms. ともづなを解かれた船は, 嵐の間は危険である.

moral

[接頭] (a) **amoral** *adj* 道徳観のない ► He is an **amoral** person, motivated only by efficiency. 彼は，効率だけを考える道徳観のない人である.

[接頭] (im) **immoral** *adj* 不道徳な，みだらな ► He led an impure and **immoral** life. 彼の生活態度は腐りきっていた.

[接頭] (im) **immoralism** *n* 背徳主義 ► an ethical viewpoint called **immoralism** 背徳主義という道徳的な考え方

[接頭] (non) **nonmoral** *adj* 非道徳的な

[接頭] (un) **unmoral** *adj* 非道徳的な ► His wife put up with his **unmoral** behavior far too long. 妻は，あまりにも長い間，夫の非道徳的な行動を我慢しすぎた.

morality

[接頭] (a) **amorality** *n* 道徳観のないこと ► Many of our institutions of learning have been turning out an increasing number of students schooled in **amorality**. 我々学術団体の多くが，道徳観を教えこまれない学生をますます多く生み出している.

[接頭] (im) **immorality** *n* 不道徳な行為，ふしだら ► a letter of admonition about the dangers of **immorality** 不道徳の危険性を忠告する文書

moralize

[接頭] (de) **demoralize** *v*

❶士気をくじく，意気喪失する ► In some cases, men become exceedingly **demoralized** when they learn that they have been passed over for promotion. 男は，場合によっては，昇格に関して無視されたことがわかると，極端に意気阻喪するものである.

❷風紀を乱す

[接頭] (im) **immoralize** *v* 不道徳にする

mortal

[接頭] (im) **immortal** *adj*

❶不死の ► No one is **immortal**. 人は死すべきものである.

❷永遠の ▸ an **immortal** work of art 不朽の芸術作品

接頭 (im) **immortality** *n* 不死，不滅

接頭 (im) **immortalize** *v* 不滅にする ▸ **immortalize** one's name 名を末代に残す

接頭 (im) **immortally** *ad* 永遠に，常に ▸ an **immortally** beautiful woman 絶世の美女

mother

接尾 (less) **motherless** *adj* 母親のない

motile

接頭 (im) **immotile** *adj* 動けない ▸ **immotile** material 動けない物体

motion

接尾 (less) **motionless** *adj* 動いていない，静止した ▸ An observer looking at a satellite in a circular equatorial orbit sees the satellite hang in a fixed spot in the sky, apparently **motionless**. 赤道円軌道で衛星を観測する者には，衛星が空の固定した点に浮いていて，一見静止しているように見える．

motivate

接頭 (ill) **ill-motivated** *adj* 不正な ▸ **ill-motivated** borrower 不正な借り手

接頭 (un) **unmotivated** *adj* 動機付けのない

motive

接尾 (less) **motiveless** *adj* 動機のない ▸ The man was accused of a seemingly **motiveless** murder. その男性は，表面上は動機のない殺人で告発された．

mount

接頭 (dis) **dismount** *v* 取り外す

接頭 (un) **unmount** *v* 取り外す ▸ **Unmount** the bolt and replace it. ボルトを取り外して交換すること．

mounted

接頭 (un) **unmounted** *adj* 取り付けられていない ▸ Proper mounting of a motor on a metal surface can reduce the temperature rise approximately 50 per cent as compared to the **unmounted** condition. 金属面の上にモーターを適切に設置すると，取り付けられていない状態に比べ，約50パーセント温度上昇が減少する．

movability

接頭 (im) **immovability** *n* 不（可）動（性） ▸ In astronomy it was the **immovability** of the earth, in history it is the independence of personality — free will. 天文学では，それは地球の不動性であったが，歴史的には人格の独立すなわち自由意志である．

movable

接頭 (im) **immovable** *adj*

❶ 固定された，動かせない ▸ become rigid or **immovable** 硬くなる，または動かなくなる

❷ 不動の ▸ **immovable** property 不動産

❸〈感情に〉動かされない ▸ an **immovable** heart 冷静な心

movably

接頭 (im) **immovably** *ad*

❶ 不動で，断固として ▸ The mountains brooded **immovably** above the river. 山々は川の上に揺るぎなくそびえていた．

❷ 固定して ▸ **immovably** supported 固定支持された

moved

接頭 (un) **unmoved** *adj* 心を動かされない，冷静な

moving

接頭 (un) **unmoving** *adj* 動かない，静止した

musical

接頭 (un) **unmusical** *adj* 非音楽的な ▸ I noticed a strange, ugly, **unmusical** distortion when playing the lower strings. 低音弦を弾いたとき，私は不快で耳障りな異常な歪みに気づいた．

mutable

接頭 (im) **immutable** *adj* 不変の，不易の ▸ The view at that

time was that all species were **immutable**, created by God. 当時の見解は，すべての種は不変であり，神によって造られたというものだった.

mutableness

接頭 (im) **immutableness** *adj* 不変性

mutably

接頭 (im) **immutably** *ad* 変わりなく，不変に ► He was one of those hopelessly and **immutably** self-confident men. 彼は，あきれるほど，そして不変の自信を持った男性たちのうちの1人でした.

muzzle

接頭 (un) **unmuzzle** *v* 言論の自由を与える

mystify

接頭 (de) **demystify** *v* わかりやすくする，明らかにする

N

nail

接頭 (un) **unnail** *v* 釘を抜く

name

接尾 (less) **nameless** *adj*

❶ 名前のない

❷ 名前を明かせない

❸ 言いようのない ▸ A **nameless** fear clutched at her heart and made her cry. 言いようのない不安が彼女の心にあふれて叫ばずにはいられなかった.

nameable

接頭 (un) **unnameable** *adj* 口に出して言えない ▸ We lived in dread of various **unnameable** calamities. 我々は, 言い表しにくい様々な災難に対する恐怖を抱きながら生きていた.

named

接頭 (un) **unnamed** *adj* 名前が出ていない, 匿名の

native

接頭 (non) **nonnative** *adj* ネイティブでない ▸ Structure documents in small modules to give the **nonnative** speaker or translator breathing room. ネイティブではない話者または翻訳者に一息つく時間を与える小さい単位で文書を構成しなさい.

natural

接頭 (un) **unnatural** *adj* 不自然な ▸ This mode of operation is **unnatural** to arc welding. この操作方法は, アーク溶接には不自然である.

naturally

接頭 (un) **unnaturally** *ad* 不自然に

nature

接頭 (ill) **ill-nature** *n* 意地悪, 不機嫌な性格

natured

接頭 (ill) **ill-natured** *adj* 意地の悪い，ひねくれた ► He is an **ill-natured** man. 彼は根性の悪い人だ.

necessarily

接頭 (un) **unnecessarily** *ad* 不必要に ► Adding the lifts and tracks to the system complicated things **unnecessarily**. リフトや軌道を装置に追加したので，不必要に複雑になった.

necessary

接頭 (un) **unnecessary** *adj* 不必要な ► eliminate **unnecessary** physical prototyping 不必要な物理的試作を行わない

need

接尾 (less) **needless** *adj* 必要のない ► **Needless** to say, the automobile radiator, the hot water heater, and . . . are all heat changers. 言うまでもなく[言う必要なく]，自動車のラジエーター，温水暖房器，および…は，すべて熱交換器である.

接尾 (less) **needlessly** *ad* 不必要に ► Not only does the file arrive late but expensive computer and communication resources are **needlessly** tied up. ファイルが遅れて到着するだけではなく，高価なコンピューターと通信機材が無駄に[不必要に]動きがとれなくなる.

negligible

接頭 (non) **nonnegligible** *adj* 無視できない ► Implicitly there is a **nonnegligible** gain in pairs. 絶対的に，対には無視できない利点がある.

negotiable

接頭 (non) **nonnegotiable** *adj* 交渉の余地のない ► If our negotiations with Japan continue as they have in the past, it is probably **nonnegotiable**. 日本との協議がこれまでと同じような形で続くなら，恐らく交渉できないであろう.

neighborly

接頭 (un) **unneighborly** *adj* 隣人らしくない

nerve

接尾 (less) **nerveless** *adj*

❶活気のない

❷落ち着いた

接頭 (un) **unnerve** *v* 気力を失わせる ► This web of friendships **unnerves** Obama's supporters on the left — and it isn't clear it will translate into support from the business community. この友好の網は，左翼のオバマ支持者たちの気力を失わせる．そして，それが経済界からの支持に変わるかどうかは明白ではない．

nerving

接頭 (un) **unnerving** *adj* 気力を失わせる ► Apple created an elaborate and **unnerving** system to enforce internal secrecy. アップル社は社内の秘密保護を強化するために，込みいってやる気をなくさせるようなシステムを作り出した．

Newtonian

接頭 (non) **non-Newtonian** *adj* 非ニュートンの ► Only the relatively simple flow of **non-Newtonian** fluids in tubes has been considered above. 以上管内の非ニュートン流体の比較的単純な流動についてのみ考察した．

nice

接頭 (un) **un-nice** *adj* 良くない，　失礼な ► a few **un-nice** words regarding his ability as a product manager プロダクトマネジャーとしての彼の能力に対する，いくつかの良くない言葉

night

接尾 (less) **nightless** *adj* 夜のない

nocent

接頭 (in) **innocent** *adj* 無害な，　無垢な ► Which is worth more, the life of an **innocent** baby or the life of a ruthless murderer? 無垢な赤ん坊と凶悪殺人犯のどちらの命が大事であろうか．

nocuous

接頭 (in) **innocuous** *adj*

❶ 害のない, 無害［無毒］の ▶ This type of virus can sneak into your system disguised as a relatively **innocuous** program. この種のウイルスは, 比較的無害のプログラムと見せかけてシステムに忍び込むことができる. ▶ Management of low-level wastes generated by the nuclear energy industry requires the use of burial sites to isolate the wastes and allow decay to **innocuous** levels. 核エネルギー産業で発生する低レベル廃棄物の管理には, 廃棄物を隔離して無害なレベルまで崩壊させられるように埋めておける場所が必要だ.

❷ 悪意のない ▶ He has achieved some notoriety as the author of the so-called Peace virus, which flashed an **innocuous** greeting on thousands of computer screens. 彼は, 何千ものコンピューターのスクリーンに悪意のない挨拶を一瞬映し出すいわゆるピースウイルスの作者として, 悪名をはせた.

❸ 当たり障りのない, 退屈な, 刺激のない ▶ There are other, **innocuous** reasons: . . ., . . ., and . . . その他に, …, …, …のような当たり障りのない理由もある.

noise

接尾 (less) **noiseless** *adj* 雑音がない, 音のしない, 静かな ▶ A **noiseless** 3-kHz channel cannot transmit binary signals at a rate exceeding 6000 bps. 雑音がない3kHzのチャネルは, 6000bpsを超える速度でバイナリー信号を送信することができない.

接尾 (less) **noiselessly** *ad* 雑音［騒音］を立てずに, 静かに ▶ Models costing under $2000 can **noiselessly** churn out up to eight pages of text each minute. 2000ドル未満のモデルで, 最高で毎分8ページにおよぶ大量のテキストの処理を静かに行う.

nominate

接頭 (in) **innominate** *adj* 無名の

normal

接頭 (ab) **abnormal** *adj* 異常な，常軌を逸した，普通でない ▶ Protective relays are compact analog networks to detect **abnormal** conditions occurring within their assigned areas. 保護継電器は，割り当てられた領域内で起こる異常な状態を検出するコンパクトなアナグロネットワークである.

normality

接頭 (ab) **abnormality** *n* 異常，普通でないこと ▶ If no **abnormalities** are detected as a result of the above, automatic operation is possible. 上記の結果，何も異常が検出されなければ，自動運転が可能となる.

normally

接頭 (ab) **abnormally** *ad* 異常に ▶ Those signals revealed **abnormally** high levels of radiation, a sure sign of serious trouble. これらの信号は，放射線レベルが異常に高いことを示し，重大な事故の確かな兆候である. ▶ The heat loss from the body is greater than the heat produced and the body temperature falls **abnormally** low. 身体から失われる熱量は発生するそれよりも多く，体温が異常に低下する.

note

接尾 (less) **noteless** *adj*

❶無名の

❷無声の

noticeable

接頭 (un) **unnoticeable** *adj*

❶ わからない ▶ The positioning resolution of many robot arms is so fine that it is virtually **unnoticeable**. ロボットアームの多くは，位置決めの解像度がとても細かく，事実上差がわからない.

❷ 人目につきにくい ▶ This is a valuable breathing space for the computer, yet so short as to be entirely **unnoticeable** to the pilot. これはコンピューターにとって一息つけるほどの価値

のある時間であるが，パイロットにとってはまったく気がつかないほどに短い時間である．

noticed

接頭 (un) **unnoticed** *adj* 目立たない

nuclear

接頭 (non) **nonnuclear** *n* 核兵器を保有していない，非核の

► The likelihood and dollar value of property damage arising from nuclear and **nonnuclear** accidents are illustrated in Fig. 3. 核事故および非核事故により生じる物的損害の予想と金額（ドル）を図3に示す．

number

接尾 (less) **numberless** *adj*

❶ 無数の ► **Numberless** birds were to be found in these latitudes. この緯度の地域では，無数の鳥が見られるはずであった．

❷ 番号のない

numbered

接頭 (un) **unnumbered** *adj*

❶ 番号の付いていない ► The colon is used to introduce a quotation, an informal table or **unnumbered** figure, an example, or an equation. コロンは，引用，非形式の表，番号の付いていない図，例，式などを導入するときに使用する．

❷ 無数の

numerable

接頭 (in) **innumerable** *adj*

❶ 無数の ► In addition, **innumerable** government documents would have to be revised. さらに，無数の官庁出版物が修正されなければならない． ► Artists called geniuses not only had exceptional talent but also produced **innumerable** masterpieces. 天才と呼ばれた画家たちは，ひときわ優れた才能があったばかりでなく，無数の傑作を描き上げた．

❷ 数え切れない ► Operational experience since then has included sea gull strikes and **innumerable** strikes from stones and other objects. その後の運航でも，カモメがぶつかってきたり，石などの物体が数え切れないほどの回数当たったりする経験をした．

numerate

接頭 (in) **innumerate** *n* 理数系に弱いこと［人］

numeric

接頭 (non) **nonnumeric** *adj* 非数字の，数字以外の ► Basically, modems ignore any **nonnumeric** characters included in phone numbers that follow an ATDx command. 基本的に，モデムは，ATDx コマンドに続く電話番号に含まれている非数字を無視する．

numerical

接頭 (non) **nonnumerical** *adj* 非数字の，数字以外の ► It must be possible for a computer to handle text and other **nonnumerical** information. コンピューターは，文字をはじめとする非数字情報も処理できなければならない．

O

obedience

接頭 (dis) **disobedience** *n* 不従順, 反抗, 違反

obedient

接頭 (dis) **disobedient** *adj* 従わない, 反抗的な

obey

接頭 (dis) **disobey** *v* 従わない, 反抗する ► I **disobeyed** the unjust teaching on same-sex marriage. 私は, 同性同士の結婚に関する不当な教えに従わなかった.

object

接尾 (less) **objectless** *adj* 目的のない

objective

接頭 (non) **nonobjective** *adj* 非客観的な

oblige

接頭 (dis) **disoblige** *v* そむく, 迷惑をかける

obliging

接頭 (dis) **disobliging** *adj* 迷惑な

observance

接頭 (non) **nonobservance** *n* 〈習慣などを〉遵守しない

observant

接頭 (non) **nonobservant** *adj* 不遵守

接頭 (un) **unobservant** *adj* 観察力のない

observed

接頭 (un) **unobserved** *adj* 観察されていない ► **Unobserved**, the weary or dejected person slumps in the bed or chair, the depressed person tends to huddle in a corner. 疲れたり落胆したりしている人は, 見られていなければベッドや椅子に沈み込み, うつ病の人は隅にうずくまる傾向がある.

obstructed

接頭 (un) **unobstructed** *adj* 遮断されていない ► The intensity is just one-fourth of that due to the **unobstructed** wave. 遮られていない波が原因で，強度はちょうどその1/4となる. ► The solar ultraviolet radiation is virtually **unobstructed** by the Martian atmosphere. 太陽からの紫外線は，火星の大気にはほとんど遮られていない.

obtainable

接頭 (un) **unobtainable** *adj*

❶ 得ることのできない ► Steels are used because they have property values which are **unobtainable** in other materials or are obtainable at higher cost. 鋼鉄は，他の材料では得られない属性値，あるいは，得られてもより高いコストがかかる属性値を持っているので，使用されている.

❷ 達成できない ► This goal is nearly **unobtainable**. この目標は，ほとんど達成できない.

obtrusive

接頭 (un) **unobtrusive** *adj* 慎み深い ► The patient requires a bag permanently in position; it must be leak-proof, **unobtrusive** under clothing, and easy to deal with. 患者は，恒久的に適所に配置されたバッグを必要とする．それは漏れが防止され，衣類の下で目立たず，取り扱いが容易でなければならない.

obtrusively

接頭 (un) **unobtrusively** *ad* 控えめに，慎み深く ► The weaknesses in the company should be stated as **unobtrusively** as possible. 社内の弱点は，できるだけ控えめに言明されるべきである. ► To reach both audiences, the advertising man defined some terms **unobtrusively**, briefly outlined a scientific problem, and . . . 両方の聴衆に関心を持たせるために，広報担当者はいくつかの用語について控えめに定義を述べ，科学的な問題を簡単に説明し，そして…

obviousness

接頭 (non) **nonobviousness** *n* 不明白，非自明性 ► Trade secrets are not patented because they do not meet the patent law standards of innovation or "**nonobviousness**." 企業秘密は，革新性もしくは「非自明性」という特許法の規準に合致しないので，特許をとることはできない．

occupied

接頭 (un) **unoccupied** *adj* 占有されていない ▶ The management allowed me to use the bathtub in the **unoccupied** next room. 管理者は，私が隣の空き部屋の浴槽を使うことを許可した． ▶ Imagine an extra atom present in the structure, occupying a position normally **unoccupied**. 余分な原子が，通常はそこにいない場所を占有して構造内にあることを想像してみなさい．

occupy

接頭 (un) **unoccupy** *v* 占有しない ▶ In a block that is **unoccupied**, all track current passes through the signal circuit and sets the signal at "clear." 占有されていないブロックでは，すべてのトラック電流は信号回路を通過して，その信号を「クリア」にセットする．

odor

接尾 (less) **odorless** *adj* 無臭の ▶ Chlordan, $C_{10}H_6Cl_8$, is a viscous, colorless, **odorless** liquid used as an insecticide. クロルデン ($C_{10}H_6Cl_8$) は，粘性，無色，無臭の液体で殺虫剤に用いられる．

odorant

接頭 (de) **deodorant** *n* 脱臭剤 ▶ Powder under his arms or use a **deodorant** if appropriate. その腋の下に粉末を塗布するかまたは，適切であれば脱臭剤を使用すること．

odorize

接頭 (de) **deodorize** *v* 不快な臭いを消す ▶ Solids are filtered out and the oil **deodorized**. 固形物はフィルターにかけられ，油は臭気を除かれる．

接頭 (de) **deodorization** *n* 臭いを消すこと，脱臭 ▶ **Deodorization** is the process of blowing hot oil with steam under a high vacuum to remove traces of volatile materials causing odor. 脱臭とは，いろいろな臭いを起こす揮発性物質のあとかたを消し去るために，高真空下で蒸気を用いて高温油脂を吹き払う過程である．

offending

[接頭] (un) **unoffending** *adj* 人にいやな気を与えない

offense

[接尾] (less) **offenseless** *adj* 悪気のない

offensive

[接頭] (in) **inoffensive** *adj* 害のない，当たり障りのない

official

[接頭] (un) **unofficial** *adj* 非公式な ▸ These countries have been in an **unofficial**, but nevertheless very real, space race. これらの国は，非公式ではあるが，事実上宇宙競争を行っている．

opened

[接頭] (un) **unopened** *adj* 開けられていない，未開封の

operable

[接頭] (in) **inoperable** *adj*

❶ 手術不可能な ▸ Advanced **inoperable** patients are frequently palliated with radiation therapy. 進行して手術不可能な患者は，放射線療法によりしばしば症状が軽減する．

❷ 運転できない ▸ Automobiles which were transported across country by rail were **inoperable** at their destination because . . . 鉄道で国内を横断して運ばれた自動車は，…のために目的地で運転できなかった．

❸ 実際的でない

operation

[接頭] (in) **inoperation** *n* 不稼働 ▸ In order to handle reliability predictions adequately, one must either consider satisfactory performance to be total operation or unsatisfactory performance to be total **inoperation**. 信頼性の予測を適切に扱うためには，満足すべき性能を全稼働とみなすか，あるいは満足できない

性能を全不稼働とみなすかしなければならない.

operative

接頭 (in) **inoperative** *adj*

❶ 無効である ► In this circuit the sweep is **inoperative** except when started by a trigger signal. この回路では, トリガー信号で始動させた場合以外は, 掃引は無効である.

❷ 稼動していない, 操業していない ► This unit usually permits immediate restoration to service of a device which may have become **inoperative**. このユニットは通常, 稼働しなくなった可能性のある装置の運転の即時復旧を可能にする.

接頭 (non) **nonoperative** *adj*

❶ 操作［運転］不能の ► In case the space traveler is unable to perform the maneuvers because of his physical condition or **nonoperative** on-board controls ... 宇宙飛行士が自分の肉体的条件のためかまたは搭載制御装置が操作不能のために操縦できない場合は, ….

❷ 実施できない

❸ 効力［効果］のない

❹ 非観血的な［手術をしない］ ► About 85% of partial small-bowel obstructions resolve with **nonoperative** treatment, while about 85% of complete small-bowel obstructions require surgery. 小腸の部分閉塞の約85％は非観血的治療で治癒するが, 小腸の完全閉塞の約85％は手術を要する.

opportune

接頭 (in) **inopportune** *adj*

❶ 時機を失した ► All of this has happened at a very **inopportune** time and, with no disrespect, an **inopportune** location. これらのすべてが, 非常に時機を逸した時に, けなすわけではないが, ふさわしくない場所で起こった.

❷ 都合の悪い, 不都合な ► They strive to calculate how frequently these **inopportune** meetings occur. こういった不都合な遭遇が起きる頻度の計算に彼らは励む.

opposed

[接頭] (un) **unopposed** *adj* 反対されていない ► The candidate was **unopposed** in the campaign. その候補は，選挙キャンペーンで反対がなかった.

order

[接頭] (dis) **disorder** *v*

❶ 混乱させる ► My desktop icons are **disordered** and do not retain the position assigned to them. 私のデスクトップ・アイコンは位置が乱れて本来の場所を保てない.

❷ 心身の調子を狂わせる

—— *n*

❶ 混乱，無秩序 ► compositional **disorder** 構成の乱れ

❷ 暴動，騒乱 ► public **disorder** 騒乱

❸ 不調，疾病 ► But recent studies have shown that the **disorder** strikes women of all socioeconomic groups, and even teenagers. しかし最近の調査で，すべての社会経済的集団で女性が，また10代の女性までも，この不調に悩まされていることがわかった. ► Dozens of **disorders** that once mystified doctors are now thought to be autoimmune. かつて医者をまどわした幾多の疾病も，いまでは自己免疫であると考えられている.

ordered

[接頭] (dis) **disordered** *adj* 無秩序な，混乱した，不調な ► It has been shown that useful device properties can also be obtained in **disordered** materials. デバイスの有用な特性というものは，雑然とした素材の中にも見出しうるということが示されている.

[接頭] (ill) **ill-ordered** *adj* 無秩序の

ordinate

[接頭] (in) **inordinate** *adj*

❶ 尋常でない，法外な ► The virus writers tend to be men in their late teens or early 20s who have spent an **inordinate** portion of their youth bathed in the glow of a computer screen. ウイルスの作者は，10代後半か20代前半の男子で発育期に途方もない時間をコンピュータースクリーンの光を浴びて過ごした者である場合が多い． ▸ Japanese car manufacturers take an **inordinate** amount of care and time dubbing new products. 日本の自動車メーカーは，度外れの手数と時間をかけて新製品を作り替えている．

❷ 過剰な ▸ The authorities have an **inordinate** fear of the masses running wild. 当局は，大衆をしたい放題にさせておくのを過剰に恐れている．

organic

接頭 (in) **inorganic** *adj*

❶ 無生物の，無機質の，非有機性の ▸ The bath should be dummy plated to remove **inorganic** impurities and charcoal filtered to remove organic impurities. 浴槽は無機質不純物を除去するために空電解を行い，有機質不純物を除去するためにチャコールフィルターで濾過しなければならない． ▸ The chemosynthetic bacteria oxidize **inorganic** compounds. 化学合成バクテリアは無機化合物を酸化する． ▸ The laser promises to be a valuable tool for drilling, cutting, and eventually milling virtually any metal or ceramic or other **inorganic** solid. レーザーは，実質的にすべての金属やセラミック，その他の非有機性の固体の穴開け，切断，最終的な切削加工を行う貴重な工具として期待されている．

❷ 自然発生的でない，人為的な

organize

接頭 (dis) **disorganize** *v*

❶ 混乱させる ▸ If the paper files are **disorganized**, the PC will only make the problem worse. もしペーパーファイルが乱れていればPCは問題をもっと悪くするだけだ．

❷ 組織を壊す，無秩序にする ▸ I felt that the United States was completely **disorganized** and didn't have even the semblance of a country. 私は，米国という組織は完全に壊れ，国家という外形さえなくしていると感じた．

organized

[接頭] (dis) **disorganized** *adj* 混乱した，乱脈な ► In medical centers and hospitals across the country, **disorganized**, underfunded, and understaffed emergency services are on the critical list. 全国の医療センターや病院において，救急医療体制の混乱，資金不足，人員不足が重大問題となっている．

[接頭] (ill) **ill-organized** *adj* まとまりの悪い

[接頭] (un) **unorganized** *adj*

❶組織化されていない，未組織の

❷無機質の

❸領域が明確でない

orient

[接頭] (dis) **disorient** *v* 方向感覚を失わせる，混乱させる

oriented

[接頭] (dis) **disoriented** *adj* 混乱した，わからなくなった ► It causes symptoms ranging from **disoriented** wandering to skin lesions to convulsions, and can lead to reproductive failure in animals that survive. それは，方向感覚錯乱性遊走から皮膚病やひきつけに及ぶ諸症状を引き起こし，なお生き残った動物たちも生殖不能になる．

orienting

[接頭] (dis) **disorienting** *adj* 方向感覚を失わせるような ► The pressure was so **disorienting**, he recalls, it was like "working down there on three martinis each." 彼が思い起こすところでは，圧力がまったく混乱して，「誰もがマーティニを3杯飲んで作業している」みたいだった．

original

[接頭] (un) **unoriginal** *adj* 独創的でない

orthodox

[接頭] (un) **unorthodox** *adj* オーソドックスでない，正統でない

▶ Since then, the Cornell professor has been vigorously promoting an **unorthodox** theory about the origin of oil and gas. それ以来，コーネル大のその教授は，石油やガスの起源に関する非正統的な理論を精力的に展開している．

own

[接頭] (dis) **disown** *v* 関係を否認する，縁を切る

owner

[接尾] (less) **ownerless** *adj* 持ち主のない

oxidization

[接頭] (de) **deoxidization** *n* 脱酸 ▶ It is thus impossible to make absolutely clean steel by any of the conventional processes requiring final **deoxidation** to prevent the CO evolution. CO 放出を防止するために最後に脱酸を必要としている在来の方法では，絶対に混ざりもののない鋼を造ることは，このように不可能である．

oxidize

[接頭] (de) **deoxidize** *v* 酸素を除く，脱酸する ▶ The normal product is fully **deoxidized**. 正常な製品は，完全に脱酸する．

[接頭] (non) **nonoxidize** *v* 酸化させない

oxidized

[接頭] (de) **deoxidized** *adj* 脱酸された ▶ Depending upon the final type of oxygen control, steels are classified as fully **deoxidized** or killed. 酸素制御の最終タイプにより，鋼鉄は完全脱酸タイプ，つまりキルドタイプとして分類される．

oxidizer

[接頭] (de) **deoxidizer** *n* 脱酸剤 ▶ This process is performed with a continuous electrode and a granular flux composed of silicates with or without **deoxidizers** and alloying elements. このプロセスは，連続電極と，脱酸剤および合金用物質を含んでいるかまたは含んでいないケイ酸塩から成る粒状のフラックスとを使ってなされる．

oxidizing

接頭 (non) **nonoxidizing** *adj* 非酸化の ▶ The molten metal bath is thus protected by a **nonoxidizing** slag, and the atmosphere is kept **nonoxidizing** by reaction with the electrodes. 溶融金属浴は，このようにして非酸化スラグにより保護されており，周辺は電極反応で非酸化状態に保たれている．

oxygenate

接頭 (de) **deoxygenate** *v* 遊離酸素を除去する

oxygenated

接頭 (de) **deoxygenated** *adj* 酸素を除去された ▶ Thus the right side of the heart serves mainly to pump **deoxygenated** blood through the lungs, while the left side pumps oxygenated blood throughout the rest of the body. このように心臓の右側部分は，主に酸素が除去された血液を肺を通して送り，左側は酸素が加えられた血液を体の他の部分全体に送り込む役目を果たす．

P

pack

接頭 (un) **unpack** *v* 開梱する，包装を解く ► It's OK to touch the power supply if you've just **unpacked** the computer. コンピューターを開梱したばかりなら電源に触れてもよい． ► troops involved in **unpacking** and erecting each missile 各ミサイルを開梱し組み立てるのに必要な中隊 ► House Republicans were still **unpacking** their boxes in the first week of January. 下院共和党議員たちは，1月の第1週はまだ荷物を開梱していた．

paid

接頭 (ill) **ill-paid** *adj* 実入りの悪い ► **ill-paid** labor 低賃金労働（者）

接頭 (un) **unpaid** *adj*

❶ 未払いの ► face stacks of **unpaid** bills 未払いの請求書の山を目の前にする

❷ 無給の ► That is the value which has been put on the voluntary, **unpaid** work members do each year. これは，メンバーが毎年行う自発的で無給の仕事に添えられた価値である．

paid-for

接頭 (un) **unpaid-for** *adj* 支払いの済んでいない

pain

接尾 (less) **painless** *adj* 苦痛のない ► The **Painless** Injection Device is a revolutionary and innovative product that eliminates the trauma associated with vaccination. 苦痛を伴わない注射器は，ワクチン接種に伴うトラウマを取り除く革新的な最先端の製品です．

paired

接頭 (un) **unpaired** *adj*

❶ 対になっていない ► The resulting cut ends with **unpaired**

bases are called sticky ends. その結果生じる切口の両端は，基部が対になっていない場合，突出末端と呼ばれる．

❷配偶者のいない

palatable

接頭 (un) **unpalatable** *adj* おいしくない ► An ordinary person finds himself in an awkward situation when his host urges him to have a second helping of an **unpalatable** dish. ひどい味の料理のおかわりをすすめられたとき，並みの大人は，ちょっとした苦境に陥る．

palpable

接頭 (im) **impalpable** *adj* 手で触ることができない，実体のない ► His own identity was fading out into a gray **impalpable** world. 彼自身の主体性が灰色の実体のない世界の中に次第に消えつつあった．

panchromatic

接頭 (non) **nonpanchromatic** *adj* 非パンクロの，全色性でない ► Panchromatic film must be used for making separation negatives, but **nonpanchromatic** film can be used for subsequent steps. 分離ネガの作製には，パンクロフィルムを用いなければならないが，次の段階には非パンクロフィルムが用いられる．

paper

接尾 (less) **paperless** *adj* ペーパーレスの，紙を使用しない ► When you "go **paperless**," you still have access to your past 18 monthly statements online to print or download. ペーパーレスに移行しても，過去18か月の口座取引をオンラインでアクセスし印刷できますし，ダウンロードもできます．

paralleled

接頭 (un) **unparalleled** *adj* 無比の，他に類を見ない ► The railroads' power is amplified by an **unparalleled** set of antitrust exemptions. 鉄道会社の影響力は，無比の独占禁止法適用除外措置により増大している．

pardonable

接頭 (un) **unpardonable** *adj* 許せない，勘弁できない

parity

接頭 (dis) **disparity** *n* 相違，不一致 ► Airbus Industry recognizes this concept and capitalizes upon the **disparities** between U.S. and foreign financing packages in its sales strategy. エアバス・インダストリー社はこの考えを認め，その販売政策における米国と外国の融資パッケージの食い違いを利用している．

parliamentary

接頭 (un) **unparliamentary** *adj* 議院の慣習に反する

parted

接頭 (un) **unparted** *adj* 分けられない

partial

接頭 (im) **impartial** *adj* 偏らない， 公平な ► **impartial** and neutral international standards 公正で中立な国際標準

partiality

接頭 (im) **impartiality** *n* 偏見のないこと，公平 ► reward and punish with **impartiality** 偏見なく賞罰を行う

partially

接頭 (im) **impartially** *ad* 偏見なく，公平に ► We **impartially** accept candidates from other universities and members of society. わが校は，他大学の出身者や社会人も公平に受け入れる．

participant

接頭 (non) **nonparticipant** *n* 不参加者， 関与しない人 ► Generally speaking, betting for **nonparticipants** is often legal, but it varies by state. 一般的に言って，不参加者を見込むことは多くの場合に正当であるが，州により異なる．

partisan

接頭 (non) **nonpartisan** *adj* 無党派の，党派に属さない ► The senior policy analyst at the **nonpartisan** research agency explains this persuasively in a fascinating new book. 無党派の

研究機関の主任政策分析員が，ある魅力的な新刊書で説得力を持ってこれを説明する． ► He generally won plaudits for his even-handed, **nonpartisan**, and unflappable approach to the highly controversial episode. 非常に議論の余地がある事例に対する，彼の公正な，党派に属さない，動じないアプローチのために，彼は世間一般の賞賛を獲得した．

—— *n* 無党派の人

party

接頭 (non) **nonparty** *adj*

❶政党と無関係の，無所属の

❷不偏不党の

—— *n* 政党と無関係の人

passable

接頭 (im) **impassable** *adj* 通行できない ► The street is **impassable**. この通りは通行ができない．

接頭 (im) **impassableness** *v* 通れないこと

接頭 (im) **impassably** *ad* 通行できずに ► It was pouring — the lane was mud, **impassably** so. 雨が激しく降っていて，路地は泥で通り抜けられなかった．

passibility

接頭 (im) **impassibility** *n* 無感覚，無感動 ► the same **impassibility** 同じ沈着さ

passible

接頭 (im) **impassible** *adj* 無感覚な，無感動な ► . . . replied the **impassible** gentleman quietly. 紳士は，…と表情をまったく変えずに答えた．

passibly

接頭 (im) **impassibly** *ad* 感動なく

passion

接尾 (less) **passionless** *adj* 感情的でない

passionate

接頭 (dis) **dispassionate** *adj* 冷静な

passive

接頭 (im) **impassive** *adj* 無表情の，感覚のない ► She went out of the room with the tray, her face **impassive** and unchanged. 盆を持って部屋を出て行く彼女の顔は，やはり無表情で頑なだった．

passiveness

接頭 (im) **impassiveness** *n* 無表情，冷静さ，冷淡さ ► The Sphinx has one hundred and fifty qualifications for **impassiveness** which you lack. スフィンクスには，あなたに欠けている150もの無感覚の資質格があります．

patented

接頭 (un) **unpatented** *adj* 特許を取っていない

path

接尾 (less) **pathless** *adj* 人跡未踏の ► The **pathless** mountain region of Alishan in the heart of Taiwan is famous for its magnificent forests and huge cypress trees. 台湾中心部にある阿里山の人跡未踏の山岳地帯は，壮大な森林と巨大なイトスギで有名である．

pathetic

接頭 (a) **apathetic** *adj*

❶無感動な，無関心な

❷冷淡な

pathetically

接頭 (a) **apathetically** *ad*

❶無関心に

❷冷淡に

patience

接頭 (im) **impatience** *n*

❶我慢できないこと，短気，焦り ► I don't seem to be able to cure my **impatience**. どうも私のせっかちな性分は直らない．

❷切望

patient

接頭 (im) **impatient** *adj* いらいらした，性急な ▶ If an **impatient** Congress retaliates against Japan and starts a trade war, no one will win. 議会がいらだって日本に報復したり貿易戦争を始めたところで，勝つ者などいない．

patiently

接頭 (im) **impatiently** *ad* 我慢できずに，待ち切れずに ▶ She was waiting **impatiently** for her son's return. 彼女は息子の帰るのが待ち遠しかった．

paved

接頭 (ill) **ill-paved** *adj* 舗装状態の悪い

接頭 (un) **unpaved** *adj* 舗装されていない ▶ It will swoop across California's coast and glide toward touchdown on the **unpaved** surface of Rogers Dry Lake. それはカリフォルニアの海岸を横切ってロジャースドライレイクの舗装していない路面に着陸しようと滑空する．

payment

接頭 (non) **nonpayment** *n* 不払い，滞納 ▶ Is it possible to be arrested for **nonpayment** of a car loan? 車のローンの不払いで逮捕されるなんてことはありうるでしょうか．

peccable

接頭 (im) **impeccable** *adj* 罪のない，申し分のない ▶ His taste was **impeccable**. 彼の趣味は非の打ち所がなかった．

pedigreed

接頭 (non) **nonpedigreed** *adj* 由緒正しくない ▶ As of last year, the company began recruiting at such **nonpedigreed** institutions as A, B, and C. 昨年には，その会社はA, B，またはCのような非有名大学で募集を開始した．

pediment

接頭 (im) **impediment** *n*

❶障害，妨害 ▶ an **impediment** to study 勉強の邪魔

❷言語障害 ▶ He has a speech **impediment**, and so he cannot

speak well. 彼には言語障害がありうまく話せない.

peeled

[接頭] (un) **unpeeled** *adj* 皮がむかれていない

peer

[接尾] (less) **peerless** *adj* 比類のない

peg

[接頭] (un) **unpeg** *v* 〈釘などを〉抜く

penetrability

[接頭] (im) **impenetrability** *n* 不可解なこと ▶ the **impenetrability** of the bureaucracy 官僚制度の不可解さ

penetrable

[接頭] (im) **impenetrable** *adj*

❶〈物質が液体・気体などを〉透過させない ▶ **impenetrable** darkness 真っ暗闇

❷〈光などを〉通さない ▶ **impenetrable** to light 光を通さない

❸入り込めない ▶ She felt herself clad in an **impenetrable** armor of falsehood. 彼女は, 自分自身が虚偽の入り込めない鎧を着ていると感じた.

❹不可解な ▶ He talked and looked at her laughing eyes, which frightened him now with their **impenetrable** look. 彼は話しながら彼女の笑っている目を見た. 不可解な目付きをしていて, 彼を恐怖に陥れた.

pennate

[接頭] (im) **impennate** *adj* 翼のない

penny

[接尾] (less) **penniless** *adj* 無一文の ▶ She went from being a **penniless** girl to owner of her own restaurant. 彼女は, 無一文からレストランのオーナーになった.

people

[接頭] (un) **unpeople** *n*

❶人間性のない人 ▶ They are mere **unpeople**. 彼らは単に人

間性のない人たちだ.

❷ (政治的に) 抹殺された人々 ► Palestinian prisoners are not "**unpeople**"; they are children of God. 捕虜となっているパレスチナ人は政治的被抹殺者ではない. 彼らは神の子である.

—— *v* …から住民をなくする ► Two villages were **unpeopled** by that disaster. 二つの村の人口があの災害によって激減した.

perceptible

接頭 (im) **imperceptible** *adj*

❶ 微小の, わずかな ► He gave me an almost **imperceptible** nod. 彼はかすかに私にうなずいてみせた.

❷ 感知できない ► The resulting degradation is **imperceptible** in a telephone communication. それによる劣化は, 電話通信では気づかれないほどである.

perception

接頭 (mis) **misperception** *n* 誤解 ► One complication that exists in learning a little about another culture is that **misperceptions** can easily occur. 別の文化について何か少し学習する際に存在する面倒な問題は, 誤解が容易に起こりうることである.

perceptive

接頭 (im) **imperceptive** *adj* 感知しない ► I was so **imperceptive** that I didn't see things very well. 私はあまり気を付けていなかったので, それをよく見ることはできなかった.

percipient

接頭 (im) **impercipient** *adj* 感知しない ► **Impercipient** collectors and gallery-curators could not distinguish the indubitable in his work. 見る目のないコレクターと学芸員は, 彼の作品の疑いの余地がない部分を見分けられなかった.

perfect

接頭 (im) **imperfect** *adj* 不完全な ► Man is **imperfect**. 人は不完全なものだ.

perfection

接頭 (im) **imperfection** *n* 不完全, 欠点 ▶ The **imperfection** of the media introduces attenuation and intersymbol interference. 媒体の欠陥が減衰と符号間干渉をもたらす. ▶ At lower temperatures, when the vibrations are reduced, the conductivity is limited by scattering from impurities and lattice **imperfections**. 低温で振動が減少すると, 不純物と格子欠陥の散在で伝導率は制限される.

perfectly

接頭 (im) **imperfectly** *ad* 不十分に, 中途半端に ▶ You may as well not do it at all than do it **imperfectly**. 中途半端にやるくらいなら, やらない方がましだ.

perforated

接頭 (un) **unperforated** *adj* ミシン目が入っていない

接頭 (im) **imperforate** *adj* 穴の開いていない ▶ Enclosed by low, **imperforate** walls, the building gives little clue as to its function. 低く穴のない壁に囲まれて, その建物は機能に関してはほとんど手掛かりを与えない.

performance

接頭 (non) **nonperformance** *n* 不履行, 不実行

performing

接頭 (non) **nonperforming** *adj* 適切に遂行しない

perishable

接頭 (im) **imperishable** *adj* 不滅の, 不朽の ▶ rich with the **imperishable** powers that are mightier than the might of kings 王の力より強大な, 不滅の力をもつ財宝を持っている

permanence

接頭 (im) **impermanence** *n*

❶ 非永続性, 非永久性, 非恒久性 ▶ This **impermanence** and the variability of the ground rules and boundary conditions of a design situation are always present. 設計状況の基本原則と境界条件が一時的なもので変わりやすいのは, いつものことで

ある.

❷ 無常 ► The author tries to compare and contrast timelessness and **impermanence**. この著者は永遠性と無常観について比較検討しようとしている.

permanent

接頭 (im) **impermanent** *adj* 永続しない, 一時的な ► **impermanent** tattoo 消えるタトゥー

permeability

接頭 (im) **impermeability** *n* 不浸透性 ► This type of rubber has excellent **impermeability**. この種のゴムは優れた不透過性を持つ.

permeable

接頭 (im) **impermeable** *adj* 〈液体・気体などを〉透過させない, 不浸透性 ► a coat **impermeable** to rain 雨を通さないコート

permissible

接頭 (im) **impermissible** *adj* 許容できない ► Such conduct is **impermissible**. そんな行動は許すことができない.

person

接頭 (non) **nonperson** *n* 存在を無視された人, 非重要人 ► Until 2000, he was something of a **nonperson** within the party. 2000年までは, 彼はそのグループではどこか存在を無視された人であった.

接頭 (un) **unperson** *n* (社会的に) 葬られた人

personal

接頭 (im) **impersonal** *adj*

❶ 個性的でない, 一般的な ► an **impersonal** remark 一般的な意見

❷ 非人称の ► the **impersonal** construction 非人称構文

personality

接頭 (im) **impersonality** *n* 個人に関しないこと, 非人間性 ► He liked the **impersonality** of urban life. 彼は都市の生活の非

個人性が好きだった.

personalize

[接頭] (de) **depersonalize** *v* 非人間的にする

persuade

[接頭] (dis) **dissuade** *v* ～しないように勧める, 思いとどまらせる ▸ She **dissuaded** him from taking money from a large investor. 彼女は彼を説得して大手投資家から資金を受けるのを諦めさせた.

persuasive

[接頭] (un) **unpersuasive** *adj* 説得力のない ▸ The argument that Article 9 should be rewritten because it is not attuned to the current international climate is singularly **unpersuasive**. 現在の国際情勢に調和していないということで第9条は改正するべきであるという議論は特に説得力がない. ▸ But just being young doesn't mean you are **unpersuasive**. しかし若いということは説得力がないということではない.

pertinence

[接頭] (im) **impertinence** *n*

❶ 無礼, 非礼 ▸ He had the **impertinence** to write me a letter like this. 彼は無礼にも僕にこんな手紙をよこした.

❷ 不適当 ▸ It was a matter out of place, an **impertinence**. それはあまりにもその場にふさわしくなかった.

pertinent

[接頭] (im) **impertinent** *adj* 無礼な, 生意気な; 不適切な ▸ an **impertinent** young man 生意気な若者 ▸ an **impertinent** remark 不適切な [生意気な] 意見

perturbed

[接頭] (un) **unperturbed** *adj* かき乱されていない, 平然とした ▸ Kayak will indeed need to paddle hard to keep ahead of the Internet giant, but English seems **unperturbed**. カヤック社は確かにそのインターネット大企業の先を行くために猛烈に櫂をこぐ必要があろう. しかしイングリッシュ氏は平然として

いる.

pervious

接頭 (im) **impervious** *adj*

❶不浸透性の, 通さない ► a fabric **impervious** to water 水を通さない布.

❷影響されない, 鈍感な ► a mind **impervious** to criticism 批判に動じない心

phosphorization

接頭 (de) **dephosphorization** *n* 脱リン ► This high-lime content is required to achieve the **dephosphorization** and S control, both characteristic of all basic steelmaking. このように石灰を高含有するには, 基本的なすべての製鋼に特有の脱リン化と硫黄調整の両者を実現することが必要である.

phosphorize

接頭 (de) **dephosphorize** *v* 脱リンする

pick

接頭 (un) **unpick** *v* 〈着物などの縫い目を〉ほどく

picked

接頭 (un) **unpicked** *adj* 収穫されていない

piety

接頭 (im) **impiety** *n* 不信心 ► When I failed in business, I thought I was being punished for my **impiety**. 事業に失敗したとき, 日ごろの不信心がたたったと思った.

pilot

接尾 (less) **pilotless** *adj* 水先案内なしの

pity

接尾 (less) **pitiless** *adj* 薄情な, 無慈悲な

place

接頭 (dis) **displace** *v*

❶取って代わる ► Colder, denser air falls and **displaces** the lighter, warm air. 冷たく密度の高い空気が下降し, 軽く暖かい空気と入れ替わる.

❷ 移動させる ► These factors act in concert to **displace** the U.S. commercial aircraft industry from a significant and growing portion of the worldwide market. これら要素が，米国の民間航空機産業を世界市場における重要かつ高成長の地位から追い出そうと，いっせいに作用している．

接尾 (less) **placeless** *adj* 場所のない ► Global capital relies on '**placeless**' tools like the internet, but the physical infrastructure those tools require are still place-bound. 国際的な資本は，インターネットのような場所を特定しない[場所のない]ツールに依存しているが，そのようなツールが必要とする実際のインフラが場所に縛られているのは変わらない．

placed

接頭 (un) **unplaced** *adj*

❶ 定置されていない，一定の地位にない

❷ 3着以内に入らない

placement

接頭 (dis) **displacement** *n*

❶ 交代，置き換え ► The **displacement** of text ripples through all the text blocks in the story. このテキストの置き換えはストーリー内のすべてのテキストブロックで次々起こります．

❷ 転位，移動 ► This is a device that generates an output voltage which is directly proportional to the relative **displacement** between the two elements of the instrument. この器械のもつ2要素間の相関転位に正比例している出力電圧を発生する装置がこれである．

planned

接頭 (ill) **ill-planned** *adj* 計画性の悪い ► an **ill-planned** move 不用意な動作，下手な手出し

接頭 (un) **unplanned** *adj* 計画されていない，無計画の ► They saw it as an **unplanned**, reflexive reaction to criticism from Wall Street. 彼らはそれをウォール街からの批判に対する，無計画で反動的な行動であるととらえた． ► Where possible, these two days — or at least the latter — should be free of business and **unplanned** visits. 可能な限り，この2日間，少なくとも第2日は仕事や突然の訪問から解放されるべき日となっています.

plasticized

接頭 (un) **unplasticized** *adj* 可塑化されていない ▶ Vinyls are available in plasticized (flexible) and **unplasticized** (rigid) types and in a variety of copolymer grades. ビニールには可塑の［可撓性のある］ものと無可塑の［可塑化されていない／剛性のある］ものならびに各種等級の共重合体のものとがある.

playing

接頭 (non) **nonplaying** *adj* プレーしない〈人〉

pleasant

接頭 (un) **unpleasant** *adj* 不愉快な ▶ The room should also be free of **unpleasant** smells. 部屋は不快な臭いもないこと. ▶ Perceiving that an **unpleasant** mood was beginning to fill the air, I softly said, "All right, I'll be a father." 僕はその場に変な空気が漂い始めたのを察して,「なるよ，父親になるよ」と小さな声で言った. ▶ Linking the three sentences together with simple conjunctions would eliminate the **unpleasant** choppy effect, but . . . 三つの文を簡単な接続詞によってつなぎ合わせると，不快なぎこちなさが消えるであろうが，… ▶ instant foods containing additives with names sounding like chemicals, soft drinks which leave only an **unpleasant** sweetness on the tongue 化学薬品のような名称の添加物が入ったインスタント食品，甘さだけがべったり［不快に］舌に残る清涼飲料水

pleasantly

接頭 (un) **unpleasantly** *ad* 不愉快に ▶ If napkins are put to dry on radiators or hot pipes, they will be **unpleasantly** stiff and abrasive when put next to the baby's skin. ナプキンを放熱器や放熱管の上に置いて乾燥させれば，赤ん坊の皮膚に触れたときに，こわばりひっかくような不快感を与えるであろう.

pleasantness

接頭 (un) **unpleasantness** *n* 不快, 不愉快なこと

please

接頭 (dis) **displease** *v* 不愉快にさせる ► If there is anything about the service that **displeases** you, go over and tell the person what the problem is. サービスに関して何か不愉快なことがあれば, その人のところへ行って何が問題か教えてやりなさい.

pleased

接頭 (un) **unpleased** *adj* 不愉快にされた ► If the apology or the acceptance do not meet the other person's expectations then it leaves one or both parties feeling **unpleased**. 謝罪もしくは謝罪の受け入れ方が相手の意に沿わない場合, どちらか一方もしくは双方が不満を覚える.

pleasing

接頭 (dis) **displeasing** *adj* 不愉快な

pleasure

接頭 (dis) **displeasure** *n* 不快, 不愉快 ► For the first year I showed my **displeasure**, but living in the same house I grew used to the dog. 私は, 最初の年は不快感を表していたが, 同じ家に住んでいるとその犬に慣れてきた. ► He recognizes friends as well as parents and shows pleasure by smiles or laughter and **displeasure** by frowns or tears. 彼は両親と同様に友人を認識し, 微笑みまたは笑いによって快感を, しかめ面または泣くことによって不快感を表した.

plot

接尾 (less) **plotless** *adj* プロットなしの

plug

接頭 (un) **unplug** *v*

❶ プラグを抜く ► **Unplug** appliances you are working on. いま作動させている装置のプラグを抜きなさい. ► You plug and **unplug** either type of cable in the same manner: always hold the cable by the connector as you push it into or pull it out of the port. どのタイプのケーブルでも同じ方法で差し込む／引き抜くこと．すなわち，ケーブルをポートに差し込む／引き抜くときにはかならずコネクターのところでケーブルを保持する． ► That is, if an investor had bought an S&P index fund and then **unplugged** his computer and phone for 20 years, he would done quite well. つまり，投資家がS&Pインデックスファンドを購入し，その後コンピューターやパソコンのプラグを20年間抜いたままにしておいたならば，彼はまさしく成功していたであろう．

❷コードを抜く ► At home, people are being told to set room temperatures at 28 ℃, use fans instead of air conditioners, and **unplug** gadgets. 家庭では室温は28℃に設定し，エアコンの代わりに扇風機を使い，小型器具類はコードを抜くように言われている．

plugged

[接頭] (un) **unplugged** *adj* プラグを抜いた

plumb

[接頭] (un) **unplumbed** *adj*

❶深さのわからない

❷配管設備のない

point

[接尾] (less) **pointless** *adj*

❶要領を得ない ► Unlike the global economy, our proclivity to get into **pointless** arguments is something we can control. 世界経済とは異なり，要領を得ない議論になりやすい我々の傾向は，制御できるものだ．

❷先のとがっていない

❸得点を取っていない

❹無意味である ► Sampling the line faster than 2H times per second is **pointless**. 毎秒2H回より高速に回線をサンプリングするのは無意味である．

polar

接頭 (non) **nonpolar** *n* 非極性, 無極 ► Consequently, this type of solid dissolves to an appreciable degree in **nonpolar** solvents. その結果, この種類の固体はかなりの程度に無極の溶媒に解ける.

polarization

接頭 (de) **depolarization** *n* 消極作用

polarize

接頭 (de) **depolarize** *v* 極性をなくす, 減極する ► Heart muscle can **depolarize** spontaneously in the absence of external stimulation. 心臓の筋肉は, 外部刺激のない状態で自発的に脱分極することができる.

接頭 (non) **nonpolarize** *v* 無極性化する, 非極性にする ► The devices trip out with very little current in the sense-wire circuit — typically less than 1 mA. IDCIs, moreover are **non-polarized**. これらの装置は, センスワイヤ回路において電流がほとんどなくてもトリップ(一般的に1mA 以下)する上, IDCI はさらに, 無極性化している.

polished

接頭 (un) **unpolished** *adj*

❶ 磨かれていない ► Some acrylic filters cost as little as . . ., while standard **unpolished** glass filters are as low as $1.00 per in2. アクリルフィルターはものによってはわずかに…である一方, 標準の磨かれていないガラスフィルターも平方インチあたり1ドル程度である.

❷ つやが出ていない ► standard **unpolished** glass filters 標準的なつや出しの塗っていないガラスフィルター

❸ 漂白されていない ► She has been eating **unpolished** natural rice for the past 40 years. 彼女は, 玄米自然食を40年も続けている. ► I remember thinking that the big bowls of **unpolished** rice hardly fitted the image of Hikaru Genji. 玄米がお茶碗に山盛りになっていて, 光源氏のイメージとは合わ

ないなあと思ったことがある.

polite

[接頭] (im) **impolite** *adj* 失礼な, 無礼な ► It is **impolite** to elbow one's way through the crowd. 人ごみの中を押し分けて通るのは失礼である.

politely

[接頭] (im) **impolitely** *ad* 無礼にも, ずけずけと ► He treated her **impolitely**. 彼は彼女を無作法に扱った.

politeness

[接頭] (im) **impoliteness** *n* 無作法

politic

[接頭] (im) **impolitic** *adj* 不得策な, 無分別な ► It would be **impolitic** to show your hand to your enemy. 敵に手の内を見せるのは得策ではない.

political

[接頭] (a) **apolitical** *adj* ノンポリの, 政治に無関心な

[接頭] (un) **unpolitical** *adj* 非政治的な ► There is no such thing as **unpolitical** art. 非政治的な芸術などない.

politicize

[接頭] (de) **depoliticize** *v* 政治色をなくす

polled

[接頭] (un) **unpolled** *adj* 投票を終わらせていない

polluted

[接頭] (un) **unpolluted** *adj* 汚染されていない

polymerization

[接頭] (de) **depolymerization** *n* 解重合 ► Such reactions include all varieties of transformations, polymerization, **depolymerization**, molecular rearrangement, oxidation-reduction reactions, etc. このような諸反応には, 変形, 重合, 解重合, 分子再調整, 酸化－還元反応などの諸変化がある.

polymerize

[接頭] (de) **depolymerize** *v* 解重合する

ponderable

接頭 (im) **imponderable** *adj* 〈効果などが〉計り知れない ▶ such **imponderable** human factors as aesthetic sensibility 美的な感受性のような量ることができない人的要因

popular

接頭 (un) **unpopular** *adj* 評判がよくない，不人気の ▶ The magnetostrictive method is **unpopular** due to the need to periodically rebias the tablet with a large permanent magnet. 磁気ひずみ法は，大型の永久磁石で周期的にタブレットを再バイアスする必要があるので人気がない． ▶ It sometimes happens that an unpleasant intruder is given the name of an **unpopular** place or country. 不快な外来物に嫌いな［評判がよくない］土地や国の名前を付けることがある．

populate

接頭 (de) **depopulate** *v* 人口を少なくする，過疎化する

populated

接頭 (de) **depopulated** *adj* 人口が少なくなった，過疎化した ▶ I have long been taking part in a campaign to solve the problems of a **depopulated** village. 私は，長い間，過疎村問題を解決するための運動に参加してきた．

接頭 (un) **unpopulated** *adj* 居住者がいない

porous

接頭 (non) **nonporous** *adj* 非多孔質性の，通気性のない ▶ Potatoes, apples, egg yolks, whole squash, and sausages are examples of foods with **nonporous** skins. じゃがいも，りんご，卵黄，丸ごとのかぼちゃ，およびソーセージなどは皮膜に通気性がない食物の例である．

possess

接頭 (dis) **dispossess** *v* 〈人から〉取り上げる

possibility

接頭 (im) **impossibility** *n* 不可能性，不可能なこと ▶ That is a virtual **impossibility**. それはまずあり得ないことだ．

possible

[接頭] (im) **impossible** *adj*

❶ 信じがたい，箸にも棒にもかからない，とても嫌な ► an **impossible** hat ひどい帽子

❷ 不可能である ► It is absolutely **impossible**. それはとうてい不可能だ.

possibly

[接頭] (im) **impossibly** *ad* どうしようもないほど，極端に ► an **impossibly** cold morning どうしようもないほど寒い朝

potent

[接頭] (im) **impotent** *adj* 無能な，無気力な ► He's **impotent** to help her. 彼は彼女を助ける能力がない.

power

[接尾] (less) **powerless** *adj*

❶ 無力な ► Social workers feel **powerless** to protect neglected children. ソーシャルワーカーは，ネグレクトされた子供たちを保護するには無力であると感じている.

❷ 効能のない

practicability

[接頭] (im) **impracticability** *n* 実行不可能性 ► The **impracticability** of executing the law has caused its repeal in several of the States. 法の執行が不可能なことから，州のいくつかでは，それは廃止された.

practicable

[接頭] (im) **impracticable** *adj*

❶ 実行不可能な ► an **impracticable** idea 実用的でない案

❷ 〈道が〉通行不可能な ► The pass is **impracticable** in winter. この峠は冬は通れない.

practicably

[接頭] (im) **impracticably** *ad* 実行不可能な程度に ► This is still **impracticably** high. これはまだ実行できないほどに高い.

practical

接頭 (im) **impractical** *adj* 実用的でない ▶ Most of these methods are outdated and **impractical**. これらの方法のほとんどは時代遅れで，実際的でない．

接頭 (un) **unpractical** *adj* 実行不可能な ▶ Magnetic power generating is not **unpractical**. 磁力発電は実行不可能ではない．

practicality

接頭 (im) **impracticality** *n* 非実際性

practically

接頭 (im) **impractically** *ad* 非実際的に

practiced

接頭 (un) **unpracticed** *adj* 訓練を積んでいない ▶ He is **unpracticed** in this kind of work. 彼はこの種の仕事に不慣れである．

precedented

接頭 (un) **unprecedented** *adj* 前代未聞の，前例のない ▶ subsidies at **unprecedented** levels 前例のない額の助成金 ▶ nuclear power which involves **unprecedented** quantities of radioactive materials 前例のない大量放射性物質を含む原子力 ▶ a phenomenon **unprecedented** in the short history of computers コンピューターの短い歴史において前例のない現象

precise

接頭 (im) **imprecise** *adj* 不正確な，不明確な ▶ Historical records are somewhat **imprecise**. 史料はある程度不正確である．

precisely

接頭 (im) **imprecisely** *ad* 不正確に，間違って ▶ He expressed himself **imprecisely**. 彼は，不正確に自己を表現した．

predictability

接頭 (un) **unpredictability** *n* 予測不可能性 ▶ The **unpredictability** of the charge density and distribution makes the effect of the ionosphere difficult to forecast. 電荷密度と分布の予測

不可能性によって電離層の影響が予測困難になっている. ▶ The most tiring aspect of the newborn baby's behavior is its **unpredictability**. 最も疲れるのは赤ん坊の行動が予測できない点である.

predictable

接頭 (un) **unpredictable** *adj* 予測できない, 予見できない ▶ The instantaneous values of noise are **unpredictable**. ノイズの瞬間的な値は予測できない. ▶ This lets you create an entertaining and **unpredictable** slide show which is fun to watch for a little while. これによって, しばらくは見ていて楽しくて先を予測することができないスライドショーを制作することができる. ▶ Radar propagation through the ionosphere fluctuates in an **unpredictable** manner. 電離層を通るレーダーの伝搬は予測できない形で変動する. ▶ Here's why fraudulently underwritten loans posed such a towering, and until now **unpredictable**, problem. 不正に引き受けられた貸し付けが, 法外かつ現在まで予見できなかった問題をもたらした理由をここに述べる.

predictably

接頭 (un) **unpredictably** *ad* 予測できず ▶ today's violently, **unpredictably** shifting business environment 今日の激しくかつ予想不可能に変化しているビジネス環境 ▶ Before our trip to the mine was done, our group would get a taste of the insurgent's ability to strike violently and **unpredictably**. 我々がその鉱山へ移動を始める前に, 暴徒の激しく予測ができない襲来能力を少しでも経験するつもりであった.

predicted

接頭 (un) **unpredicted** *adj* 予測できない ▶ Changes or developments under the shipbuilding contract add **unpredicted** weight topside. 造船契約に基づく変更や開発で, 予測されなかった重量が上甲板に追加される.

pregnable

接頭 (im) **impregnable** *adj* 難攻不落の，〈態度などが〉断固とした ▸ The general pronounced the fortress **impregnable**. 将軍はその要塞が不落であると断言した.

接頭 (im) **impregnably** *ad* 堅固な方法で ▸ The sight of that bland, **impregnably** righteous face has been enough to make their blood run cold. その穏やかな，堅固に高潔な顔は，彼らに血の凍る思いをさせるのに十分であった.

prejudiced

接頭 (un) **unprejudiced** *adj* 偏見のない ▸ That is an unbiased view — an **unprejudiced** view — of the matter. それが偏見のない[公平な]意見だ.

接頭 (un) **unprejudicedly** *ad* 偏見なく

premeditated

接頭 (un) **unpremeditated** *adj* 計画的でない

prepared

接頭 (ill) **ill-prepared** *adj* 準備不足の ▸ be **ill-prepared** for disaster 災害への準備が十分でない ▸ He was **ill-prepared**. 彼は，準備不足だった.

接頭 (un) **unprepared** *adj* 準備ができていない ▸ You don't dare show up **unprepared** because he understands your work and he has his own position on its value. 彼は君の仕事も自身の地位の価値もよくわきまえているため，君はあえて準備もせずに姿を現さなくてもよいだろう.

prepossessing

接頭 (un) **unprepossessing** *adj* 〈外見などが〉良くない

prescriptible

接頭 (im) **imprescriptible** *adj* 法令に拘束されない，〈時効などで〉消滅できない ▸ **imprescriptible** right 無時効の権利

prescription

接頭 (non) **nonprescription** *adj* 処方箋なしで買える

presented

接頭 (ill) **ill-presented** *adj*

❶示し方が不適切な

❷保存状態が悪い

press

接頭 (de) **depress** *v*

❶消沈させる

❷活力を弱める ▸ Simultaneously, interleukin-1 acts on the body's central thermostat, causing a fever, which may **depress** viral activity and enhance the immune response. 同時に，再生白血(球)素−1が身体中枢定温装置に作用して熱を発生し，それによりウイルスの活動が弱まり免疫反応を高める．

pressed

接頭 (de) **depressed** *adj*

❶元気のない，弱体化された ▸ In the guinea pig, ascorbic acid depletion results in **depressed** immunological response, and high vitamin C dosage increases cell division. モルモット実験ではアスコルビン酸の消耗が免疫反応の弱体化という結果を示し，高用量のビタミンCの服用は細胞分裂を増加させている．

❷不景気な

pressurize

接頭 (de) **depressurize** *v* 減圧する ▸ The cushion contains seven air bladders that are pressurized or **depressurized** according to the flight maneuver. そのクッションには飛行運動に応じて加圧あるいは減圧できる7つの空気袋が入っている．

pressurized

接頭 (de) **depressurized** *adj* 減圧された ▸ It is now possible to measure these dynamic hull-pressure and shaft forces in a **depressurized** towing tank. これら動的船体圧力と減圧された曳行タンクの軸力を計測することが今では可能である．

接頭 (un) **unpressurized** *adj* 加圧されていない ▸ The problems can be eliminated by using an **unpressurized** atomizing process. その問題は，加圧されない霧状化工程を利用することによって解決することができる．

pretentious

接頭 (un) **unpretentious** *adj* 見栄をはらない，控えめな ► It was a very small, **unpretentious** Catholic school for girls with only one class of fewer than 50 pupils in each school year. 一学年一クラス50名弱という実にひっそりとした［控えめな］，カトリック系の女学校だった．

pretentiously

接頭 (un) **unpretentiously** *ad* 控えめに

price

接尾 (less) **priceless** *adj* 値がつけられない，非常に貴重な ► Sometimes these are of little value before contracting but **priceless** after an award. 契約前はほとんど無価値でありながら，一度賞が決定すると金で買えないほど貴重になる場合がある． ► The Japanese regard the three of four days when the blossoms come out as **priceless**. 日本人は，桜の花が咲くこの3，4日に無上の［非常に貴重な］価値を置く．

priced

接頭 (un) **unpriced** *adj*

❶ 値がついていない ► an **unpriced** purchase order 値を指定しない買い注文

❷ たいへん貴重な ► The result should be that the scarcity of **unpriced** natural resources is a factor that is included in the market price. その結果，貴重な天然資源が不足すれば市場価格に影響を及ぼすことになる．

principled

接頭 (un) **unprincipled** *adj* 節操のない，道義心のない ► An **unprincipled** person follows no moral code, has no integrity, and should not be trusted. 道義心のない人間は，道徳に従わず，不誠実であり，信用するに値しない．

printable

接頭 (un) **unprintable** *adj* 〈言葉などが〉印刷するのに適さない, 印刷できない, 不穏当な

printing

接頭 (non) **nonprinting** *adj* 印刷していない, 非印刷の ► The **nonprinting** parts should be painted over with ink- and water-resistant lacquer. 非印刷箇所は, 耐インクラッカーおよび耐水ラッカーで塗りあげること. ► Both the printing and **non-printing** areas are at the same level. 印刷面と印刷してない面は両方とも高さは同じである.

privileged

接頭 (un) **unprivileged** *adj* 特権のない

probability

接頭 (im) **improbability** *n* 起こりそうにないこと ► Impossibility should never be confused with **improbability**. 不可能は, 起こりそうにないことと決して混同するべきではない.

probable

接頭 (im) **improbable** *adj*

❶起こりそうにない ► The statement sounds **improbable**. その話は本当とは思えない.

❷ありそうもない

接頭 (im) **improbably** *ad* ありそうもなく ► His performance was **improbably** good. 彼の演技は信じられないくらいよかった.

problematic(al)

接頭 (un) **unproblematic(al)** *adj* 問題のない ► The security values serve the function of helping oneself to fit in and adapt in an **unproblematic** way to society. 安全という価値観があることにより, 人は問題なく社会参加への道をたどることができる.

problematic(al)ly

接頭 (un) **unproblematic(al)ly** *ad* 問題なく

procedural

[接頭] (non) **nonprocedural** *adj* 非手順(式)の ▸ It is almost impossible to query a network-model database using **nonprocedural**, English-based query languages such as SQL. 非手順式の，SQL のような英語主体の問い合わせ言語を使用してネットワークモデルのデータベースを照会することはほとんど不可能である．

processed

[接頭] (un) **unprocessed** *adj* 未処理の ▸ Fiber, which stimulates the bowel, is found in fresh fruit and vegetables, in cereals (especially **unprocessed** bran or porridge) and in wholemeal bread. 腸を刺激する繊維は新鮮な果物や野菜，穀物(特に未加工のぬかやポリッジ)，全麦パンに含まれている．

productive

[接頭] (non) **nonproductive** *adj* 非生産的な ▸ **Nonproductive** time includes setup time, changing of parts, equipment failure, etc. 非生産的な時間には，準備期間，部品交換，器材故障などがある．

[接頭] (un) **unproductive** *adj* 非生産的な ▸ For years, multinationals simply accepted the **unproductive** and hugely corrupt business practices. 長年にわたって，多国籍企業は非生産的で際限なく腐敗したビジネス慣習を容易に受け入れてきた．

productively

[接頭] (un) **unproductively** *ad* 非生産的に

professional

[接頭] (non) **nonprofessional** *adj* ノンプロの，非専門職の
—— *n* ノンプロ，非専門職 ▸ Positions which involve management of both professionals and **nonprofessionals** bring a median income of $45,000 with only a few subordinates. 専門職，非専門職にかかわらず，管理職の地位にある人は部下が少しいるだけだが収入の中央値は45,000 ドルである． ▸ But it's a helpful way of thinking for us **nonprofessionals**. し

かし，それは我々のようなノンプロにとっては有効な考え方である．

接頭 (un) **unprofessional** *adj*

❶専門外の ▸ Pontellier had brought her sketching materials, which she sometimes dabbled with in an **unprofessional** way. ポンテリアはスケッチ用具を持ってきていたが，プロフェッショナルとは程遠いやり方で使ってみるに過ぎないこともあった．

❷職業倫理に反する

profit

接頭 (non) **nonprofit** *adj* 非営利の ▸ The show is being sponsored by a **nonprofit** group. そのショーは非営利団体の後援を受けている． ▸ He is on a total of six corporate and four **nonprofit** boards. 彼は全部で六つの会社の取締役会と四つの非営利団体の理事会に所属している．

—— *n* 非営利団体 ▸ The man works for five **nonprofits**. その男性は五つの非営利団体で働いている． ▸ The **nonprofit** corporation received all of the assets of the forerunner of ABC Co. その非営利団体はABC社の前身のすべての資産を受け取った． ▸ The man told him that **nonprofits** needed a revenue source apart from fundraising and occasional one-off corporate contributions. 非営利団体は資金調達や臨時の一回限りの企業の出資とは別に財源が必要であると，その男性は彼に話した．

接尾 (less) **profitless** *adj* 儲からない ▸ But profits evaporated, creating an era of so-called **profitless** prosperity in the middle of the decade. しかし，利益は消えてなくなり，その10年間の中頃にはいわゆる利益なき繁忙という時代になっていた．

profitable

接頭 (un) **unprofitable** *adj* 儲からない，利益の上がらない ▸ The bus company has stopped running the **unprofitable** route. バス会社は，利益の上がらない路線の運行を停止した． ▸ In the United States, any effort to eliminate an **unprofitable** train line, or to abandon an uneconomic branch line, for example, often requires lengthy public hearings. アメリカではたとえば鉄道の利益の出ていない路線を廃止したり経済性の低い支線を廃線にする場合，長期にわたる公聴会が必要となる.

profitmaking

[接頭] (non) **nonprofitmaking** *adj* 営利を追求しない

proliferation

[接頭] (non) **nonproliferation** *n* 〈核兵器などの〉拡散防止の

promising

[接頭] (un) **unpromising** *adj* 見込みのない，将来性のない

prompted

[接頭] (un) **unprompted** *adj* 〈言動が〉他から強制されたものではない

pronounceable

[接頭] (un) **unpronounceable** *adj* 発音しにくい ▶ such risky areas as investment banking and **unpronounceable** derivatives 投資銀行業務や発音しにくい金融派生商品などのリスクを伴う分野

proof

[接頭] (dis) **disproof** *n* 反駁，反証

proper

[接頭] (im) **improper** *adj* 不適切な，下品な，正しくない ▶ I must apologize for the **improper** words I used. 私は，自分の使った不適切な発言に対してお詫びする.

properly

[接頭] (im) **improperly** *ad* 不適切に，誤って ▶ **improperly** write something 書き間違える

properness

[接頭] (im) **improperness** *n* 不適当

proportion

[接頭] (dis) **disproportion** *n* 不均衡

proportional

接頭 (dis) **disproportional** *adj* 釣り合っていない ► Does that one man wield power grossly **disproportional** to his economic stake in the company? ある人間が，その会社における経済的なかかわり合いにまったく不釣り合いな力量を発揮することができるだろうか.

proportionate

接頭 (dis) **disproportionate** *adj* 不釣り合いな ► Its width was **disproportionate** to its length. その幅はその長さに不釣り合いであった. ► a **disproportionate** burden 不釣り合いな負担

proportionately

接頭 (dis) **disproportionately** *ad* 不釣り合いに ► It seems likely that this distinction accounts, in part, for the **disproportionately** small representation of women today in the professional fields of science and technology. この差異は，科学と技術の職業分野において今日の女性が占める数が不釣り合いに小さいことを部分的に説明しているように見える.

proportioned

接頭 (ill) **ill-proportioned** *adj* 不釣り合いな

proprietary

接頭 (non) **nonproprietary** *adj* 所有権のない，非専売の ► The newest CAD/CAM company to switch to **nonproprietary** hardware is ABC Inc. 専売権を持たないハードウェアを販売することに切り換えた最も新しいCAD/CAMの会社はABC社である.

propriety

接頭 (im) **impropriety** *n* 間違い，不適当，不正 ► He waved off suggestions of **impropriety**. 彼は不適切な提案を拒絶した.

protected

接頭 (un) **unprotected** *adj*

❶ 保護されていない ► All the **unprotected** copper is eaten

away from the laminate, leaving the desired conductive pattern. 保護処理なしの銅はすべて腐食して薄層から削られ，その結果所望の導電パターンが得られる.

❷ 無防備な ► Corrosive vapors can eat away the internal parts of **unprotected** machines. 腐食性の蒸気は無防備の機械の内部部品を腐食してしまう. ► Contamination may be transmitted to you through cracks or abrasions on your **unprotected** hands. 汚染は無防備な手にあるひび割れや擦り傷から伝染することがある.

prove

接頭 (un) **unprove** *v* 立証しない ► But skeptics have pointed out that much of that total is "**unproven.**" しかし，懐疑的な人たちは，その合計量の多くが「未確認」であることを指摘してきた.

接頭 (dis) **disprove** *v* 反対のことを証明する ► The earlier idea, that full-fledged bacteria arise from nonliving material by spontaneous generation, has been **disproved** by careful elimination of living bacteria from the nonliving material. 成熟したバクテリアは自然発生により無生物から生ずる，という初期の考え方は，無生物から生のバクテリアを注意深く排除したことで誤りであることが証明された.

proved

接頭 (un) **unproved** *adj* 立証されていない

proven

接頭 (un) **unproven** *adj* 立証されていない，試されていない

► Furthermore, attempts to use **unproven** technology on commercial aircraft usually involve unacceptable risk and investment. さらに，立証されていない技術を民間航空機に利用しようとすれば受け入れがたいリスクや投資を伴う.

provided

接頭 (un) **unprovided** *adj*

❶ 備え付けられていない ► I had seen how they left their

watchmen **unprovided** with a boat. 彼らが一隻のボートも警備員に与えずにいたのを見た.

❷準備されていない

provident

接頭 (im) **improvident** *adj*

❶先見性のない, 将来に備えない ▸ He has no savings — he is **improvident**. 彼は, 金の蓄えがない. すなわち, 倹約心がない.

❷ 性急な, 不用意な ▸ in an **improvident** manner 不用意な態度で

providently

接頭 (im) **improvidently** *ad* 性急に, 先見性なく, 先のことを考えずに ▸ He lived **improvidently** for the moment. 彼は, 当面その日暮らしで生活した.

provoked

接頭 (un) **unprovoked** *adj* 挑発されたものではない

prudence

接頭 (im) **imprudence** *n*

❶無分別, 軽率 ▸ She deeply regretted her **imprudence**. 彼女は自分の軽率さを深く後悔した.

❷ ずうずうしさ, 不謹慎 ▸ If that is called **imprudence**, I wonder what would be called a thoughtful provision against the vicissitudes of fortune. それを不謹慎と言うのであれば, 運命の移り変わりを思慮深く考えて備えることは何なのだろう.

prudent

接頭 (im) **imprudent** *adj*

❶厚かましい, ずうずうしい ▸ I thought it would be **imprudent** of him to settle so early. 彼がそんなにも早く落ち着くのは, ずうずうしいと思った.

❷無分別な, 軽率な ▸ Do you think that my Father will ever be reconciled to this **imprudent** connection? この軽率な関係に, 父が納得するとでも思いますか.

prudently

接頭 (im) **imprudently** *ad* 軽率に，軽々しい態度で

public

接頭 (non) **nonpublic** *adj* 非公開の ► He also admitted that he “abused his relationship” with federal law enforcement to get **nonpublic** information and trade on it. 彼はさらに，連邦法の執行についての「彼の関連性を悪用」し，非公開情報を得てそれに関する取引をしたと認めた．

published

接頭 (un) **unpublished** *adj* 未発表の ► The manuscripts must be **unpublished**, but if the selection committee recognizes an already published manuscript, it can be subject to selection. 応募作品は未発表のものでなければならないが，すでに発表されたものでも選考委員会が認めたものは選考対象とする．

pulsating

接頭 (non) **nonpulsating** *adj* 鼓動しない ► The conventional polyphase motor develops a smooth **nonpulsating** torque and is essentially a constant-speed motor. 従来の多相電動機はスムーズな無脈動トルクを発生させる，本質的には定速電動機である．

pulse

接尾 (less) **pulseless** *adj*

❶脈拍のない

❷生気[活気]のない

punished

接頭 (un) **unpunished** *adj* 処罰されない

pure

接頭 (im) **impure** *adj* 純粋でない，不純な ► The outer layers are slightly **impure** diamond. 外側の層は，わずかに不純物の混じったダイヤモンドである．

purity

接頭 (im) **impurity** *n*

❶不純物, 混入物 ► The stability of these compounds varies with the water and metallic **impurity** present. これらの化合物の安定性は, 水と存在する金属質の不純物によって変わる.

❷不純, 不潔, 不道徳

purpose

接尾 (less) **purposeless** *adj* 目的のない, 意味のない ► In fact, there is no such thing as a **purposeless** life. 事実, 意味のない人生というものはありません.

put down

接頭 (un) **unputdownable** *adj* 〈読書などが〉途中でやめられない

Q

qualification

接頭 (dis) **disqualification** *n*

❶不適格，失格（処分）

❷資格剥奪

qualified

接頭 (ill) **ill-qualified** *adj* 適任でない ▸ an **ill-qualified** teacher 能力の劣った教師

接頭 (un) **unqualified** *adj*

❶資格のない，不適格な ▸ While I appreciate the sincerity of his desire to serve, I find him to be **unqualified** as a candidate for this organization. 彼の働きたいという希望の真剣さを評価するものの，私が見るところでは彼にはこの組織の候補者としての資格はない.

❷無条件の ▸ the need for **unqualified** adherence to a philosophy of respect for life 人命尊重思想の無条件の遵守の必要性

qualify

接頭 (dis) **disqualify** *v*

❶不適格とする ▸ Nothing **disqualifies** a writer faster than factual mistakes. 事実の誤認ほど急速に著作者の不適格性を問うものはない.

❷資格を剥奪する ▸ He **disqualified** one candidate when she admitted she paid an ad agency to write her presentation. 彼は，ある候補者がお金を支払って自分のプレゼンテーションを広告会社に書かせたことを認めると，彼女の資格を剥奪した.

quench

接尾 (less) **quenchless** *adj* 癒やせない

quenchable

接頭 (un) **unquenchable** *adj*

❶〈火や明かりなどを〉消せない
❷水冷できない

questionable

[接頭] (un) **unquestionable** *adj* 疑いのない ▶ It's **unquestionable** that rising unemployment is one of the most pressing issues in the industrial world. 失業率が上昇していることは，産業界での急を要する問題のひとつであることに疑いの余地はない.

questionably

[接頭] (un) **unquestionably** *ad* 疑いなく ▶ Were this indeed the case, then democracy would **unquestionably** be the best form of government. これが実態だとすると，民主主義は文句なしに[疑いなく]最高の政治形態です.

questioned

[接頭] (un) **unquestioned** *adj* 疑いのない

questioning

[接頭] (un) **unquestioning** *adj* 疑いを持たない

questioningly

[接頭] (un) **unquestioningly** *ad* 疑いなく ▶ a new show that **unquestioningly** presents demonstrations of paranormal feats 超常的な芸当の実演を無条件に見せる新しいショー

quiet

[接頭] (dis) **disquiet** *v* 平静を失わせる，心を乱す

[接頭] (un) **unquiet** *adj* 不安な

quieting

[接頭] (dis) **disquieting** *adj* 不安にする ▶ From Norway and Denmark came the same **disquieting** signals. ノルウェーやデンマークから同様に人を不安にするような徴候が出ている.

quietude

[接頭] (dis) **disquietude** *n* 不安，心配

quote

[接頭] (un) **unquote** *v* 引用を終わる

R

racial

接頭 (non) **nonracial** *adj* 人種差別をしない

radioactive

接頭 (non) **nonradioactive** *adj* 放射能を含まない，非放射性の ► A deeper aquifer contains toxic, **nonradioactive** materials. 深い帯水層は，有毒な非放射性物質を含んでいる.

rail

接尾 (less) **railless** *adj* 無軌道の

rain

接尾 (less) **rainless** *adj* 雨の降らない ► The clear, **rainless** winter gave place to spring and the giant cactus burst into flower. すっきりと晴れて雨の降らなかった冬が春になり，巨大なサボテンの花が咲いた.

random

接頭 (non) **nonrandom** *n* 任意でない，　無作為でない ► However, as expansion proceeds, the distribution might become **nonrandom** and require an interconnection to randomize the distributions. しかしながら，拡張が進むと分配が無作為でなくなることがあるので，その分配を無作為化する内部干渉が必要になることがある.

randomness

接頭 (non) **nonrandomness** *n* 非任意，規則正しいこと ► The overflow traffic itself acquires a **nonrandomness**, whose character is described by more sophisticated expressions. オーバーフローした交通それ自身には規則正しさが備わっていて，その特性はより精巧な表現によって表される.

rational

接頭 (ir) **irrational** *adj*

❶ 理性のない ► One often makes seemingly **irrational** decisions. 人はしばしば，一見不合理な[理性のない]結論を出す. ► The state television not only contributes to but encourages an already widespread tendency for the **irrational**. 国営のテレビは，すでに広がっている無分別の[理性のない]傾向を助長するばかりか，奨励さえもする.

❷ 不合理な ► The sick child probably needs more comforting than usual and may have many apparently **irrational** fears. 病気の子供はおそらくいつもより一層元気づけられる必要があり，多くの明らかに不合理な怖れを抱いていることがある. ► If he had not been **irrational** in composing this music, a well-known song that we sing today would not exist. 彼の理屈に合わない[不合理な]作曲行為がなされなかったとしたら，今日私たちが愛唱する歌の一つは存在しなかっただろう.

❸ 無理[非有理]の ► This was despite the fact that Pythagoras had known it to be an **irrational** number back in the days of ancient Greece. これは，ピタゴラスがそれは無理数となることを古代ギリシャの時代に分かっていた事実に反した.

rationality

[接頭] (ir) **irrationality** *n* 理性のなさ，分別のなさ

rationally

[接頭] (ir) **irrationally** *ad*

❶ 無分別に ► A few **irrationally** told flight attendants they wanted to leave the plane. 若干の人が，無分別にも飛行機から降りたいと接客乗務員に告げた.

❷ 不合理に ► The stock's miserable run under Immelt isn't nearly as bad as it looks because the price was **irrationally** high when he got the job. イメルト就任後の株価の貧弱な推移は，就任時の株価が不合理に高かったので，見かけほどは悪くない.

ravel

[接頭] (un) **unravel** *v* 〈糸や謎を〉解く ► **Unravel** the video disc player line cord and ... ビデオディスクプレーヤーのライン

コードをほどき, …. ► be important in **unraveling** the chemistry of other elements 他の元素の化学的性質を解くうえで重要である ► Long before scientists even began to **unravel** the mysteries of this remarkable system, the ancients were aware of immunity. 科学者たちがこのすばらしいシステムの謎を解き明かし始めるはるか以前にさえ古代人は免疫について知っていた.

ray

接尾 (less) **rayless** *adj* 光線のない

reach

接頭 (un) **unreached** *adj*

❶到達していない ► The linear chains still contain **unreached** portions which are capable of flowing under heat and pressure. 線形連鎖でもまだ加熱および加圧下において流動性のある, 到達していない部分がある.

❷及んでいない ► The ultimate goal is to narrow disparities by extending prosperity to those **unreached** by China's economic miracle. 最終目標は, 繁栄が及んでいない地域にまで繁栄を拡大させる中国の奇跡的な経済成長で格差を縮めることである.

reacted

接頭 (un) **unreacted** *adj* 未反応の ► This **unreacted** magnesium has the potential to act as ... この未反応のマグネシウムは, …として作用する可能性がある.

reactive

接頭 (non) **nonreactive** *adj* 無反応性の ► Hydrophilic silicones are **nonreactive** fluids that have been modified for slight or complete solubility in water. 親水性シリコンは水に微溶解ないし完全溶解するように改良された無反応性流体である.

read

接頭 (ill) **ill-read** *adj* 教養のない

接頭 (un) **unread** *adj* 読まれていない ► The other day I transferred my **unread** books from the bookshelf to a small cardboard box marked "To be read" in large characters. 先日，そうした読んでいない本を「未読」と大書きした小さなダンボール箱に移し替えた．

readable

接頭 (un) **unreadable** *adj*

❶判読できない ▶ What is the process of converting readable data into **unreadable** characters to prevent unauthorized access? 権限のないアクセスを防ぐための，可読データを不可読文字に変換するプロセスはどのようなものか．

❷読んでも面白くない

reader

接頭 (non) **nonreader** *n* 本を読まない人

ready

接頭 (un) **unready** *adj* 用意されていない，準備されていない

real

接頭 (non) **nonreal** *adj* ノンリアルの ▶ Remote teaching requires transmission in real or **nonreal** time of highly varied images. 遠隔授業を行う場合，非常に多様な映像をリアルタイムあるいはノンリアルタイムで送信する必要がある．

接頭 (un) **unreal** *adj* 現実的でない，実在しない

realistic

接頭 (un) **unrealistic** *adj* 非現実的な ▶ The figure of 150,000 subscribers is **unrealistic**. 契約者数15万人という数字は非現実的である． ▶ It is **unrealistic** to expect service quality to be consistent and similar across different countries. 違った国に，一貫した，同様の質のサービスを期待することは現実的ではない． ▶ The proliferation of route awards, new airline entries, and **unrealistic** fare discounts has contributed to the current financial crisis in the airline industry. 路線認可の急増，新しい航空会社の参入，および非現実的な料金割引が，現在の航空会社の財務危機の原因となっている．

realistically

接頭 (un) **unrealistically** *ad* 非現実的に

reality

接頭 (un) **unreality** *n* 非現実性

realizable

接頭 (un) **unrealizable** *adj* 実現できない ► An oscillator in which the loop gain is exactly unity is an abstraction that is completely **unrealizable** in practice. ループゲインが正確に単一な発信機は実際にはまったく実現できない抽象概念である.

realized

接頭 (un) **unrealized** *adj* 実現されていない, 帳簿上の ► Microsoft tries to find pockets of **unrealized** revenue and then figures out what to make. マイクロソフトは帳簿上の収入額を見つけ, それで何を作ることができるかを計画する.

reason

接尾 (less) **reasonless** *adj*

❶道理に合わない, 分別のない

❷理由のない ► The exception to which I refer is that of the patient who had the sudden attacks of **reasonless** depression. 理由がなく突然落ち込んだ患者は私の述べた例外である.

接頭 (un) **unreason** *n* 不合理, 不条理

reasonable

接頭 (un) **unreasonable** *adj*

❶理由のない, 適正でない ► It was also decided that with this multiplicity of services it was **unreasonable** to restrict customers to the use of only one channel at a time. このサービスの多様性について, 一度に1チャンネルしか使ってはいけないと, 顧客に制限するのは不合理であるということも決定された. ► The contractor did rely on it, and it would be **unreasonable** to permit the defendant to revoke its offer. 請負会社はそれを頼りにしていて, 被告側にそのオファーの取り消しを

許すことは理屈に合わないであろう.

❷ 筋が通っていない ► The husband's argument is not altogether **unreasonable**. 亭主の言い分も, まんざら筋が通っていないこともない. ► It stated that applying fuel surcharges to the overall rate was "**unreasonable**" and put an end to the practice. それによると, 全料金に燃油サーチャージを適用することは「適正ではなく」, 徴収を中止した.

reasonably

接頭 (un) **unreasonably** *ad* 理由なく, 不合理に ► interfere **unreasonably** with the comfortable enjoyment of life and property 人生と財産を快適に享受することを不合理に妨害する ► He can be replaced only with the Funder's approval (which shall not be **unreasonably** withheld). 彼は出資者の承認(これは理由なく阻止してはならない)によってのみ交代させることができる.

reasoned

接頭 (un) **unreasoned** *adj* 不合理な

reasoning

接頭 (un) **unreasoning** *adj* 思慮のない

received

接頭 (ill) **ill-received** *adj* 評判の悪い

reck

接尾 (less) **reckless** *adj* 無謀な, 無茶な ► But such pride can quickly become chauvinistic or **reckless**. しかし, そのような誇りは, すぐに排外主義的または無謀なものとなる. ► Minkow admitted adopting Conspirator A's false assertions with **reckless** disregard for the truth. ミンコウ氏は, 無謀にも真実を無視して, 共謀者 A の嘘の主張を採用したと認めた.

接尾 (less) **recklessly** *ad* 無謀に ► Youth can perhaps be said to be a time when one forges ahead **recklessly** with the enterprising spirit characteristic of the young. 若さというものは, その年齢特有の進取性によってがむしゃらに[無謀に]進ん

でいく時代と言えるかもしれない.

reclaimable

接頭 (ir) **irreclaimable** *adj* 回復できない ▶ If there are financial problems, it is wise to take legal advice early before matters become **irreclaimable**. 金銭的問題がある場合, 事態が回復不能になる前に早期に法的助言を得ることが賢明である.

recognizable

接頭 (un) **unrecognizable** *adj* 見分けられない ▶ The date or time specified on the command line was **unrecognizable**. コマンド行で指定された日付または時刻が認識不可能だった.

recognized

接頭 (un) **unrecognized** *adj* 認識されていない ▶ Endometriosis is an often **unrecognized** disease that afflicts anywhere from 4 million to 10 million American women and is a major cause of infertility. 子宮内膜症は多くの場合, 認識されていない病気で, 米国では400万〜1000万人ほどの女性が罹患し, 不妊の主要な原因となる.

recoil

接尾 (less) **recoilless** *adj* 反動のない

reconcilable

接頭 (ir) **irreconcilable** *adj* 和解できない; 折り合いがつかない; 相容れない ▶ They may vary and seem very different, but they are not **irreconcilable**. 彼らは変化し非常に相違しているようであるが, 和解できなくはない.

reconstructed

接頭 (un) **unreconstructed** *adj* 時代遅れの

recorded

接頭 (un) **unrecorded** *adj* 記録されていない ▶ Because of extinct tribes with **unrecorded** languages, the number of languages formerly spoken is impossible to assess. 記録に残っていない言語を使用していた種族が絶滅してしまったため, 以前話されていた言語の数を推定することは不可能である.

recurring

接頭 (non) **nonrecurring** *adj* 反復しない, 非経常的な ▸ It said most of the **nonrecurring** costs for the Boeing 757 and 767 and the McDonnell Douglas F-18 were incurred on corporate balance sheets before 1984. ボーイング757と767およびマクダネルダグラスF-18の経常外費用の大部分は, 1984年より前の同社バランスシート上でのものであるとされた.

redeemable

接頭 (ir) **irredeemable** *adj* 買い戻しができない

接頭 (un) **unredeemable** *adj* 償還不能な

redeemed

接頭 (un) **unredeemed** *adj* 償還されていない

reducible

接頭 (ir) **irreducible** *adj* 縮小できない

reel

接頭 (un) **unreel** *v* 〈ひもやテープなどを〉巻き戻す

refined

接頭 (un) **unrefined** *adj* 精製されていない ▸ The alanine, leucine, isoleucine and other pro-fat amino acids contained in **unrefined** mash for rice vinegar work to suppress the insulin. 米酢もろみ[未精製マッシュ]に含まれているアラニン, ロイシン, イソロイシン, といった抗肥満アミノ酸が, インスリンの働きを抑制する.

reflected

接頭 (un) **unreflected** *adj*

❶反省していない

❷反射されていない

reflecting

接頭 (un) **unreflecting** *adj*

❶反射しない ▸ There was the danger of being drugged by the miasma that rose from this **unreflecting** surface. ここには, このくすんだ[反射しない]表面から立ち上る不吉な雰囲気

に麻痺させられそうな危険があった.

❷反省しない

reflective

[接頭] (un) **unreflective** *adj* 無反省の

refundable

[接頭] (non) **nonrefundable** *adj* 返金不可の

refutable

[接頭] (ir) **irrefutable** *adj* 反論できない ► There is **irrefutable** proof that they own the only original print of this image. 彼らがこの画像の唯一のオリジナルプリントを所有するという反論できない証拠がある.

regard

[接頭] (dis) **disregard** *v* 無視する ► The program **disregards** data to or from the circuits. プログラムは, 回路の入出力データを無視する.

regarded

[接頭] (ill) **ill-regarded** *adj* 不評の

[接頭] (un) **unregarded** *adj* 顧みられない

regenerate

[接頭] (un) **unregenerate** *adj* 改心しない ► The Spirit of God is absent in the **unregenerate** person's life. 改心しない人の人生には神の精神は存在しない.

registered

[接頭] (un) **unregistered** *adj* 登録されていない

regular

[接頭] (ir) **irregular** *adj*

❶不規則な, でこぼこな ► There are special sections which are rolled at **irregular** intervals. 不規則な間隔でローラーをかける特別な部分がある.

❷不整形の, 不定形の ► Diamond has also been found as **irregular** microcrystalline clumps up to a millimeter or so in size. ダイヤモンドは, 大きさが1ミリ程度までの不定形の微晶質

のかたまりでも見つかっている.

❸法に反した, 反則的な

regularity

[接頭] (ir) **irregularity** *n* 不規則性, 不揃い, 反則 ▶ surface **irregularities** 表面の不規則 ▶ In general, material damage accumulates at the stress concentration that normally accompanies the particle, void, or surface **irregularity**. 一般に, 材料の破損は, 普通, 粒子, 空隙, または表面のでこぼこ[不規則性]に伴う応力の集中部分で多く生じる.

regularly

[接頭] (ir) **irregularly** *ad* 不規則的に, 不法に, 不揃いに ▶ The crystals of highest purity are often **irregularly** shaped. 最高純度の水晶はしばしば形が不揃いだ. ▶ The finished weight of **irregularly** shaped or badly flawed crystals is often very much less. 不規則な形をしていたり, ひどい傷があったりする水晶は, 仕上り重量が非常に小さくなることが多い.

regulate

[接頭] (de) **deregulate** *v* 規制緩和する ▶ However, in the U.S. and other countries whose telecommunications industries have been **deregulated** ... しかし, 米国をはじめとする電気通信産業の規制緩和が行われている国々においては, …. ▶ Since freight railroads were **deregulated** in 1980, the number of large, so-called Class I railroads has shrunk from 40 to seven. 貨物鉄道の規制が1980年に緩和されて以来, いわゆるクラスIの大型鉄道会社の数は40社から7社に減少した.

[接頭] (un) **unregulate** *v* 規制しない ▶ In Mexico, negative campaigning is illegal, but the law never contemplated social media, which are **unregulated**. メキシコでは, ネガティブキャンペーンは不法行為であるが, 法律の規制を受けていないソーシャルメディアについてはまともに考慮されていない.

regulated

[接頭] (un) **unregulated** *adj*

❶ 規制されていない ▶ How about the recession? It was brought about by greedy banks and the **unregulated** market. 景気後退についてはどうか. 景気後退は貪欲な銀行と規制されていないマーケットによりもたらされた. ▶ What IPOs used to do almost exclusively now sometimes happens in that burgeoning and largely **unregulated** marketplace. IPO がほとんど独占的に行ってきたことが, 今ではその急成長している, 規制のない市場においてしばしば行われる. ▶ In a competitive environment including **unregulated** long distance carriers and users, not all players may perceive ... 規制されていない長距離通信会社, およびユーザーなどの競争的な環境においては, すべての関係者が…と気付いているとはかぎらない.

❷ 調整されていない ▶ supply the panel lamps and **unregulated** d.c. for the relay パネルランプや無調整直流電流を継電器用に供給する

regulation

接頭 (de) **deregulation** *n* 規制緩和の ▶ **Deregulation** in continental Europe will clearly occur in a slower and more ponderous way than in the US, UK, or Japan. 大陸欧州の規制緩和は, 米国, 英国, また日本におけるよりももっとゆっくりと, しかももっと慎重に起こることは明確である.

regulatory

接頭 (de) **deregulatory** *adj* 規制緩和, 自由化 ▶ Any moves toward rapid **deregulatory** measures are, consequently, fraught with political difficulties. 急速に規制緩和手段を取ろうとする動きはどれも結果的に政治的困難を伴う.

rehearsed

接頭 (ill) **ill-rehearsed** *adj* リハーサルが十分でない

reheated

接頭 (un) **unreheated** *adj* 再加熱されていない

reinforced

[接頭] (un) **unreinforced** *adj* 強化されていない ► an ordinary **unreinforced** concrete pipe 強化されていない，通常のコンクリート導管 ► The stiffness, strength, toughness, and creep and fatigue resistance of polyacetals are higher than those of other **unreinforced** crystalline thermoplastics. ポリアセタール樹脂の硬さ，強度，頑丈さ，およびクリープと疲労に対する抵抗力は，他の非強化結晶サーモプラスチックよりも高い． ► One disadvantage of **unreinforced** rubber packings is that they are subject to extrusion. 補強されていないゴムパッキンの弱点の一つは押し出しを受けやすいことである．

related

[接頭] (un) **unrelated** *adj* 無関係の ► Some voltages or currents are **unrelated** to the signal. その信号と無関係な電圧または電流がある． ► Sell virtually every asset **unrelated** to bedrock banking. 基本の銀行業務に関係のない資産はほとんどすべて売り払え． ► He spent several minutes ticking through a laundry list of victories **unrelated** to Wall Street. 彼はウォール街とは無関係の長い勝利リストをチェックしながら数分を過ごした． ► An engineer may be part of the integration team while working on several **unrelated** projects. エンジニアは，無関係のいくつかのプロジェクトで働いていながら，総合チームに入ることができる． ► Nursing care in a large number of **unrelated** conditions may involve anticipating possible difficulties in breathing or relieving existing ones. それぞれ関連のない多くの条件の下での看護には多くの呼吸困難が予想されたり呼吸が楽になったりすることもある．

relational

[接頭] (non) **nonrelational** *adj* 関係のない ► a **nonrelational** database 関係モデルに基づかないデータベース

relent

[接尾] (less) **relentless** *adj*

❶執拗な，粘り強い ▶ Scientists are afraid that the **relentless** Halley's mania is bound to result in disappointment. 科学者は，諦めの悪いハレー彗星マニアが間違いなく落胆することになるのを懸念している.

❷無慈悲な，容赦ない ▶ Under Ballmer, a **relentless** salesman as persistent as a piston striking steel, Microsoft's enterprise-software division generated $15 billion in sales last year. ピストンが鉄を打つように粘り強くそして無慈悲ともいえる営業マンのバルマー氏のもとで，マイクロソフト社の企業担当部門は，昨年150億ドルの売り上げを達成した.

❸絶え間ない ▶ Postwar history has been characterized by a **relentless** pursuit of prosperity and Japan's emergence as an economic power. 戦後の歴史の特徴と言えば，絶え間ない繁栄を追求し，日本が経済大国となったことである.

接尾（less） **relentlessly** *ad* 執拗に，容赦なく ▶ It's all about execution, setting a few simple goals and **relentlessly** pushing to achieve them. それは実行がすべてである，すなわちわかりやすい目標をいくつか決め，それらを容赦なく推進し，達成することである. ▶ At the same time, other countries **relentlessly** educated their people. 同時に，ほかの国々は厳しくその国民を教育した.

relenting

接頭（un） **unrelenting** *adj*（断固として）譲らない ▶ In contrast to the public school system, which faces **unrelenting** fiscal pressures, the for-profit sector has been growing in recent years. 厳しい財政圧力に直面している公立の学校制度とは対照的に，営利目的の部門は近年成長している.

relevance

接頭（ir） **irrelevance** *n* 無関係，不適切

relevant

接頭（ir） **irrelevant** *adj*

❶～に関連のない，無関係な ▶ This is completely **irrelevant**

to pronunciation. これは，発音には全く関係がない． ▶ In a progress report, obscure design information is **irrelevant** unless it has a direct bearing on the progress of the project. 進捗状況レポートでは，それがプロジェクトの進行に直接的な影響を与えない限り，あまり重要ではない設計情報は問題とならない． ▶ Women can show that gender is **irrelevant** to quality work and professionalism. 女性たちは，性別と質の高い仕事やプロ意識とは無関係であることを示すことができる． ▶ When he was first asked in a deposition to identify the hedge fund that was investing in the case, his attorney objected that the question was **irrelevant**. 彼が嘱託尋問で，投資していたヘッジファンドについて確認するように最初に要求されたとき，彼の弁護士はその問題は無関係であると異議を唱えた．
❷ 重要でない ▶ Orkut, Google's first social network, was born alongside Facebook in 2004 but is largely **irrelevant** outside of Brazil. オーカットはグーグルの最初のソーシャルネットワークであり，2004年にフェイスブックと並んで生まれたが，ブラジル国外ではほとんど重要でない．

reliability

接頭 (un) **unreliability** *n* 信頼できないこと ▶ The risks of increased **unreliability** must be balanced against the improvements which may be achieved. 信頼性を損なうリスクが増すので，実現される改良と釣り合いを取る必要がある．

reliable

接頭 (un) **unreliable** *adj* 信頼できない ▶ The boasts of terrorists for the sake of publicity are notoriously **unreliable**. テロリストが何を言っても，それは周知の通り信頼性のないものである． ▶ If a snap-action switch or toggle mechanism is not used, a very simple but **unreliable** switch can be made. スナップアクション・スイッチまたはトグル機構が使用されていない場合，非常に単純であるが信頼できないスイッチができてしまう．

reliably

接頭 (un) **unreliably** *ad* 信頼できずに

relieved

接頭 (un) **unrelieved** *adj* 〈不安などが〉和らげられない

religion

接頭 (ir) **irreligion** *n* 無信仰

religious

接頭 (ir) **irreligious** *adj* 無信仰の, 不信心な

接頭 (un) **unreligious** *adj* 無宗教の, 無信心な

relish

接頭 (dis) **disrelish** *v* 嫌う

remarkable

接頭 (un) **unremarkable** *adj* 目立たない, 平凡な ▸ At a glance, the point of sale (POS) system might seem like an **unremarkable** tool for business, but many retail managers do not use or even know about numerous functions it has. POS システムは事業の道具としては一見平凡なものに見えるかもしれませんが, 小売業の経営者はその多彩な機能を使ったこともなければ存在さえ知らないことも多いのです.

remember

接頭 (dis) **disremember** *v* 忘れる

remitting

接頭 (un) **unremitting** *adj* 〈根気などが〉弱まらない

remorse

接尾 (less) **remorseless** *adj* 無慈悲な, 容赦ない

removable

接頭 (ir) **irremovable** *adj* 除去できない ▸ Most wireless headsets have inside and rechargeable but **irremovable** power packs. 大部分のワイヤレスのヘッドセットは, 再充電可能ではあるが取り外しのできない電源パックを内部に備えている.

renewable

[接頭] (non) **nonrenewable** *adj* 再生不可能な

repair

[接頭] (dis) **disrepair** *n* 修復不可能, 破損状態 ▶ The tenant left the premises in **disrepair**. その入居者は施設を破損したままにした.

repaired

[接頭] (un) **unrepaired** *adj* 修理されていない ▶ Even in the daytime its broken shutter, left **unrepaired**, remained closed. 昼日中でも, 破れ放題の雨戸が閉めたままにしてあった.

reparable

[接頭] (ir) **irreparable** *adj* 修理できない, 修復できない ▶ The situation isn't **irreparable**. その状況は修復できないことはない. ▶ Further efforts could cause **irreparable** damage to the garment. さらなる作用によってその衣服に修理不能の損傷が生じることがある. ▶ Top auto executives warn that such a sales rate will do **irreparable** damage to the industry if it continues indefinitely. 自動車会社の経営首脳陣は, このような販売価格をいつまでも続けると, 業界は取り返しのつかない[修復できない]損失を被ることになると警告している.

repeatable

[接頭] (un) **unrepeatable** *adj* 繰り返しはできない ▶ An unprecedent and **unrepeated** event took place in Geneva in July 1955. 1955年6月, ジュネーブで先例がなくその後も起きそうにない出来事が発生した.

repetitive

[接頭] (non) **nonrepetitive** *adj* 反復しない, 非反復の ▶ At an early age (5 and younger), it is important to make symmetrical, **nonrepetitive** movements. 幼少期(5歳以下)では, 対称的な非反復運動をすることが重要である.

replaceable

[接頭] (ir) **irreplaceable** *adj* 取り換えられない, かけがえのな

い ▶ His death was my grandmother losing an only son, my mother a husband of more than 10 years, and my younger sister and I an **irreplaceable** father. 彼の死は，祖母は一人息子を失い，母は十数年連れ添った夫と死に別れ，僕と妹はかけがえのない父を亡くすことを意味した．

reported

[接頭] (un) **unreported** *adj* 報告されていない

represent

[接頭] (mis) **misrepresent** *v* 誤って［偽って］伝える ▶ If the company **misrepresented** facts about properties or the owners, the investors could force the lender to take the loans back at full value. 同社が所有権または所有者について事実を誤って伝えた場合，投資家は貸し手にローンを全額戻すことを強制できる．

representational

[接頭] (non) **nonrepresentational** *adj* 非具象的な

representative

[接頭] (un) **unrepresentative** *adj* (～を) 代表していない

represented

[接頭] (un) **unrepresented** *adj* 〈議会などに〉代表を送っていない

repressible

[接頭] (ir) **irrepressible** *adj* 抑制できない

reproachable

[接頭] (ir) **irreproachable** *adj* 欠点のない

reputable

[接頭] (dis) **disreputable** *adj* 評判の悪い，みっともない

repute

[接頭] (dis) **disrepute** *n* 不評，悪評，不人気

research

[接頭] (ill) **ill-researched** *adj* 調査が不徹底な

[接頭] (un) **unresearched** *adj* 研究されていない ▶ People

send out appallingly **unresearched** and generic requests. 人々は, 驚くほどに調査が不十分で包括的な要求を出してくる.

reserved

接頭 (un) **unreserved** *adj* 遠慮のない

resettable

接頭 (non) **nonresettable** *adj* 非リセット(式)の, リセットできない ▸ **Nonresettable** or one-shot IDCIs are recommended when a single immersion renders appliances unsafe or unreliable. 1回浸漬して器具に安全性がなかったり信頼がおけない場合は, 非リセット式または, ワンショット IDCI を推奨する.

resident

接頭 (non) **nonresident** *n* 非居住者

—— *adj*

❶〈ソフトウェアなどが〉非常駐の ▸ a **nonresident** program 非常駐型プログラム

❷ 非居住の ▸ These companies, financed by stock sales to **nonresident** as well as resident investors, constructed irrigation projects. これらの会社は, 居住投資家と同じく非居住投資家への株式の売却による資金で灌漑施設を建設した.

residential

接頭 (non) **nonresidential** *adj* 非居住用の ▸ At the same time, let's broaden the definition of eligible investment assets to include **nonresidential** buildings. 同時に, 適格とされる投資財産の定義を広げて非住居用ビルを含めることにしよう.

resist

接尾 (less) **resistless** *adj* 無抵抗の

resistance

接頭 (non) **nonresistance** *n* 無抵抗

resistant

接頭 (non) **nonresistant** *adj* 無抵抗の, 非抵抗性の ▸ Thus **nonresistant** bacteria can be transformed into resistant ones by exposure to a medium in which ... このようにして非抵抗性バクテリアを…である培地にさらすことにより，抵抗性バクテリアに変えることができる.

resistible

接頭 (ir) **irresistible** *adj*

❶ 抵抗できない ▸ The **irresistible** force of technological change has led even the most hard-line of PTT monopolies into a reappraisal of their national telecommunication policies. 技術変化のいやおうのない[抵抗できない]力は，最も変わりにくいPTTの独占ですら，国の遠距離通信政策の見直しへと向かわせている.

❷ 非常に魅力的な ▸ The taste of burnt rice and soy sauce blended well together, and this indescribably fragrant taste I found **irresistible**. お焦げと醤油の味がうまく混じり合い，何とも香ばしい味が非常に魅力的だった. ▸ For the couple, the educational opportunities were **irresistible**. そのカップルにとって，教育の機会は非常に魅力的であった.

resistibly

接頭 (ir) **irresistibly** *ad* 抵抗できずに，いや応なく ▸ Retailers have been drawn **irresistibly** toward an event that occurs only once every 75 years. 小売業者たちは，75年に1回しかめぐってこないイベントにいや応なく引きつけられている.

resisting

接頭 (un) **unresisting** *adj* 抵抗しない ▸ When one splits at one blow an **unresisting** piece without any knots, the result is a straight, nicely shaped piece of firewood. 節目のない素直なところを割るときは，本当に一発で，素直な美しい形の薪に仕上がる.

resolute

接頭 (ir) **irresolute** *adj* 決断力のない

resolvable

接頭 (un) **unresolvable** *adj* 解決できない ▸ Why is this crisis

so **unresolvable**? この危機はなぜそんなに解決できないものなのであろうか.

resolved

接頭 (un) **unresolved** *adj* 未解決の ▸ Turbulence modeling is **unresolved**. 乱気流のモデリングは未解決である. ▸ By the time of the September board meeting, one big issue remained **unresolved**. 9月の役員会までには一つの大きな問題が未解決のままであった.

respect

接頭 (dis) **disrespect** *n* 失礼, 無礼 ▸ He showed **disrespect** for the PM by ignoring his advice. 彼は, 総理大臣のアドバイスを無視するという無礼を働いた.

respective

接頭 (ir) **irrespective** *adj*

❶ ～に関係なく ▸ Freight trains increasingly are run on schedules, leaving at the appointed time **irrespective** of the cars and tonnage then available. 貨物列車はますます定刻に運行するようになり, 指定された時刻に, それまでに集まった貨車やトン数に関係なく出発する. ▸ We need a strategy or a set of strategies that can be successful almost **irrespective** of what the world looks like. 我々は, 世界がどのようになるかにほとんど関係なく成功できる計画を必要とする.

❷ ～にかかわりなく ▸ All convalescent patients, **irrespective** of age, should be encouraged to rest for at least an hour every afternoon, preferably on the bed where they can really relax. すべての回復期の患者は, 年齢にかかわりなく, 午後はいつも少なくとも1時間, 望ましくは本当にくつろぐことができるベッドで休むことを奨励されるべきである. ▸ In addition there may be an expiry date, which must be observed **irrespective** of the date on which the drops are opened. さらには有効期限があり, 点眼液を開栓した日付にかかわらずその期限には注意しなければならない.

responsibility

接頭 (ir) **irresponsibility** *n*

❶ 無責任, 責任無能力 ► Staff members should avoid any comments implying parental inadequacy, **irresponsibility**, or other fault as the cause of FTT. スタッフは, 発育不全(FTT)の原因として親の不適格性, 無責任, またはその他の過失を暗示するいかなる発言も避けなければならない.

❷ 無責任な行為 [人] ► That **irresponsibility** will become a thing of the past if the leader gets his way. リーダーが自分の意思を貫徹すれば, その無責任は過去のものになる.

responsible

接頭 (ir) **irresponsible** *adj* 無責任な ► There's an **irresponsible** and nonsensical statement for you! 何と無責任で無意味な発言でしょう. ► They are approaching it in the most **irresponsible** way possible. 彼らは, それ以上は考えられないような無責任なやり方で, それに取り組んでいる. ► I sometimes get angry at the extremely **irresponsible** way in which color is complacently used. あまりにも無責任な色使いが平然となされているのにはときに腹が立つ. ► Worst of all, he said, was the ballooning U.S. debt, which had prompted him to stop buying long-term bonds from the "**irresponsible** and fiscally inept" government. 彼が言うには, 何よりも悪いのは膨れあがる米国の負債であって, そのために彼は「無責任で財政的に能力を欠いた政府」から長期債を買うのをやめてしまった.

responsive

接頭 (ir) **irresponsive** *adj* 反応のない

接頭 (un) **unresponsive** *adj* 反応が鈍い ► Initially they may be shocked and **unresponsive**, however much the death was expected. 最初はショックを受け, 反応できなくなるが, そのような死は予想されていたものである.

rest

接尾 (less) **restless** *adj* 気が休まらない, 落ち着かない ► If

the patient is **restless** and fails to sleep, other drugs may be prescribed. もし，患者が気が落ち着かず，睡眠を取ることができないなら，他の薬を処方する場合もある． ▶ In spite of his eagerness to get home, he is often **restless** and depressed, finding it hard to settle down. 彼は，家に帰りたいと強く願っていたにもかかわらず，しばしば不安を覚えたりふさぎ込んだりして，気持ちを落ち着けるのは難しいと感じている．

接頭 (un) **unrest** *n* (政治的な) 不安，不穏，動揺 ▶ The **unrest** was spreading throughout the nation. 社会的不安感が国中に広がった． ▶ Take oil prices, which soared recently as **unrest** set in across the Middle East. 石油価格を見てみよう．石油価格は中東で政情不安が広がり始めた最近になって急騰した． ▶ Business leaders cannot be bystanders, he says, adding that he's concerned that the Occupy Wall Street movement is a harbinger of social **unrest**.「ビジネスリーダーは傍観者であることはできない」と彼は言って,「ウォール街を占拠せよ運動」は社会不安の前兆ではないかと心配している旨を付け加えた．

restrained

接頭 (un) **unrestrained** *adj* 抑制されていない

restraint

接頭 (un) **unrestraint** *n* 無抑制，無拘束

restrict

接頭 (de) **derestrict** *v* 統制 [制限] を解除する

接頭 (un) **unrestrict** *v* 制限しない，拘束しない ▶ It was most important to ensure that the bore in the weld region was **unrestricted**. 溶接部の穴は制限されないことを確実にすることが最も重要であった．

restrictive

接頭 (non) **nonrestrictive** *adj* 非制限的な

retrievable

接頭 (ir) **irretrievable** *adj* 取り返しのつかない ▶ any irreversible and **irretrievable** commitments of resources 非可逆で取り返しできない資源の投入

returnable

接頭 (non) **nonreturnable** *adj* 回収不能の, 返却されない ▶ Note: there is a **nonreturnable** deposit of 10% of the total due for all bookings. ご注意: 予約される場合は(たとえキャンセルしても)支払うべき総額の10%は返却されない保証金となります.

reverence

接頭 (ir) **irreverence** *n* 無礼, 非礼

reverent

接頭 (ir) **irreverent** *adj* 無礼な ▶ His job offers are littered with **irreverent** and indefensible "conditions." 彼の求人には, 応募者側にとって無礼で防ぎようがない「条件」が満載だった.

reversible

接頭 (ir) **irreversible** *adj*

❶ 撤回できない, もとに戻せない ▶ The trend to telecommunication deregulation is **irreversible**. 遠隔通信許認可規制撤廃の動きは, もとに戻せない[撤回できない]. ▶ Global connectivity through trade has remained strong, and is likely to be an **irreversible** trend, for at least two reasons. 貿易を通した世界の結びつきは強いままで, 少なくとも二つの理由で, この傾向はもとに戻りそうにない.

❷ 不可逆的な ▶ With the coolant gone, superheated steam could have triggered a series of **irreversible** reactions leading to a meltdown of the fuel and ... 冷却剤がなくなって, 加熱蒸気が一連の非可逆反応を生起させて燃料と…のメルトダウンを引き起こした可能性がある. ▶ The outside world sees China as a rising economic power, a nation with seemingly **irreversible** economic momentum. 諸外国は中国を, 新興の経済大国で, 表面上不可逆的な経済の勢いをもつ国とみなしている. ▶

The cooling achievable by an **irreversible** process is represented in Fig.1. 不可逆過程によって得られる冷却を図1に示す.

reversibly

[接頭] (ir) **irreversibly** *ad*

❶ もとに戻せずに ► Under heat and pressure, the powder melts and flows into all parts of the mold cavity, the resin cross-links thus becoming **irreversibly** hardened. 熱と圧力を受けると粉末は溶けて鋳型の空洞のすべての部分に流入し, それによって樹脂のクロスリンクが非可逆的に硬化される.

❷ 不可逆的に ► Heat flows **irreversibly** from a high- to a low-temperature zone. 熱は, 高温の部分から低温の部分へと不可逆的に流れる. ► It poisons the enzyme **irreversibly**. それは不可逆的に酵素の作用を損なわせる. ► Climate change will **irreversibly** alter the planet. 気候変動が惑星を不可逆的に変える.

reversing

[接頭] (non) **non-reversing** *adj* 反転不能の, 非逆転の ► Gas turbines are arranged in a variety of ways to drive a ship, using **non-reversing** gears, reversing gears, and electric drives of various types. ガスタービンは, 非逆転装置, 逆転装置, 多種の電気駆動を用いて船を様々なやり方で動かせるようになっている.

revised

[接頭] (un) **unrevised** *adj* 未修正の, 未改正の ► The book is still **unrevised**. その本はまだ改訂されていない.

revocable

[接頭] (ir) **irrevocable** *adj* 取り消せない ► This involves an **irrevocable** error. これには, 修正できない[取り消せない]エラーがある.

rewarded

[接頭] (un) **unrewarded** *adj* 報われない

rewarding

[接頭] (un) **unrewarding** *adj* 報いのない

rib

[接尾] (less) **ribless** *adj* 補強材のない

righteous

[接頭] (un) **unrighteous** *adj* 高潔でない，邪悪な

rigid

[接頭] (non) **nonrigid** *adj* 硬くない ► be designed to fill rigid and **nonrigid** containers such as glass, metal, plastic, paper, etc. ガラスや金属，プラスチック，紙など，硬い容器にも硬くない容器にも使えるように設計されている

rim

[接尾] (less) **rimless** *adj* 縁なしの ► At 60, even in a clean white shirt and **rimless** spectacles, Page still looks like a farmer. 60歳になって，清潔な白いシャツを着て，縁のない眼鏡をかけてもページは農夫のように見える.

ripe

[接頭] (un) **unripe** *adj* 〈果実などが〉熟していない ► What acids do **unripe** fruits have? 熟していない果物にはどのような酸が含まれているか.

rivaled

[接頭] (un) **unrivaled** *adj* 競争相手のない，比類のない ► Fine ceramic is **unrivaled** in strength. ファインセラミックは，比類のない強度を持っている. ► It stands **unrivaled** in the world. それは世界に比類がない. ► benefits from our **unrivaled** experience and know-how 他が太刀打ちできない経験とノウハウから得られる利点

robe

[接頭] (dis) **disrobe** *v* 衣服を脱ぐ

roll

[接頭] (un) **unroll** *v*

❶〈巻かれた紙やテープなどを〉開く，巻き戻す ► She places

the new sheet on the bed and tucks it in, then **unrolls** it to meet the soiled sheet. 看護師は新しいシートをベッドの上に置き，その端を押し込み，そして汚れたシートに接するまで巻き戻す.

❷ 明らかにする ► The ride **unrolled** a pristine scene of success. こうして運転するうちに成功への本来の姿が見えた.

roof

接尾 (less) **roofless** *adj* 屋根のない

接頭 (un) **unroof** *v* 屋根をはがす

root

接尾 (less) **rootless** *adj* 根のない，不安定な ► The **rootless** lifestyle made school difficult to keep up with, so he had to quit in fifth grade. その不安定な生活スタイルでは学校についていくのが難しくなり，彼は5年生でやめざるをえなかった.

接頭 (un) **unroot** *v* 根絶する

rotational

接頭 (ir) **irrotational** *adj* 交互に変わらない ► For fluids of low viscosity, such as air or water, **irrotational** flow may be approached in a free vortex. 例えば空気または水などのような粘度が低い液体では，自由渦内で渦なし流れに近くなることがある.

routine

接頭 (non) **non-routine** *adj* 非日常的な，非恒常的な ► **non-routine** work 非定型業務

rudder

接尾 (less) **rudderless** *adj*

❶ 舵のない

❷ 指導者のいない

ruffled

接頭 (un) **unruffled** *adj* 動揺していない

rule

接尾 (less) **ruleless** *adj* 制約されない

ruly

接頭 (un) **unruly** *adj* 規則に従わない，言うことを聞かない ► A Government oceanographer abruptly realized he was looking at the mysterious natural engine that drives El Niño, the **unruly** fluctuation of weather. 政府の海洋学者は，不規則な天候の変動であるエルニーニョを動かす神秘的な自然のエンジンを見ているのだと突然実感した．

Russian

接頭 (non) **non-Russian** *adj* 非ロシアの ► The **non-Russian** Slavs looked up to the Russians. 非ロシア系スラブ民族はロシア人を尊敬した．

rust

接尾 (less) **rustless** *adj* 錆びない，錆びていない ► The **rustless** chain has outstanding corrosion resistance because its surface is Ni-plated. この錆びないチェーンは，表面にニッケルメッキを施しているので，優れた耐腐食性を備えている．

rusting

接頭 (non) **nonrusting** *adj* 非錆質の ► **Nonrusting** siding nails are often set flush with the surface of the wood, in which case puttying is unnecessary. 不錆性のサイディング用釘は，木材の表面と同一面まで沈めることがあり，その場合は，パテ盛りは不要である．

ruth

接尾 (less) **ruthless** *adj* 無慈悲な ► Which is worth more, the life of an innocent baby or the life of a **ruthless** murderer? 無垢な赤ちゃんと凶悪殺人犯，どちらの命が大事でしょうか．

接尾 (less) **ruthlessness** *n* 無慈悲さ ► He had a nice balance between academic **ruthlessness** and people skills. 彼は，学問的な非情さ［無慈悲さ］と人との関係づくりのうまさのよいバランス感覚を持っていた．

S

saddle

［接尾］(less) **saddleless** *adj* サドルのない

［接頭］(un) **unsaddle** *v* 〈馬から〉鞍を外す

safe

［接頭］(un) **unsafe** *adj* 安全でない，危険な ► Even for the most tolerant crops a concentration of boron exceeding 4mg/liter is considered **unsafe**. 最も耐性のある穀物でさえ，4mg/L を超えるホウ素が濃縮することは危険だと考えられる．

said

［接頭］(un) **unsaid** *adj* 〈思っていることなどを〉口に出さない

salable

［接頭］(un) **unsalable** *adj* 売れない

salinize

［接頭］(de) **desalinize** *v* 塩分を除く，脱塩する

［接頭］(de) **desalinization** *n* 脱塩すること，　脱塩 ► Dual-purpose reactors have been proposed for water **desalinization** plants: the heat generated would be used in both A and B. 二重目的原子炉は水の脱塩用プラントとしてもくろまれている．つまり発生熱が A と B との両者において利用されるのである．

salt

［接頭］(de) **desalt** *v* 脱塩する

［接尾］(less) **saltless** *adj* 塩気のない，塩分のない ► Enjoy our collection of **saltless** recipes submitted, reviewed and rated by B society. B 協会が評価し，チェックして提出した塩分のないレシピのコレクションをお楽しみください．

salted

［接頭］(de) **desalted** *adj* 脱塩した ► How far inland **desalted** water can be pumped is another issue. どの程度まで内陸に脱

塩水を輸送するかは，また別問題である．

sane

接頭 (in) **insane** *adj* 正気でない ▸ It is just the ramblings of an **insane** person. それは，正気ではない人間のとりとめのない話にすぎない．

sanely

接頭 (in) **insanely** *ad* 正気でなく，非常識に ▸ It's profit expectations — they're **insanely** optimistic. それは利益予想であるので，彼らは非常識にも楽観的である．

sanitary

接頭 (in) **insanitary** *adj* 不衛生な ▸ The resurgence of diseases such as cholera and plague is due largely to the rapid growth of **insanitary** urban areas. コレラやペストといった疾病の復活は，不衛生な都市の急速な拡大によるところが非常に大きい．

接頭 (un) **unsanitary** *adj* 不衛生な ▸ The cells shown in the photographs were in an unkept and **unsanitary** state. 写真に写っている独房は，ほったらかしで不衛生な状態であった．

sanity

接頭 (in) **insanity** *n* 狂気の沙汰，愚かしいこと

sap

接尾 (less) **sapless** *adj*

❶樹液のない

❷活力のない

satiable

接頭 (in) **insatiable** *adj* 飽きることのない，貪欲な ▸ Then, between the ages of 1 and 6, appetite increases, often becoming **insatiable**. その後，1～6歳の間に食欲は増し，貪欲なまでになる．

satisfaction

接頭 (dis) **dissatisfaction** *n* 不満，　不満の種 ▸ There is a general **dissatisfaction** with ... 一般に，…に対して不満があ

る. ▸ **dissatisfaction** with the company's strategy 会社の戦略に対する不満

satisfactory

接頭 (dis) **dissatisfactory** *adj* 不満足な, 不満の原因となる ▸ The judge was **dissatisfactory** to anyone. その判決は, 誰にとっても不満であった.

接頭 (un) **unsatisfactory** *adj* 不満足な, 不十分な ▸ In such cases amplitude modulation is **unsatisfactory**. このような場合, 振幅変調は満足のいくものではない. ▸ An **unsatisfactory** paint job can be caused by any of the following: 塗装作業は, 次の不具合のどれによっても結果が不良になる.

satisfied

接頭 (dis) **dissatisfied** *adj* 不満足な ▸ Even so, I have never felt particularly **dissatisfied**. そうであったとしても, 私は特に不満を感じたことはなかった. ▸ Women often are made technical copy editors on the theory that they are less likely than men to become **dissatisfied** with a static job. 女性は男性に比較して静的な仕事に不満足を感じることが少ないとの理論で技術資料の編集者にされることがある.

接頭 (un) **unsatisfied** *adj* 不満な, 満たされていない

satisfy

接頭 (dis) **dissatisfy** *v* 不満に思う ▸ Naturally the Indians were **dissatisfied** with the situation in which they found themselves, and ... アメリカ原住民は, 当然に自分たちが置かれている立場を不満に思っていた.

satisfying

接頭 (un) **unsatisfying** *adj* 満足できない ▸ Most people do not like to be restricted to items which they probably regard as **unsatisfying** and inadequately "filling." ほとんどの人は嫌いなもの[満足できない]ものや満喫できないと感じるものに限定されたくない.

saturate

接頭 (de) **desaturate** *v* 非飽和させる ▶ In the packet shifting mechanism, the saturated ESR signal is partially **desaturated** by a shift of the resonance line due to the change of local field. パケットシフティング機構では，ESR 飽和信号は，地域磁場の変化による共鳴線のシフトによって部分的には非飽和となる．

接頭 (un) **unsaturate** *v* 飽和しない ▶ The fatty acids may be **unsaturated**, having one or more carbon atoms in the chain joined by two bonds as in oleic acid. 脂肪酸は，一つ以上の炭素原子がオレイン酸のように二重結合によって連鎖に入っているため飽和されていない．

saturated

接頭 (non) **nonsaturated** *adj* 不飽和の ▶ Under the action of heat alone, a **nonsaturated** carbide can fix hydrogen, and finally yield compounds analogous to petroleum. 不飽和のカーバイドは，熱の作用だけで水素を固定することができ，結局，石油に類似した化合物を作り出す．

接頭 (un) **unsaturated** *adj* 不飽和状態の ▶ A typical oil gas consists of saturated and **unsaturated** hydrocarbons, and . . . 典型的な油性ガスは飽和および不飽和炭化水素でできており，….

saturation

接頭 (un) **unsaturation** *n* 不飽和状態 ▶ **Unsaturation** is measured as iodine value, calculated as the percent iodine absorbed by the fat. 不飽和はヨウ素価として測定される．すなわち，脂質に吸収されたヨウ素のパーセンテージで表される．

saved

接頭 (un) **unsaved** *adj* 未セーブの，保存していない ▶ Power failures, glitches, human error, or even program error can cause you to lose valuable, **unsaved** data. 電源故障，誤作動，ヒューマンエラーなど，またはプログラムエラーでさえ，セーブし

ていない貴重なデータが失われる原因になることがある.

savory

接頭 (un) **unsavory** *adj* (道徳的に)好ましくない ▸ Sometimes we try to justify this **unsavory** business on the cynical ground that by rationing out the means of violence we can somehow control the world's violence. 我々は時に, 武器を供給することにより何とかして世界中で起きている暴力を鎮静化するという皮肉な論拠によりこの好まれざる任務を正当化しようとしている. ▸ That leaves Lipitor users in the odd position of rooting for Ranbaxy, a company with some **unsavory** history. このことはリピトール使用者を, よろしくない経歴を持つ会社ランバクシー社の設立にとって奇妙な立場に置くことになる.

say

接頭 (un) **unsay** *adj* 〈前言を〉取り消す

scale

接頭 (de) **descale** *v* 湯あかを取り除く

scathed

接頭 (un) **unscathed** *adj*

❶ 無事で ▸ Why were extinctions so selective, devastating some species while leaving others virtually **unscathed**? 一部の種を壊滅させる一方で他の種はほとんど無事に残るように, なぜ絶滅がそのように選択的に起きたのか.

❷ 無傷の ▸ Meanwhile, Google's competitor Baidu seemed to hum along **unscathed**. 一方グーグルの競合バイドゥは無傷で好調のようであった. ▸ There are some who claim my pacifism is unrealistic and ask what I would do were Japan attacked, but the adversary would not escape **unscathed**. 私の平和主義は非現実的であると主張し, 日本が攻撃されたらどうするのかと尋ねる者もいた. しかし敵は無傷では逃げられなかった.

scent

接尾 (less) **scentless** *adj* 無臭の，無香性の

scheduled

接頭 (non) **nonscheduled** *adj* 不定期の ► ABC sometimes operates aircraft on a **nonscheduled** basis. ABC社は不定期便の航空機を運航することがある.

接頭 (un) **unscheduled** *adj* 予定していない，臨時の ► **Unscheduled** trains are not unusual in the sightseeing season. 観光シーズンには臨時列車は珍しくない.

schooled

接頭 (un) **unschooled** *adj* 学校教育を受けていない

scientific

接頭 (non) **nonscientific** *adj* 非科学的な ► There are three types of **nonscientific** sampling, namely: (1) purposive sampling, (2) incidental sampling, and (3) quota sampling. 非科学的サンプリングには3種類あり，それらは，(1) 有意サンプリング，(2) 偶発的サンプリング，(3) 割り当てサンプリングである.

接頭 (un) **unscientific** *adj* 非科学的な ► The creation model is **unscientific** for a number of reasons. その創造モデルは多くの理由で非科学的であるといえる.

scientifically

接頭 (un) **unscientifically** *ad* 非科学的に

score

接尾 (less) **scoreless** *adj* 無得点の ► The Whitecaps remained unbeaten with a **scoreless** draw against the Philadelphia Union on Saturday. 土曜日の試合でホワイトカップスは，フィラデルフィア・ユニオンと0対0で引き分けた.

scramble

接頭 (un) **unscramble** *v*

❶ 〈状態を〉もとに戻す

❷ 〈暗号などを〉解読する

scrambling

接頭 (un) **unscrambling** *adj*

❶解読する

❷スクランブルを解く ► Special receivers may contain **unscrambling** devices which cause the receiver to synchronize and produce a normal picture. 特別の受信機には，同期を取り正常画像を生成するためにスクランブルを解く装置が入っていることがある.

screened

接頭 (un) **unscreened** *adj*

❶遮蔽されていない

❷ふるいにかけていない，保安検査を受けていない

❸〈映画が〉上映されていない

screw

接頭 (un) **unscrew** *adj* ねじを緩める

scripted

接頭 (un) **unscripted** *adj* 台本のない，即興の，計画に入っていない，思いがけない ► There was so much one could learn in an **unscripted** hour with Jobs that my top editors at Fortune in New York City timed trips so that they could tag along on my windows with him. 思いがけないジョブズ氏との面会には，学べるものが多くあったため，ニューヨークの「フォーチュン」誌のトップ・エディターは滞在時間を延ばすほどであった. このため彼らは私のインタビューに付き合うことができた.

scrupulous

接頭 (un) **unscrupulous** *adj* 不謹慎な，破廉恥な

scrutable

接頭 (in) **inscrutable** *adj* 不可解な，計り知れない ► If a person or their expression is **inscrutable,** it is very hard to know what they are really thinking or what they mean. 人や表現が不可解である場合，その人が本当に考えていることやその表現

が意味することを理解するのは非常に難しい.

接頭 (in) **inscrutably** *ad* 不可解そうに ▸ He replied **inscrutably**, "What you focus on in life is what you create." 彼は,「人生で人が最も集中すべきは何を創造するかということなのだ」と不可解そうに答えた.

seal

接頭 (un) **unseal** *v* 封印を解く, 開封する

sealed

接頭 (un) **unsealed** *adj*

❶封をしていない

❷押印されていない

seam

接尾 (less) **seamless** *adj* 縫い目［継ぎ目］のない, シームレスの ▸ Tubular steel products are classified according to two principal methods of manufacture, namely the welded and **seamless** methods. 管状の鋼鉄製品は, 二つの主要な製造法, すなわち溶接法とシームレス法によって分類される.

接尾 (less) **seamlessly** *ad* 途切れなく, 常に ▸ Only Raytheon's Patriot system can **seamlessly** communicate with other U.S. launchers in the area. レイソン社のパトリオットシステムだけがこの地域の米国製の発射装置と常に通信することができる.

searchable

接頭 (un) **unsearchable** *adj* 調査できない, 不可解な, 究明できない ▸ how to make a page **unsearchable** in blog search ブログ検索で検索できないようにするには

seasonable

接頭 (un) **unseasonable** *adj* 季節外れの ▸ reduce crop damage caused by **unseasonable** frosts 季節外れの結霜による作物の被害を減らす

seasonably

接頭 (un) **unseasonably** *ad* 季節外れに

seasoned

接頭 (un) **unseasoned** *adj* 味付けされていない

seat

接頭 (un) **unseat** *v*

❶〈人やものをもとのところから〉外す ▶ A nonlubricated-plug valve may use a tapered plug with a mechanical lifting device that **unseats** the plug. 非潤滑式プラグバルブでは，プラグを外す機械式持ち上げ装置があるテーパー付きプラグが使用されている．

❷〈もとの状態などを〉取り戻す ▶ pool their resources to **unseat** traditional U.S. market dominance 伝統的なアメリカの市場支配の席を奪うために資源をプールする

sectarian

接頭 (non) **nonsectarian** *adj* 特定の宗派［会派］に属さない ▶ It is easy to embrace the idea of **nonsectarian** spiritual values when we focus on a few key ones: kindness, courage, willingness, self-control, and honesty. いくつかの重要なこと，すなわち優しさ，勇気，意欲，自制心，誠実さなどに注目すれば，どの宗派にも属さない精神的価値観を受け入れることは簡単である．

secure

接頭 (in) **insecure** *adj* 自信のない，不安定な，不安な ▶ The unfamiliarity of hospital combines with any pain or uncomfortable procedures to disturb the child and make him feel **insecure**. 不慣れな病院の雰囲気と何らかの痛みや不快な処置が合わさって，子どもを動揺させ，不安な気持ちにさせる． ▶ The patient will probably feel **insecure** and need the support of those around him. 患者はおそらく不安を感じるので，周りの人のサポートを必要とする．

secured

接頭 (un) **unsecured** *adj*

❶安全でない

❷ 無担保の ► For instance, an investment in U.S. Treasuries carries lower risk (we hope) than an **unsecured** credit card line. たとえば，米国財務省証券への投資は，無担保の貸出限度額よりリスクは低い（ことを願う）.

security

接頭 (in) **insecurity** *adj* 不安定，不確実 ► Well-grounded, affable, nary a twitch of neurosis or **insecurity** about him. 十分な教育を受け，丁寧で，彼については人格障害や不安感は感じられなかった.

seed

接尾 (less) **seedless** *adj* 種なしの

seeded

接頭 (un) **unseeded** *adj*

❶ 種のない

❷ ノーシードの

seeing

接頭 (un) **unseeing** *adj* 目の見えない

seemly

接頭 (un) **unseemly** *ad* 下品な，見苦しい ► It is disgusting to see them making an **unseemly** spectacle of themselves by singing drunkenly in the street at the top of their lungs. 彼らが街中で放吟しつつ酩酊の醜態をさらすのは，見るだに不快だ.

► The **unseemly** state of affairs in the Diet makes a mockery of my sermon that each and every one of them can transform politics. 国会の見苦しい現状は，彼らのだれもが政治を変えることができるという私の訓戒を嘲笑している.

seen

接頭 (un) **unseen** *adj* (目に)見えない，予測できない ► But it nonetheless generates a degree of cooperation **unseen** at large organizations. しかし，それにもかかわらず，それは大きな組織ではいまだ例がないほどの協力関係を作り出す.

segregate

[接頭] (de) **desegregate** *v* 人種差別をなくす

segregated

[接頭] (un) **unsegregated** *adj*

❶分離されない

❷人種差別をしない

select

[接頭] (de) **deselect** *v*

❶訓練から外す

❷拒否する

❸除外する

selective

[接頭] (non) **nonselective** *adj* 非選択性の，非選択的な，選択しない

[接頭] (un) **unselective** *adj* 無作為の，任意の ► It is not allowed to cover the heat pipes with **unselective** coating. 無作為に選んだ［任意の］被覆材でヒートパイプをカバーすることは許されていない．

self

[接頭] (non) **nonself** *adj* 非自己の ► One of the more devastating errors of the immune system involves its failure to distinguish between self and **nonself**, resulting in so-called autoimmune diseases. 免疫系のさらに破壊的な誤りの一つは，自己と非自己の区別ができないことであり，その結果いわゆる自己免疫疾患を引き起こすことになる．

[接尾] (less) **selfless** *adj* 利己心のない，無私無欲の

selfconscious

[接頭] (un) **unselfconscious** *adj* 自分を意識しない

selfconsciously

[接頭] (un) **unselfconsciously** *ad* 自分を意識せずに

selfish

[接頭] (un) **unselfish** *adj* 利己的でない ► I will forever be

grateful for his **unselfish** willingness to share and teach. 私は，彼の，分かち合い，教えようという無私の積極的な献身に永遠に感謝するであろう．

selfishly

接頭 (un) **unselfishly** *ad* 利己的でなく， 寛大に ▶ In the meantime, all we can do is to work patiently, fearlessly, and **unselfishly** to an end that we think is right. しばらくの間，我々のできることは，正しいと思うことを終わりまで，根気よく，恐れずに，寛大に取り組むことである．

sensate

接頭 (in) **insensate** *adj* 感覚のない

sense

接頭 (non) **nonsense** *n* 無意味なこと，ナンセンス ▶ Any competent economics instructor would give you an F if you asserted the same sort of **nonsense** on an exam. あなたが試験で同じように無意味なことを主張した場合，どんな有能な経済学講師でもあなたに不可を与えるだろう． ▶ He was an author who belonged to the school of writing known as **nonsense** literature which came into vogue at one period before the war. 彼は戦前の一時期に台頭したナンセンス文学と呼ばれる一派に属する作家であった．

接尾 (less) **senseless** *adj*

❶ 無意味な，ナンセンスな ▶ The December 1st tragedy in Kansas City was a sad and **senseless** action. 12月1日にカンザスシティーで起きた悲劇は，悲しくそして意味のない行為であった．

❷ 感覚のない，人事不省の

sensibility

接頭 (in) **insensibility** *n* 無感知，無感覚

sensible

接頭 (in) **insensible** *adj* 感知しない，感覚のない ▶ **Insensible** losses (evaporative free water losses from the skin and respiratory tract in a ratio of 2:1) account for about 1/2 of maintenance needs. 不感[感覚がない]喪失(2: 1の割合で皮膚と気道から蒸発することによる自由水の喪失)は，維持必要量の約1/2を占める.

sensitive

接頭 (in) **insensitive** *adj*

❶ 感度が低い ► RDX is high-melting, fairly **insensitive**, and the most powerful compound in common use. RDXは融点が高く，適度に感度が低く，一般的な用途では最も強力な接着剤である.

❷ 影響を受けない ► The nozzle is **insensitive** to the rate at which liquid is delivered to it. ノズルは液が流れてくる速さには影響を受けない. ► The best insulators are **insensitive** to moisture and adhere well to the electrodes. 絶縁体は，湿気の影響を受けず，電極によく接着するものが最良である.

❸ 無神経な ► That analogy is both overstated and **insensitive**. そういう類推は大げさだし，無神経だ. ► I have no faith in writers who have an **insensitive** palate. 私は無神経な趣味の文筆家を信用しない.

sensitivity

接頭 (in) **insensitivity** *n* 不感度，無感性 ► TNT derives its important virtues from its relative **insensitivity** to shock and its convenient melting point. TNTは，相対的に衝撃に無感性であり，融点が手ごろであることを長所としている. ► A decrease in contractions in the large intestine or an **insensitivity** of the rectum to the presence of stool results in severe, chronic constipation. 大腸の収縮が減少したり，直腸が大便の存在に無感性であると，重症の慢性便秘になります.

sensitize

接頭 (de) **desensitize** *v*

❶ 感度を減ずる ► The FAA plans to **desensitize** the aircraft when they are in dense traffic areas to cut down on spectrum usage. FAA は航空機が交通量の大なる区域にあるときにはスペクトル使用を減らすように，航空機の感度を抑制するプランがある．

❷ フィルムの感光度を下げる

sensitizer

[接頭] (de) **desensitizer** *n* 減感剤，感度抑制剤 ▸ The most common moisture is Composition B, which contains about 60% RDX, 40% TNT, and some wax as a **desensitizer**. 最も普通の水分は合成物 B であり，これは約60% の RDX，40% の TNT，および感度抑制剤としてワックスを若干含んでいる．

sentimental

[接頭] (un) **unsentimental** *adj* 感傷的でない

separable

[接頭] (in) **inseparable** *adj*

❶ 分離できない ▸ an electrical circuit that has been fabricated as an **inseparable** assembly of circuit elements in a single structure 単一構造で回路要素の不可分な[分離できない]組立品として製作された電気回路

❷ 切り離せない ▸ China's achievements in revolution and construction are **inseparable** from support by the people of the world. 革命と建設における中国の成功は，世界の人々からの支援と切り離せない．

serial

[接頭] (non) **nonserial** *adj*

❶ 非逐次(的)な ▸ A **nonserial** DP (Degree of Polymerization) problem can be represented in monadic or polyadic form. 非連続性 DP (重合度) 問題は一価元素または多価元素の形状で表される．

❷ 非連続(性)の ▸ In an AND/OR graph representation of **nonserial** problems, edges may connect nodes at any two arbitrary levels. 非逐次的問題の AND/OR グラフ表示においては，エッジはノードを二つの任意レベルのどちらかに接続す

る.

❸順次発生しない

served

[接頭] (ill) **ill-served** *adj* 役に立たない

serviceable

[接頭] (un) **unserviceable** *adj* 役に立たない, 使用できない ▸ The company undertook to repair or replace certain **unserviceable** high-pressure turbines at no extra cost to the USAF. その会社は, 実用にならなくなった高圧タービンを USAF への追加料金なしで修理または交換することを引き受けた.

set

[接頭] (ill) **ill-set** *adj* 取り付けの悪い

[接頭] (un) **unset** *v* 設定を解く ▸ This sets and **unsets** a category to print the category name with its entry. これによって, カテゴリー名を入力と共にプリントするためのカテゴリーがセットされ, セットが外される.

settle

[接頭] (un) **unsettle** *v* 不安定にする, 不安にする

settled

[接頭] (un) **unsettled** *adj*

❶解決されてない ▸ clarify some points previously left **unsettled** 前には解決せずに残されていたいくつかの点を明らかにする

❷不安定にされた ▸ The weather remains **unsettled**. 天気がぐずついている. ▸ Rather than shake up the already **unsettled** company by implementing a new approach ... すでに不安定になった会社を新しい方法で再編するのではなく, ….

settling

[接頭] (un) **unsettling** *adj*

❶不安にする ▸ Probably the most **unsettling** discovery is an adverse model basin report. おそらく, 最も人を不安にする発見は, 反対モデルベイスンレポートであろう.

❷ 解決されていない ▸ The same set of **unsettling** problems is afflicting all the world's developed countries, but still nobody knows what to do about them. 世界中の先進国で解決されていない問題が生じて同じように困っているのに，みんなどうしてよいかわからない．

sewered

接頭 (un) **unsewered** *adj* 下水のない ▸ **unsewered** areas 下水設備のない地域

sex

接頭 (un) **unsex** *n*

❶ 性的能力を失わせる

❷ 性の特徴を失わせる

sexy

接頭 (un) **unsexy** *adj* 魅力のない ▸ Iron Planet, based across the bay from Silicon Valley in Pleasanton, is as **unsexy** as it gets. アイアンプラネットはシリコンバレーから湾を隔てたプレサントンに本拠を置く企業であるが，魅力は全くない．

shade

接尾 (less) **shadeless** *adj* 日陰のない

shaded

接頭 (non) **nonshaded** *adj* 日陰ではない ▸ In the shaded area the daytime CO_2 evolution rate was higher than the nighttime rate and in the **nonshaded** area the inverse was observed. 日陰の領域では，日中の CO_2発生率は夜間の発生率より高かったが，日陰ではない領域では逆の現象が観察された．

接頭 (un) **unshaded** *adj*

❶ 陰になっていない ▸ Induced currents in the shaded coil cause the flux in the shaded portion of the pole to lag the flux in the **unshaded** portion. 日陰になったコイルの誘導電流により，極板の日陰の部分のフラックスが日陰になっていない部分のフラックスを遅れさせる．

❷ 日陰ではない，日の当たる ▸ The **unshaded** region represents the major application area for today's servosystems. 日陰にならない領域が今日のサーボシステムの主な応用分野である.

shadow

[接尾] (less) **shadowless** *adj* 光が遮られてない

shakable

[接頭] (un) **unshakable** *adj* 〈気持ちや信念などを〉動かしがたい

shaken

[接頭] (un) **unshaken** *adj* 揺るがない

shame

[接尾] (less) **shameless** *adj* 恥を知らない，ずうずうしい

shape

[接尾] (less) **shapeless** *adj* 形のない，定形のない ► Natural gas is colorless, **shapeless** and odorless; a combustible gaseous mixture that gives off a great deal of energy when burned. 天然ガスは，無色，無形，無臭の可燃性混合ガスで，燃やすと大量のエネルギーを出す.

shaped

[接頭] (ill) **ill-shaped** *adj* 不格好な

[接頭] (un) **unshaped** *adj* 形のない

shared

[接頭] (un) **unshared** *adj* 分配されていない，共有されていない ► Communication problems at the bicultural negotiation table are contingent upon shared and **unshared** values. 二文化間の交渉テーブルで発生するコミュニケーション上の問題は価値観を共有しているかどうかによる.

sheathe

[接頭] (un) **unsheathe** *adj* 〈刀などを〉さやから抜く

shielded

[接頭] (un) **unshielded** *adj* 保護［シールド］されていない ► employing polyethylene as a dielectric spacer between two uniformly spaced, **unshielded** wires 間隔が一様で，シールドされていない2本のワイヤ間の絶縁スペーサーとしてポリエチレンを使用して，…

shift

[接尾] (less) **shiftless** *adj* 無能な，気力のない

[接頭] (un) **unshift** *adj* (パソコンなどの) シフトを解除する

ship

[接頭] (un) **unship** *v* 〈船から〉 荷を下ろす ► The quarantine station chief may give instructions to the master of the vessel etc. to **unship** or produce the cargo for an examination. 検疫所長は，検査を行うため当該船舶の長に対して，当該貨物を陸揚げし，または提出する旨を指示することができる.

shod

[接頭] (un) **unshod** *adj* 靴を履いていない

shoe

[接尾] (less) **shoeless** *adj* 靴を履いていない

shrink

[接頭] (non) **nonshrink** *adj* 縮まない

shrouded

[接頭] (un) **unshrouded** *adj* 覆いかぶされていない ► analyze shrouded and **unshrouded** impellers シュラウドありおよびシュラウドなしのインペラーを分析する

sight

[接尾] (less) **sightless** *adj* 目の見えない ► Several pellets were lodged in his eyes, leaving him **sightless**. 何発かの弾丸が彼の目に打ち込まれた，その結果彼は視力を失った[目が見えなくなった].

[接頭] (un) **unsight** *adj* 調べることなく

sightliness

[接頭] (un) **unsightliness** *n* 見場の悪さ ► the **unsightliness** of an enormous pit mine in the distance 遠方にある巨大な縦穴式採掘場の見場の悪さ

sightly

接頭 (un) **unsightly** *adj* 目障りな ▶ In hanging out the wash, the housewife arranges it neatly on the clothes line so it dries quickly and does not look **unsightly**. 洗濯物を干すにしても，主婦は，バランスよく乾きやすく見苦しくないように工夫して干す. ▶ The city should remove **unsightly** signboards such as those telling motorists to "drive slowly." 市当局は見境なく設置されている「速度を落とせ」などの目障りな標識を取り除くべきだ.

signed

接頭 (un) **unsigned** *adj* 署名のない

significant

接頭 (in) **insignificant** *adj*

❶ 重要でない，大きくない ▶ . . . because you may waste energy on replying to **insignificant** messages that should be reserved for more important matters. …より重要なことのために保存しておくべきエネルギーを重要度の低いメッセージに対応するために適用することになりかねないので ▶ The Minamata Disease problem is not so simple or **insignificant** that it can be written off in an article that merely says "there are lots of sham patients." ただ「ニセ患者が多い」と記事に書いて済ませられるほど水俣病問題は単純でも重要でないわけでもない.

❷ わずかな ▶ The convection currents set up in the confined spaces are **insignificant** and can cause little heat transfer. 狭い空間での対流は問題にはならず，伝熱もわずかだ. ▶ In the last five years, female students in his program have increased from an **insignificant** number to 10 percent. 最近の5年間で彼のプログラムに参加する女子学生は微々たる［わずかな］人数から10パーセントへと増加した. ▶ . . . but repeatedly describing them as financially **insignificant** to him, merely recreational and simply a way to spice up an otherwise drab weekend. …であるが，それらは彼にとって金銭的にはわずかであり，単に気晴らしで，そうでもしなければ退屈な週末に趣を添えるものだと繰り返し述べている．

similar

接頭 (dis) **dissimilar** *adj* 似ていない，異なった ► This is best achieved through a constraint analysis that allows for direct comparisons of **dissimilar** opportunities vying for limited resources. これは，限られた資源を求めて競争している異なる機会を直接比較できる，制約解析を通して達成するのが最もよい．

similarity

接頭 (dis) **dissimilarity** *n* 相違

sin

接尾 (less) **sinless** *adj* 罪のない

sincere

接頭 (in) **insincere** *adj*

❶ 誠意のない

❷ 偽善的な，わざとらしい ► Using a casual expression for a major favor sounds rude and using a very polite expression for a minor favor sounds **insincere**. ひとかたならぬ世話を受けた相手にくだけた表現を使うと失礼に響き，反対に些細なことに丁重なお礼を言うとわざとらしく感じる．

sincerity

接頭 (in) **insincerity** *n* 不誠実，不誠意

singular

接頭 (non) **nonsingular** *adj* 非特異な ► It is easy to calculate the coefficient matrix B provided that S is **nonsingular**. S が非特異だとすれば，係数行列 B を計算することは容易である．

sinkable

接頭 (un) **unsinkable** *adj* 〈船などが〉 沈むことのない ► Seventy-three years after the "**unsinkable**" Titanic plowed into an iceberg and slowly slipped beneath the waves, . . . 「不沈船」

タイタニック号が氷山に激しくぶつかり波のなかにゆっくりと吸い込まれてから73年を経て，…

sinusoidal

接頭 (non) **nonsinusoidal** *adj* 非正弦曲線の ► Examples are direct-current, alternating-current, **nonsinusoidal**, digital, and transient circuit theory. 例としては，直流，交流，非正弦，デジタル，および過渡回路理論などがある． ► Circuits with **nonsinusoidal** waveforms are analyzed by breaking the waveform into a series of sinusoidal waves of different frequencies known as a Fourier series. 非正弦波形を持つ回路は，波形をフーリエ級数として知られる一連の周波数の異なる正弦波に分解することによって分析される．

skid

接頭 (non) **nonskid** *adj* スリップしない

skill

接頭 (de) **deskill** *v* 〈作業などを〉単純化する

skilled

接頭 (un) **unskilled** *adj* 熟練していない〈人など〉 ► Among the advantages of using solderless connectors are uniformity of installation, simple operation by **unskilled** operators, and optimum rate of attachment. ソルダーレス端子を使う利点は，取り付けが均一で，未熟なオペレーターでも簡単にできそして組み立て量を最適化できることである．

skillful

接頭 (un) **unskillful** *adj* 未熟な

skimmed

接頭 (un) **unskimmed** *adj* 脂肪を取り除いていない ► Whole, or **unskimmed**, milk is a unique fluid because it contains every food requirement, with the exception of vitamin C and iron. 全乳すなわち脱脂していない牛乳は，ビタミンCおよび鉄分を除くすべての栄養素を含んでいる点で唯一無二の飲料である．

skin

[接尾] (less) **skinless** *adj* 皮なしの ► These boneless, **skinless** filets are 99% fat-free and great for grilling. この骨なし皮なしの肉は，99 %脂分を落としており，グリルするのに最適です.

sleep

[接尾] (less) **sleepless** *adj* 眠れない

sleeve

[接尾] (less) **sleeveless** *adj* 袖なしの

slip

[接頭] (non) **nonslip** *adj* スリップ止め加工した

smiling

[接頭] (un) **unsmiling** *adj* 笑わない

smoke

[接尾] (less) **smokeless** *adj* 煙の出ない，無煙の ► In modern firearms, gunpowder has largely been superseded by nitrocellulose-based and other **smokeless** explosives. 最新の小火器において，火薬はほとんどニトロセルロース系など無煙の爆薬に取って代わられた.

smoker

[接頭] (non) **nonsmoker** *n* 非喫煙者 ► Smoking also has substantial effects on the health of **nonsmokers**. 喫煙は，非喫煙者の健康にも実質的な影響を及ぼす.

smoking

[接頭] (non) **nonsmoking** *adj* 禁煙の，非喫煙の ► fifty **nonsmoking** men who underwent coronary-bypass surgery 心臓バイパス手術を受けた50人の非喫煙男性

snap

[接頭] (un) **unsnap** *v* スナップを外す

snarl

[接頭] (un) **unsnarl** *v* もつれをほぐす

soap

[接尾] (less) **soapless** *adj* 石鹸のない

sociable

接頭 (un) **unsociable** *adj* 非社交的な，交際嫌いな ▶ Are cats really **unsociable**? 猫には本当に社交性はないのか.

social

接頭 (a) **asocial** *adj*

❶反社会的な

❷社交性のない

接頭 (un) **unsocial** *adj* 非社会的な

sold

接頭 (un) **unsold** *adj*

❶売れ残りの ▶ The shop was overstocked with **unsold** goods. その店は，売れ残り品で在庫過剰であった. ▶ The products were left **unsold**. その製品は売れ残りとなった.

❷売れていない ▶ The novels are unpublished and the screenplay **unsold**. これらの小説は出版されておらず，映画のシナリオは売れていない.

solicited

接頭 (un) **unsolicited** *adj* 求めたものではない ▶ supervisors offering **unsolicited** advice and guidance 頼まれてもいない忠告や指導をする監督者

soluble

接頭 (dis) **dissoluble** *adj* 分解できる，溶解できる

接頭 (in) **insoluble** *adj*

❶溶解しない，非溶解性の，不溶性の ▶ It is **insoluble** in alcohol. それはアルコールに溶けない［溶解しない］. ▶ . . . to stabilize high-available chlorine for bleaching purposes without obtaining detrimental **insoluble** materials. …有害な非溶解性物質を入手しなくても漂白目的に入手性が高い塩素を安定化するために…

❷解くことのできない，解決できない

solution

接頭 (dis) **dissolution** *n* 分解，　溶解 ▶ The electrochemical

potential for a given metal in solution measured relative to a standard electrode determines the **dissolution** rate of the metal or alloy. 基準電極に比例して計測された溶液中のある金属に対する電気機械のポテンシャルが，金属または合金の溶解速度を決める．

solvable

接頭 (dis) **dissolvable** *adj* 分解できる，溶解できる ► **dissolvable** plastic wafers 溶解性プラスチックウエハ

solve

接頭 (dis) **dissolve** *v*

❶ 溶解する，分解する ► If there is any bleeding, it means that a component in the paint has **dissolved** the coloring material in the rust. 何か流れ出しているとすれば，それはペイントの成分が錆の中の色素を溶かし出している証拠である．

❷ 〈議会などを〉解散する

solved

接頭 (dis) **dissolved** *adj* 溶解した ► Molten iron as produced in the blast furnace from iron ore contains considerable amounts of **dissolved** carbon. 溶鉱炉で鉄鉱石から生産された溶銑は，溶解した炭素を相当量含む．

接頭 (un) **unsolved** *adj* 解決されていない ► The cause of the accident has been **unsolved** until now. 事故の原因は，不明のまま今日に至っている．

solvency

接頭 (in) **insolvency** *n* 支払い不能，債務超過 ► The country is careening toward **insolvency** and housing starts are down. その国は債務超過に傾きつつあり，住宅建築着工は減少している．

solvent

接頭 (in) **insolvent** *adj* 支払い不能の，破産した ► In response, the agency, which seized the **insolvent** mortgage giants in September ... それに応えて，支払い不能に陥った住宅ロー

ン大手を9月に取得した当局は……

sonance

[接頭] (dis) **dissonance** *n* 不協和, 不調和, 不一致

sonant

[接頭] (dis) **dissonant** *adj* 調和しない, 一致しない

song

[接尾] (less) **songless** *adj* 歌のない

sophisticated

[接頭] (un) **unsophisticated** *adj* 複雑でない, 巧妙でない ► Until recently, both hardware and software to handle large backups was fairly **unsophisticated**. 最近まで, 大量のバックアップを処理するハードウェアとソフトウェアは両方ともかなり洗練を欠いていた.

soul

[接尾] (less) **soulless** *adj* 魂のこもっていない ► He has taken a swipe at action films that rely too much on computerized effects, calling them "a **soulless** enterprise." 彼は, アクション映画はコンピューター効果に頼りすぎていて,「魂のこもっていない娯楽」だと非難した.

sound

[接尾] (less) **soundless** *adj* 無音の, 静かな ► Dr. Yamasaki found that he could create a **soundless** space anywhere by using a method that counteracts, or rather cancels, noise. 山崎博士は効果を打ち消す, すなわちノイズをキャンセルする方法を用いればどこでも無音の空間を作ることができることを発見した.

[接頭] (un) **unsound** *adj* 健全でない, 不安定な, 信頼できない

sounding

[接頭] (ill) **ill-sounding** *adj* 響きの悪い ► an **ill-sounding** name 響きの悪い名前

soundness

[接頭] (un) **unsoundness** *n* 不健全さ ► No one can be a poet

without a certain **unsoundness** of mind. 心にある種の不健全さがないと詩人にはなれない.

space

[接尾] (less) **spaceless** *adj*

❶無限の

❷場所をとらない

sparing

[接頭] (un) **unsparing** *adj* 寛大な, 気前のよい

spark

[接尾] (less) **sparkless** *adj* 無火花の ► We have integrated the controller with our switches in such a way that they are **sparkless**. 我々は, このコントローラーをスイッチに組み込み火花が出ないようにした.

speakable

[接頭] (un) **unspeakable** *adj* 言いようのない, 言葉では言い表せない

specialized

[接頭] (un) **unspecialized** *adj* 特化されていない, 分化していない

specific

[接頭] (non) **nonspecific** *adj* 特定的でない

specified

[接頭] (un) **unspecified** *adj* 不特定の ► Backlash is usually **unspecified** and is highly dependent on . . . バックラッシュは通常不指定であり, …に大きく影響される. ► men to play golf with women for **unspecified** purposes. 特別の目的もなく女性たちとゴルフに興じる男たち

speck

[接尾] (less) **speckless** *adj* 斑点のない

spectacular

[接頭] (un) **unspectacular** *adj* 豪華でない, ぱっとしない ► The sight, however, was decidedly **unspectacular**. しかし眺めは

まったく映えなかった. ▶ It is an **unspectacular** work which seems to present little change for its progress, little reward for all the trouble it takes. それは, 手間ばかりかかって一向に代わり映えのしない地味な仕事だ.

speech

接尾 (less) **speechless** *adj* (驚きなどにより)言葉をなくした, 絶句した

spent

接頭 (ill) **ill-spent** *adj* 浪費された ▶ **ill-spent** money 死に金

接頭 (un) **unspent** *adj* 〈金銭などが〉費やされていない

spine

接尾 (less) **spineless** *adj* 決断力のない ▶ When I come across young people who are exceptionally sensible, I somehow find them weak and **spineless**. 私は妙にもの分かりのいい若者を見ると, 何か弱々しく, たよりない気がしてしまう. ▶ He's **spineless**. あの男はからきし意気地がない.

spirit

接尾 (less) **spiritless** *adj* 活気のない

spiritual

接頭 (un) **unspiritual** *adj* 精神的でない ▶ Can a Christian remain **unspiritual**? クリスチャンは非精神的でいることができるのか.

spiritually

接頭 (un) **unspiritually** *ad* 精神的でなく, 物質的に

spoiled

接頭 (un) **unspoiled** *adj* 損なわれていない ▶ Discover the **unspoiled** charms of the Celebes. セレベス島の魅力的な自然を見つけよう.

spoilt

接頭 (un) **unspoilt** *adj* 損なわれていない

spoken

接頭 (un) **unspoken** *adj* 無言の, 言外の, 暗黙の ▶ I think I

learned from my father the **unspoken** language or instincts that go back thousands of years. 私は数千年もさかのぼる暗黙のビジネス言語または才能を父から学んだと思う. ► I even witnessed Japanese-style **unspoken** communication and personality projection at work. 私は仕事の場において，日本式の以心伝心や腹芸さえ目撃しました.

spool

接頭 (un) **unspool** *v*

❶〈映画を〉上映する

❷糸巻きからほどく

sporting

接頭 (non) **nonsporting** *adj*

❶スポーツと無縁の，猟犬の資質を欠いた

❷突然変異が起きにくい

接頭 (un) **unsporting** *adj* スポーツマンらしくない

sportsmanlike

接頭 (un) **unsportsmanlike** *adj* スポーツマンらしくない，スポーツ精神にもとる

spot

接尾 (less) **spotless** *adj* 汚れ[しみ]がない

spotted

接頭 (un) **unspotted** *adj* 汚れ[斑点]のない

spring

接尾 (less) **springless** *adj*

❶ばねが付いていない ► The invention relates to a **springless** valve engine mechanism for fuel engines, comprising a plurality of combustion cylinders and respective pistons. 本発明は，内燃エンジンのバネを使用しないエンジン機構に関するものであり，複数の燃焼シリンダーとそれぞれのピストンとを備えている.

❷元気のない

stability

[接頭] (in) **instability** *n*

❶ 不安定性 ▶ There is evidence of **instability**. 不安定性の証拠がある. ▶ When such directional **instability** is suspected, it is advisable to check with a model test spiral maneuver and ... そのような方向不安定性が疑われるときは，モデルテストスパイラル運動によって確認することが望ましく，… ▶ The **instability** observed is believed to be one which had been predicted earlier and is known as the kink **instability**. 観測された不安定性は，あらかじめ予想されていたものと考えられ，キンク不安定性として知られている.

❷ (政治的) 不安定性 ▶ It's a recipe for social and political **instability** or even chaos. それは，社会および政治の不安定性への対策，さらには混沌状態への対策でさえある. ▶ Commodity prices, political **instability**, and monetary problems are certainly out there. 物価，政治的不安定，金融などの問題は，確実にそこにある.

stabilization

[接頭] (de) **destabilization** *n* 不安定 ▶ Some take it as an article of faith that the U.S. went to war to secure Iraqi oil and prevent **destabilation** of the region. 米国はイラクの石油を確保し地域の不安定化を防止するために開戦したということを信条としている人もいる.

stabilize

[接頭] (de) **destabilize** *v* 不安定化させる

stabilizing

[接頭] (de) **destabilizing** *adj* 不安定である ▶ He was worried that it would be too **destabilizing** for the company. 彼は，それによって会社があまりに不安定になるだろうと悩んでいた.

stable

[接頭] (un) **unstable** *adj* 不安定な ▶ A switch or relay can be used, but their contact resistance tends to be **unstable** when passing small electric currents. スイッチまたはリレーは使用可能だが，接触抵抗は，微小電流が流れると変わりやすくなりがちだ． ► Should foreign investors worry about planting roots in seismically **unstable** areas? 海外投資家は地震が多く不安定な地域に根を下ろすことを心配すべきなのか． ► This action provides adequate steering moments for control even though the missile may be aerodynamically **unstable**. この動作によって，ミサイルが空気力学的に不安定であったとしても，十分な操舵モーメントが与えられる．

stably

接頭 (un) **unstably** *ad* 不安定に

stack

接頭 (un) **unstack** *v* 積み上げたものを崩す ► Automatic equipment for stacking and **unstacking** cases, for emptying and filling cases with bottles or cartons . . . is used. ケースを山のように積み上げたり，積み上げた山からケースを取り出したり，またケースに瓶やカートンを詰めたりケースからこれらを取り出したりする自動機器が使用されている．

stain

接尾 (less) **stainless** *adj*

❶錆びない

❷ステンレス製の ► Unless otherwise specified, all parts in direct contact with the product shall be made of **stainless** steel. 特に指定のない限り，製品に直接接触する部品は，すべてステンレス・スティールを使用するものとする．

stained

接頭 (un) **unstained** *adj* 汚れのない ► Then apply a thin wash coat of shellac over both the stained and **unstained** stripes to seal the wood pores. 次に木材の穴をシールするために，汚れのあるストライプと汚れのないストライプの両方にセラックニスの薄いウォッシュコートを塗布する．

stamped

[接頭] (un) **unstamped** *adj*

❶スタンプが押されていない

❷〈切手などが〉貼られていない

standard

[接頭] (non) **nonstandard** *adj*

❶非標準的な，標準外の ► While ISO has standardized certain protocols, other **nonstandard** protocols also exist. 国際標準化機構が特定のプロトコルを標準化する一方，他の標準外のプロトコルもまた存在する.

❷規格外の ► The government publishes standard parts descriptions for . . . and issues precise rules governing the preparation of descriptions for **nonstandard** parts. 政府は，…について規格部品の明細書を発行し，規格外部品の明細書の作成を抑制する厳密な規定を公布する.

standardized

[接頭] (non) **nonstandardized** *adj* 規格化されていない ► The **nonstandardized** items that adversely affect telecommunications are . . . 電気通信に悪影響を及ぼす，規格化されていない項目は…である.

star

[接尾] (less) **starless** *adj* 星の出ていない ► On the dark, **starless** night of March 12, a sixteen-year old boy slowly walked up the trail across the pastures by the mill trench. 3月12日の星も出ていない暗い夜に，16歳の少年は溝のそばの牧草地を横切って小道をゆっくりと登っていった.

starred

[接頭] (ill) **ill-starred** *adj* 星回りの悪い ► an **ill-starred** destiny 不運な運命

starter

[接頭] (non) **nonstarter** *n* 最初から可能性のない人

state

接尾 (less) **stateless** *adj*

❶ 市民権のない, 国籍のない ► The president announced that such so-called **stateless** Russian speakers in the Baltics would be allowed to enter Russia without a visa. 大統領は, バルト諸国のいわゆる国籍のないロシア語話者は, ビザなしでロシアに入国することを許可すると発表した.

❷ 国境のない

stated

接頭 (un) **unstated** *adj* 述べられていない ► The group leader has supported the **unstated** need of the group and made it visible. グループのリーダーは, グループに必要な説明されていないものを確認し, それを明確にした.

steady

接頭 (non) **nonsteady** *adj* 不安定な ► Because of the unavoidable heat leak into substances cooled by this process, the extremely low temperatures obtained are always **nonsteady**. この方法で冷却した物質への熱もれは避けられないので, 得られた超低温は常に不安定である.

接頭 (un) **unsteady** *adj* 不安定な ► This may be due to **unsteady** velocities or to alternating forces. これは不安定な速度または交番応力によるものと考えられる. ► Carpet on the floor reduces noise, while also making it less likely that an **unsteady** patient will trip or slip. 床に敷かれたカーペットは騒音を軽減し, 一方で不安定な患者がつまずきにくくまたすべりにくくする.

steady-state

接頭 (un) **unsteady-state** *adj* 不安定な状態の ► Such a process is known as an **unsteady-state** process. このようなプロセスは, 不安定状態プロセスと呼ばれている.

stem

接尾 (less) **stemless** *adj* 柄[茎]のない

step

接頭 (mis) **misstep** *n* 失策 ▸ Many of the stocks of our Fastest-Growing companies appear to be "priced for perfection"— meaning that a slight **misstep** could send them tumbling. わが国の最も速く成長している企業の株の多くは,「完全性に高値がついている」ように見える. すなわち, わずかな失策がそれらを転落させうることを意味している.

sterile

接頭 (non) **nonsterile** *adj* 非無菌の ▸ These can facilitate sterilizing within the package or they can be used to package items that are sold **nonsterile**. これらはパッケージの中で殺菌できるようになっているか, もしくは非無菌状態で販売されている商品の包装に使用される.

stick

接頭 (non) **nonstick** *adj* 焦げ付かない, 付着しない

接頭 (un) **unstick** *v* 〈くっついているもの同士を〉離す, はがす

stinting

接頭 (un) **unstinting** *adj* 惜しみない ▸ Van Winkle does it by an **unstinting** focus on quality, a lot of viral marketing, and a little bit of luck. ファン・ヴィンクル氏はそれを, 品質向上に惜しみない努力を払い, バイラル・マーケティング手法を多用し, そして少しの運を活かして実行している. ▸ Cherishing Japan's peace Constitution born of the horrors of war, the Japanese people have made **unstinting** efforts for peace for over half a century. 戦争への恐怖から生まれた日本の平和憲法を大事に守りながら, 日本国民は半世紀以上にわたって平和維持への惜しみない努力をしてきた.

stintingly

接頭 (un) **unstintingly** *ad* 惜しみなく ▸ The university professor **unstintingly** gave her love and devotion. その大学教授は, 彼女に献身の愛を惜しみなく与えた. ▸ There should also be an explicit provision enabling Japan to contribute **unstintingly** to international peace in protecting the lives and property of people worldwide. 日本が惜しみなく，世界中の生命や財産を保護することによって世界平和に惜しみなく貢献できる明白な規定を作らなければならない．

stone

[接尾] (less) **stoneless** *adj*

❶石のない

❷〈果実などの〉核のない ► The **stoneless** dried plums are prepared by taking out the stone from each plum separately using a special punch. その種なし乾燥プラムは特別なパンチを使用して個々のプラムから別々に種を取り除いて作られる．

stop

[接頭] (non) **nonstop** *adj* ノンストップの ► People are rewarded with a **nonstop** thrill ride in which a mock spaceship climbs, banks and even reaches the speed of light. 人々は，昇ったり，傾斜飛行したり，光の速さまでも出せる模擬宇宙船のスリルに富んだノンストップ飛行を楽しんだ．

[接頭] (un) **unstop** *v* 〈瓶などの〉栓を抜く

stoppable

[接頭] (un) **unstoppable** *adj* 阻止できない，止められない ► Dell faces the seemingly **unstoppable** Apple juggernaut. デルは止めることができそうもないアップルの圧倒的な勢力に直面している．

storage

[接頭] (non) **nonstorage** *n* 非貯蔵式の ► In a **nonstorage** tube the only light utilized is that reaching a particular point on the tube's light-sensitive unit while .... 非貯蔵式のチューブでは，使用される唯一の光はチューブの光感受ユニット上の特定の点に到達する光であるが，その一方….

strained

[接頭] (un) **unstrained** *adj* 緊張しない

strap

接尾 (less) **strapless** *adj*

❶〈婦人服などの〉肩ひものない

❷吊革のない

接頭 (un) **unstrap** *v*〈ひもなどを〉緩める

strength

接尾 (less) **strengthless** *adj*

❶強度のない ► These data show that tensile strength of cometary material is distinct enough from **strengthless** material. これらのデータによると，彗星の物質の抗張力は，強度のない物質とは明らかに異なる．

❷力がない ► He woke in the morning so unrefreshed and **strengthless** that he sent for the doctor. その朝，彼は気分がすぐれず体に力が入らなかったので医者を呼んでもらった．

stressed

接頭 (un) **unstressed** *adj* 強調されていない ► What is the **unstressed** vowel in February? "February" でアクセントのない母音はどれか．

string

接頭 (un) **unstring** *v*〈弦などを〉緩める，外す

structured

接頭 (un) **unstructured** *adj* 組織的でない ► a gigantic **unstructured** mess 巨大で組織化されていない混乱状態

strung

接頭 (un) **unstrung** *adj*〈弦などを〉緩めた，外した

stuck

接頭 (un) **unstuck** *adj* 剥がれた，くっついていない ► On two occasions, the cursor froze and could not be **unstuck**. 二度にわたってカーソルは固着して，もとの状態に戻すことができなかった．

studied

接頭 (un) **unstudied** *adj*

❶知識のない
❷準備なしの

stuff

接頭 (un) **unstuff** *v* 詰め込まない ► Poultry may be stuffed or **unstuffed**. 鶏肉には詰め物をしてもよいし，詰めなくてもよい.

subscribe

接頭 (un) **unsubscribe** *v*

❶〈登録や講読などを〉取り消す

❷署名をしない ► The group won't be interested in your subscribe/**unsubscribe** requests. グループはあなたの署名入り／署名なしのどちらの要求にも関心を持たないであろう.

substantial

接頭 (in) **insubstantial** *adj* 実体のない，非現実的な ► However, this characterization proves to be too **insubstantial** for the promises of the minimal theory to be properly satisfied. けれども，この説明は，最小理論の有望性があまりにも非現実的なため，適切に理解されないことがわかる.

接頭 (un) **unsubstantial** *adj* 実体のない ► That's the most **unsubstantial** argument I've ever heard. それは，私が聞いた中で最も内容のない議論である.

substantially

接頭 (in) **insubstantially** *ad* 非現実的に

接頭 (un) **unsubstantially** *ad* 実体がなく，根拠なく

substantiated

接頭 (un) **unsubstantiated** *adj* 立証されていない ► He also propounded his **unsubstantiated** hypothesis. 彼は，立証されてない仮説も提起した.

successful

接頭 (un) **unsuccessful** *adj* 不成功の，不首尾の ► Attempts to confirm these findings have been **unsuccessful** as yet. これらの調査結果を確認しようとしたが，今のところ不成功に終

わっている. ▶ The **unsuccessful** investment has to be written off. 不成功に終わった投資は, 帳簿から消さなければならない. ▶ I think both the successful and **unsuccessful** should taste something bitter at least once. 順調な人もうまくいかない人も, 一度は苦い思いを味わうべきである. ▶ Germanium planar transistors using germanium oxide as the surface mask proved **unsuccessful** in early work because of the unsuitable nature of germanium oxide. 表面マスクとして酸化ゲルマニウムを利用するゲルマニウムプレーナートランジスターは, 酸化ゲルマニウムの性質が不適合であったため初期の製作で不出来なことが判明した.

successfully

接頭 (un) **unsuccessfully** *ad* 不成功に ▶ The plaintiffs' main response to these actions has been to try, **unsuccessfully**, to squelch them. これらの行動に対する原告の主な反応は彼らを黙らせようとする試みであったが, 不成功に終わっている. ▶ In 2008 the railroads tried, **unsuccessfully**, to dismiss Neuwirth's suit, which is now awaiting a decision on whether the court will certify its class. 2008年, 鉄道会社はニューワースの訴訟を却下しようとしたが, 不成功に終わり, この訴訟は現在, 法廷がそのクラスを認めるかどうかの決定を待っている.

sufferable

接頭 (in) **insufferable** *adj* 耐えられない, 我慢できない

sufficiency

接頭 (in) **insufficiency** *n* 不十分, 不適当, 不足 ▶ The booster and the repeater make up for the **insufficiency** of remote powering voltages or excessive attenuation for particularly long lines. 昇圧機と中継器は, 遠隔パワリング電圧の不足や, 特別長い回線の過剰減衰を補う.

sufficient

接頭 (in) **insufficient** *adj* 十分でない, 不適当な ▶ **Insuffi-**

cient energy is transferred to the liquid to produce waves. 不十分なエネルギーが液体に伝えられて波をつくる. ► Proportional control is **insufficient** to control a motor under varying loads. 比例制御は, 負荷が変化するときのモーターの制御には不適当だ. ► The data available, however, are **insufficient** to permit the precise location or detailed description of this phenomenon. しかし, 入手できるデータは, この現象の精確な位置を示すかまたは詳細に説明できるようにするには不十分である.

sugar

接尾 (less) **sugarless** *adj* 砂糖の入っていない, 無糖の ► The sweetener used in **sugarless** gums and mints can rapidly cause liver failure in dogs. シュガーレス [無糖の] ガムに使用している人工甘味料とミントは, 犬の急性肝臓疾患を起こす可能性がある.

suitable

接頭 (un) **unsuitable** *adj* 不適当な ► In general they are too violent and therefore **unsuitable** as propellants. 一般的に, それらは特性が激しすぎ, そのために推進剤として不適である.

suited

接頭 (ill) **ill-suited** *adj* 不適な, 不似合いな ► be **ill-suited** to mass production 大量生産に適していない

接頭 (un) **unsuited** *adj*

❶不向きな, 適当でない

❷釣り合わない, 両立しない

sulfurization

接頭 (de) **desulfurization** *n* 脱硫 ► Further improvements include the provision of equipment for flue gas **desulfurization** at sintering plants and **desulfurization** of coke-oven gas. さらなる改善策には, 焼結施設の煙道ガス脱硫装置の取り付けおよびコークス炉ガスの脱硫がある.

sullied

接頭 (un) **unsullied** *adj* 汚されていない ► They were about to get what they asked for, but it would not be an **unsullied** blessing. 彼らは要求していたものを手に入れようとしていたが, まったくけがれない祝福とはならないであろう.

sun

接尾 (less) **sunless** *adj* 日の当たらない, 日光がささない

sung

接頭 (un) **unsung** *adj*

❶ 歌にされていない

❷ 讃えられていない, 無名の ► I was especially sensitive to the banker's self-pity, because even as they carried on in Davos about how unfair life was to them, I was preparing for the memorial service of an **unsung** hero. ダボスで彼らが人生の不公平さを嘆いた時でさえ, ある無名の英雄のために追悼会を計画していたこともあって, 私は銀行家の自己憐憫の情には特に敏感であった.

superable

接頭 (in) **insuperable** *adj*

❶ 〈川などが〉越えられない ► The Mississippi River seemed an **insuperable** barrier. ミシシッピー川は越えられない障害のように見えた.

❷ 克服できない ► The obstacles are awe-inspiring, but not theoretically **insuperable**. 恐れ多いと感じるほどの障害ではあるが, 理論的には打破できないことではない. ► Bewildered by a seemingly **insuperable** recession, the Japanese people seemed to lose all reason. なかなか克服できない不況にうろたえて, 日本人はすべての良識を失っているようだった.

supercharged

接頭 (un) **unsupercharged** *adj* 過給されていない, 無過給の ► an **unsupercharged** engine 無過給エンジン

supervise

接頭 (non) **nonsupervise** *v* 監視しない ▶ Transfer during communication can be **nonsupervised**. 通信中の転送は監視できない.

supervised

接頭 (un) **unsupervised** *adj* 非監視型の

supper

接尾 (less) **supperless** *adj* 夕食抜きの ▶ Traveled till quite dark, when we were forced to halt for the night at a place where there was no water; and of course we all slept **supperless**. 真っ暗になるまで歩いたので, その晩は水もないような場所に泊まらざるを得なかったし, もちろん, みんなが夕食抜きでベッドに入った.

support

接頭 (non) **nonsupport** *n*

❶扶養義務不履行

❷不支持, 援助しないこと

supportable

接頭 (in) **insupportable** *adj* 耐えられない, 我慢できない

接頭 (un) **unsupportable** *adj* 支えられない, 支持[擁護]できない

supported

接頭 (un) **unsupported** *adj* 支持[立証]されていない ▶ By accepting his responsibility, the writer throws away the simple writing tricks of using **unsupported** statements, . . . 自分の責任を引き受けることによって, 著作者は立証されていない所説を使用するという単純な著述上の策略を放棄する. ▶ High-voltage wires and cables use multilayer wrappings of both **unsupported** and supported Teflon. 高圧線および高圧ケーブルは, 支持されていないテフロンと支持されているテフロンの両方を使った多層包装を採用している.

sure

接頭 (un) **unsure** *adj* 確信のない, 自信のない ► If you are **unsure** about which mode is appropriate for your application, . . . 自分のアプリケーションにどのモードが適しているかについて確信がない場合は, … ► Many people are **unsure** of just what multimedia computing is for, and whether there is a market for it. マルチメディアコンピューティングがいったい何のためなのか, また果たしてその市場があるのだろうかということについて多くの人は確信をもっていない.

surpassable

接頭 (un) **unsurpassable** *adj* このうえない

接頭 (un) **unsurpassably** *ad* これ以上ないというほどに ► My friend and I immediately became her pupils on the spot and had the nerve to converse with her in **unsurpassably** broken English. 友人と僕もさっそく即席の生徒となり, これ以上はないほどのブロークン・イングリッシュでずうずうしくも彼女と話をした.

surpassed

接頭 (un) **unsurpassed** *adj* 比類のない, 無類の ► If most of the drawing work entails revising or modifying a large library, CAD software is **unsurpassed**. もし製図業務のほとんどが大きなライブラリーの見直しや修正を伴うなら, CAD ソフトウェアにまさるものはない.

surprising

接頭 (un) **unsurprising** *adj* 驚くほどではない ► Given this fact, it is **unsurprising** that people put money on a pedestal. これがあっては, 人々が金銭至上主義になるのはしかたありません [驚くほどではありません].

surprisingly

接頭 (un) **unsurprisingly** *ad* 驚くほどでなく ► They are, **unsurprisingly**, normal men and women who overwhelmingly put their families first. 彼らは, 驚くことではなく, 断然自分

の家族を最重視する当たり前の男性と女性である. ► Railroads and shippers are, **unsurprisingly**, divided over the issue of whether rates accurately reflect costs. 鉄道会社や運送会社は, 驚くことではないが, その料金がコストを正確に反映しているかどうかという論点について意見が分かれている.

susceptible

接頭 (in) **insusceptible** *adj* 受け入れない

suspected

接頭 (un) **unsuspected** *adj* 疑われていない ► Direct observation of the edges of oxidized specimens by the electron microscope has shown new and **unsuspected** crystal habits in the corrosion film. 酸化された試料のエッジを電子顕微鏡で直接観察することによって, 腐食膜内での新たなそして思いもよらない晶癖が明らかになった.

suspecting

接頭 (un) **unsuspecting** *adj* 疑っていない ► Some **unsuspecting** investors will doubtless be delighted to learn of their participation. 中には彼らが参加することに喜びを感じている疑うことのない投資家もいる. ► Thus the infection can be spread from computer to computer by **unsuspecting** users who either swap disks or send programs to one another over telephone lines. こうして感染は, ディスクを交換したり電話回線を使ってプログラムを送るような, 疑いをもたないユーザーによってコンピューターからコンピューターへと広がる可能性がある.

sustainable

接頭 (un) **unsustainable** *adj* 支持できない, 支えられない, 維持 [持続] できない ► an **unsustainable** financial burden 支え切れない財政上の重荷

sustainably

接頭 (un) **unsustainably** *ad* 支持できないように, 支えられないように ► We could end the crisis of **unsustainably** rising

U.S. health care costs. 私たちは，米国の医療費が維持できないほどに上昇する危機に終止符を打つことができたであろうに．

sweetened

接頭 (un) **unsweetened** *adj* 糖分が入っていない；甘味を加えていない ▶ Use artificial sweeteners, **unsweetened** fruit juices, low calorie drinks and "unfrosted" cereals. 人口甘味料，無添加フルーツジュース，低カロリー飲料，および「糖分無添加」シリアルを使用しなさい． ▶ Dried, frozen or **unsweetened** tinned fruit may be acceptable alternatives to raw, fresh fruit if that is unavailable. 乾燥，冷凍，あるいは甘みを付けていない缶詰の果物は，生の新鮮な果物が入手できない場合，これらの代替品として受け入れてもよい．

swerving

接頭 (un) **unswerving** *adj* 不動の

symmetric(al)

接頭 (a) **asymmetric(al)** *adj*

❶ 非対称的な ▶ An **asymmetric(al)** waveform has pulses of different amplitudes, e.g. +190 V and −210 V. 非対称的波形は異なる振幅パルスをもっている．すなわち＋190ボルトと−210ボルトである． ▶ Various means were used to produce an **asymmetric** output wave so that the advantage of the equivalent of a dc power supply could be maintained. 非対称形出力波を出すためにいろいろな方法がとられ，その結果直流電源と等価である利点を維持することができた．

❷ 不均整な

symmetrical

接頭 (non) **nonsymmetrical** *adj* 非対称的な ▶ If . . ., the intermolecular forces will be very large compared to those of a **nonsymmetrical** shape. もし…であれば，その分子間の力は非対称形の分子間の力に比べて極めて大きい． ▶ Low-density polyethylene contains many more side branches which create **nonsymmetrical** areas of low density and therefore low intermolecular attraction. 低密度ポリエチレンは，低密度の，したがって分子間の引力の小さい非対称部分をつくる側枝をはるかに多く持っている.

接頭 (un) **unsymmetrical** *adj* 非対称形の ▶ In addition to tubing, porthole extrusion is used to produce hollow **unsymmetrical** shapes in aluminum alloys. アルミ合金で中空の非対称形のものを製造するには，チュービングの他にポートホール押し出し法を使用する.

symmetrically

接頭 (un) **unsymmetrically** *ad* 非対称形に ▶ If . . . , and plate stiffeners located **unsymmetrically**, the design may become difficult to fabricate . . . 補強板が非対称に取り付けられたりしているならば，その設計では組み立てが難しくなるかもしれない.

symmetry

接頭 (a) **asymmetry** *n*

❶ 非対称性，非対称 ▶ An **asymmetry** results which produces optical activity. 光学的活動を生ずる非対称が生ずる. ▶ Furthermore, it is not possible to use the same equipment at the subscriber and exchange end, bearing in mind the intrinsic **asymmetry** of the transmission. さらに，送信に固有の非対称性を考慮すると，同じ機器を加入者および交換端末に対して使用するのは不可能である.

❷ 不均整

接頭 (dis) **dissymmetry** *n* 非対称 ▶ While the **dissymmetry** can be reduced by turning the rotor faster, . . . 一方，ローターを速く回転させることによって，非対称性を減じることができるが，….

sympathetic

接頭 (un) **unsympathetic** *adj* 思いやりのない，冷淡な

symptomatic

接頭 (a) **asymptomatic** *adj* 兆候のない，無症状の

symptomatically

接頭 (a) **asymptomatically** *ad* 兆候なく，無症状に

synchronous

接頭 (a) **asynchronous** *adj* 非同期の ▶ This mode uses **asynchronous** communications for commands and data. このモードではコマンドとデータに非同期の通信を使用している. ▶ AC motors can be divided into two major categories: **asynchronous** motors (inductive motors) and synchronous motors. 交流モーターは，非同期モーター［誘導モーター］と同期モーターの二つに大別される.

synchronously

接頭 (a) **asynchronously** *ad* 非同期式に ▶ At the moment, international digital connections are made through network-node interfaces, which are operated **asynchronously**. さしあたり，国際計数連絡は，非同期式に作動する回路網接続点インタフェースを通じて行われる.

systematic

接頭 (un) **unsystematic** *adj* 非体系的な ▶ The country's groundwater resources are being exploited in an **unsystematic** way, with no regard for the longer term. その国の地下水源は非系統的に使用されており，より長期に亘る考慮はされていない.

T

tact

接尾 (less) **tactless** *adj* 機転のきかない

tail

接尾 (less) **tailless** *adj* 尾のない

tainted

接頭 (un) **untainted** *adj* 汚染されていない

talent

接尾 (less) **talentless** *adj* 才能のない ► We are all **talentless** on the show and can do nothing without writers. 我々は全員ショーに関しては才能がなく，作家なくしては何もできない.

tamable

接頭 (un) **untamable** *adj* 飼いならせない ► While many of his countrymen viewed Afghanistan as an **untamable** place, Drummond was smitten. 多くの同郷人が，アフガニスタンを服従させる[飼いならす]ことができない地域と見ている最中，ドラモンドは一撃を食らった.

tamed

接頭 (un) **untamed** *adj* 人の手が入っていない，加工されていない ► Taiwan had only been a Japanese colony for six years and was still an **untamed** place subject to epidemics like malaria and cholera. 当時の台湾は日本領となってまだ6年で，マラリア，コレラなどの伝染病が蔓延する未開の[人の手が入っていない]土地でした.

tangible

接頭 (in) **intangible** *adj*

❶ 実体のない，手で触れることができない ► Because of their **intangible** nature, software products are difficult to trace and troubleshoot during development. ソフトウェア製品は実

体がないため，開発中にトレースしたり問題解決を行ったりするのが困難だ.

❷漠然としている ▸ The talents and the abilities that make a good technical writer are largely **intangible**. 優れたテクニカルライターになる素質と能力はおしなべて漠然としている.

❸無形の ▸ Think about how each of these entries contributes to the tangible and **intangible** success and well-being of America. これらの項目のそれぞれが米国の有形無形の成功や繁栄にどう寄与しているかについて考えてみよう. ▸ Japan is a country that designates and honors living national treasures and **intangible** cultural properties in traditional culture, crafts, and more. 日本は，伝統的な文化，工芸などにおける人間国宝や無形文化財を指定し，栄誉を与える国である.

—— *n* 無形のもの，無形財産 ▸ Someone must decide which data to use and how to evaluate the **intangibles** quantitatively. どのデータを使い，どのようにして実体のないものを量的に見積もるかを，だれかが決めなければならない.

tangle

接頭 (un) **untangle** *v* 〈もつれなどを〉解く，〈問題などを〉解決する ▸ In revising, you may help **untangle** a confusing passage by sorting ideas into simple sentences. 改訂の際にアイデアを単純な文章に分類することにより，絡みあった節を解きほぐすことできるかもしれない.

tapped

接頭 (un) **untapped** *adj* 未開拓の ▸ This **untapped** low-end smartphone segment is a key to the company's future. この未開拓の低価格なスマートフォンという区分はその企業にとって鍵になる.

tarnished

接頭 (un) **untarnished** *adj* 汚されていない

taste

接頭 (dis) **distaste** *n* 嫌悪，不愉快 ▸ The volunteer should be

sensitive to the patient's feelings and in no way show any **distaste**. ボランティアは，患者の感情を敏感に察知し，けっして嫌悪感を表してはならない.

接尾 (less) **tasteless** *adj*

❶無味乾燥な

❷味のない ▸ Pure water is **tasteless** and odorless. 純水は無味無臭である.

❸悪趣味な ▸ I would like the city to stop running buses painted in **tasteless** colors. 私は市に悪趣味な色のバスを走らせるのを止めてもらいたい.

接尾 (less) **tastelessness** *n* 味がないこと ▸ The writings of such people are often reminiscent of the **tastelessness** of instant foods. そういう人の文章は，しばしばインスタント食品のような味気なさを覚える.

tasteful

接頭 (dis) **distasteful** *adj* 不愉快な，嫌な ▸ I myself get on the phone and accept any kind of work, even work that's **distasteful** to me. 私は自分で電話に出て，たとえ自分にとって不愉快なものであっても，あらゆる種類の仕事を引き受けている.

tastefulness

接頭 (dis) **distastefulness** *n* 不快感，嫌悪感 ▸ Rather, **distastefulness** stems from understanding something wrong. むしろ，嫌悪感はなにかについて誤解することによって生ずる.

taught

接頭 (un) **untaught** *adj* 教えられたものでない，自然の

tear

接尾 (less) **tearless** *adj* 泣かない，涙の出ない

technical

接頭 (non) **nontechnical** *adj*

❶非技術的な ▸ There is a difference of opinion as to the degree to which engineers should be involved in both technical and **nontechnical** decisions. 技術者が技術的な決定と非技術的な決定の両方にかかわるべき程度については，意見の相違がある．

❷ 非技術系の ► The product should be designed with the **nontechnical** user in mind. その製品は，非技術系のユーザーを念頭に置いて設計されなければならない．

tempered

[接頭] (ill) **ill-tempered** *adj* 不機嫌な ► an **ill-tempered** bull 不機嫌な雄牛

[接頭] (un) **untempered** *adj* 〈鉄などが〉焼き入れされていない

tenable

[接頭] (un) **untenable** *adj*

❶ 〈論理などが〉支持できない ► All confirmed, the situation was **untenable**. すべては立証されたが，その状況は支持できない． ► At the time these measurements were made they were taken as conclusive proof that a corpuscular theory was **untenable**. そして測定がなされたときこれらは粒子説は擁護できないという最終的な証拠とみなされた．

❷ 維持できない ► It's clear that pension financing will collapse, social security costs will balloon, and the nation's financing will be **untenable**. 年金資金が底をつき，社会保障費は増大し，国家の財政は維持できないことは明白である．

tenanted

[接頭] (un) **untenanted** *adj* 〈土地や家屋などが〉賃貸されていない，空いている

term

[接尾] (less) **termless** *adj*

❶ 無条件の ► He finally approved a **termless** surrender, allowing the troop to land in southern Italy. 最終的に彼は無条件降伏を認め，その結果その部隊が南イタリアに上陸できた．

❷ 無制限の

terminal

接頭 (non) **nonterminal** *adj*

❶ 非終端の ► The token-flow graph can be decomposed into modular token-flow subgraphs corresponding to all **nonterminal** nodes in the tree. このトークンフロー図は，ツリーの非終端ノードのすべてに対応するモジュラートークンフロー部分図に分割することができる.

❷ 非終期の ► Can a **nonterminal** event of the cell cycle be used for phytoplankton species-specific growth rate estimation? 細胞周期の非終期事象は植物プランクトンの種特異的成長率の推測に利用できるであろうか.

tested

接頭 (un) **untested** *adj* 試されていない

tethered

接頭 (un) **untethered** *adj* 放たれた，解放された ► At the age of 58, Susan Lyne found herself as **untethered** as she had been back in Berkeley. 58歳になったとき，スーザン・ラインはかつてバークリーにいたときのような解放感を感じた.

thank

接尾 (less) **thankless** *adj* 感謝されない ► The job they do is **thankless**. 彼らのやっていることは，ありがたいものではない.

thankful

接頭 (un) **unthankful** *adj* 感謝しない ► Is there a Bible verse on **unthankful** people? 聖書には，感謝しない人々のための節はあるのか.

theism

接頭 (a) **atheism** *n* 無神論，神を信じないこと

theist

接頭 (a) **atheist** *n* 無神論者

theistic

接頭 (a) **atheistic** *adj* 無神論の

thermal

接頭 (non) **nonthermal** *adj* 非熱式の ▶ This overlap means that a strong spike at the edge of one channel will be felt in the adjacent one as **nonthermal** noise. このオーバーラップとは，一つのチャネルの縁の強いスパイクが隣接するチャネルの縁で熱ではないノイズとして感じられることである．

think

接頭 (un) **unthink** *v* 考えることを止める

thinkable

接頭 (un) **unthinkable** *adj* 考えられない，想像できない ▶ The reordering in some of the other categories seems almost **unthinkable**. 他のカテゴリーの中の何かを再注文することは考えられない． ▶ Such a requirement would have been **unthinkable** a few years earlier. このような要件は数年前までは考えられないことであった． ▶ Nearly everybody agrees that raising the entire Titanic would be both technologically and financially **unthinkable**. タイタニック全体を引き揚げるのは，技術的にも財政的にも考えられないということにほとんどすべての人が同意している．

thinking

接頭 (un) **unthinking** *adj* 思慮のない

接頭 (un) **unthinkingly** *ad* 無分別に ▶ As I said earlier, the people are only half paying attention to the Constitution and may well **unthinkingly** accept the idea of rewriting it. 私が前に述べたように，国民は憲法にさほど関心を持っておらず，何の考えもなしに改正を受け入れるのはもっともなことである．

thought

接尾 (less) **thoughtless** *adj* 思慮のない，不注意な

接尾 (less) **thoughtlessly** *ad* 思慮なく，不注意に，下手に ▶ The Americans were worried that if they **thoughtlessly** created an elite, the Japanese people would rise up as a powerful nation once again. 下手にエリートをつくると，この日本人という民族は再び強力な国家をつくってしまうとアメリカ人は恐れていた．

thought-of

接頭 (un) **unthought-of** *adj* 思いもよらない

thread

接頭 (un) **unthread** *v* 〈もつれたものなどを〉ほどく ▶ This article describes what text blocks are and how to manipulate them, how text blocks are threaded, and how you can **unthread** and rethread them. この記事では，テキストブロックとは何か，どのようにそれらを扱うか，テキストブロックにどのように筋が付けられるか，どのようにそれらの筋をもとに戻して筋を付け直すかについて説明する．

threaten

接頭 (un) **unthreatened** *adj* 脅かされない ▶ It is also one of the last places on earth where the wolf roams **unthreatened** by man. そこは，オオカミが人間たちに脅かされないで勝手に動き回る地球上で最後の土地の一つでもある．

thrift

接尾 (less) **thriftless** *adj* 節約しない，金遣いの荒い

tide

接尾 (less) **tideless** *adj* 潮汐［潮の満ち干］のない

tidy

接頭 (un) **untidy** *adj* だらしない

tie

接頭 (un) **untie** *v* 〈結び目などを〉ほどく ▶ **untie** a package 小包をほどく

tied

接頭 (un) **untied** *adj* 〈結び目やひもなどが〉解かれた

time

接尾 (less) **timeless** *adj* 時間に関係のない，無限の ▶ Experience 180 degree views of **timeless** sunrises over the Sierra

Madre. 時間を忘れる[時間に関係のない]シエラマドレに昇る日の出が180度の眺望で見ることができます.

timed

[接頭] (ill) **ill-timed** *adj* 時機を失した, タイミングの悪い ▶ She was in no humor to receive Henry's **ill-timed** addresses with favor. 彼女は, ヘンリーのタイミングのよくない求婚を喜んで受け入れる気分になかった.

timely

[接頭] (un) **untimely** *adj* 時機を失した ▶ Now, deeply aware of the doomsday clock, Rick Corman has the **untimely** job of planning his company's future. 現在, リック・コーマン氏は自分の死を意識しており, 時機を失してはいるが会社の将来の計画を立てる仕事に取り組んでいる. ▶ The petals cling to life tenaciously "as though loth or afraid to die rather than drop **untimely**, preferring to rot on her stem." 花弁はなかなか散らず, 死を嫌い恐れるかのように, 茎にしがみついたまま[時機を失したまま]色あせて枯れていく.

tire

[接尾] (less) **tireless** *adj* 疲れない, 飽きない

[接尾] (less) **tirelessly** *ad* 疲れを知らずに ▶ Robots will **tirelessly** repeat the path precisely. ロボットは疲れることなくその経路を正確に繰り返す.

tiring

[接頭] (un) **untiring** *adj* 疲れを知らない

[接頭] (un) **untiringly** *ad* 疲れることなく ▶ Once properly instructed, the computer executes its routines faithfully, **untiringly**, yielding to no boredom or carelessness. 適切な命令を与えると, コンピューターは, 忠実に, 疲れ知らずに, 倦怠感や不注意を示さずそのルーチンを実行する.

titled

[接頭] (un) **untitled** *adj* 題名のない

told

接頭 (un) **untold** *adj*

❶言語に絶する

❷数え切れない，無数の ► A reactor meltdown and explosion caused **untold** death and suffering. 原子炉溶融と爆発で，無数の死者と被害を引き起こした. ► An **untold** number were making his "I'm with Coco" graphic their own profile picture on Facebook. 数え切れない人たちが「Coco と共に」の画像をフェイスブック上の自分たちのプロフィール写真にしていた.

tolerable

接頭 (in) **intolerable** *adj* 許容しがたい ► Heavy-duty protective relay systems detect all **intolerable** system conditions. 高負荷保護リレーシステムはすべての許容できないシステム状態を検出する. ► Danish Prime Minister . . . called the situation "**intolerable** and extremely worrying." デンマークの…首相はその状況を「許し難くてこの上なく厄介である」と表現した.

tolerance

接頭 (in) **intolerance** *n*

❶不寛容 ► **Intolerance** for corruption is the sine qua non of MCC deal making. 違法行為を許容しないことは，MCC 取引をする場合の必須条件である.

❷不耐性，過敏症

tolerant

接頭 (in) **intolerant** *adj*

❶不耐性の ► Between 30 million and 50 million people in the United States are lactose **intolerant**. 米国では3000万～5000万人が乳糖不耐性を示します.

❷不寛容な，偏狭な

tonal

接頭 (a) **atonal** *adj*〔音楽〕無調の

tonality

接頭 (a) **atonality** *n*〔音楽〕無調性

tone

接尾 (less) **toneless** *adj*

❶音調のない

❷活力のない

tooth

接尾 (less) **toothless** *adj*

❶歯のない ▸ After the blade has been rotated, the drive gear continues to turn, but slips on the **toothless** portion of the driven gear. ブレードを回した後も駆動ギアは回転し続けるが，駆動ギアの歯のない部分で滑る．

❷威力のない

touchable

接頭 (un) **untouchable** *adj*

❶手の届かない，触ることのできない，実体のない ▸ Former President Luiz Lula da Silva called Brazil's judiciary a "black box" that's "**untouchable.**" 元大統領のルイス・ルラ・ダ・シルヴァ氏は，ブラジルの司法制度は「触れることのできない」「ブラックボックス」だと呼んだ．

❷触れてはならない

touched

接頭 (un) **untouched** *adj* 手を付けていない ▸ No cities went **untouched** by the collapse in price over the past few years. 過去数年において価格破壊により被害を受けなかった都市はない． ▸ The money I had put aside for my mother's post-operative care was kept **untouched** and added to my sense of futility. 母の手術後の養生に備えて用意したお金がそのまま残ったのも，私のむなしさに拍車をかけた．

towed

接頭 (un) **untoward** *adj* 運の悪い，不利な

toxic

接頭 (non) **nontoxic** *adj* 毒(性)がない，無毒の ▸ The fiber is relatively narrow (approx. 2 mm) and said to be **nontoxic**. そ

の繊維は比較的細く（約2mm），毒性がないといわれている．
▸ **Nontoxic** to plants and animals, penicillin is toxic to many growing Eubacteria. ペニシリンは，植物や動物に対しては無毒であるが，多くの増殖中の真正細菌に対しては有毒である．

trace

[接尾]（less） **traceless** *adj* 〈犯罪などの〉痕跡がない

track

[接尾]（less） **trackless** *adj* 足跡のない

tractable

[接頭]（in） **intractable** *adj*

❶ 手に負えない ▸ Such plans would make the debt problem **intractable** by weakening the IMF and the World Bank. そのような計画は，IMFと世界銀行を弱体化させて債務問題を手に負えないものにする．

❷ 扱いにくい ▸ For **intractable** problems, approximate solutions should be used. 扱いにくい問題では，近似解を用いるとよい．

traditional

[接頭]（non） **nontraditional** *adj* 非伝統的な

trained

[接頭]（ill） **ill-trained** *adj* しつけの悪い，取り付け方が間違っている

[接頭]（un） **untrained** *adj* 訓練を受けていない ▸ We are concerned here only with the major manual input methods that can be executed by **untrained** operators. 訓練されていないオペレーターが実行できる主な手動入力方法のみ不安があります．

trammeled

[接頭]（un） **untrammeled** *adj* 妨げられない

transferred

[接頭]（non） **nontransferred** *adj* 非移転の，ノントランスファー

的な ▸ Two modes are used to generate a plasma: transferred arc and **nontransferred** arc. プラズマを発生させるのに二つのモード，すなわちトランスファーアークとノントランスファーアークがある．

translated

接頭 (mis) **mistranslated** *adj* 誤訳された ▸ In the negotiation, another example is 35,000, **mistranslated** by the interpreter as 35 million. その交渉においてもう一つの例は，35,000が通訳によって3500万として誤訳されたことである．

transparent

接頭 (non) **nontransparent** *adj* 非透過の，透明でない ▸ This allows a terminal not only to make use of one B channel in the **nontransparent** mode for the needs of basic telephony but also ... これにより端末は基本的な電話通信に必要な非透過モードにおいて，B チャンネルを1個利用できるようにするばかりでなく，…もできるようになる．

traveled

接頭 (un) **untraveled** *adj* 旅行したことがない

treat

接頭 (ill) **ill-treat** *v* 虐待する，冷遇する，酷使する ▸ If you **ill-treat** a horse, it won't race for you and you won't win with it. 馬を雑に扱えば，思うように走ってくれないしレースに勝てない．

treated

接頭 (ill) **ill-treated** *adj* 虐待された ▸ I can not allow you to be **ill-treated**. 君が虐待されるのを僕は黙って見ていられない． ▸ an **ill-treated** child 被虐待児

接頭 (un) **untreated** *adj* 未処理の ▸ Operation of a water supply may involve either plain chlorination, which is addition of chlorine to otherwise **untreated** water, or ... 給水業務では，塩素をそれ以外の方法では処理されない水に塩素を添加する単純な塩素処理，または…が行われる．

tried

接頭 (un) **untried** *adj* 試されたことがない

trivial

接頭 (non) **nontrivial** *adj* 些細でない，重要な，簡単でない ▶ Detecting low-flying aircraft is **nontrivial** in part because propagation over the earth's horizon is weak. 低飛行航空機の探知は，地平線上の伝播力が幾分弱いためもあり，簡単でない．

trod

接頭 (un) **untrod** *adj* 踏まれていない，人跡未踏の

troubled

接頭 (un) **untroubled** *adj* 心を乱されない

true

接頭 (un) **untrue** *adj* 真実でない ▶ This assessment of scopes as crude technology has turned out to be **untrue**. 原油処理技術の領域に関するこの評価は，正しくないことがわかった． ▶ In creating an "image" of his company as an alert, aggressive, capable organization, it is never necessary for the writer to make **untrue** statements. 機敏で，積極的で，能力が高い組織という自分の会社の「イメージ」を作るために，虚偽の表現を用いることは著作者にはけっして必要ではない．

trust

接頭 (dis) **distrust** *v* 信じない，疑う ▶ Some users still **distrust** the sampled traces that DSOs provide, no matter how fast the sampling rate. サンプリング速度がいかに速くても，ユーザーのなかには，DSO が提供しているサンプルのトレース結果を信用していないものがやはりいる．

—— *n* 不信，疑惑 ▶ create **distrust** and uncertainty in the minds of foreign customers dealing with American firms 米国企業と取引している外国の顧客の心に不信感とためらいを生じさせる

接尾 (less) **trustless** *adj* 信用できない ▶ The information we

have received for so long has proven to be **trustless**. 我々が長年にわたり得てきた情報は信用できないことがわかった.

trustful

接頭 (dis) **distrustful** *adj* 信じがたい ► The nation is increasingly **distrustful** of the federal government. 国民は, 連邦政府をますます信用しなくなる.

trustworthiness

接頭 (un) **untrustworthiness** *n* 不信 ► If the negotiations are not going well, the perception of impatience may be construed as **untrustworthiness** by Japanese negotiators not familiar with U.S. customs. 交渉がうまくいかないときは, アメリカの習慣に不慣れな日本人交渉者が性急さを感じてそれを不信感と解釈しているのかも知れない.

trustworthy

接頭 (un) **untrustworthy** *adj* 信頼できない

truth

接頭 (un) **untruth** *n* 虚偽, 真実でないこと

truthful

接頭 (un) **untruthful** *adj* 偽りの, 真実でない ► Great attention should be paid to the **untruthful** report. 偽りの報告に多くの注意を払うべきである.

tube

接尾 (less) **tubeless** *adj* 〈タイヤなどが〉チューブレスの

tuck

接頭 (un) **untuck** *v* 〈まくりあげたものを〉 もとに戻す ► Support her while your helper brushes out any crumbs, **untucks** the bottom layers of bedding and rolls them up to the patient's back. 看護師がゴミをブラシで掃き出し, 最下にある寝具をたくし上げ, 患者の背中まで巻き上げるまで患者を支えなさい.

tucked

接頭 (un) **untucked** *adj* 〈包みなどが〉 ほぐれた ► Wrinkled

sheets, crumbs in the bed, and **untucked** bedclothes all contribute to restlessness. しわくちゃのシーツ，寝具内のごみくず，はみ出している寝具，これらすべてが睡眠の妨げとなる．

tune

接尾 (less) **tuneless** *adj* 調子外れの

tuned

接頭 (un) **untuned** *adj* 調子がずれている

turned

接頭 (un) **unturned** *adj* ひっくり返されていない，裏返しではない

tutored

接頭 (un) **untutored** *adj* 知識のない

twist

接頭 (un) **untwist** *v* 〈よじれやねじれなどを〉もとに戻す

typical

接頭 (a) **atypical** *adj* 変則的な，例外的な ▶ My situation is perhaps **atypical** in that I am older and my wants are simple. 私の方が年齢が高くて私の欲望が単純である点で，例外的なのかもしれない． ▶ Soft cheeses may be spoiled by gas production, excessive acidity, improper development of surface flora, and contamination with **atypical** molds. 軟かいチーズは，ガス発生，過酸性，表面フローラの異常な成長，変則的カビの汚染などにより損なわれることがある．

接頭 (un) **untypical** *adj* 典型的でない ▶ It is **untypical** of Jim to make such a mistake. そんな間違いをするとはジムらしくない．

typically

接頭 (a) **atypically** *adj* 例外的に ▶ Even if all 60 pay and attend, that will be an **atypically** small conference. 60人全員が会費を払って出席したとしても，それは例外的に小規模な会合であろう．

U

understanding

接頭 (mis) **misunderstanding** *n* 誤解 ▸ Confusion or **misunderstanding** may result, but on the other hand, negotiators may get more than they actually expect or deserve via this technique. 混乱や誤解が起こることもあるが，一方では，交渉者はこの技術によって，実際に予想されるかまたは受けるに値するよりも多くのものを得ることがある．

uniform

接頭 (non) **nonuniform** *adj*

❶ 不均質な，不均一な ▸ Warping of bars will result, and **nonuniform** wall thickness will occur in tubes. 結果としてバーにたわみが生じ，チューブの壁厚が不均一になる． ▸ In solar cells, the **nonuniform** generation of carriers within the junction plane gives rise to a concentration gradient along the junction plane. 太陽電池では，接合面内のキャリアの不均一な発生は，接合面に沿って濃度勾配を引き起こす． ▸ The first and probably the most important was to provide a method for applying uniform radial compression to the welding ring without causing **nonuniform** distortion. 一番目でおそらく最も重要なことは，溶接リングに不斉一な歪みを生じさせないで半径方向に均等に圧縮を加える方法を示すことである．

❷ 非一様な ▸ The charge-ratio method is an electrostatic method where the grid is laid out on a **nonuniform** pattern. 電荷率方式は，格子構造が非一様形態で構築されている場合の静電方式である．

uniformity

接頭 (non) **nonuniformity** *n* 不均質性 ▸ The slot effect is caused by the variation of reluctance torque, which is due to the magnetic **nonuniformity** presented by the slot openings. スロッ

ト効果は，リラクタンストルクの変動により生ずるが，これはスロット開口部に現れる不均一磁界によるものである．

union

接頭 (dis) **disunion** *n*

❶分割，分離

❷不統一

接頭 (non) **nonunion** *adj* 労働組合に加入していない，非組織の，労働組合員を雇用しない

unite

接頭 (dis) **disunite** *v* 分離させる

unity

接頭 (non) **nonunity** *n* 非単一性 ▸ For a speed increaser, the **nonunity** ratio is less than 1; for a decreaser, greater than 1. 加速装置の場合，非単一性率は1より小さくなり，減速装置は1より大きくなる．

usable

接頭 (un) **unusable** *adj*

❶使いものにならない ▸ If the synchronizing signals are caused to vary at random but predetermined rates, the signal is **unusable** in conventional receivers. もし同期信号がランダムであるが所定のレートで変動させられるなら，その信号はこれまでの受信機には使用できない．

❷使われない ▸ The open hearth became an important user of hitherto **unusable** iron and steel scrap. 平炉は，これまで使用されなかった鉄や鋼のスクラップの重要な使用者となった． ▸ Plastic parts become hard and **unusable** in time, but you can prolong their life by washing them in warm water with a little washing-up liquid. ビニール部品は使っているとこわばり使えなくなるが，少量の洗剤で温水中で洗濯すれば寿命を延ばすことができる．

use

接頭 (dis) **disuse** *v* 使用をやめる ▸ Cotton-covered wire formerly was extensively used in receiver manufacturing but has been **disused** owing to the fact that ... 綿で被覆した電線は，かつては受信機の製造に広く使われていたが，…という事実が明らかになって廃止されている.

—— *n* 使われないこと ▸ The word has passed into complete **disuse**. その言葉は，まったく使われなくなった.

接頭 (ill) **ill-use** *n* 酷使

接頭 (non) **nonuse** *n* 不使用

接尾 (less) **useless** *adj* 役に立たない ▸ Regardless of capabilities, an interactive graphic system is **useless** if it cannot conform to your needs. 能力がどうあろうと，対話型グラフィックシステムは，あなたの必要性に合致しないならば役に立たない. ▸ No matter how **useless** parents and state may be, people of individuality will emerge and develop. 親や国がどんなにだめでも，個性のある人間は現れ，育つ.

used

接頭 (dis) **disused** *adj* 廃止された

接頭 (un) **unused** *adj*

❶ 使われていない ▸ In general, very little **unused** chlorine capacity exists in the industry. 一般的に，業界には使用されない塩素生産量はわずかしか存在しない.

❷ 慣れていない

usual

接頭 (un) **unusual** *adj* 異常な，普通でない ▸ With proper care in selecting and applying limit switches, a life of 20 million operations is not **unusual**. リミット・スイッチを適切に選択し応用すれば，操作回数2,000万回という寿命は異常ではない. ▸ **Unusual** structures may require special maintenance procedures. 特別な構造では特殊な保全手続きが必要になることがある.

usually

接頭 (un) **unusually** *ad*

❶異常に，普通でなく ▸ It shows the advantage of water over other fluids, a result of its **unusually** low viscosity. 水の他の液体に対する長所は，粘度が非常に低いということである.
❷非常に ▸ Nobody will respond unless they have particularly good memories or are **unusually** good-natured. よほど記憶力のいいやつか，よほど人のいいやつじゃないと話に乗ってこない.

utile

[接頭] (in) **inutile** *adj* 無用の，無益の

utterable

[接頭] (un) **unutterable** *adj* 言葉に表せない

V

valid

接頭 (in) **invalid** *adj*

❶ 無効の，妥当でない ▶ When a collision is detected, the transceiver puts a special **invalid** signal on the cable to insure that . . . 衝突が検知されると，そのトランシーバーは特殊な無効信号をケーブルに送信し，…を確実に認識するようにする． ▶ Unless a check is signed, it is **invalid**. 小切手は，署名されていなければ無効である．

❷ 根拠がない

validate

接頭 (in) **invalidate** *v* 無効になる ▶ A contract is **invalidated** if only one party signs it. 当事者の一方だけが署名をしただけでは，契約は無効になる．

valuable

接頭 (in) **invaluable** *adj* とても高価な，貴重な ▶ The multitude of artifacts already examined are **invaluable**, not simply for their rarity but for . . . 検証済みの芸術作品の多くは，それが稀少であるだけではなく…であるために貴重なものである． ▶ Plasmids are an **invaluable** tool in recombinant DNA technology. プラスミドは，組み換え DNA 技術において，非常に貴重な道具となっている． ▶ A bed-tray is **invaluable** for the patient who has to have his meals in bed. ベッドトレイは，ベッドで食事をしなければならない患者にとって非常に貴重である． ▶ The companionship and friendship of an understanding volunteer can be **invaluable** to both the patient and the community psychiatric nurse. 理解があるボランティアの仲間意識や友情が，患者と地域の精神科の看護師の両方にとって非常に貴重でありうる．

valuation

接頭 (de) **devaluation** *n* 〈平価の〉切り下げ, 〈価値の〉低下 ► Commodity prices are going up, and the **devaluation** of the U.S. dollar will help support energy prices over the long term. 一次産品の価格は上がりつつあり, 米ドルの価値の低下が長期的にエネルギー価格を支えるうえで役に立つであろう.

value

接頭 (de) **devalue** *v* 〈価値などを〉低下させる

接尾 (less) **valueless** *adj* 価値のない ► This means that what is normally regarded as **valueless** waste should now be regarded as recyclable material. つまり, 通常価値のないごみとみなされているものは, リサイクル可能な材料とみなすべきだということである.

vaporized

接頭 (un) **unvaporized** *adj* 蒸発していない ► The **unvaporized** liquid is continually removed as the still or bottom product. 気化していない液体は, 蒸留器生産物または残留生産物として継続的に除去される.

variable

接頭 (in) **invariable** *adj* 変えることのできない

—— *n* 不変量, 不変数 ► K and θ are the **invariables**. K と θ は不変量である.

variably

接頭 (in) **invariably** *ad*

❶ 変わることなく, 不変に, 常に, いつも ► Satellite launchings are **invariably** made toward the east, since the earth rotates in that direction. 衛星の打ち上げは必ず東に向けられるが, それは地球がその方向に回転しているからだ. ► Even if they have a miai, therefore, they are **invariably** turned down. だから, せっかくお見合いをしてもいつも断られてしまう.

❷ 必ず ► Virulent phages **invariably** kill their hosts. 毒性ファージは, 必ず宿主を殺す. ► The girls who were bright students were almost **invariably** good at English. 女生徒で勉強ができる子は，ほとんどと言っていいほど［ほとんど必ず］英語もできた.

variant

接頭 (in) **invariant** *adj.* 不変の，変化しない，一様の ► The line codes used for echo suppression must be **invariant** with respect to time in the event of storage of the pulse responses. エコー抑制に用いる回線コードは，パルス応答を蓄積する場合には，時間に関して不変でなければならない.

varnished

接頭 (un) **unvarnished** *adj*

❶ ありのままの，ごまかしのない ► This is how to get the **unvarnished** truth about how a piece of software actually performs. これは一片のソフトウェアが実際にはどのように性能を発揮するかについてごまかしのない事実を知る方法である.

❷ ニスを塗っていない ► I was amazed when I read the card that accompanied the rice tub of **unvarnished** cypress wood. 櫃材の白木のお櫃にそえられたカードを読んで，私は茫然とした.

veil

接頭 (un) **unveil** *v*

❶ ベールをはがす

❷ 公表する，発表する ► A new version was **unveiled** a year later. 1年後に新しい版が発表された. ► Jobs sometimes uses the occasion to **unveil** important initiatives. ジョブズ氏は重要なイニシアティブを公表するため，この好機を使用した. ► At the F8 event in September, he **unveiled** something called a timeline to replace Facebook's aging profile pages. 9月に行われたF8イベントにおいて彼は，フェイスブック社の古くなったプロフィール・ページにとって代わるタイムラインと呼ばれるものを発表した.

veiling

接頭 (un) **unveiling** *n* 〈計画などを〉明らかにすること ▶ In the short time since its **unveiling**, sales have reportedly maintained a fivefold lead over competing personal productivity applications. それが明らかになってからの短い時間に，売り上げは競合する個人向け生産性アプリケーションに対して5倍のリードを維持していると伝えられている．

ventilated

接頭 (ill) **ill-ventilated** *adj* 換気の悪い

接頭 (non) **nonventilated** *adj* 非換気の ▶ **Nonventilated** means so constructed as to provide no intentional circulation of external air through the enclosure. 意図的にエンクロージャーの外の空気を中に入れて循環させたりしないような構造の非換気手段．

接頭 (un) **unventilated** *adj* 換気されていない ▶ Carboxyhemoglobin rose from 1.25% to 1.77% after exposure in the ventilated room, and to 2.28% after exposure in the **unventilated** room. 一酸化炭素ヘモグロビンは，換気された部屋では1.25パーセントから1.77パーセントに上昇し，換気されていない部屋では，2.28パーセントまで上昇した．

ventilating

接頭 (non) **nonventilating** *adj* 無風の ▶ **Nonventilating** conditions may be present over an area for several days as a result of certain meteorological phenomena. ある種の気象現象の結果として，ある区域で数日間無風状態となることがある．

verbal

接頭 (non) **nonverbal** *adj* 言葉を用いない ▶ Negotiations may be marked by various signals, both verbal and **nonverbal**. 交渉は，さまざまな信号，すなわち言葉を用いるものと言葉を用いないものの両方で特徴付けられる．

versed

接頭 (un) **unversed** *adj* ～に精通していない

view

接尾 (less) **viewless** *adj*

❶目に見えない

❷意見を持たない

vigorous

接頭 (in) **invigorous** *adj* 不愉快な

vincibility

接頭 (in) **invincibility** *n* 無敵, 不敗 ► On that Friday morning he had the look of **invincibility** that appears to have characterized him all his life, but that sometimes is stripped away by sadness. その金曜の朝, 彼は無敵の様相であった. それは彼の生涯の特徴であったけれども, 時に悲しみでその無敵さは剥がされる.

vincible

接頭 (in) **invincible** *adj* 無敵の ► Harumafuji wrapped up the Emperor's Cup by defeating the seemingly **invincible** Hakuho on July 23 in a long-awaited showdown. 日馬富士は7月23日, ファンが待ち望んでいた決戦で, 無敵のように思われた白鵬を倒して天皇賜杯を制した.

violable

接頭 (in) **inviolable** *adj* 侵害することのできない ► Nor should the outline developed at the start of a project be considered to be **inviolable**. また, プロジェクトの開始時に策定されたアウトラインを絶対に変更不可能と考えるべきでもない. ► When . . . one must be sure to understand that the people of that country have their ideas and feelings which are absolutely **inviolable**. …の場合, その国の人々にはなんぴとにも侵すことのできない思想や感情があることをきちんと悟るべきである.

violate

接頭 (in) **inviolate** *adj* 侵害されない, 不可侵の ► As we have had the opportunity to learn from Hitler, Starlin, and Mao Zedong, this freedom alone must be **inviolate**. ヒトラー，スターリン，毛沢東で人類は学習しましたから，この自由だけは不可侵としなければなりません．

violence

接頭 (non) **nonviolence** *n* 非暴力

violent

接頭 (non) **nonviolent** *adj* 非暴力の

virulent

接頭 (non) **nonvirulent** *adj* 毒性がない，無毒(性)の ▸ It is possible that some plasmids became permanently **nonvirulent**. プラスミドのいくつかは，永久に無毒になった可能性がある．

viscous

接頭 (non) **nonviscous** *adj* 非粘性の ▸ . . . , whereas irrotational flow is possible only for an ideal or **nonviscous** fluid. …，一方，非回転流は，理想流体または非粘性流体でのみ可能である．

visible

接頭 (in) **invisible** *adj*

❶ 見えない ▸ All the text in a story is threaded together as though an **invisible** thread runs through every word. …， ストーリー内のテキストは，すべての言葉に見えない糸が通っているかのように，すべてが一つの筋に結ばれている． ▸ The **invisible** nature of radiation does stir emotions and feed paranoiac imaginations. 放射能は目に見えないため動揺を与え，偏執的な妄想をもたらす． ▸ In dry atmosphere at 25℃ the oxide film on iron is 15-50 A thick and is **invisible**. 25℃の乾燥した大気中では，鉄につく酸化膜は厚さが15～50 Aで，目には見えない． ▸ The result could be an even greater number of **invisible** addicts. その結果，目に見えない常用者はさらに多数となりうる． ▸ Popularity — it is something like an **invisible** gas and immediately moves away. 人気――それは

見えないガスみたいなものなので，すぐに離れていく．
❷無視されている

vision

接尾 (less) **visionless** *adj* 見通しのない ► Without this you are doomed to a **visionless** future and endless mediocrity. これをしなければ，君たちには希望のない将来と永遠に続く平凡な人生が運命づけられている．

vital

接頭 (non) **nonvital** *adj* 活気のない，重要でない ► This subsystem performs **nonvital** operating functions such as starting, running at the prescribed speeds, slowing down, and stopping. このサブシステムは，起動，指示速度による運転，減速，停止など重要でない運転機能を果たす．

voice

接頭 (non) **nonvoice** *n* 音声なしの ► This new system has as its primary goal the integration of voice and **nonvoice** services. この新しいシステムは音声サービスと非有声サービスの統合を主要目的としている．

接尾 (less) **voiceless** *adj*
❶無言の，声が出せない
❷発言権のない

接尾 (less) **voicelessness** *n* 声の出ないこと

voiced

接頭 (un) **unvoiced** *adj* 口に出さない

volatile

接頭 (in) **involatile** *adj* 蒸発しない，不揮発性の ► The most volatile components evaporate first, but with all crude oils there will undoubtedly be a residue left which is virtually **involatile**. 最も揮発性のある成分がまず蒸発するが，あらゆる原油で疑う余地なく，ほとんど不揮発性の残留物が出る．

接頭 (non) **nonvolatile** *adj* 揮発しない，不 [非] 揮発性の ► All **nonvolatile** carbonaceous materials are deposited on the catalyst as coke and are ... 不揮発性炭質はすべて触媒上にコークとして沈着し，…. ▶ With steam distillation, a volatile material can be separated from **nonvolatile** impurities. 水蒸気蒸留によって，揮発性の成分を不揮発性の不純物から分離することができる. ▶ This command stores the active configuration parameters in **nonvolatile** memory as one of two user-defined profiles. この命令によって，二つのユーザー定義プロファイルの一つとして非揮発性メモリーにアクティブ設定パラメーターが保存される. ▶ Yet **nonvolatile** (distillate) fuels are burned to advantage in these engines which cannot be rigorously identified as true diesels. しかし，非揮発（蒸留液）燃料は，本物のディーゼルとは厳密には認められないこれらのエンジンで効果的に燃焼する.

voluntarily

接頭 (in) **involuntarily** *ad*

❶ 不随意に ▶ A small baby has no control over this muscle and its bladder empties immediately and **involuntarily**. 小さな赤ん坊はこの筋肉をコントロールできず，その膀胱は直ちにかつ不随意に空になる.

❷ 思わず，無意識に ▶ He looked so serious that I **involuntarily** hid myself and chuckled. 彼の姿があまりにも真剣なので，私は思わず身を隠し，くすくす笑ってしまった. ▶ "This is it!" I exclaimed **involuntarily** when I came to this passage. この一節に出合って，私は思わず［無意識に］「これだ！」と叫んだ.

voluntary

接頭 (in) **involuntary** *adj*

❶ 不本意な

❷ 非自発的な ▶ Nonetheless, there is no similar protection in cases of imprisonment to serve a sentence or of **involuntary** admission into a mental institution. それにもかかわらず，刑に服するための拘禁または精神病院への非自発的な入院の場

合，同様の保護はない．

❸ 無意識の ▸ The **involuntary** escape of urine or the emptying of the bowel is a very distressing and humiliating experience. 無意識の尿漏れや排便は非常に悩ましく，屈辱的な経験である．

vote

接尾 (less) **voteless** *adj* 選挙権のない

voting

接頭 (non) **nonvoting** *adj* 投票権のない

vulcanized

接頭 (un) **unvulcanized** *adj* 硫黄処理した，硫化した ▸ For example, **unvulcanized** rubber will dissolve in solvents in which vulcanized rubber will only swell. 例えば，加硫されていないゴムは，加硫されたゴムならば膨らむだけのソルベントによって溶ける．

vulnerable

接頭 (in) **invulnerable** *adj* 不死身の，へこたれない ▸ This ship was **invulnerable** even if as many as four of her watertight compartments were flooded. 水密区画が四つも水浸しになろうとも，この船は大丈夫であった．

W

waged

[接頭] (un) **unwaged** *adj* 定職のない，失業した

wanted

[接頭] (un) **unwanted** *adj*

❶望まれない ► In logic systems, noise refers to any **unwanted** voltage appearing at the input of a logic circuit. 論理装置の場合，ノイズとは論理回路の入力端に現れる好ましくない電圧のことをいう． ► His demands appeared to amount to less than $10 million — small potatoes for a billionaire like Forstmann but an **unwanted** nuisance nonetheless. 彼の要求は1千万ドル(フォーストマンのような億万長者にとっては小額であるが，望まれないやっかいな額ではある)には及ばないと思われた．

❷不要の，必要としない ► return **unwanted** goods 不用品を返品する

war

[接尾] (less) **warless** *adj* 戦争のない ► The pioneers of a **warless** world are the young men who refuse military service. 戦争のない世界の牽引者は，兵役を拒否する若者たちである．

warrant

[接頭] (un) **unwarrant** *v* 正当化しない ► The excess of enthusiasm raised the prices of western land to a figure which was entirely **unwarranted** when considered in view of the earning power. 過度の熱気によって西部の土地価格は，収益力の観点から考慮すると全く正当とは考えられない数字まで高騰した．

warrantable

[接頭] (un) **unwarrantable** *adj* 正当化できない

warranted

接頭 (un) **unwarranted** *adj* 正当化されていない ▸ The White House blasted Landrieu's ploy as "**unwarranted** and outrageous." ホワイトハウスはランドリュー氏の策略を「正当性がなく，かつ良識に欠ける」と非難した. ▸ All people have the right to be free of **unwarranted** interference with their private lives, their families, and their homes. すべての人は，各自の私生活，家族，家庭に対する不当な干渉から守られる権利を有する.

wary

接頭 (un) **unwary** *adj* 注意の足りない，不注意な

washed

接頭 (un) **unwashed** *adj* 洗っていない

watched

接頭 (un) **unwatched** *adj* 注意されていない

water

接頭 (un) **unwater** *v*

❶ 水を抜く ▸ During construction the dam site must be **unwatered** so that the foundation may be prepared. 工事中，ダム現場は基礎工事ができるよう水を抜いておく必要がある.

❷ 乾燥させる ▸ The passages must be **unwatered** for inspection and maintenance. 通路は，検査やメンテナンスのために乾燥させておく必要がある.

接尾 (less) **waterless** *adj*

❶ 水のない，干上がった

❷ 水のいらない〈料理〉

❸ 乾式の

wave

接尾 (less) **waveless** *adj* 波の立たない

wavering

接頭 (un) **unwavering** *adj* 動揺しない

waveringly

[接頭] (un) **unwaveringly** *ad* 動揺せずに

weapon

[接尾] (less) **weaponless** *adj* 武器を持たない ► If evil men were not now and then slain, it would not be a good world for **weaponless** dreamers. 悪人が処刑されないのであれば，武器を持たない夢想家にとってよい世界とはいえない．

wearing

[接頭] (non) **nonwearing** *adj* 消耗しない ► The mechanical electronic technology exists to put these **nonwearing**, high-energy beams to work on the factory floor. 機械電子技術の役目は，これらの消耗しない高エネルギーのビームを工場で運転できるようにすることである．

weary

[接尾] (less) **weariless** *adj* 疲労していない

wearying

[接頭] (un) **unwearying** *adj* 疲れない

wed

[接頭] (un) **unwed** *adj* 結婚しない，未婚の

weight

[接尾] (less) **weightless** *adj* 無重力の ► While traveling in orbit, his body is **weightless**. 軌道を飛行している間，彼の身体には重さがない． ► The astronaut must be able to work alone in a **weightless** condition in a near vacuum environment. 宇宙飛行士は，真空に近い環境で，かつ無重力状態で，たった一人で作業できなければならない．

welcome

[接頭] (un) **unwelcome** *adj* 歓迎されない ► Forstmann, a life-long gambler, has found himself back in the limelight and in the center of an **unwelcome** scandal. 生涯を通じてのギャンブラーであるフォーストマンは，自分が脚光を浴び，歓迎されないスキャンダルの中心にいることに気が付いた． ► By then many Chinese had written off Google as an **unwelcome** outsider with less reliable service. その時までに多くの中国人は，信頼できるサービスがなく歓迎されない外来者だとしてグーグルの名前を消してしまっていた．

welcoming

接頭 (un) **unwelcoming** *adj* 歓迎しない

well

接頭 (un) **unwell** *adj* 気分がよくない ► Kumiko was **unwell** for the past few days and was staying away from work. 久美子は二，三日，体の調子がすぐれずに，勤めを休んでいた． ► If the diet is not followed, the patient may become **unwell** and if he is then not treated he may lose consciousness and die. 規定食を続けることができなくなると，患者は衰弱し，治療を受けられなくなれば，意識を失い死亡してしまうかもしれない．

wheel

接尾 (less) **wheelless** *adj* 車輪の付いていない，無輪の

white

接頭 (non) **nonwhite** *adj* 非白人の

wholesome

接頭 (un) **unwholesome** *adj* 健康に悪い

wieldly

接頭 (un) **unwieldy** *adj* 扱いにくい ► Such trains can be **unwieldy** and difficult to control. そのような列車は扱いにくく制御が困難なことがある．

wife

接尾 (less) **wifeless** *adj* 妻のいない，独身の

willed

接頭 (ill) **ill-willed** *adj* 悪意をもった

willing

接頭 (un) **unwilling** *adj* 気が進まない ► **unwilling** consent いやいやながらの同意 ► The consensus these days is that tough business conditions have made people **unwilling** to take job risks. 最近では，人々は，困難な業務条件の下では，仕事のリスクを負うのに抵抗があるということが，一致した意見である． ▶ The general contractor must face the fact that a subcontractor who is losing money could be an **unwilling** member of the project team. 総合建設請負業者は，損をする下請け業者がプロジェクトチームに気が進まないながらメンバーとして加わっている場合があるという事実に直面しなければならない． ▶ If we are **unwilling** to take initiative and work for change, how can we fault the students for being apathetic and apolitical? 我々がイニシアティブをとり，改革のために働こうとしなければ，冷淡で政治に関心のない学生たちを非難できるはずがない．

willingly

接頭 (un) **unwillingly** *ad* 気乗りせずに

willingness

接頭 (un) **unwillingness** *n* 気が進まないこと ▶ Rather, it is the people's **unwillingness** to confront the past. むしろ過去に立ち向かうことは人々にとって気の進まないことである．

wind

接頭 (un) **unwind** *n* 〈緊張などが〉ほぐれる ▶ 5:45PM. Time to **unwind**. The Battle of Britain combat game is up and running. 午後5時45分，緊張が解ける時間．バトルオブブリテンの戦闘ゲームが始まる．

接尾 (less) **windless** *adj* 風のない，無風の

window

接尾 (less) **windowless** *adj* 窓のない ▶ If that team wants to invest, it will bring it to the full NEA partnership, which meets every Monday in a **windowless** conference room. そのチームが投資を希望するのであれば，NEA と全面的な提携を結ぶことができるであろう．経営者たちは毎週月曜日に窓のない会議室で会合を開いている．

wing

接尾 (less) **wingless** *adj* 翼のない

winnable

接頭 (un) **unwinnable** *adj* 勝ち取れない ▶ William Westmoreland had deliberately downplayed the strength of the North Vietnamese, deepening U.S. involvement in an **unwinnable** war. ウィリアム・ウェストモアランド氏は故意に北ベトナム兵の力を過小評価し，その結果アメリカは勝ち取れない戦争の泥沼にはまっていった.

wire

接尾 (less) **wireless** *adj* 無線[ワイヤレス]の ▶ The television camera is a device used to pick up and translate a scene into an electrical signal called video for transmission by cable or **wireless** broadcasting. テレビカメラは，映像を撮り，それを有線放送あるいは無線放送で送信するための，ビデオといわれる電気信号に変換するのに用いられる機器である. ▶ Google acquired a tiny **wireless** startup called Android in 2005. グーグル社は2005年にアンドロイドと呼ばれる小さな無線通信新興企業を買収した. ▶ Paul Jacobs is a distinguished electrical engineer in his own right, with more than 40 **wireless**-technology and -device patents to his name. ポール・ジェイコブズ氏は著名な電気技術者であり，40件以上のワイヤレス技術および装置に関する自分名義の特許を所有している.

—— *n* 無線 ▶ It was 12:15 when the first call for help was sent out on the **wireless**. 救助を求める第一信が無線で発信されたのは12:15だった.

wise

接頭 (un) **unwise** *adj* 賢明でない，愚かな ▶ With current technology, it is **unwise** to have satellites spaced much closer than 4 degrees in the 360-degree equatorial plane. 現在の技術では，360度の赤道面内に4度より近い間隔で衛星を配置するのは賢明ではない. ▶ Besides, it was thought **unwise** to lighten the stick forces too much in case the aircraft was accidentally overstressed. おまけに，航空機に不慮の過大な負荷が加わっている場合，操縦桿に加える力を軽減しすぎるのは賢明ではないと考えられた. ► We are hard-wired to do nothing in most cases, even when the data tell us that's **unwise**. データによるとたとえ愚かな判断であっても我々はほとんどの場合本来何もしないようにできている.

wisely

接頭 (un) **unwisely** *ad* 愚かに ► Taken aback, we remained silent for a while, but then Yoko **unwisely** ventured to ask "You said 'level'. . . ?" 私たちは驚いて黙ったが，よせばいいのに(愚かにも)陽子ちゃんは「平ら…ですか」と質問した.

wished

接頭 (un) **unwished** *adj* 望まれていない ► Love and Death are two **unwished** guests. Nobody can rule over them. 愛と死は望まれない来客だ. だれもこれらをコントロールすることはできない.

wished-for

接頭 (un) **unwished-for** *adj* 望んでいない

wisher

接頭 (ill) **ill-wisher** *n* 他人の不幸を願う人

wit

接尾 (less) **witless** *adj* 知恵のない，愚かな

接尾 (less) **witlessly** *ad* 愚かに ► No longer did he **witlessly** climb the narrow trees. もはや彼は細い木を登るという愚かなことはしなかった.

witnessed

接頭 (un) **unwitnessed** *adj*

❶ 目撃されていない ► **unwitnessed** everyday occurrences 気付かないうちに過ぎてゆく日々の出来事

❷ 〈五官などに〉感知されない

witting

接頭 (un) **unwitting** *adj* 気が付かない ▸ The dapper Italian technocrat could emerge as a savior of the world financial system or as its **unwitting** assassin. このこざっぱりした身なりのイタリア人テクノクラートは，世界の金融システムの救世主または気付かないでその暗殺者として現れたであろう．

wittingly

接頭 (un) **unwittingly** *ad* 気が付かずに，うっかり ▸ Forgetting is something one does **unwittingly** and not something one can do intentionally.「忘れる」とは，どう考えてみても，ついうっかり行うことであって，意図的にできることではない． ▸ There the virus was **unwittingly** reproduced by the employees. そこで，ウイルスは，従業員によって，はからずも複写された．

womanly

接頭 (un) **unwomanly** *adj* 女性らしくない

wonted

接頭 (un) **unwonted** *adj* 普通でない

word

接尾 (less) **wordless** *adj*

❶無言の

❷言葉にならない

work

接尾 (less) **workless** *adj* 仕事のない，失業した

workable

接頭 (un) **unworkable** *adj*

❶実行できない

❷加工できない ▸ The technology also helps Ford trim costs by not having to replace **unworkable** parts. この技術によりフォードは，加工できない部品を交換することなく，経費を削減することができる．

worldliness

接頭 (un) **unworldliness** *n* 世俗的でないこと

worldly

接頭 (un) **unworldly** *adj* 世俗的でない

worn

接頭 (un) **unworn** *adj*

❶摩耗していない

❷傷んでいない

worth

接尾 (less) **worthless** *adj* 価値のない ► The check is **worthless** unless it is signed. 小切手は，サインがなければ価値がない． ► Discovered in 1970 by a scientist at Sandoz, the drug was nearly abandoned as **worthless**. サンド社の科学者により1970年に発見されたその薬は，無価値としてほとんど放棄されていた． ► Land near Clifton, Kansas, which had earlier been considered **worthless**, sold in 1887 at $6000 a quarter section. カンサス州クリフトン近くの土地は，かつては価値がないと考えられていたが，1887年には1平方マイルの1/4が6000ドルで売られた．

worthy

接頭 (un) **unworthy** *adj* ～する価値がない ► For me, to be called "base" was like being told I was **unworthy** to live. 私にとって「卑怯だ」と言われることは「お前は生きている価値がない」というのと同じです．

woven

接頭 (non) **nonwoven** *adj* 不織の ► Plastics are produced in **nonwoven** fabric-like constructions. プラスチック生成物は不織布状の構造になっている．

wrap

接頭 (un) **unwrap** *v* 〈包みなどを〉開ける

wrinkle

接頭 (un) **unwrinkle** *v* しわを伸ばす，しわが伸びる

written

[接頭] (ill) **ill-written** *adj* 書き方が不適切な

[接頭] (un) **unwritten** *adj*

❶ 書かれていない，成文化されていない ▶ In Japan there seems to be an **unwritten** law that certain kinds of ethnic jokes are best not made in public. 日本では，ある種のエスニック・ジョークは，公の場ではあまり口にしないほうがよいという不文律があるらしい.

❷ 慣習となっている ▶ Everyone is aware of the **unwritten** caste system. 慣習となっているカースト制度についてだれもが承知している.

Z

zip

接頭 (un) **unzip** *v*

❶〈圧縮したファイルなどを〉解凍する

❷ジッパーを開ける

接尾 (less) **zipless** *adj* ジッパーの付いていない

zipped

接頭 (un) **unzipped** ジッパーが閉じていない ► If someone is walking along with his fly **unzipped** or her blouse unbuttoned,... 誰かがズボンのジッパーを留め忘れて歩いていたり，ブラウスのボタンを留め忘れて歩いたりしていたら，…

反意語索引

A

abase …… 34
abasement …… 35
abnormal …… 244
abnormality …… 244
abnormally …… 244
acritical …… 101
ageless …… 12
ahistorical …… 187
aimless …… 14
aimlessly …… 15
airless …… 15
amoral …… 236
amorality …… 236
apathetic …… 261
apathetically …… 261
apolitical …… 274
armless …… 23
artless …… 24
asocial …… 342
asymmetric(al) …… 362
asymmetry …… 363
asymptomatic …… 364
asymptomatically …… 364
asynchronous …… 364
asynchronously …… 364
atheism …… 369
atheist …… 369
atheistic …… 369
atonal …… 373
atonality …… 373
atypical …… 379
atypically …… 379

B

backless …… 33
baseless …… 34
beardless …… 35
blameless …… 38
bloodless …… 39
bodiless …… 39
borderless …… 39
bottomless …… 40
boundless …… 40
brainless …… 40
breathless …… 41
breathlessness …… 41
brimless …… 42
brushless …… 42

C

careless …… 46
carelessly …… 46
cashless …… 46
causeless …… 47
changeless …… 51
cheerless …… 54

D

E

F

G

godless ········ 176
godlessly ········ 176
godlessness ········ 176
graceless ········ 177
gracelessly ········ 177
gracelessness ········ 177
groundless ········ 179
groundlessly ········ 179
groundlessness ········ 179
guideless ········ 180
guileless ········ 180
guilelessly ········ 180
guilelessness ········ 180
guiltless ········ 180
guiltlessness ········ 180
gutless ········ 181
gutlessly ········ 181

H

hairless ········ 182
hairlessness ········ 182
handless ········ 182
hapless ········ 183
haplessly ········ 183
haplessness ········ 183
harmless ········ 184
harmlessly ········ 184
harmlessness ········ 184
hatlessly ········ 185
heartless ········ 186
heartlessly ········ 186
heartlessness ········ 186
heedless ········ 186
heedlessly ········ 186
heedlessness ········ 186
helpless ········ 186
helplessly ········ 186
helplessness ········ 187
homeless ········ 188
homelessness ········ 188
hopeless ········ 189
hopelessly ········ 190
hopelessness ········ 190
humorless ········ 191
humorlessly ········ 192
humorlessness ········ 192

I

ill-advised ········ 11
ill-advisedly ········ 11
ill-affect ········ 11
ill-affected ········ 11
ill-aimed ········ 15
ill-argued ········ 23
ill-arranged ········ 24
ill-assorted ········ 27
ill-attended ········ 28
ill-balanced ········ 33
ill-behaved ········ 36
ill-boding ········ 39
ill-bred ········ 41
ill-breeding ········ 41
ill-conceived ········ 75
ill-conditioned ········ 77

J

K

O

P

T

U

unwrap ··· 401
unwrinkle ··· 401
unwritten ··· 402
unzip ··· 403
unzipped ··· 403
useless ··· 382

V

valueless ··· 385
viewless ··· 388
visionless ··· 390
voiceless ··· 390
voicelessness ··· 390
voteless ··· 392

W

warless ··· 393
waterless ··· 394
waveless ··· 394
weaponless ··· 395
weariless ··· 395
weightless ··· 395
wheelless ··· 396
wifeless ··· 396
windless ··· 397
windowless ··· 397
wingless ··· 398
wireless ··· 398
witless ··· 399
witlessly ··· 399
wordless ··· 400
workless ··· 400
worthless ··· 401

Z

zipless ··· 403

和英索引

あ

アークの出ない　nonarcing〈22〉
愛のない　loveless〈223〉
相容れない　incompatible〈68〉, irreconcilable〈299〉
愛国心の欠如　incivism〈55〉
愛されていない　unloved〈223〉
相性が合わない　uncongenial〈79〉
空いている　untenanted〈368〉
曖昧さ　indetermination〈114〉
曖昧でない　unambiguous〈17〉, unequivocal〈139〉
曖昧でないこと　unambiguousness〈17〉
曖昧でなく　unambiguously〈17〉, unequivocally〈139〉
曖昧な　noncommittal〈66〉, unclear〈56〉
曖昧に　indefinitely〈110〉
アイロンがけの要らない　noniron〈207〉
青白い　bloodless〈39〉
青二才の　beardless〈35〉
明かされていない　undisclosed〈118〉
あからさまな　unashamed〈25〉
飽きない　tireless〈372〉
明らかな　uncoverable〈100〉
明らかに　unambiguously〈17〉
明らかにする　demystify〈239〉, disclose〈57〉, unclose〈58〉, uncover〈99〉, unroll〈317〉
明らかにすること　unveiling〈387〉
飽きることのない　insatiable〈321〉
あきれるほど　hopelessly〈190〉
悪意のある　ill-intentioned〈203〉

悪意のない　guileless〈180〉, innocuous〈243〉
悪意をもった　ill-disposed〈121〉, ill-willed〈396〉
～に悪影響を与える　ill-affect〈11〉
悪趣味な　tasteless〈367〉
アクセスできない　inaccessible〈4〉
アクセントのない　unaccented〈3〉
悪評　disrepute〈309〉
開けられていない　unopened〈250〉
開ける　unclose〈58〉, unwrap〈401〉
あごのない　chinless〈54〉
浅い考えで　incautiously〈47〉
足のない　footless〈166〉
足のない状態　footlessness〈166〉
脚のない　legless〈215〉, limbless〈217〉
味がないこと　tastelessness〈367〉
味付けされていない　unseasoned〈328〉
味のない　tasteless〈367〉
足跡のない　trackless〈375〉
焦り　impatience〈261〉
頭の悪い　clueless〈59〉
当たり障りのない　innocuous〈243〉, inoffensive〈250〉
悪化　degradation〈178〉
悪化する　degenerate〈174〉
扱いにくい　intractable〈375〉, unhandy〈182〉, unmanageable〈226〉, unwieldy〈396〉
厚かましい　imprudent〈288〉
圧縮解除　decompression〈73〉
圧縮されていない　uncompressed〈73〉
圧縮データをもとに戻す　decompress〈73〉
圧縮できない　incompressible〈73〉
圧倒的に　incomparably〈68〉
圧力を下げる　decompress〈73〉
当てにならない　undependable〈111〉

当てのない　aimless〈14〉
当てもなく　aimlessly〈15〉
穴の開いていない　imperforate〈265〉
雨の降らない　rainless〈293〉
誤った考え　misconception〈75〉
誤った処置　mishandling〈182〉
誤った伝達　miscommunication〈67〉
誤って　improperly〈285〉
誤って知らされる　misinformed〈199〉
誤って伝える　misrepresent〈309〉
誤り　inaccuracy〈5〉
誤りのない　inerrant〈140〉
誤りを犯さない　unerring〈140〉
誤ることなく　unerringly〈140〉
争いを好まない　noncontentious〈89〉
洗っていない　unwashed〈394〉
ありそうもない　improbable〈282〉, unlikely〈217〉
ありそうもなく　improbably〈282〉
ありのままの　artless〈24〉, unvarnished〈386〉
合わない　disagree〈13〉, ill-fitting〈162〉
合わないこと　disagreement〈14〉
哀れ　haplessness〈183〉
哀れな　hapless〈183〉
安価な　inexpensive〈147〉, less-expensive〈147〉
安価に　inexpensively〈147〉
暗号を解く　decode〈59〉
安全でない　unsafe〈320〉, unsecured〈328〉
安全な　harmless〈184〉
案内人がいない　guideless〈180〉
アンバランス　imbalance〈33〉
アンバランスな　imbalanced〈33〉
暗黙の　unspoken〈346〉

い

言いようのない　ineffable〈130〉, nameless〈240〉, unspeakable〈345〉
言いようのない状態で　indefinably〈109〉
言うことを聞かない　indocile〈124〉, unruly〈319〉
家のない　homeless〈188〉
家のないこと　homelessness〈188〉
硫黄処理した　unvulcanized〈392〉
イオン化していない　unionized〈207〉
イオンを除去する　deionize〈206〉
意外な　unexpected〈146〉, unlooked-for〈223〉
錨を上げる　unmoor〈235〉
息を切らした　breathless〈41〉
意気喪失する　demoralize〈236〉
意気地なく　gutlessly〈181〉
意気地のない　gutless〈181〉
違憲　unconstitutionality〈87〉
違憲の　unconstitutional〈86〉
意見を持たない　viewless〈388〉
石のない　stoneless〈353〉
意識がないこと　unconsciousness〈83〉
意識していない　unconscious〈82〉
意識を失った　unconscious〈82〉
異質の　inhomogeneous〈188〉
維持できない　unsustainable〈361〉, untenable〈368〉
意地の悪い　ill-natured〈241〉
異常　abnormality〈244〉
異常な　abnormal〈244〉, unusual〈382〉
異常に　abnormally〈244〉, unusually〈382〉
意地悪　ill-nature〈240〉
急がない　unhurried〈192〉
傷んでいない　unworn〈401〉
位置を変えさせる　dislocate〈221〉

一時的な　impermanent〈266〉
一様でない　uneven〈141〉
一様の　invariant〈386〉
一列になっていない　unaligned〈15〉
一貫性がなく　inconsistently〈85〉
一貫性のない　inconsistent〈85〉, disconnected〈81〉, discontinuous〈91〉
一致しない　disaccord〈5〉, disagree〈13〉, discordant〈76〉, dissonant〈344〉, incompatible〈68〉, incongruent〈80〉, inconsonant〈85〉
一致しないで　incongruently〈80〉, incongruously〈80〉
一定の地位にない　unplaced〈269〉
一点の曇りもない　immaculate〈225〉
いつになく　uncharacteristically〈52〉
一般的な　impersonal〈266〉
いつも　invariably〈385〉
偽って伝える　misrepresent〈309〉
偽りの　untruthful〈378〉
偽りのない　unfeigned〈158〉
偽る　disguise〈181〉
移動　displacement〈269〉
移動させる　dislodge〈222〉, displace〈268〉
糸くずの付いていない　lintless〈219〉
意図的でない　unintended〈202〉
糸巻きからほどく　unspool〈347〉
委任状のない　noncommissioned〈65〉
命のない　lifeless〈216〉
違反　disobedience〈247〉, nonconformance〈79〉
違反行為　misconduct〈77〉
衣服を着ていない　uncovered〈100〉
衣服を脱がされた　undressed〈126〉
衣服を脱がせる　undress〈126〉
衣服を脱ぐ　disrobe〈317〉
違法　illegitimacy〈215〉, unlawfulness〈214〉

違法な　illegitimate〈215〉
違法に　illegally〈215〉
違法の　illegal〈215〉, unlawful〈213〉
意味のない　fruitless〈172〉, meaningless〈230〉, purposeless〈290〉
いや応なく　inescapably〈140〉, inevitably〈142〉, irresistibly〈311〉
いや気　disinclination〈197〉, indisposition〈121〉
いや気を持たせる　disgust〈181〉
癒やせない　quenchless〈291〉
いやな　distasteful〈367〉, impossible〈276〉
いやな感じの　ill-favored〈156〉
いらいらした　impatient〈262〉
威力のない　toothless〈374〉
色あせない　fadeless〈152〉
異論のない　uncontested〈90〉, undisputed〈122〉
いわれのない　groundless〈179〉
陰気な　cheerless〈54〉
インク抜き　deinking〈201〉
インクを消す　deink〈200〉
インクを消すこと　deinking〈201〉
印刷していない　nonprinting〈282〉
印刷するのに適さない　unprintable〈282〉
印刷できない　unprintable〈282〉
印象的でない　unimpressive〈196〉
引用を終わる　unquote〈292〉

う

受け入れない　insusceptible〈361〉
受け入れられない　unacceptable〈3〉
動いていない　motionless〈237〉
動かされない　immovable〈238〉
動かしがたい　unshakable〈336〉
動かせない　immobile〈233〉, immovable〈238〉
動かない　unmoving〈238〉

動かなくする　immobilize〈234〉
動けない　immobile〈233〉, immotile〈237〉
〈コントロールなどを〉失った　disabled〈2〉
薄明かりの　ill-lit〈220〉
薄味の　flavorless〈163〉
歌にされていない　unsung〈358〉
歌のない　songless〈344〉
疑いなく　doubtlessly〈125〉, undoubtedly〈125〉, unquestionably〈292〉, unquestioningly〈292〉
疑いのない　doubtless〈125〉, undoubted〈125〉, unquestionable〈292〉, unquestioned〈292〉
疑いのないこと　doubtlessness〈125〉
疑いの余地がない　unimpeachable〈196〉
疑いの余地なく　unimpeachably〈196〉
疑い深い　incredulous〈101〉
疑いを持たない　unquestioning〈292〉
疑う　distrust〈377〉
疑うような目つきで　incredulously〈101〉
疑う余地なく　incontestably〈89〉
疑う余地のない　incontestable〈89〉
疑っていない　unsuspecting〈361〉
疑われていない　unsuspected〈361〉
内気な　undemonstrative〈111〉
打ち砕かれない　uncrushable〈102〉
打ち解けない　uncommunicative〈67〉
打ち負かすことのできない　unbeatable〈35〉
うっかり　inadvertently〈11〉, unwittingly〈400〉
うっかりした　inadvertent〈10〉
美しくない　unbeautiful〈36〉, unhandsome〈182〉
移す　dislocate〈221〉
訴えられない　unappealable〈19〉
移り気　inconstancy〈86〉
移り気な　inconstant〈86〉

腕のない　armless〈23〉, limbless〈217〉
奪う　disfranchise〈170〉, incapacitate〈45〉
奪うこと　incapacitation〈45〉
奪うことのできない　inalienable〈15〉
うまく調整されていない　uncoordinated〈95〉
埋められていない　unfilled〈160〉
埋めることができない　unbridgeable〈42〉
裏返しではない　unturned〈379〉
売れていない　unsold〈342〉
売れない　unsalable〈320〉
売れ残りの　unsold〈342〉
浮気　inconstancy〈86〉
浮気な　inconstant〈86〉
うわ薬をかけていない　unglazed〈176〉
うわ薬を除去する　deglaze〈176〉
運の悪い　untoward〈374〉
運転できない　inoperable〈250〉
運転不能の　nonoperative〈251〉

え

柄のない　stemless〈351〉
えも言われぬ　ineffable〈130〉
永遠に　immortally〈237〉
永遠の　ageless〈12〉, immortal〈236〉
影響されない　impervious〈268〉
影響を受けていない　uninfected〈198〉
影響を受けない　insensitive〈332〉, unaffected〈12〉
英国(人)らしくない　un-English〈137〉
永続しない　impermanent〈266〉
永続的な　indissoluble〈122〉
栄養不良の　ill-fed〈158〉
営利を追求しない　nonprofitmaking〈285〉
得がたい　inaccessible〈4〉

得ることのできない　unobtainable〈248〉
縁を切る　disown〈255〉
延々と　endlessly〈136〉
延期できない　inextensible〈150〉
縁起の悪い　inauspicious〈30〉
援助しないこと　nonsupport〈359〉
塩分のない　saltless〈320〉
塩分を除く　desalinize〈320〉
遠慮のない　unreserved〈310〉

お

尾のない　tailless〈365〉
おいしくない　unpalatable〈258〉
追い出す　dislodge〈222〉, unhouse〈190〉
老いない　ageless〈12〉
押印されていない　unsealed〈327〉
凹凸　unevenness〈141〉
覆いかぶされていない　unshrouded〈337〉
大きくない　insignificant〈338〉
大雑把に　carelessly〈46〉
オーソドックスでない　unorthodox〈254〉
冒されていない　uncorrupted〈97〉
おかしなことに　incongruously〈80〉
置き換え　displacement〈269〉
遅らされない　unhindered〈187〉
遅らせる　discourage〈98〉
行われていない　uncommitted〈66〉
起こりそうにない　improbable〈282〉
起こりそうにないこと　improbability〈282〉
抑え切れない　inextinguishable〈150〉
納まりの悪い　inhospitable〈190〉
教えにくいこと　indocility〈124〉
教えられたものでない　untaught〈367〉

惜しみない　unstinting〈352〉
惜しみなく　unstintingly〈352〉
汚染されていない　uncontaminated〈88〉, unpolluted〈274〉, untainted〈365〉
汚染物質の除去　decontamination〈89〉
汚染物質を除去する　decontaminate〈88〉
恐れ知らずの　fearless〈157〉
恐れず(に)　fearlessly〈157〉
恐れていない　unafraid〈12〉
恐れない　undaunted〈106〉
恐れを知らない　dauntless〈106〉
落ち着いた　nerveless〈242〉
落ち着かない　restless〈313〉
汚点のない　unblemished〈38〉
音のしない　noiseless〈243〉
男らしく　unmanly〈226〉
落とす　abase〈34〉
落とすこと　abasement〈35〉
衰えない　unabated〈1〉
驚くべき　incredible〈100〉
驚くほどでなく　unsurprisingly〈360〉
驚くほどではない　unsurprising〈360〉
同じ基準で測れない　incommensurable〈64〉
脅かされない　unthreatened〈371〉
覚えがない　guiltless〈180〉
思いがけない　unexpected〈146〉, unscripted〈326〉
思い違い　misconception〈75〉
思いとどまらせる　dissuade〈267〉
思いもよらない　unthought-of〈371〉
思いもよらぬほど　inconceivably〈74〉
思いやりのない　inconsiderate〈84〉, uncharitable〈53〉, unsympathetic〈363〉
思いやりのなさ　inconsiderateness〈84〉

面白みがない　mirthless〈232〉
思わず　involuntarily〈391〉
親不孝な　unfilial〈160〉
及んでいない　unreached〈295〉
折り合いがつかない　irreconcilable〈299〉
愚かしい　brainless〈40〉
愚かしいこと　insanity〈321〉
愚かな　clueless〈59〉, unwise〈398〉, witless〈399〉
愚かなこと　inadvisability〈11〉
愚かに　unwisely〈399〉, witlessly〈399〉
降ろす　unload〈220〉, unloading〈221〉
終わっていない　unfinished〈160〉
終わりがないこと　endlessness〈136〉
終わることのない　unending〈136〉
恩知らず　ingratitude〈178〉
音声なしの　nonvoice〈390〉
音調のない　toneless〈374〉

か

加圧されていない　unpressurized〈280〉
害のない　innocuous〈243〉, inoffensive〈250〉
害を及ぼさない形で　harmlessly〈184〉
階級のない　classless〈56〉
解禁する　decriminalize〈101〉
解決されていない　unsettled〈334〉, unsettling〈334〉, unsolved〈343〉
解決できない　inextricable〈151〉
解決する　untangle〈366〉
解決できない　insoluble〈342〉, unresolvable〈311〉
外国人　non-citizen〈54〉
解雇する　discharge〈52〉
開梱する　unpack〈257〉
解散　disbandment〈34〉
解散する　disband〈34〉, dissolve〈343〉

開示しないこと　nondisclosure〈118〉
解重合　depolymerization〈274〉
解重合する　depolymerize〈274〉
回収されていない　uncollected〈61〉
回収不可能な　uncollectable〈60〉, uncollectible〈61〉
回収不能の　nonreturnable〈315〉
塊状になっていない　nonagglomerated〈13〉
改心しない　unregenerate〈301〉
改善されていない　unimproved〈197〉
外装を施していない　unclad〈55〉
解体　disbandment〈34〉
解体する　deconstruct〈87〉, demobilize〈234〉, disband〈34〉, dismantle〈227〉
開店休業状態の　inactive〈7〉
解凍する　unfreeze〈170〉, unzip〈403〉
解読する　decode〈59〉, unscramble〈325〉, unscrambling〈326〉
ガイドのない　guideless〈180〉
飼いならせない　untamable〈365〉
開発されていない　unexploited〈149〉
開封する　unseal〈327〉
回復できない　irreclaimable〈299〉
解放された　disengaged〈137〉, untethered〈369〉
解放する　discharge〈52〉, disembarrass〈134〉, disengage〈137〉, unbridle〈42〉, unleash〈214〉
解明不可能な　unelucidated〈134〉
買い戻しができない　irredeemable〈300〉
解離　dissociation〈27〉
改良されていない　unimproved〈197〉
変えられずに　inalterably〈16〉
変えられない　inalterable〈16〉, unchangeable〈51〉
顧みられない　unregarded〈301〉
変えることのできない　invariable〈385〉
顔のないこと　facelessness〈152〉

書かれていない　unwritten〈402〉
〜にかかわりなく　irrespective〈312〉
書き方が不適切な　ill-written〈402〉
鍵のない　keyless〈211〉, lockless〈221〉
かき乱されていない　unperturbed〈267〉
過給されていない　unsupercharged〈358〉
核のない　stoneless〈353〉
家具が取り付けられていない　unfurnished〈173〉
欠くことのできない　unexpendable〈147〉
隠されていない　undisguised〈120〉
拡散防止の　nonproliferation〈285〉
確実に　indisputably〈121〉, undoubtedly〈125〉
確証されていない　uncorroborated〈97〉
確信のない　uncertain〈49〉, unsure〈360〉
確信していない　unconvinced〈94〉
確認しない　disconfirm〈79〉
確認できない　unidentified〈194〉
核兵器を保有していない　nonnuclear〈245〉
学問のない　unlearned〈214〉
学寮制でない　noncollegiate〈61〉
陰になっていない　unshaded〈335〉
かけがえのない　irreplaceable〈308〉
加工されていない　untamed〈365〉
加工できない　unworkable〈400〉
がさつな　ill-kept〈211〉
飾らない　unaffected〈12〉
飾られていない　unadorned〈9〉
舵のない　rudderless〈318〉
過剰な　inordinate〈252〉
ガスケットが付いていない　ungasketed〈174〉
風のない　windless〈397〉
風通しの良い　airless〈15〉
数え切れない　incalculable〈44〉, innumerable〈245〉, untold〈373〉

数え切れないこと　incalculability〈44〉
数えられていない　uncounted〈98〉
数えられない　uncountable〈98〉
可塑化されていない　unplasticized〈270〉
過疎化した　depopulated〈275〉
過疎化する　depopulate〈275〉
型ができていない　unformed〈169〉
硬くない　nonrigid〈317〉
形なく　formlessly〈167〉
形のない　formless〈167〉, shapeless〈336〉, unshaped〈336〉
形のないこと　formlessness〈167〉
形の悪い　ill-formed〈169〉
肩ひものない　strapless〈354〉
偏らない　impartial〈259〉, unbias(s)ed〈37〉
～する価値がない　unworthy〈401〉
価値のない　valueless〈385〉, worthless〈401〉
勝ち取れない　unwinnable〈398〉
活気のない　inanimate〈18〉, nerveless〈242〉, nonvital〈390〉, pulseless〈289〉, spiritless〈346〉
活気のない状態で　inanimately〈18〉
活気を弱める　de-energize〈136〉
学校教育を受けていない　unschooled〈325〉
合体されていない　unincorporated〈197〉
合致しないこと　disagreement〈14〉
活動しない　inactive〈7〉
活力のない　sapless〈321〉, toneless〈374〉
活力を弱める　depress〈280〉
稼動していない　inoperative〈251〉
過度に　unduly〈127〉
過度の　undue〈127〉, immoderate〈234〉
必ず　invariably〈385〉
金遣いの荒い　thriftless〈371〉
可能性のない人　nonstarter〈350〉

カバーを外す　uncover〈99〉
過敏症　intolerance〈373〉
カフェインを取り除いた　decaffeinated〈44〉
カプセルに包まれていない　unencapsulated〈135〉
カプセルになっていない[入っていない]　noncapsulated〈45〉
我慢できずに　impatiently〈262〉
我慢できない　insufferable〈356〉, insupportable〈359〉
我慢できないこと　impatience〈261〉
神にささげていない　unhallowed〈182〉
神の存在を否定して　godlessly〈176〉
神を信じないこと　atheism〈369〉
神を認めない　godless〈176〉
神を認めないこと　godlessness〈176〉
紙を使用しない　paperless〈258〉
加盟していない　unaffiliated〈12〉, unaligned〈15〉
仮面をはぐ　unmask〈228〉
体が不自由な　helpless〈186〉
軽々しい態度で　imprudently〈289〉
可愛らしくない　unlovely〈223〉
皮がむかれていない　unpeeled〈263〉
皮なしの　skinless〈341〉
変わっていない　unchanged〈51〉
変わらない　unchanging〈51〉
変わりなく　immutably〈239〉
変わりやすい　inconstant〈86〉
変わりやすいこと　inconstancy〈86〉
変わりやすく　inconstantly〈86〉
変わることなく　invariably〈385〉
考えてもみない　undreamed-of〈126〉
考えられない　unthinkable〈370〉
考えることを止める　unthink〈370〉
感覚のない　unfeeling〈158〉, impassive〈261〉, insensate〈331〉, insensible〈331〉, senseless〈331〉

換気されていない　unventilated〈387〉
換気の悪い　ill-ventilated〈387〉
環境に対する配慮がない　ungreen〈179〉
～に関係なく　irrespective〈312〉
関係のない　nonrelational〈304〉
関係を絶つ　disaffiliate〈12〉, dissociate〈26〉
関係を否認する　disown〈255〉
歓迎されない　ill-loved〈223〉, unwelcome〈395〉
歓迎しない　unwelcoming〈396〉
感光度を下げる　desensitize〈332〉
監護権のない　noncustodial〈104〉
観察されていない　unobserved〈247〉
観察力のない　unobservant〈247〉
監視しない　nonsupervise〈359〉
乾式の　waterless〈394〉
感謝されない　thankless〈369〉, unappreciated〈20〉
感謝しない　unthankful〈369〉
感謝の気持ちのない　ungrateful〈178〉
慣習となっている　unwritten〈402〉
慣習にとらわれない　unconventional〈94〉
鑑賞する目がない　inappreciative〈20〉
感傷的でない　unsentimental〈333〉
感情的でない　passionless〈260〉
感情を表さない　emotionless〈134〉, unemotional〈134〉
頑丈でない　infirm〈161〉
関心のない　uninterested〈203〉
完成していない　undone〈125〉
間接的に　indirectly〈118〉
間接の　indirect〈117〉
関節のない　jointless〈208〉
感染していない　uninfected〈198〉
完全な　undamaged〈105〉
乾燥させる　unwater〈394〉

寛大でない　unforgiving〈167〉, ungenerous〈175〉
寛大な　unsparing〈345〉
寛大に　unselfishly〈331〉
簡単でない　nontrivial〈377〉
感知されない　unwitnessed〈399〉
感知しない　imperceptive〈264〉, impercipient〈264〉, insensible〈331〉
感知できない　imperceptible〈264〉
感知できないくらいの　inappreciable〈20〉
感度が低い　insensitive〈332〉
感度抑制剤　desensitizer〈333〉
感度を減ずる　desensitize〈332〉
感動なく　impassibly〈260〉
かんぬきを外す　unbar〈34〉
完璧さ　infallibleness〈154〉
完璧に　infallibly〈154〉
勘弁できない　unpardonable〈259〉
甘味を加えていない　unsweetened〈362〉
関与しない人　nonparticipant〈259〉
管理されていない　unadopted〈9〉
管理職でない　nonexecutive〈144〉
関連なく　immaterially〈229〉
～に関連のない　irrelevant〈305〉

き

気が進まない　unwilling〈396〉
気が進まないこと　indisposition〈121〉, unwillingness〈397〉
気が付かずに　unknowingly〈211〉, unwittingly〈400〉
気が付かない　unaware〈32〉, unknowing〈211〉, unwitting〈400〉
気が休まらない　restless〈313〉
気の進まない　disinclined〈197〉
気をつけない　mindless〈232〉
気を取られている態度で　inattentively〈29〉
聞いたことのない　unheard〈185〉, unheard-of〈185〉

議院の慣習に反する　unparliamentary〈259〉
消えた　unlit〈220〉
消えてなくなる　disappear〈19〉
消える　disappear〈19〉
規格外の　nonstandard〈350〉
規格化されていない　nonstandardized〈350〉
聞きとりにくい　indiscernible〈118〉
聴き取れない　inaudible〈29〉
聴き取れないこと　inaudibility〈29〉
効き目のない　inefficacious〈131〉
企業形態でない　noncorporate〈95〉
危険な　unsafe〈320〉
危険にさらされていない　uncompromised〈74〉
危険のない　acritical〈101〉
期限の定めのない　undated〈105〉
聞こえない　unheard〈185〉
聞こえないように　inaudibly〈29〉
儀式ばらない　unceremonious〈49〉
希釈していない　undiluted〈116〉
傷が付いていない　undamaged〈105〉
傷のない　flawless〈164〉, unblemished〈38〉
傷を受けていない　unharmed〈184〉
規制緩和　deregulatory〈303〉
規制緩和する　deregulate〈302〉
規制緩和の　deregulation〈303〉
規制されていない　unregulated〈302〉
規制しない　unregulate〈302〉
季節外れに　unseasonably〈327〉
季節外れの　unseasonable〈327〉
偽善的な　insincere〈339〉
規則正しいこと　nonrandomness〈293〉
規則に従わない　unruly〈319〉
基礎のない　baseless〈34〉

期待していない　inexpectant〈146〉, unhoped-for〈190〉
期待していなかった　unexpected〈146〉
期待はずれの行事　nonevent〈142〉
汚く　uncleanly〈56〉
貴重な　invaluable〈384〉, priceless〈281〉, unpriced〈281〉
気づいていない　unconscious〈82〉
機転のきかない　undiplomatic〈117〉, tactless〈365〉
気取らない　unaffected〈12〉, unassuming〈27〉
気乗りせずに　unwillingly〈397〉
揮発しない　nonvolatile〈390〉
厳しい　inclement〈57〉, uncompromising〈74〉
気分がすぐれない　indisposed〈121〉
気分がよくない　unwell〈396〉
基本的でない　nonessential〈140〉
気前のよい　unsparing〈345〉
気前のよくない　ungenerous〈175〉
気まぐれな　inconstant〈86〉
気味の悪い　uncanny〈44〉
機密扱いでない　unclassified〈56〉
機密を解除する　declassify〈56〉
決めていない　undecided〈106〉
虐待された　ill-treated〈376〉
虐待する　ill-treat〈376〉
逆方向通勤　incommutation〈68〉
逆方向通勤者　incommuter〈68〉
キャップを外す　uncap〈45〉
救済できない　cureless〈103〉
休止　inactivity〈8〉
休止中の　inactive〈7〉
吸収性のない　unabsorbent〈3〉
牛乳を含まない　nondairy〈105〉
究明できない　unsearchable〈327〉
寄与しない　noncontributory〈91〉

教育のない　unlearned〈214〉
教育不足の　ill-educated〈130〉
教育を受けていない　uneducated〈130〉
強化されていない　unreinforced〈304〉
教化しない　unedifying〈129〉
境界のない　borderless〈39〉
狂気の沙汰　insanity〈321〉
行儀の悪い　ill-behaved〈36〉, ill-mannered〈227〉
競業避止の　noncompete〈69〉
強硬な　uncompromising〈74〉
凝縮されていない　uncondensed〈76〉
凝縮できない　incondensable〈76〉, incondensible〈77〉
強制されたものではない　unprompted〈285〉
強制されない　unconstrained〈87〉
強制的でない　unforced〈166〉
矯正できない　incorrigible〈96〉
矯正不能　incurability〈103〉
競争相手のない　unrivaled〈317〉
競争禁止の　noncompete〈69〉
競争しない　noncompete〈69〉
競争のない　noncompetitive〈69〉, uncontested〈90〉
競争力のない　noncompetitive〈69〉, uncompetitive〈70〉
強調されていない　unstressed〈354〉
強度のない　strengthless〈354〉
器用に　flawlessly〈164〉
恐怖心のなさ　fearlessness〈157〉
莢膜のない　noncapsulated〈45〉
興味がない　disinterested〈203〉, uninterested〈203〉
興味のない　uninteresting〈204〉
興味のないこと　disinterest〈203〉
共有されていない　unshared〈336〉
教養のない　illiterate〈220〉, ill-read〈295〉, uncultivated〈102〉, uncultured〈103〉, unlettered〈216〉

狭量な　illiberal〈216〉
強力な　unbeatable〈35〉
虚偽　untruth〈378〉
極性をなくす　depolarize〈273〉
極端に　impossibly〈276〉
御し難い　indocile〈124〉
居住者がいない　unpopulated〈275〉
拒絶できない　undeclinable〈107〉
拒否　disclaimer〈55〉
拒否する　deselect〈330〉
許容しがたい　intolerable〈373〉
許容できない　impermissible〈266〉, inadmissible〈9〉, unacceptable〈3〉
許容できないほどに　inadmissibly〈9〉
嫌う　dislike〈217〉, disrelish〈307〉
切られた　disconnected〈81〉
切られていない　uncut〈104〉
嫌われた　disliked〈217〉
切り下げ　devaluation〈385〉
キリスト教徒にふさわしくない　unchristian〈54〉
切り離す　decouple〈98〉, disconnect〈81〉, uncouple〈98〉, undock〈124〉, unjoint〈208〉
切り離せない　inextricable〈151〉, inseparable〈333〉
気力喪失　disintegration〈202〉
気力のない　shiftless〈337〉
気力を失わせる　unnerve〈242〉, unnerving〈242〉
切る　disconnect〈81〉
記録されていない　unrecorded〈299〉
議論の余地なく　inarguably〈23〉, incontestably〈89〉, indisputably〈121〉
議論の余地のない　inarguable〈22〉, incontestable〈89〉, incontrovertible〈92〉, indisputable〈121〉, unarguable〈22〉
議論を引き起こさない　uncontroversial〈92〉
疑惑　disbelief〈36〉, distrust〈377〉

均一でない　inequable〈138〉
禁煙の　nonsmoking〈341〉
緊急性　immediacy〈231〉
…の均衡を失わせる　unbalance〈33〉
緊張しない　unstrained〈353〉
緊迫した　breathless〈41〉

く

苦もなく　effortlessly〈132〉
食い違い　inconsistency〈85〉, mismatch〈228〉
空気のない　airless〈15〉
偶然に　unintentionally〈203〉
茎のない　stemless〈351〉
釘を抜く　unnail〈240〉
鎖から解放する　unchain〈50〉
鎖を解かれた　unchained〈50〉
駆除する　disinfest〈199〉
駆逐する　dislodge〈222〉
崩す　unstack〈349〉
口に出さない　unsaid〈320〉, unvoiced〈390〉
口に出して言えない　unnameable〈240〉, unmentionable〈231〉
口の重い　incommunicable〈67〉, incommunicative〈67〉
口下手の　ineloquent〈133〉
靴を履いていない　shoeless〈337〉, unshod〈337〉
苦痛　discomfort〈63〉
苦痛のない　painless〈257〉
屈曲のない　uninflected〈199〉
屈しない　unbowed〈40〉
屈折しない　uninflected〈199〉
くっついていない　unstuck〈354〉
区別できない　indistinctive〈122〉, indistinguishable〈123〉
雲のない　cloudless〈58〉
曇りのない　unclouded〈58〉

曇りを取る　defog〈165〉
鞍を外す　unsaddle〈320〉
暗い　ill-lit〈220〉
比べものにならない　matchless〈228〉
繰り返しはできない　unrepeatable〈308〉
軍備縮小　disarmament〈23〉
訓練から外す　deselect〈330〉
訓練されてない　indisciplined〈118〉
訓練を受けていない　untrained〈375〉
訓練を積んでいない　unpracticed〈277〉

け

毛を抜く　unhair〈182〉
計画されていない　unplanned〈269〉
計画性の悪い　ill-planned〈269〉
計画的でない　unpremeditated〈279〉
計画に入っていない　unscripted〈326〉
経験のない　unexperienced〈147〉, uninitiated〈200〉
経験不足の　inexperienced〈147〉
軽罪　misdemeanor〈110〉
経済的でない　noneconomic〈129〉, uneconomical〈129〉
形式ばらない　informal〈168〉
芸術のわからない　inartistic〈25〉
軽率　imprudence〈288〉, indiscretion〈119〉
軽率さ　incautiousness〈47〉, inconsiderateness〈84〉, indiscreetness〈119〉
軽率な　imprudent〈288〉, incautious〈47〉, inconsiderate〈84〉, indiscreet〈119〉, unconsidered〈84〉
軽率に　ill-advisedly〈11〉, imprudently〈289〉, inadvertently〈11〉, incautiously〈47〉, indiscreetly〈119〉
経年していない　unaged〈13〉
啓発しない　unedifying〈129〉
怪我をしていない　uninjured〈200〉

けしからん　inexcusable〈144〉, disgraceful〈177〉
下水のない　unsewered〈335〉
消すことのできない　ineffaceable〈130〉, inerasable〈139〉, inextinguishable〈150〉
消せない　unquenchable〈291〉
けた違いの　incomparable〈68〉
結果を欠いて　inconsequently〈84〉
結合されない　uncombined〈62〉
結合を解く　decouple〈98〉
結婚しない　unwed〈395〉
結婚に適さない　unmarriageable〈228〉
結晶化していない　uncrystallized〈102〉
欠席　nonattendance〈28〉
決断力のない　irresolute〈311〉, spineless〈346〉
決着のつかない　indecisive〈107〉
決着のできない　indeterminable〈114〉
決定的でない　inconclusive〈76〉, indecisive〈107〉
決定的な　unbeatable〈35〉
欠点　demerit〈232〉, disadvantage〈10〉, imperfection〈265〉
欠点のない　faultless〈156〉, irreproachable〈309〉, unmarred〈228〉
結論に達しない　inconclusive〈76〉
結論に達しないで　inconclusively〈76〉
下品　indecorum〈108〉, indelicacy〈110〉
下品な　illiberal〈216〉, improper〈285〉, indecent〈106〉, indelicate〈110〉, unmannerly〈227〉, unseemly〈329〉
煙の出ない　smokeless〈341〉
減圧　decompression〈73〉
減圧された　depressurized〈280〉
減圧する　decompress〈73〉, depressurize〈280〉
原因不明の　unknown〈212〉
現役でない　inactive〈7〉
嫌悪　disfavor〈156〉, disgust〈181〉, distaste〈366〉
嫌悪感　dislike〈217〉, distastefulness〈367〉

嫌悪感を抱かせる　disgusting〈181〉
限界のない　unbounded〈40〉
言外の　unspoken〈346〉
減感剤　desensitizer〈333〉
元気なく　cheerlessly〈54〉
元気のない　cheerless〈54〉, depressed〈280〉, listless〈220〉, springless〈347〉
研究されていない　unresearched〈309〉
減極する　depolarize〈273〉
現金が要らない　cashless〈46〉
現金化しにくい　illiquid〈219〉
現金不足の　illiquid〈219〉
減結合　decoupling〈98〉
減結合する　decouple〈98〉
健康的でない　unhealthy〈185〉
健康に良くない　unhealthy〈185〉
健康に悪い　unwholesome〈396〉
堅固な方法で　impregnably〈279〉
言語障害　impediment〈262〉
言語に絶する　indescribable〈112〉, ineffable〈130〉, untold〈373〉
検査を受けていない　unchecked〈54〉
減磁　degauss〈174〉
現実的ではない　unreal〈296〉
検出されていない　undetected〈114〉
検出不能な　undetectable〈114〉
健全でない　unsound〈344〉
言質を与えない　noncommittal〈66〉
限定しない　nonfinite〈160〉
見当違いに　inconsequently〈84〉
憲法違反の　unconstitutional〈86〉
厳密でないこと　inexactness〈143〉
賢明でない　unwise〈398〉
幻滅　disenchantment〈135〉

幻滅感　disillusionment〈194〉
幻滅させる　disillusion〈194〉
幻滅を感じた　disillusioned〈194〉
権利放棄書　disclaimer〈55〉
権利を放棄する　disclaim〈55〉
言論の自由を与える　unmuzzle〈239〉
幻惑を覚ますこと　disillusion〈194〉

こ

故意でない　inadvertent〈10〉, unintentional〈203〉
故意でなく　unintentionally〈203〉
好意的でない　unflattering〈163〉
硬化していない　uncured〈103〉
硬化しない　nonhardenable〈183〉
高価でない　less-expensive〈147〉
高価な　invaluable〈384〉
効果なく　fruitlessly〈172〉, ineffectually〈131〉
効果の上がらない　ineffectual〈130〉
効果のない　fruitless〈172〉, ineffective〈130〉, inefficient〈131〉, nonoperative〈251〉, unavailing〈31〉
効果のなさ　ineffectiveness〈130〉
豪華でない　unspectacular〈345〉
公開　disclosure〈58〉
公開されていない　undisclosed〈118〉
降格　degradation〈178〉
降格させる　degrade〈178〉
交換できない　incommutable〈67〉, inconvertible〈94〉
好奇心のない　incurious〈104〉
攻撃できない　unassailable〈26〉
高潔でない　unrighteous〈317〉
交互に変わらない　irrotational〈318〉
交際嫌いな　unsociable〈342〉
控除できない　nondeductible〈108〉

交渉の余地のない　nonnegotiable〈241〉
向上意欲をそぐ　disincentive〈197〉
校正されていない　uncalibrated〈44〉
光線のない　rayless〈295〉
拘束されない　unbounded〈40〉, uncommitted〈66〉, unconstrained〈87〉, unfettered〈159〉
拘束しない　unrestrict〈314〉
拘束力のない　nonbinding〈38〉
交代　displacement〈269〉
公認の　unaccredited〈5〉
効能のない　powerless〈276〉
公表する　unveil〈386〉
興奮しない　inexcitable〈143〉
公平　impartiality〈259〉
公平な　impartial〈259〉, indifferent〈115〉
公平に　impartially〈259〉
巧妙でない　unsophisticated〈344〉
効率の悪い　inefficient〈131〉
効率の悪さ　inefficiency〈131〉
考慮されない　unconsidered〈84〉
効力のない　noneffective〈130〉, nonoperative〈251〉
声が出せない　voiceless〈390〉
声の出ないこと　voicelessness〈390〉
越えられない　insuperable〈358〉
コードの付いていない　cordless〈95〉
コードレスの　cordless〈95〉
コードを抜く　unplug〈271〉
氷を取り除く　deice〈194〉
誤解　misconception〈75〉, misinterpretation〈204〉, misperception〈264〉, misunderstanding〈380〉
誤解される　misinformed〈199〉
誤解する　misinterpret〈204〉
誤解の余地がない　unambiguous〈17〉

誤解を招く　misleading〈214〉
互換性がない　incompatible〈68〉
呼吸困難　breathlessness〈41〉
呼吸困難の　breathless〈41〉
呼吸不能　breathlessness〈41〉
酷使　ill-use〈382〉
酷使する　ill-treat〈376〉
国籍のない　stateless〈351〉
告訴されていない　uncharged〈53〉
克服できない　insuperable〈358〉
ごくわずかの　inappreciable〈20〉
焦げ付かない　nonstick〈352〉
心にとどめない　unmindful〈232〉
心を動かされない　unmoved〈238〉
心を乱されない　untroubled〈377〉
心を乱す　disquiet〈292〉
個人に関しないこと　impersonality〈266〉
個人の　noncorporate〈95〉
個性的でない　impersonal〈266〉
個性のない　faceless〈152〉
個性のないこと　facelessness〈152〉
答えのない　unanswered〈18〉
答えることのできない　unanswerable〈18〉
国境のない　stateless〈351〉
固定された　immovable〈238〉
固定した　immobile〈233〉
固定して　immovably〈238〉
固定する　immobilize〈234〉
鼓動しない　nonpulsating〈289〉
異なった　dissimilar〈339〉
言葉が不明瞭なこと　inarticulateness〈25〉
言葉が不明瞭に　inarticulately〈24〉
言葉で表せない　inexpressible〈149〉

言葉で言い表せない　indescribable〈112〉, unspeakable〈345〉
言葉で言い表せないくらい　indescribably〈112〉
言葉に表せない　unutterable〈383〉
言葉にならない　inarticulate〈24〉, wordless〈400〉
言葉の曖昧な　inexplicit〈149〉
言葉をなくした　speechless〈346〉
言葉を用いない　nonverbal〈387〉
子供のいない　childless〈54〉
このうえない　unsurpassable〈360〉
好ましくない　disagreeable〈14〉, disliked〈217〉, undesirable〈112〉, unenviable〈138〉, unfavorable〈156〉, unsavory〈324〉
好ましくないこと　undesirability〈112〉
好ましくなく　undesirably〈113〉
好まれない　ill-loved〈223〉
好みに合わない　uncongenial〈79〉
語尾変化をしない　indeclinable〈107〉, uninflected〈199〉
ごまかしのない　unvarnished〈386〉
誤訳された　mistranslated〈376〉
雇用に適さない　unemployable〈135〉
これ以上ないというほどに　unsurpassably〈360〉
壊すことのできない　unbreakable〈41〉
壊れていない　unbroken〈42〉
壊れにくい　unbreakable〈41〉
困窮していない　nondistressed〈123〉
根拠がない　invalid〈384〉
根拠なく　groundlessly〈179〉, unsubstantially〈355〉
根拠のない　baseless〈34〉, bottomless〈40〉, causeless〈47〉, groundless〈179〉, unfounded〈170〉, ungrounded〈179〉
根拠の弱い　ill-founded〈170〉
混雑していない　uncrowded〈102〉
痕跡がない　traceless〈375〉
根絶する　unroot〈318〉
混入物　impurity〈289〉

コンピューター化していない　noncomputerized〈74〉
混乱　disarray〈24〉, disorder〈252〉
混乱させる　disarrange〈24〉, dislocate〈221〉, disorder〈252〉, disorganize〈253〉, disorient〈254〉
混乱した　disordered〈252〉, disorganized〈254〉, disoriented〈254〉
混乱するようなところがない　uncluttered〈59〉

さ

再加熱されていない　unreheated〈303〉
際限なく　endlessly〈136〉
際限のない　boundless〈40〉, illimitable〈218〉
採算が取れない　uneconomic〈129〉
最初から可能性のない人　nonstarter〈350〉
再生不可能な　nonrenewable〈308〉
才能のない　talentless〈365〉
債務超過　insolvency〈343〉
採用されない　unadopted〈9〉
先のことを考えずに　improvidently〈288〉
先のとがっていない　pointless〈272〉
作者不明の　unattributed〈29〉
削除されていない　unexpurgated〈150〉
避けられない　inevitable〈142〉
下げる　abase〈34〉, degrade〈178〉
些細でない　nontrivial〈377〉
支えられない　unsupportable〈359〉, unsustainable〈361〉
支えられないように　unsustainably〈361〉
左遷　degradation〈178〉
定かでない　ill-defined〈109〉
雑音がない　noiseless〈243〉
雑音を立てずに　noiselessly〈243〉
殺菌　disinfection〈198〉
殺菌性のある　disinfectant〈198〉
察しのない　inconsiderate〈84〉

雑然と　formlessly〈167〉
砂糖の入っていない　sugarless〈357〉
砂糖をまぶしていない　unfrosted〈172〉
悟らせる　undeceive〈106〉
サドルのない　saddleless〈320〉
錆びていない　rustless〈319〉
錆びない　rustless〈319〉, stainless〈349〉
差別(待遇)をしない　nondiscriminatory〈120〉
妨げない　unblock〈38〉
妨げられない　untrammeled〈375〉
さやから抜く　unsheathe〈336〉
触ることのできない　untouchable〈374〉
酸化させない　nonoxidize〈255〉
参加者が少ない　ill-attended〈28〉
賛成できない　uncomfortable〈64〉
酸素を除去された　deoxygenated〈256〉
酸素を除く　deoxidize〈255〉
3着以内に入らない　unplaced〈269〉
散漫な　incompact〈68〉

し

肢のない　limbless〈217〉
シームレスの　seamless〈327〉
シールドされていない　unshielded〈336〉
支援されていない　unbacked〈33〉
潮の満ち干のない　tideless〈371〉
塩気のない　saltless〈320〉
資格のない　ineligible〈133〉, unauthorized〈30〉, unqualified〈291〉
資格剥奪　disqualification〈291〉
資格を剥奪する　disqualify〈291〉
自活　independence〈111〉
時間に関係のない　timeless〈371〉
士気をくじく　demoralize〈236〉

時機を失した　ill-timed〈372〉, inopportune〈251〉, untimely〈372〉
識別されていない　undistinguished〈123〉
識別できない　nondiscriminatory〈120〉, undiscriminating〈120〉
識別不能な　undistinguishable〈123〉
識別力のない　indiscriminating〈120〉
刺激のない　innocuous〈243〉, uninspired〈201〉
自己主張しない　unassertive〈26〉
仕事のない　workless〈400〉
仕事のない状態　joblessness〈208〉
指示を受けていない　uninstructed〈201〉
支持されていない　unbacked〈33〉, unsupported〈359〉
支持できない　unsupportable〈359〉, unsustainable〈361〉, untenable〈368〉
支持できないように　unsustainably〈361〉
史実と異なる　unhistorical〈188〉
史実に合わずに　unhistorically〈188〉
事実無根　groundlessness〈179〉
事実無根の　groundless〈179〉
自主　independence〈111〉
自主的に　independently〈112〉
自信のない　insecure〈328〉, unsure〈360〉
静かな　airless〈15〉, noiseless〈243〉, soundless〈344〉
静かに　noiselessly〈243〉
沈むことのない　unsinkable〈339〉
私生の　illegitimate〈215〉
自制心のない　incontinent〈90〉
自制心を失って　incontinently〈90〉
自制不可能なこと　incontinence〈90〉
自然な　artless〈24〉, inartificial〈25〉
自然の　untaught〈367〉
自然発生的でない　inorganic〈253〉
持続できない　unsustainable〈361〉
時代遅れの　uncool〈95〉, unreconstructed〈299〉

従わない　disobedient〈247〉, disobey〈247〉
仕立ての悪い　ill-cut〈104〉
失格(処分)　disqualification〈291〉
しっかりと守られていない　ill-guarded〈180〉
失脚させる　unhorse〈190〉
失業　joblessness〈208〉, unemployment〈135〉
失業した　unwaged〈393〉, workless〈400〉
失業中の　jobless〈208〉, unemployed〈135〉
失禁　incontinence〈90〉
失禁して　incontinently〈90〉
失禁の　incontinent〈90〉
しつけの悪い　ill-trained〈375〉
実現されていない　unrealized〈297〉
実現できない　unrealizable〈297〉
実行困難な　unfeasible〈157〉
実行できない　unworkable〈400〉
実行できないこと　infeasibility〈157〉, infeasibleness〈158〉
実行不可能性　impracticability〈276〉
実行不可能な　impracticable〈276〉, infeasible〈157〉, unpractical〈277〉
実行不可能な程度に　impracticably〈276〉
実在しない　unreal〈296〉
実在しないこと　nonentity〈137〉
実際的でない　inoperable〈250〉
実際にはできない　infeasible〈157〉
失策　misstep〈352〉
実施できない　nonoperative〈251〉
失踪　disappearance〈20〉
質素な　unadorned〈9〉
実体がなく　unsubstantially〈355〉
実体のない　bodiless〈39〉, formless〈167〉, impalpable〈258〉, incorporeal〈96〉, insubstantial〈355〉, unsubstantial〈355〉, intangible〈365〉, untouchable〈374〉
実体のないこと　incorporeity〈96〉

失調性の　incoordinated〈95〉
実直な　guileless〈180〉
失墜すること　abasement〈35〉
ジッパーが閉じていない　unzipped〈403〉
ジッパーの付いていない　zipless〈403〉
ジッパーを開ける　unzip〈403〉
疾病　disorder〈252〉
質問されていない　unasked〈25〉
実用的でない　impractical〈277〉
執拗な　relentless〈304〉
執拗に　relentlessly〈305〉
失礼　disrespect〈312〉
失礼な　impolite〈274〉, uncourteous〈99〉, un-nice〈242〉
自動化されていない　noncomputerized〈74〉
指導者のいない　rudderless〈318〉
自発的な　unconstrained〈87〉
支払いの済んでいない　unpaid-for〈257〉
支払い不能　insolvency〈343〉
支払い不能の　insolvent〈343〉
縛られていない　unbound〈40〉, unconfined〈79〉
支払われていない　undischarged〈118〉
シフトを解除する　unshift〈337〉
自分の立場を決めていない　uncommitted〈66〉
自分を意識しない　unselfconscious〈330〉
自分を意識せずに　unselfconsciously〈330〉
脂肪分のない　fatless〈155〉, nonfat〈155〉
脂肪を取り除いていない　unskimmed〈340〉
～から資本を引き揚げる　disinvest〈205〉
締まりのない　incompact〈68〉
しみがない　spotless〈347〉
市民権のない　stateless〈351〉
示し方が不適切な　ill-presented〈280〉
湿っていない　undamped〈105〉

霜を取り除く　defrost〈171〉
邪悪な　unrighteous〈317〉
弱体化された　depressed〈280〉
釈放する　discharge〈52〉
社交性のない　asocial〈342〉
謝罪する気がない　unapologetic〈19〉
遮断されていない　unobstructed〈247〉
遮断する　de-energize〈136〉
遮蔽されていない　unscreened〈326〉
邪魔されない　undisturbed〈123〉, unhindered〈187〉
車輪の付いていない　wheelless〈396〉
自由にする　disengage〈137〉
自由意志論　indeterminism〈115〉
自由化　deregulatory〈303〉
自由裁量でない　nondiscretionary〈119〉
収穫されていない　unpicked〈268〉
住居に適していない　uninhabitable〈199〉
収縮させていない　nonconstricted〈87〉
修正していない　unmodified〈235〉
集中した　undivided〈124〉
重点を置かない　de-emphasize〈134〉
重点を置かないこと　de-emphasis〈134〉
柔軟性がない　inflexible〈164〉
修復できない　irreparable〈308〉
修復不可能　disrepair〈308〉
十分でない　insufficient〈356〉
十分に検討されていない　ill-argued〈23〉
…から住民をなくする　unpeople〈263〉
重要でない　immaterial〈229〉, inconsequential〈83〉, indifferent〈115〉, insignificant〈338〉, irrelevant〈305〉, nonessential〈140〉, nonvital〈390〉, unimportant〈196〉
重要でないこと　immateriality〈229〉, inconsequentialness〈83〉, indifference〈115〉, unimportance〈196〉

重要でなく　immaterially〈229〉
重要な　nontrivial〈377〉
従来のものではない　unconventional〈94〉
修理されていない　unrepaired〈308〉
修理できない　irreparable〈308〉
就労不能　incapacity〈45〉
樹液のない　sapless〈321〉
縮刷版ではない　unabridged〈2〉
熟していない　unripe〈317〉
縮小できない　irreducible〈300〉
縮退した　degenerated〈174〉
熟練していない　unskilled〈340〉
手術不可能な　inoperable〈250〉
手術をしない　nonoperative〈251〉
受精されない　unfertilized〈159〉
主体性　independence〈111〉
潤滑されていない　nonlubricated〈224〉
循環の　endless〈135〉
順次発生しない　nonserial〈333〉
遵守しない　nonobservance〈247〉
純粋でない　impure〈289〉
純粋な　unadulterated〈10〉
順応性のない　inelastic〈132〉
準備ができていない　unprepared〈279〉
準備されていない　unprovided〈287〉, unready〈296〉
準備なしの　unstudied〈354〉
準備不足の　ill-equipped〈139〉, ill-prepared〈279〉
使用を廃止する　decommission〈65〉
使用をやめる　disuse〈381〉
使用できない　unavailable〈31〉, unserviceable〈334〉
消イオン　deionization〈206〉
消イオンの　deionized〈207〉
上映されていない　unscreened〈326〉

上映する　unspool〈347〉
消化が悪い　indigestible〈116〉
消化できない　indigestible〈116〉
消化不良　indigestion〈116〉
消化不良になった　indigestive〈116〉
消化不良の　indigestive〈116〉
障害　impediment〈262〉
障害のある　disabled〈2〉
障害のない　unimpeded〈196〉
償還されていない　unredeemed〈300〉
償還不能な　unredeemable〈300〉
正気でない　insane〈321〉
正気でなく　insanely〈321〉
常軌を逸した　abnormal〈244〉
商業に関係のない　uncommercial〈65〉
消極作用　depolarization〈273〉
条件反応を消去する　decondition〈77〉
消磁　degauss〈174〉, demagnetization〈225〉
消磁された　unmagnetized〈226〉
消磁状態の　demagnetizing〈226〉
消磁する　demagnetize〈225〉
消磁できる　unmagnetizable〈225〉
正直さ　guilelessness〈180〉
消失　disappearance〈20〉
消失する　disappear〈19〉
上手でない　inexpert〈147〉
招待されていない　uninvited〈206〉
招待しない　disinvite〈206〉
正体を暴く　unmask〈228〉
承知しない　disapprove〈22〉
消沈させる　depress〈280〉
焦点の合っていない　unaligned〈15〉, unfocused〈165〉
譲渡移転ができない　unalienable〈15〉

商道徳に反する　uncommercial〈65〉
消毒　disinfection〈198〉
消毒する　disinfect〈198〉
消毒用の　disinfectant〈198〉
蒸発していない　unvaporized〈385〉
蒸発しない　involatile〈390〉
消費されていない　unconsumed〈88〉
上品さのないこと　gracelessness〈177〉
証明が可能な　incontrovertibly〈92〉
消滅できない　imprescriptible〈279〉
消耗しない　nonwearing〈395〉
将来性のない　futureless〈173〉, unpromising〈285〉
将来性のないこと　futurelessness〈173〉
将来に備えない　improvident〈288〉
除外する　deselect〈330〉
除去する　unclog〈57〉
除去できない　irremovable〈307〉
職業倫理に反する　unprofessional〈284〉
触媒作用で促進させない　uncatalyze〈47〉
触媒作用で促進されない　uncatalyzed〈47〉
植民地状態を解く　decolonize〈61〉
食用に適さない　inedible〈129〉, uneatable〈129〉
食欲をそそらない　unappetizing〈20〉
植林されていない　unforested〈166〉
除湿　dehumidification〈191〉
除湿された　dehumidified〈191〉
除湿している　dehumidifying〈191〉
除湿する　dehumidify〈191〉
女性らしくない　unwomanly〈400〉
除霜の　defrosting〈172〉
除隊　demobilization〈234〉
除隊させる　demobilize〈234〉
処罰されない　unpunished〈289〉

処罰の対象から外す　decriminalize〈101〉
処方箋なしで買える　nonprescription〈279〉
署名のない　unsigned〈338〉
署名をしない　unsubscribe〈355〉
所有権のない　nonproprietary〈286〉
書類で立証されていない　undocumented〈125〉
地雷を除去する　demine〈232〉
知らされていない　unenlightened〈137〉, uninformed〈199〉
知らずに　unknowingly〈211〉
知らない　unknowing〈211〉
調べることなく　unsight〈337〉
知られていない　unknown〈212〉
自立して　independently〈112〉
支離滅裂　incoherence〈60〉
支離滅裂に　incoherently〈60〉
支離滅裂にする　disjoint〈208〉
支離滅裂の　disjointed〈208〉
思慮なく　thoughtlessly〈370〉
思慮の足りない　ill-advised〈11〉
思慮のない　ill-judged〈209〉, mindless〈232〉, thoughtless〈370〉, unreasoning〈298〉, unthinking〈370〉
思慮のないこと　inattentiveness〈29〉
知ることができない　unknowable〈211〉
印の付いていない　unmarked〈228〉
素人っぽく　inexpertly〈148〉
素人っぽさ　inexpertness〈148〉
しわが伸びる　unwrinkle〈401〉
しわにならない　uncrushable〈102〉
しわを伸ばす　unwrinkle〈401〉
人為的な　inorganic〈253〉
侵害されない　inviolate〈388〉
侵害することのできない　inviolable〈388〉
神経が太い　fearless〈157〉

親交がない　unfamiliar〈154〉
信仰心のない　faithless〈153〉
人口が少なくなった　depopulated〈275〉
人口を少なくする　depopulate〈275〉
申告されていない　undeclared〈107〉
紳士らしくない　ungentlemanly〈175〉
人事不省の　senseless〈331〉
信じがたい　distrustful〈378〉, impossible〈276〉
信じない　distrust〈377〉, incredulous〈101〉, unbelieving〈37〉
信じない人　unbeliever〈37〉
真実でない　untrue〈377〉, untruthful〈378〉
真実でないこと　untruth〈378〉
人種差別をしない　nonracial〈293〉, unsegregated〈330〉
人種差別をなくす　desegregate〈330〉
尋常でない　inordinate〈252〉
信じようとしない　unbelieving〈37〉
信じられない　inconceivable〈74〉, incredible〈100〉, unbelievable〈36〉
信じられないこと　incredibility〈100〉
信じられないほど　incredibly〈100〉, unbelievably〈37〉
信じられないほどの　uncanny〈44〉
心身障害　disability〈1〉
心身の調子を狂わせる　disorder〈252〉
神聖でない　unholy〈188〉
人跡未踏の　pathless〈261〉, untrod〈377〉
親切でない　unfriendly〈171〉
身体障害　disability〈1〉
心配　disquietude〈292〉, unease〈128〉, uneasiness〈128〉
心配事がない　careless〈46〉
心配そうに　uneasily〈128〉
心配な　uneasy〈128〉
尋問されない　unchallenged〈51〉
信用しない　disbelieve〈37〉
信用できない　trustless〈377〉

信用を傷つける　discredit〈100〉
信用を傷つけるような　discreditable〈101〉
信頼できずに　unreliably〈307〉
信頼できない　unreliable〈306〉, unsound〈344〉, untrustworthy〈378〉
信頼できないこと　unreliability〈306〉
信頼できる　unfailing〈152〉
森林の伐採　deforestation〈166〉
森林を伐採する　disafforest〈12〉

す

遂行されていない　unaccomplished〈5〉
衰退しやすい　degenerative〈175〉
水門のない　lockless〈221〉
水冷できない　unquenchable〈291〉
数字以外の　nonnumeric〈246〉, nonnumerical〈246〉
ずうずうしい　imprudent〈288〉, shameless〈336〉, imprudence〈288〉
好きでない　dislike〈217〉
救いがたい　incurable〈103〉
救いようがなく　hopelessly〈190〉
すぐに興奮しない　inexcitable〈143〉
スクランブルを解く　unscrambling〈326〉
ずけずけと　impolitely〈274〉
すごい　incredible〈100〉
筋が通っていない　unreasonable〈297〉
筋の通らない　illogical〈222〉
勧められない　inadvisable〈11〉, unadvisable〈11〉
勧められないこと　inadvisability〈11〉
〜しないように勧める　dissuade〈267〉
スタンプが押されていない　unstamped〈350〉
捨てる　discard〈46〉, unlearn〈214〉
ステンレス製の　stainless〈349〉
素直でない　indirect〈117〉, indocile〈124〉
スナップを外す　unsnap〈341〉

ずば抜けた　incomparable〈68〉
すべてを網羅していない　inexhaustive〈144〉
すべてを網羅せずに　inexhaustively〈145〉
スポーツ精神にもとる　unsportsmanlike〈347〉
スポーツと無縁の　nonsporting〈347〉
スポーツマンらしくない　unsporting〈347〉, unsportsmanlike〈347〉
住みにくい　inhospitable〈190〉
住むことのできない　unlivable〈220〉
スリップしない　nonskid〈340〉
スリップ止め加工した　nonslip〈341〉
ずるさがないこと　guilelessness〈180〉
澄んだ　noncrystalline〈102〉

せ

性の特徴を失わせる　unsex〈335〉
誠意のない　insincere〈339〉
成果のない　fruitless〈172〉
生気のない　inanimate〈18〉, pulseless〈289〉
生気のない状態で　inanimately〈18〉
請求者がいない　unclaimed〈56〉
性急な　impatient〈262〉, improvident〈288〉
性急に　improvidently〈288〉
制御できない　uncontrollable〈92〉, ungovernable〈177〉
制限しない　unrestrict〈314〉
制限を解除する　derestrict〈314〉
生彩のない　colorless〈61〉
静止　inactivity〈8〉
静止した　motionless〈237〉, unmoving〈238〉
政治色をなくす　depoliticize〈274〉
政治に無関心な　apolitical〈274〉
誠実でない　unfaithful〈153〉
誠実な　guileless〈180〉
成熟していない　unaged〈13〉

生殖力のない　infertile〈159〉
精神的でない　unspiritual〈346〉
精神的でなく　unspiritually〈346〉
精製されていない　unrefined〈300〉
整然とした　uncluttered〈59〉
静態の　inactive〈7〉
成長しない　nongrowing〈179〉
精通していない　unacquainted〈6〉, unfamiliar〈154〉, unversed〈387〉
精通していないこと　unfamiliarity〈154〉
性的能力を失わせる　unsex〈335〉
正当化されていない　unwarranted〈394〉
正当化しない　unwarrant〈393〉
正当化できない　ill-justified〈209〉, unjustifiable〈209〉, unwarrantable〈393〉
正当な理由のない　ill-founded〈170〉
正統性がない　illegitimate〈215〉
正統でない　unorthodox〈254〉
政党と無関係の　nonparty〈260〉
征服できない　unconquerable〈82〉
成文化されていない　unwritten〈402〉
生命のない　inanimate〈18〉
生命をもっていないこと　inanimateness〈18〉
制約されない　ruleless〈318〉
整列されていない　unaligned〈15〉
清廉潔白　incorruption〈97〉
清廉潔白な　incorruptible〈97〉
責任無能力　irresponsibility〈313〉
世俗的でない　unworldly〈401〉
世俗的でないこと　unworldliness〈401〉
絶縁されていない　uninsulated〈201〉
絶縁体　nonconductor〈78〉
接近不可能性　inaccessibility〈4〉
絶句した　speechless〈346〉

設計の悪い　ill-designed〈112〉
石鹸のない　soapless〈341〉
節操のない　unprincipled〈281〉
接続されていない　unconnected〈81〉
絶対確実性　infallibility〈153〉
絶対確実な　infallible〈154〉
絶対的な　unequivocal〈139〉
絶対的に　unequivocally〈139〉
絶対の　incontrollable〈92〉
絶対間違いのない　infallible〈154〉
切断　disconnection〈82〉
接地されていない　ungrounded〈179〉
設定されていない　unestablished〈140〉
設定を解く　unset〈334〉
節度なく　immoderately〈234〉
節度のない　immoderate〈234〉
説得力のない　unconvincing〈94〉, unpersuasive〈267〉
設備の不十分な　ill-equipped〈139〉
切望　impatience〈261〉
絶望　hopelessness〈190〉
絶望的な　hopeless〈189〉, uncorrectable〈96〉
説明されていない　unaccounted-for〈5〉
説明されることなく　unexplained〈148〉
説明できない　indefinable〈109〉, inexplainable〈148〉, inexplicable〈148〉, inexpressible〈149〉, unaccountable〈5〉
説明できないくらい　unaccountably〈5〉
説明できないほどに　inexplicably〈148〉
節約しない　thriftless〈371〉
拙劣な　inartificial〈25〉
背中のない　backless〈33〉
狭苦しい　incommodious〈66〉
責められることのない　blameless〈38〉
栓を抜く　uncork〈95〉, unstop〈353〉

選挙権のない　voteless〈392〉
宣言していない　undeclared〈107〉
漸減する　decrescent〈101〉
先見性なく　improvidently〈288〉
先見性のない　improvident〈288〉
全色性でない　nonpanchromatic〈258〉
宣誓を拒否する人　nonjuror〈209〉
戦争のない　warless〈393〉
前代未聞の　unheard〈185〉, unheard-of〈185〉, unprecedented〈277〉
選択しない　nonselective〈330〉
線引きできない　uncrossed〈102〉
選別されていない　ill-assorted〈27〉
選別せずに　indiscriminatingly〈120〉
専門外の　unprofessional〈284〉
占有されていない　unoccupied〈249〉
占有しない　unoccupy〈249〉
前例のない　unprecedented〈277〉
洗練されていない　inelegant〈133〉, uncultured〈103〉

そ

相違　disparity〈259〉, dissimilarity〈339〉
騒音を立てずに　noiselessly〈243〉
操業していない　inoperative〈251〉
相互連結していない　noninterconnecting〈203〉
操作不能の　nonoperative〈251〉
装飾されていない　ungarnished〈174〉
送信不能な　undeliverable〈110〉
想像できない　inconceivable〈74〉, unimaginable〈195〉, unthinkable〈370〉
想像できないほどに　unimaginably〈195〉
想像もつかない　inconceivable〈74〉
想像もつかないほど　inconceivably〈74〉
想像力のない　unimaginative〈195〉

相続権を奪う　disinherit〈200〉
騒乱　disorder〈252〉
即時性　immediacy〈231〉
測定されていない　unmeasured〈231〉
測定できない　immeasurable〈230〉
束縛を解く　disenthrall〈137〉
側面から　indirectly〈118〉
底がない　bottomless〈40〉
底なしの　bottomless〈40〉
損なわれていない　unspoiled〈346〉, unspoilt〈346〉
損なわれない　unimpair〈195〉
組織化されていない　unorganized〈254〉
組織的でない　unstructured〈354〉
組織を壊す　disorganize〈253〉
阻止できない　unstoppable〈353〉
育ちの悪い　ill-bred〈41〉
育ちの悪さ　ill-breeding〈41〉
即興の　unscripted〈326〉
素っ気ない　flavorless〈163〉
そつなく　flawlessly〈164〉
そつのない　flawless〈164〉
袖なしの　sleeveless〈341〉
備え付けられていない　unprovided〈287〉
そむく　disoblige〈247〉
粗野　indelicacy〈110〉
粗野な　ill-bred〈41〉, illiberal〈216〉, indelicate〈110〉, uncourteous〈99〉, uncouth〈99〉
粗野なこと　ill-breeding〈41〉
損(失)のない　lossless〈223〉
存在しない　inexistent〈145〉, nonexistent〈145〉
存在しないもの　nonexistence〈145〉
存在を無視された人　nonperson〈266〉
ぞんざいに　carelessly〈46〉, unceremoniously〈49〉

損失　disadvantage〈10〉
損傷を受けていない　undamaged〈105〉, uninjured〈200〉

た

他に類を見ない　unparalleled〈258〉
他の支配を受けない　independent〈111〉
退院する　discharge〈52〉
退化　degeneration〈175〉
退化しやすい　degenerative〈175〉
戴冠式を済ませていない　uncrowned〈102〉
退屈させる　uninspiring〈201〉
退屈な　innocuous〈243〉
大事なことを知らない　ill-informed〈199〉
対照的でない　noncontrastive〈91〉
退色　discoloration〈62〉, discoloring〈62〉
退色する　discolor〈61〉
大切なことを知らない　ill-informed〈199〉
体調の悪い　ill-conditioned〈77〉
帯電していない　uncharged〈53〉
滞納　nonpayment〈262〉
退廃　degeneration〈175〉
退廃する　degenerate〈174〉
代表していない　unrepresentative〈309〉
代表を送っていない　unrepresented〈309〉
たいへん貴重な　unpriced〈281〉
台本のない　unscripted〈326〉
怠慢な　inattentive〈29〉
タイミングの悪い　ill-timed〈372〉
題名のない　untitled〈372〉
体力を減退させる　decondition〈77〉
絶え間ない　relentless〈304〉
耐えられない　insufferable〈356〉, insupportable〈359〉, unbearable〈35〉, unendurable〈136〉

耐えられないほど　unbearably〈35〉
絶えることのない　undying〈127〉
耕されていない　uncultivated〈102〉
妥協しない　uncompromise〈73〉, uncompromising〈74〉
助けを受けない　unassisted〈26〉
助けを借りない　unaided〈14〉
讃えられていない　unsung〈358〉
正しくない　improper〈285〉
たちの悪い　ill-conditioned〈77〉, ill-disposed〈121〉
立場を決めていない　uncommitted〈66〉
脱衣　undressing〈126〉
脱イオン　deionization〈206〉
脱塩　desalinization〈320〉
脱塩した　desalted〈320〉
脱塩する　desalinize〈320〉, desalt〈320〉
脱塩すること　desalinization〈320〉
脱酸　deoxidization〈255〉
脱酸剤　deoxidizer〈255〉
脱酸された　deoxidized〈255〉
脱酸する　deoxidize〈255〉
脱湿　dehumidification〈191〉
脱脂の　nonfat〈155〉
脱臭　deodorization〈249〉
脱臭剤　deodorant〈249〉
脱水　dehydration〈192〉
脱水状態　dehydration〈192〉
脱水する　dehydrate〈192〉
達成されていない　unmet〈232〉
達成できない　unachievable〈6〉, unattainable〈28〉, unobtainable〈248〉
脱硫　desulfurization〈357〉
脱リン　dephosphorization〈268〉
脱リンする　dephosphorize〈268〉
妥当でない　invalid〈384〉

たとえようもなく　indescribably〈112〉
他人の不幸を願う人　ill-wisher〈399〉
種なしの　seedless〈329〉
種のない　unseeded〈329〉
楽しくない　joyless〈209〉
食べられない　inedible〈129〉
食べることができない　uneatable〈129〉
魂のこもっていない　soulless〈344〉
だます　disguise〈181〉
試されたことがない　untried〈377〉
試されていない　unproven〈287〉, untested〈369〉
たゆまぬ　unflagging〈162〉
頼るものもなく　helplessly〈186〉
堕落することのない　incorruptible〈97〉
だらしない　untidy〈371〉, unkempt〈211〉
短気　impatience〈261〉
断固とした　impregnable〈279〉, inexorable〈145〉
断固として　immovably〈238〉
炭酸が入っていない　noncarbonated〈45〉
単純化する　deskill〈340〉
短所　demerit〈232〉, disadvantage〈10〉
炭素を除去する　decarbonize〈46〉
断続的に　discontinuously〈91〉
弾力性のない　inelastic〈132〉

ち

小さな　inconsiderable〈84〉
地位にない　unplaced〈269〉
地位を下げる　degrade〈178〉
知恵のない　witless〈399〉
チェックされていない　unchecked〈54〉
チェックしない　uncheck〈53〉
チェック(マーク)を外す　uncheck〈53〉

近づきがたいほどに　inaccessibly〈4〉
近づきにくい　inaccessible〈4〉, ungetatable〈175〉
〜と違って　unlike〈217〉
近寄りがたい　unapproachable〈21〉
力がない　strengthless〈354〉
力強くない　gutless〈181〉
知識のない　unstudied〈354〉, untutored〈379〉
知識の不足　incognizance〈60〉
恥辱　disgrace〈177〉
地図に載っていない　uncharted〈53〉, unmapped〈228〉
知性のない　unintelligent〈202〉
父親のいない　fatherless〈155〉
父が亡くなった　fatherless〈155〉
縮まない　nonshrink〈337〉
秩序立っていないこと　formlessness〈167〉
知能のない　unintelligent〈202〉
血の気のない　bloodless〈39〉
注意されていない　unwatched〈394〉
注意の足りない　unwary〈394〉
注意深くない　uncautious〈47〉
注意を引かない　inconspicuous〈86〉
注意を引かないように　inconspicuously〈86〉
忠告を受けていない　unadvised〈11〉
中止　discontinuity〈90〉
中止する　discontinue〈90〉
忠実でない　disloyal〈223〉, unfaithful〈153〉
中断　discontinuity〈90〉
中断する　discontinue〈90〉
躊躇しない　unhesitating〈187〉
躊躇なく　unhesitatingly〈187〉
中途半端に　imperfectly〈265〉
チューブレスの　tubeless〈378〉
注目されない　unheeded〈186〉

中立　nonalignment〈16〉
中立の　colorless〈61〉, indifferent〈115〉, nonaligned〈15〉
超自然的な　unearthly〈128〉
兆候なく　asymptomatically〈364〉
兆候のない　asymptomatic〈364〉
調査が不徹底な　ill-researched〈309〉
調査できない　unsearchable〈327〉
調子がずれている　untuned〈379〉
調子外れの　tuneless〈379〉
調整されていない　uncoordinated〈95〉, unmodulated〈235〉, unregulated〈302〉
潮汐のない　tideless〈371〉
挑発されたものではない　unprovoked〈288〉
帳簿上の　unrealized〈297〉
調理していない　uncooked〈95〉
調和しない　dissonant〈344〉, incongruent〈80〉, inconsonant〈85〉
調和しないで　incongruently〈80〉
調和のとれない　inharmonious〈184〉
賃貸されていない　untenanted〈368〉

つ

対になっていない　unpaired〈257〉
付いていない　unaccompanied〈4〉
ついてくる　inevitable〈142〉
費やされていない　unspent〈346〉
通気性のない　nonporous〈275〉
通行できずに　impassably〈260〉
通行できない　impassable〈260〉
通行不可能な　impracticable〈276〉
使いものにならない　unusable〈381〉
疲れない　tireless〈372〉, unwearying〈395〉
疲れることなく　untiringly〈372〉
疲れを知らずに　tirelessly〈372〉

疲れを知らない　inexhaustible〈144〉, unflagging〈162〉, untiring〈372〉
疲れを知らないこと　inexhaustibleness〈144〉
疲れを知らないように　inexhaustibly〈144〉
使われていない　unused〈382〉
使われない　unusable〈381〉
使われないこと　disuse〈381〉
付き添わない　unchaperon〈51〉
付き添われていない　unattended〈28〉
月の出ていない　moonless〈235〉
継ぎ目なしの　endless〈135〉
継ぎ目のない　seamless〈327〉
～につきものの　inevitable〈142〉
尽きることなく　inexhaustibly〈144〉
尽きることのない　inexhaustible〈144〉
償いようのない　inexpiable〈148〉
償われていない　inexpiate〈148〉
作りの悪い　ill-constructed〈87〉
都合の悪い　inopportune〈251〉
つじつまの合わないこと　inconsistency〈85〉
慎みのない　immodest〈234〉
慎み深い　unobtrusive〈248〉
慎み深く　unobtrusively〈248〉
つながっている　unbroken〈42〉
常に　immortally〈237〉, invariably〈385〉, seamlessly〈327〉
つばのない　brimless〈42〉
翼のない　impennate〈263〉, wingless〈398〉
潰す　dismantle〈227〉
妻のいない　wifeless〈396〉
つまらない　ungiving〈176〉, uninteresting〈204〉
積み上げたものを崩す　unstack〈349〉
罪のない　guiltless〈180〉, harmless〈184〉, impeccable〈262〉, sinless〈339〉
罪のないこと　guiltlessness〈180〉

詰め込まない　unstuff〈355〉
詰め物をしていない　unconstructed〈87〉
つやが出ていない　unpolished〈273〉
釣り合いのとれていない　unbalanced〈33〉
釣り合っていない　disproportional〈286〉
釣り合わない　incongruous〈80〉, unsuited〈357〉
吊革のない　strapless〈354〉
つれない　heartless〈186〉

て

手が届かない　unaffordable〈12〉
手で触れることができない　impalpable〈258〉, intangible〈365〉
手に負えない　incorrigible〈96〉, intractable〈375〉
手の届かない　untouchable〈374〉
手のない　handless〈182〉
手を付けていない　untouched〈374〉
手を離す　unhand〈182〉
低下　debasement〈35〉, degradation〈178〉, devaluation〈385〉
低下させる　debase〈34〉, devalue〈385〉
定義されていない　undefined〈109〉
定義できない　indefinable〈109〉
提携していない　unaffiliated〈12〉, unaligned〈15〉
定形のない　shapeless〈336〉
低減していない　undiminished〈117〉
抵抗しない　unresisting〈311〉
抵抗できずに　irresistibly〈311〉
抵抗できない　irresistible〈311〉
停止する　deactivate〈6〉
定職のない　unwaged〈393〉
ディスインフレーション　disinflation〈199〉
ディスクのない　diskless〈121〉
訂正されていない　uncorrected〈96〉
定置されていない　unplaced〈269〉

手入れが行き届いていない　ill-maintained〈226〉
手入れされていない　ill-kept〈211〉, uncared-for〈46〉
手落ち　inefficiency〈131〉
敵意を除く　disarming〈23〉
敵意を除くように　disarmingly〈23〉
適応していない　unaccommodated〈4〉
適応性のない　inelastic〈132〉
適応できない　inadaptable〈8〉
適合しない　uncongenial〈79〉
適合できない　unadaptable〈8〉
適さない　disagree〈13〉
適していない　unfit〈162〉
適正でない　unreasonable〈297〉
適切に遂行しない　nonperforming〈265〉
適切に文書化されていない　ill-documented〈125〉
適当でない　unsuited〈357〉
できない　incapable〈45〉, unable〈2〉
できないこと　inability〈1〉
適任でない　ill-qualified〈291〉
適用できない　inapplicable〈20〉
でこぼこな　irregular〈301〉, uneven〈141〉
でたらめな　indiscriminate〈119〉
撤回できない　irreversible〈315〉
撤去する　dismantle〈227〉
徹底していない　nonexhaustive〈144〉
徹底的でない　inexhaustive〈144〉
徹底的でなく　inexhaustively〈145〉
撤廃する　unban〈34〉
転位　dislocation〈221〉, displacement〈269〉
典型的でない　untypical〈379〉
伝達できない　incommunicable〈67〉
伝達できない状態　incommunicability〈67〉
伝達不良　miscommunication〈67〉

転置　dislocation〈221〉
伝導しない　nonconducting〈78〉

と

同意しない　disagree〈13〉
動員解除　demobilization〈234〉
透過させない　impenetrable〈263〉, impermeable〈266〉
道義心のない　unprincipled〈281〉
動機付けのない　unmotivated〈237〉
動機のない　motiveless〈237〉
凍結していない　unfrozen〈172〉
動作に上品さのないこと　gracelessness〈177〉
動じない　unfaze〈156〉
どうしようもない　hopeless〈189〉, incurably〈103〉
どうしようもないほど　impossibly〈276〉, hopelessly〈190〉
どうしようもなく　helplessly〈186〉
投資をやめる[減らす]　disinvest〈205〉
どうすることもできないこと　helplessness〈187〉
統制を解除する　decontrol〈92〉, derestrict〈314〉
当選困難な　unelectable〈132〉
当然の　inevitable〈142〉
胴体のない　bodiless〈39〉
到達していない　unreached〈295〉
導通していない　nonconducting〈78〉, nonconductive〈78〉
同等でない　unequal〈138〉
道徳観のない　amoral〈236〉
道徳観のないこと　amorality〈236〉
道徳的　illicit〈216〉
党派に属さない　nonpartisan〈259〉
投票権のない　nonvoting〈392〉
投票を終わらせていない　unpolled〈274〉
糖分が入っていない　unsweetened〈362〉
透明でない　nontransparent〈376〉

透明な　noncrystalline〈102〉
動揺　unrest〈314〉
動揺していない　unruffled〈318〉
動揺しない　unflappable〈163〉, unwavering〈394〉
動揺せずに　unwaveringly〈395〉
道理に合わない　reasonless〈297〉
登録されていない　unregistered〈301〉
遠い昔の　immemorial〈231〉
通さない　impenetrable〈263〉, impervious〈268〉
ドープ処理されていない　undoped〈125〉
通れないこと　impassableness〈260〉
解かれた　untied〈371〉
解き放つ　disentangle〈137〉
途切れない　unbroken〈42〉
途切れなく　seamlessly〈327〉
解く　unbind〈38〉, uncoil〈60〉, undo〈124〉, unravel〈294〉, untangle〈366〉
解くことのできない　insoluble〈342〉
毒(性)がない　nontoxic〈374〉, nonvirulent〈389〉
毒ガスなどの除去　decontamination〈89〉
毒ガスなどを除去する　decontaminate〈88〉
得策でない　inadvisable〈11〉
独自性　inimitability〈195〉
独自に　independently〈112〉
特色のない　featureless〈158〉, indistinctive〈122〉
独身の　wifeless〈396〉
独創性のない　uninspired〈201〉
独創的でない　unoriginal〈254〉
特徴的でない　nondiscriminatory〈120〉
特徴のない　featureless〈158〉, uncharacteristic〈52〉
特徴のないこと　facelessness〈152〉
特徴のない状態　featurelessness〈158〉
特徴のないように　featurelessly〈158〉

特定的でない　nonspecific〈345〉
特定の宗派[会派]に属さない　nonsectarian〈328〉
特定の宗派に限定されない　nondenominational〈111〉
特定の目的に当てられていない　unappropriated〈21〉
得点を取っていない　pointless〈272〉
独特の　inimitable〈195〉
匿名の　faceless〈152〉, unnamed〈240〉
独立(心)　independence〈111〉
独立させる　decolonize〈61〉
独立して　independently〈112〉
溶けない　infusible〈173〉
途中でやめられない　unputdownable〈290〉
土地を持っていない　landless〈213〉
特化されていない　unspecialized〈345〉
特許を取っていない　unpatented〈261〉
ドックから出す　undock〈124〉
特権のない　unprivileged〈282〉
突然に　unexpectedly〈146〉
突然変異が起きにくい　nonsporting〈347〉
どっちつかずに　indecisively〈107〉
どっちつかずの　indecisive〈107〉
取って代わる　displace〈268〉
とてつもない　incredible〈100〉
とても嫌な　impossible〈276〉
とても高価な　invaluable〈384〉
止まることなく　unceasingly〈48〉
止まることのない　unceasing〈48〉
飛べない　flightless〈164〉
途方もなく　incredibly〈100〉
留め金を外す　unclasp〈56〉
止めどなく　endlessly〈136〉
止められない　unstoppable〈353〉
止める　immobilize〈234〉, inactivate〈7〉

友達のいない　friendless〈171〉
ともづなを解かれた　unmoored〈235〉
ともづなを解く　unmoor〈235〉
友なしで　friendlessly〈171〉
取り上げる　dispossess〈275〉
取り返しのつかない　immedicable〈231〉, irretrievable〈314〉
取り換えられない　irreplaceable〈308〉
取り消し　undoing〈125〉
取り消す　unsay〈324〉, unsubscribe〈355〉
取り消せない　irrevocable〈316〉
取り付け方が間違っている　ill-trained〈375〉
取り付けない　unattached〈27〉
取り付けの悪い　ill-set〈334〉
取り付けられていない　unmounted〈237〉
取り除く　disburden〈42〉, unburden〈43〉
取り外す　dismantle〈227〉, dismount〈237〉, undress〈126〉, unfix〈162〉, unmount〈237〉
取り戻す　unseat〈328〉
努力することなく　effortlessly〈132〉
努力を必要としない　effortless〈132〉
努力を必要としないこと　effortlessness〈132〉
〈受話器などを〉取る　unhook〈189〉
取るに足らない　inconsequent〈83〉, inconsiderable〈84〉, unconsidered〈84〉
取るに足らないこと　inconsequentiality〈83〉
取るに足らないように　inappreciably〈20〉
鈍感な　impervious〈268〉
貪欲な　insatiable〈321〉

な

名を汚す　disgrace〈177〉
直すことのできない　uncorrectable〈96〉
治っていない　uncured〈103〉

治らない　incurable〈103〉, incurably〈103〉
仲のよくない　inharmonious〈184〉
泣かない　tearless〈367〉
慰めようもなく　inconsolably〈85〉
慰められない　inconsolable〈85〉
納得していない　unconvinced〈94〉
何事もない　uneventful〈142〉
何もしないこと　inaction〈6〉
生意気な　impertinent〈267〉
名前が出ていない　unnamed〈240〉
名前のない　nameless〈240〉
名前を明かせない　nameless〈240〉
鉛を含んでいない　unleaded〈214〉
波の立たない　waveless〈394〉
涙の出ない　tearless〈367〉
悩まされない　unmolested〈235〉
並びの悪い　ill-arranged〈24〉
慣れていない　unaccustomed〈6〉, unused〈382〉
難攻不落の　impregnable〈279〉, inexpugnable〈150〉
ナンセンス　nonsense〈331〉
ナンセンスな　senseless〈331〉
なんとなく　indefinably〈109〉

に

荷を下ろす　unburden〈43〉, unship〈337〉
似合わない　ill-fitting〈162〉, unbecoming〈36〉
煮え切らないで　indecisively〈107〉
臭いを消す　deodorize〈249〉
臭いを消すこと　deodorization〈249〉
肉のない　meatless〈231〉
逃げられない　inescapable〈140〉
逃げることのできない　unescapable〈140〉
ニスを塗っていない　unvarnished〈386〉

偽情報　disinformation〈199〉
日光がささない　sunless〈358〉
似ていない　dissimilar〈339〉
入手できない　unavailable〈31〉
入手不可能　unavailability〈30〉
乳製品などを含まない　nondairy〈105〉
任意でない　nondiscretionary〈119〉, nonrandom〈293〉
任意の　unselective〈330〉
認可された　unaccredited〈5〉
認可されていない　unauthorized〈30〉
人気のない　unfashionable〈155〉
人間以外の　nonhuman〈191〉
人間性のない人　unpeople〈263〉
人間でない　nonhuman〈191〉
認識されていない　unrecognized〈299〉
認識しない　incognizant〈60〉
認識の不足　incognizance〈60〉
任命されていない　noncommissioned〈65〉

ぬ

縫い目のない　seamless〈327〉
脱がされた　unclothed〈58〉
脱がす　unclothe〈58〉
抜く　unpeg〈263〉

ね

値がついていない　unpriced〈281〉
値がつけられない　priceless〈281〉
根のない　rootless〈318〉
根も葉もない　groundless〈179〉
ネイティブでない　nonnative〈240〉
ねじを緩める　unscrew〈326〉
粘り強い　relentless〈304〉

値引き　discount〈97〉
値引きする　discount〈97〉
眠れない　sleepless〈341〉
狙いどころが悪い　ill-aimed〈15〉
燃焼していない　unburned〈43〉
年代不詳の　undated〈105〉

の

能率的でない　inefficient〈131〉
能力がない　incapable〈45〉
能力を奪う　disable〈2〉
ノーシードの　unseeded〈329〉
望まれていない　undesired〈113〉, unwished〈399〉
望まれない　unwanted〈393〉
望んでいない　unwished-for〈399〉
のっぺり　expressionless〈149〉
のっぺりした　faceless〈152〉
伸びない　inextensible〈150〉, inextensional〈150〉
述べられていない　unstated〈351〉
飲むことができない　undrinkable〈127〉
のらりくらりと　inefficiently〈132〉
ノンストップの　nonstop〈353〉
ノントランスファー的な　nontransferred〈375〉
ノンバンク　nonbank〈34〉
ノンフィクション　nonfiction〈159〉
ノンプロ　nonprofessional〈283〉
ノンプロの　nonprofessional〈283〉
ノンポリの　apolitical〈274〉
ノンリアルの　nonreal〈296〉

は

葉のない　leafless〈214〉
葉を落とす　defoliate〈165〉

歯のない　toothless〈374〉
配管設備のない　unplumbed〈272〉
配偶者のいない　unpaired〈257〉
廃止された　disused〈382〉
廃止する　disestablish〈140〉
排出する　discharging〈53〉
背徳主義　immoralism〈236〉
入り込めない　impenetrable〈263〉
破壊できない　indestructible〈113〉
ばかげた　illogical〈222〉
馬鹿な　brainless〈40〉
はがす　unstick〈352〉
計り知れない　immeasurable〈230〉, imponderable〈275〉, inscrutable〈326〉, measureless〈230〉, unfathomable〈156〉, inestimable〈140〉
剥がれた　unstuck〈354〉
覇気がない　cheerless〈54〉
破棄できない　indefeasible〈108〉
吐き出す　disgorge〈176〉
馬具を取り外す　unharness〈185〉
薄情　heartlessness〈186〉
薄情な　pitiless〈268〉
薄情に　heartlessly〈186〉
漠然と　indefinitely〈110〉
漠然とした　indefinable〈109〉
漠然としている　intangible〈365〉
剥奪する　disbar〈34〉
剥落する　nonadherent〈9〉
暴露　disclosure〈58〉
暴露しないこと　nondisclosure〈118〉
暴露する　disclose〈57〉, uncloak〈57〉
刷毛のない　brushless〈42〉
破産した　insolvent〈343〉
箸にも棒にもかからない　impossible〈276〉

恥知らずの　dishonorable〈189〉
恥をかく　disgraceful〈177〉
恥を感じない　unabashed〈1〉
恥を知らない　shameless〈336〉, unashamed〈25〉, unblushing〈39〉
場所のない　placeless〈269〉
場所をとらない　spaceless〈345〉
恥ずかしくもなく　unashamedly〈25〉
外した　unstrung〈354〉
外す　disjoint〈208〉, unhook〈189〉, unlatch〈213〉, unload〈220〉, unseat〈328〉, unstring〈354〉
破損状態　disrepair〈308〉
裸にする　unclothe〈58〉
裸の　unclad〈55〉
場違いの　incongruous〈80〉
発音が不明瞭なこと　inarticulateness〈25〉
発音が不明瞭に　inarticulately〈24〉
発音しにくい　unpronounceable〈285〉
発芽していない　ungerminated〈175〉
はっきり言えない　inarticulate〈24〉
はっきり言わない　inexplicit〈149〉
はっきりしない　inaudible〈29〉, indefinite〈109〉, indistinct〈122〉
はっきりと決められない　indeterminate〈114〉
バックルを外す　unbuckle〈42〉
発言権のない　voiceless〈390〉
発見されていない　undiscovered〈119〉
伐採　deforestation〈166〉
発達途上の　unformed〈169〉
ぱっとしない　unspectacular〈345〉
発表　disclosure〈58〉
発表しないこと　nondisclosure〈118〉
発表する　unveil〈386〉
果てしない　boundless〈40〉, endless〈135〉
果てしなく続く　endlessly〈136〉

果てしなさ　endlessness〈136〉
花の咲かない　flowerless〈165〉
花のない　flowerless〈165〉
離す　disengage〈137〉, unstick〈352〉
放す　unhitch〈188〉
放たれた　untethered〈369〉
羽根のない　featherless〈158〉
羽根のない状態　featherlessness〈158〉
ばねが付いていない　springless〈347〉
母親のない　motherless〈237〉
はばかることなく　guilelessly〈180〉
破滅の原因　undoing〈125〉
ばらばらにされた　disjointed〈208〉
ばらばらにする［なる］　disintegrate〈201〉
貼られていない　unstamped〈350〉
バランスの悪い　ill-balanced〈33〉
…のバランスを失わせる　unbalance〈33〉
晴れた　cloudless〈58〉
破廉恥な　unscrupulous〈326〉
パワー不足の　gutless〈181〉
反英雄　nonhero〈187〉
反感　disgust〈181〉
反抗　disobedience〈247〉
反抗する　disobey〈247〉
反抗的な　disobedient〈247〉
番号の付いていない　unnumbered〈245〉
番号のない　numberless〈245〉
ハンサムでない　unhandsome〈182〉
反社会的な　asocial〈342〉
反射されていない　unreflected〈300〉
反射しない　unreflecting〈300〉
反自由主義　illiberalism〈216〉
反証　disproof〈285〉

ひ

非営業的な　uncommercial〈65〉
非永続性　impermanence〈265〉
非営利団体　nonprofit〈284〉
非営利の　noncommercial〈65〉, nonprofit〈284〉
非音楽的な　unmusical〈238〉
非会員　nonmember〈231〉
非外交的な　undiplomatic〈117〉
非開示　nondisclosure〈118〉
非階層式の　non-hierarchical〈187〉
非介入　nonintervention〈205〉
控えめな　undemonstrative〈111〉, unpretentious〈281〉
控えめに　unobtrusively〈248〉, unpretentiously〈281〉
非科学的な　nonscientific〈325〉, unscientific〈325〉
非科学的に　unscientifically〈325〉
比較できないこと　incomparability〈68〉
比較できないほどに　incommensurably〈64〉
比較にならない　incomparable〈68〉
比較にならないくらい　incomparably〈68〉
非核の　nonnuclear〈245〉
非核分裂性の　nonfissionable〈161〉
日陰ではない　nonshaded〈335〉, unshaded〈335〉
日陰のない　shadeless〈335〉
非画像　nonimage〈194〉
非活性化　deactivation〈7〉
非活性化させる　deactivate〈6〉
光が遮られてない　shadowless〈336〉
挽かれていない　unground〈179〉
非換気の　nonventilated〈387〉
非観血的な　nonoperative〈251〉
非監視型の　unsupervised〈359〉
非干渉性　incoherency〈60〉
非干渉性の　noncoherent〈60〉
美観を損なう　disfigure〈160〉

非技術系の　nontechnical〈367〉
非技術的な　nontechnical〈367〉
非喫煙者　nonsmoker〈341〉
非喫煙の　nonsmoking〈341〉
引き剥がされた　unglued〈176〉
非揮発性の　nonvolatile〈390〉
非逆転の　non-reversing〈316〉
非客観的な　nonobjective〈247〉
非吸湿性の　non-hygroscopic〈193〉
非競合の　noncompetitive〈69〉
非凝集の　nonagglomerated〈13〉
非協力　noncooperation〈95〉
非協力的な　uncooperative〈95〉
非極性　nonpolar〈273〉
非極性にする　nonpolarize〈273〉
非居住者　nonresident〈310〉
非居住の　nonresident〈310〉
非居住用の　nonresidential〈310〉
非キリスト教徒　non-Christian〈54〉
非金属　nonmetal〈232〉
非金属の　nonmetallic〈232〉
非駆出性　non-ejection〈132〉
非具象的な　nonrepresentational〈309〉
非グリセリド　nonglyceride〈176〉
非経済的な　uneconomic〈129〉
非芸術的な　inartificial〈25〉, inartistic〈25〉
非芸術的に　inartistically〈25〉
非経常的な　nonrecurring〈300〉
非結晶　noncrystalline〈102〉
非結晶の　noncrystallized〈102〉
非決定論　indeterminism〈115〉
非決定論者　indeterminist〈115〉
非決定論的　indeterministic〈115〉

ひげのない　beardless〈35〉
非現実性　unreality〈297〉
非現実的な　insubstantial〈355〉, unrealistic〈296〉
非現実的に　insubstantially〈355〉, unrealistically〈297〉
非行　misconduct〈77〉
非公開の　nonpublic〈289〉
非恒久性　impermanence〈265〉
飛行禁止　no-fly〈165〉
非拘禁の　noncustodial〈104〉
非公式　informality〈168〉
非公式な　unofficial〈250〉
非公式に　informally〈168〉
非公式の　informal〈168〉
非恒常的な　non-routine〈318〉
非控除の　nondeductible〈108〉
非合法　illegitimacy〈215〉, unlawfulness〈214〉
非合法の　illegal〈215〉, illegitimate〈215〉, unlawful〈213〉
非互換性　incompatibility〈68〉
非細胞の　noncellular〈48〉
非酸化の　nonoxidizing〈256〉
非自己の　nonself〈330〉
非磁性の　nonmagnetic〈225〉
非実在　nonexistence〈145〉
非実際性　impracticality〈277〉
非実際的に　impractically〈277〉
非自動の　nonautomatic〈30〉
ビジネス以外　nonbusiness〈43〉
非自発的な　involuntary〈391〉
非自明性　nonobviousness〈248〉
非社会的な　unsocial〈342〉
非社交的な　unsociable〈342〉
非習慣性の　nonaddictive〈8〉
非終期の　nonterminal〈369〉

非自由主義　illiberalism〈216〉
非収縮の　nonconstricted〈87〉
非終端の　nonterminal〈369〉
非宗派的な　undenominational〈111〉
非重要人　nonperson〈266〉
非常勤の　nonexecutive〈144〉
非晶形　noncrystalline〈102〉
非常識に　insanely〈321〉
非常駐の　nonresident〈310〉
非衝突　noncollision〈61〉
非情な　unmerciful〈231〉
非常に　uncommonly〈66〉, unusually〈382〉
非常に貴重な　priceless〈281〉
非常に魅力的な　irresistible〈311〉
微小の　imperceptible〈264〉
非消耗性の　nonconsumable〈87〉
非食料品　nonfood〈165〉
非信者　nonbeliever〈37〉
非侵襲性の　noninvasive〈205〉
非人道的行為　inhumanity〈191〉
非人道的な　inhumane〈191〉
非侵入式の　noninvasive〈205〉
非数字の　nonnumeric〈246〉, nonnumerical〈246〉
非正弦曲線の　nonsinusoidal〈340〉
非制限的な　nonrestrictive〈314〉
非整合性　incommensurability〈64〉
非生産　degeneration〈175〉
非生産的な　nonproductive〈283〉, unproductive〈283〉
非生産的に　unproductively〈283〉
非錆質の　nonrusting〈319〉
非政治的な　unpolitical〈274〉
非成長の　nongrowing〈179〉
非政府の　nongovernmental〈177〉

非接触(性)の　noncontact〈88〉, noncontacting〈88〉
非接着性の　nonadherent〈9〉
非選挙の　non-electoral〈132〉
非線形性　nonlinearity〈219〉
非線形の　nonlinear〈218〉
非選択性の　nonselective〈330〉
非選択的な　nonselective〈330〉
非戦闘員　noncombatant〈62〉
非戦闘の　noncombat〈62〉
非専売の　nonproprietary〈286〉
非専門家　nonexpert〈147〉
非専門職　nonprofessional〈283〉
非専門職の　nonprofessional〈283〉
非相関性　noncorrelation〈96〉
非層状の　nonlaminar〈213〉
非組織の　nonunion〈381〉
非体系的な　unsystematic〈364〉
非対称　asymmetry〈363〉, dissymmetry〈363〉
非対称形に　unsymmetrically〈363〉
非対称形の　unsymmetrical〈363〉
非対称性　asymmetry〈363〉
非対称的な　asymmetric(al)〈362〉, nonsymmetrical〈362〉
非多孔質性の　nonporous〈275〉
非単一性　nonunity〈381〉
非弾性的な　inelastic〈132〉
非弾性の　inelastic〈132〉
非断定的な　nonassertive〈26〉
非逐次(的)な　nonserial〈333〉
非嫡出の　illegitimate〈215〉
非直線性　nonlinearity〈219〉
非直線の　nonlinear〈218〉
非貯蔵式の　nonstorage〈353〉
非通電にされた　de-energized〈137〉

ひっくり返されていない　unturned〈379〉
びっくりする　disconcert〈75〉
日付の付いていない　undated〈105〉
日付のない　dateless〈105〉
必須の　indispensable〈121〉
筆舌に尽くしがたい　ineffable〈130〉
必然性　inevitability〈142〉
必然的に　inescapably〈140〉, inevitably〈142〉
必然の　unescapable〈140〉
匹敵しがたい　unmatchable〈228〉
匹敵するものがない　unequaled〈138〉
必要としない　unwanted〈393〉
必要のない　needless〈241〉
非抵抗性の　nonresistant〈310〉
否定する　disclaim〈55〉, disconfirm〈79〉
否定できない　incontestable〈89〉, undeniable〈111〉
非手順(式)の　nonprocedural〈283〉
非鉄の　nonferrous〈159〉
非電子的　nonelectrolytic〈133〉
非伝染性の　noncommunicable〈67〉
非伝統的な　nonconventional〈93〉, nontraditional〈375〉
非伝導の　nonconducting〈78〉
非電導の　nonconductive〈78〉
非透過の　nontransparent〈376〉
非同期式に　asynchronously〈364〉
非同期の　asynchronous〈364〉
非同調　nonconformity〈79〉
非道徳的な　nonmoral〈236〉, unmoral〈236〉
非同盟　nonalignment〈16〉
非同盟の　nonaligned〈15〉, unaligned〈15〉
非特異な　nonsingular〈339〉
人通りが少なく　unfrequently〈171〉
人通りがない　unfrequented〈170〉

人にいやな気を与えない　unoffending〈250〉
人の手が入っていない　untamed〈365〉
人目につきにくい　unnoticeable〈244〉
非日常的な　non-routine〈318〉
非ニュートンの　non-Newtonian〈242〉
否認　disclaimer〈55〉
否認者　disclaimer〈55〉
否認する　disallow〈16〉, disapprove〈22〉, disclaim〈55〉
非任意　nonrandomness〈293〉
非人間性　impersonality〈266〉
非人間的な　inhuman〈190〉, inhumane〈191〉
非人間的にする　dehumanize〈191〉, depersonalize〈267〉
非人称の　impersonal〈266〉
ひねくれた　ill-natured〈241〉
非熱式の　nonthermal〈370〉
非燃焼性の　noncombustible〈63〉
非粘性の　nonviscous〈389〉
日の当たらない　sunless〈358〉
日の当たる　unshaded〈335〉
非の打ちどころなく　faultlessly〈156〉
非の打ちどころのない　faultless〈156〉, flawless〈164〉
非の打ちどころのないこと　faultlessness〈156〉
非能率(性)　inefficiency〈131〉
非能率的な　inefficient〈131〉
非能率的に　inefficiently〈132〉
火の気のない　fireless〈161〉
非破壊的な　nondestructive〈113〉
非白人の　nonwhite〈396〉
非パンクロの　nonpanchromatic〈258〉
批判的でない　acritical〈101〉, uncritical〈101〉
非反復の　nonrepetitive〈308〉
批判力のない　uncritical〈101〉
響きの悪い　ill-sounding〈344〉

非ヒステリシスの　nonhysteretic〈193〉
非標準的な　nonstandard〈350〉
被覆されていない　uncoated〈59〉
非腐食性　noncorrosive〈97〉
非武装化する　demilitarize〈232〉
非武装の　unarmed〈24〉
非物質化する　dematerialize〈229〉
非物質性　immateriality〈229〉
非物質論　immaterialism〈229〉
非ブランドの　nonbranded〈41〉
非文法的な　ungrammatical〈178〉
非分裂の　nondividing〈124〉
非変調の　unmodulated〈235〉
非包括的な　incomprehensive〈73〉
非方向性の　nondirectional〈118〉
非放射性の　inactive〈7〉, nonradioactive〈293〉
非暴力　nonviolence〈389〉
非暴力の　nonviolent〈389〉
非飽和させる　desaturate〈323〉
暇のない　leisureless〈216〉
秘密扱いでない　nonclassified〈56〉
非民主的な　undemocratic〈110〉
非無菌の　nonsterile〈352〉
ひもを解く　unlace〈213〉
非有機性の　inorganic〈253〉
非有理の　irrational〈293〉
非溶解性の　insoluble〈342〉
評価しがたい　inestimable〈140〉
表現が乏しい　unexpressive〈150〉
表現されない　unexpressed〈149〉
標準外の　nonstandard〈350〉
表情なく　expressionless〈149〉
表情に乏しく　expressionlessly〈149〉

非溶性の　nonconsumable〈87〉
費用のかからない　inexpensive〈147〉
漂白されていない　unpolished〈273〉
評判がよくない　unpopular〈275〉
評判の悪い　disreputable〈309〉, ill-famed〈154〉, ill-received〈298〉, infamous〈155〉
開く　unfold〈165〉, unfurl〈173〉, unroll〈317〉
非リセット(式)の　nonresettable〈310〉
非理想的　nonideal〈194〉
非流動性の　illiquid〈219〉
非良心的な　unconscionable〈82〉
非履歴現象の　nonhysteretic〈193〉
非倫理的な　unethical〈141〉
比類のない　peerless〈263〉, unrivaled〈317〉, unsurpassed〈360〉
ひるまない　unflinching〈165〉
非礼　impertinence〈267〉, irreverence〈315〉
非励起の　nonexcited〈143〉
非レーザーの　nonlaser〈213〉
非連続(性)の　nonserial〈333〉
非連続の　noncontiguous〈90〉
疲労していない　weariless〈395〉
非ロシアの　non-Russian〈319〉
非ロック式の　nonlocking〈222〉
非論理的な　illogical〈222〉
敏感でない　indiscriminating〈120〉
ヒンジを外す　unhinge〈187〉
頻度が低い　infrequent〈170〉
頻繁でない　infrequent〈170〉
貧乏でない　nondistressed〈123〉

ふ

負の投資を行う　disinvest〈205〉
無愛想な　inhospitable〈190〉

不安　disquietude⟨292⟩, unease⟨128⟩, uneasiness⟨128⟩, unrest⟨314⟩
不安そうに　uneasily⟨128⟩
不安な　insecure⟨328⟩, uneasy⟨128⟩, unquiet⟨292⟩
不安にする　disquieting⟨292⟩, unsettle⟨334⟩, unsettling⟨334⟩
不安定　destabilization⟨348⟩, insecurity⟨329⟩
不安定化させる　destabilize⟨348⟩
不安定性　instability⟨348⟩
不安定である　destabilizing⟨348⟩
不安定な　incalculable⟨44⟩, inconstant⟨86⟩, insecure⟨328⟩, nonsteady⟨351⟩, rootless⟨318⟩, unsound⟨344⟩, unstable⟨348⟩, unsteady⟨351⟩
不安定な状態の　unsteady-state⟨351⟩
不安定に　unstably⟨349⟩
不安定にされた　unsettled⟨334⟩
不安定にする　unsettle⟨334⟩
不案内な　ill-informed⟨199⟩
不意の　unbidden⟨38⟩, unceremonious⟨49⟩
不一致　disagreement⟨14⟩, discordance⟨76⟩, disparity⟨259⟩, dissonance⟨344⟩, incompatibility⟨68⟩, inconcinnity⟨75⟩, incongruence⟨80⟩, incongruity⟨80⟩, nonconformity⟨79⟩
フィルムの感光度を下げる　desensitize⟨332⟩
封をしていない　unsealed⟨327⟩
封印を解く　unseal⟨327⟩
風紀を乱す　demoralize⟨236⟩
風味のない　flavorless⟨163⟩
不運　haplessness⟨183⟩, unhappiness⟨183⟩
不運な　ill-fated⟨155⟩, inauspicious⟨30⟩, luckless⟨224⟩, unlucky⟨224⟩
不運にも　haplessly⟨183⟩, unluckily⟨224⟩
不衛生な　insanitary⟨321⟩, unsanitary⟨321⟩
不易の　immutable⟨238⟩
無遠慮な　immodest⟨234⟩, unceremonious⟨49⟩
フォーマットされていない　nonformatted⟨168⟩, unformatted⟨168⟩
不穏　unrest⟨314⟩
不穏当な　unprintable⟨282⟩

不快　discomfort〈63〉, displeasure〈271〉, unpleasantness〈271〉
不快感　distastefulness〈367〉
不快感を与える　uncomfortable〈64〉
不快感を持つ　uncomfortable〈64〉
不開示　nondisclosure〈118〉
不快な　disagreeable〈14〉, uncomfortable〈64〉, uncomfortable〈64〉
不快な臭いを消す　deodorize〈249〉
不快に　undesirably〈113〉
不可解そうに　inscrutably〈327〉
不可解な　bottomless〈40〉, impenetrable〈263〉, incomprehensible〈72〉, inexplainable〈148〉, inexplicable〈148〉, inscrutable〈326〉, unsearchable〈327〉
不可解なこと　impenetrability〈263〉, incomprehensibility〈72〉
不可解なことに　incomprehensibly〈72〉
不可解にも　inexplicably〈148〉
不可逆的な　irreversible〈315〉, irreversibly〈316〉
不確実　insecurity〈329〉
不確実さ　uncertainty〈50〉
不確実性　uncertainty〈50〉
不確実な　uncertain〈49〉
不拡張　inextension〈150〉
不確定　indetermination〈114〉
不確定性　indeterminacy〈114〉
不確定の　indeterminate〈114〉
不可欠な　indispensable〈121〉
不可抗争　incontestability〈89〉
深さのわからない　unplumbed〈272〉
不可思議な　unaccountable〈5〉
不可侵の　inviolate〈388〉
不可争性　incontestability〈89〉
不格好な　ill-shaped〈336〉, ungainly〈174〉
不活性化　inactivation〈7〉
不活性化された　inactivated〈7〉

不活性化する　inactivating〈7〉
不活性の　inactive〈7〉
不活発　inactivity〈8〉
不活発化させる　deactivate〈6〉
不活発な　inactive〈7〉
不活発に　inactively〈8〉
不稼働　inoperation〈250〉
不可能性　impossibility〈275〉
不可能である　impossible〈276〉
不可能なこと　impossibility〈275〉
不可避性　inevitability〈142〉
不可避的に　inescapably〈140〉, inevitably〈142〉
不可避の　inescapable〈140〉, inevitable〈142〉, unavoidable〈31〉, undeniable〈111〉
不可分の　inalienable〈15〉
不干渉　noninterference〈204〉, nonintervention〈205〉
不完全　imperfection〈265〉
不完全さ　incompleteness〈71〉
不完全性　incompleteness〈71〉
不完全な　imperfect〈264〉, incomplete〈70〉, inexact〈143〉
不完全に　incompletely〈71〉
不感度　insensitivity〈332〉
不寛容　intolerance〈373〉
不寛容な　intolerant〈373〉
不機嫌な　disgruntled〈179〉, ill-humored〈192〉, ill-tempered〈368〉
不機嫌な性格　ill-nature〈240〉
不規則性　irregularity〈302〉
不規則的に　irregularly〈302〉
不規則な　irregular〈301〉
不吉な　ill-boding〈39〉, inauspicious〈30〉
不吉な方法で　inauspiciously〈30〉
不揮発性の　involatile〈390〉, nonvolatile〈390〉
不気味な　unearthly〈128〉

不朽の　imperishable〈265〉
不器用さ　inexpertness〈148〉
不器用な　handless〈182〉
不器用に　inexpertly〈148〉
不協和　disharmony〈184〉, dissonance〈344〉
武器を持たない　weaponless〈395〉
不均一な　inhomogeneous〈188〉, nonuniform〈380〉, uneven〈141〉
不均一に　inhomogeneously〈189〉
不均衡　disequilibrium〈139〉, disproportion〈285〉, imbalance〈33〉, incoordination〈95〉, unbalance〈33〉
不均質　unevenness〈141〉
不均質性　nonuniformity〈380〉
不均質な　inhomogeneous〈188〉, nonuniform〈380〉, uneven〈141〉
不謹慎　imprudence〈288〉
不謹慎な　unscrupulous〈326〉
不均整　asymmetry〈363〉
不均整な　asymmetric(al)〈362〉
復員　demobilization〈234〉
複雑でない　uncomplicated〈71〉, unsophisticated〈344〉
復調　demodulation〈235〉
復調する　demodulate〈235〉
不屈の　unconquerable〈82〉, uncrushable〈102〉
不敬に　godlessly〈176〉
不景気な　depressed〈280〉
不経済な　uneconomical〈129〉
不潔　impurity〈289〉
不潔な　unclean〈56〉
不潔に　uncleanly〈56〉
不決断　indetermination〈114〉
不減衰の　undamped〈105〉
不健全さ　unsoundness〈344〉
不健全な　unhealthy〈185〉
不幸　haplessness〈183〉, unhappiness〈183〉

不幸な　hapless〈183〉, infelicitous〈158〉, unfortunate〈169〉, unhappy〈183〉, unlucky〈224〉
不幸にも　haplessly〈183〉, unfortunately〈169〉, unhappily〈183〉, unluckily〈224〉
不公平　inequity〈139〉, unfairness〈153〉
不公平な　inequitable〈139〉, unfair〈152〉, unjust〈209〉
不公平に　inequitably〈139〉, unfairly〈153〉
不合理　unreason〈297〉
不合理な　illogical〈222〉, inconsequential〈83〉, irrational〈293〉, unreasoned〈298〉
不合理に　irrationally〈294〉, unreasonably〈298〉
無作法　discourtesy〈99〉, ill-breeding〈41〉, impoliteness〈274〉, incivility〈55〉, indecency〈106〉, indecorum〈108〉, indelicacy〈110〉
無作法な　graceless〈177〉, ill-mannered〈227〉, immodest〈234〉, indecent〈106〉, indecorous〈108〉, mannerless〈227〉, unceremonious〈49〉, uncivil〈55〉, uncourteous〈99〉, unmannered〈227〉, unmannerly〈227〉
無作法なこと　gracelessness〈177〉
無作法に　gracelessly〈177〉, indecorously〈108〉, unceremoniously〈49〉
不参加　nonattendance〈28〉
不参加者　nonparticipant〈259〉
不賛成　disapproval〈22〉
不死　immortality〈237〉
不死の　deathless〈106〉, immortal〈236〉
不支持　nonsupport〈359〉
不自然な　unnatural〈240〉
不自然に　unnaturally〈240〉
ふしだら　immorality〈236〉
不実行　nonperformance〈265〉
不実な　faithless〈153〉
無事で　unscathed〈324〉
不死身の　invulnerable〈392〉
不従順　disobedience〈247〉, indocility〈124〉

不十分　inadequacy〈8〉, insufficiency〈356〉
不十分な　ill-conceived〈75〉, inadequate〈9〉, incomplete〈70〉, unsatisfactory〈322〉
不十分に　imperfectly〈265〉, inadequately〈9〉
不出廷　nonappearance〈20〉
不出頭　nonappearance〈20〉
不首尾の　unsuccessful〈355〉
不受理　nonacceptance〈4〉
不純　impurity〈289〉
不純な　impure〈289〉
不純物　impurity〈289〉
不純物のない　unalloyed〈16〉
不遵守　nonobservant〈247〉
不使用　nonuse〈382〉
不消化の　indigested〈116〉
不正直な　dishonest〈189〉
不正直に　dishonestly〈189〉
不承諾　nonacceptance〈4〉, noncompliance〈71〉
不承知　disapproval〈22〉, nonacceptance〈4〉, nonagreement〈14〉
不浄な　unholy〈188〉
不条理　unreason〈297〉
腐食しない　incorruptible〈97〉
不織の　nonwoven〈401〉
侮辱　indignity〈116〉
不信　disbelief〈36〉, distrust〈377〉, untrustworthiness〈378〉
不信感　incredulity〈101〉
不信心　impiety〈268〉, infidelity〈160〉
不信心な　irreligious〈307〉, ungodly〈176〉
不親切な　inconsiderate〈84〉, kindless〈211〉, unkind〈211〉
不親切に　unkindly〈211〉
不浸透性　impermeability〈266〉, impermeable〈266〉
不浸透性の　impervious〈268〉
不信任　nonconfidence〈78〉

不侵略　nonaggression〈13〉
不粋　inelegance〈133〉
不随意に　involuntarily〈391〉
不正　impropriety〈286〉, injustice〈209〉
不正行為　injustice〈209〉, misbehavior〈36〉
不正な　ill-motivated〈237〉
不正な手段　indirection〈118〉
不正に　dishonestly〈189〉
不誠意　insincerity〈339〉
不正確　inaccuracy〈5〉, inexactitude〈143〉, inexactness〈143〉
不正確な　imprecise〈277〉, inaccurate〈5〉, incorrect〈96〉, inexact〈143〉
不正確に　imprecisely〈277〉, incorrectly〈96〉, inexactly〈143〉
不整形の　irregular〈301〉
不成功に　unsuccessfully〈356〉
不成功の　unsuccessful〈355〉
不整合(面)　unconformity〈79〉
不整合の　unconformable〈79〉
不誠実　disloyalty〈223〉, faithlessness〈153〉, insincerity〈339〉
不誠実な　disingenuous〈199〉, faithless〈153〉
不誠実に　faithlessly〈153〉
不鮮明な　unclear〈56〉
不相応な状態で　incommensurately〈65〉
武装解除　disarmament〈23〉
武装解除する　disarm〈23〉
武装しないで　unarmed〈24〉
不足　insufficiency〈356〉
付属していない　unaccompanied〈4〉
不揃い　irregularity〈302〉
不揃いに　irregularly〈302〉
ふたがとられた　uncovered〈100〉
ふたのない　lidless〈216〉
不耐性　intolerance〈373〉
不耐性の　intolerant〈373〉

不確かな　uncertain〈49〉
不確かに　uncertainly〈50〉
不断の　uninterrupted〈204〉
負担をなくす　unburden〈43〉
不治　incurability〈103〉
不治の　cureless〈103〉, incurable〈103〉
縁なしの　rimless〈317〉
付着しない　nonstick〈352〉
不注意　inadvertence〈10〉, inattention〈28〉
不注意な　careless〈46〉, heedless〈186〉, inadvertent〈10〉, inattentive〈29〉, incautious〈47〉, mindless〈232〉, thoughtless〈370〉, unwary〈394〉
不注意に　carelessly〈46〉, inadvertently〈11〉, thoughtlessly〈370〉
不忠実　disaffection〈12〉, disloyalty〈223〉
不忠実な　faithless〈153〉
不調　disorder〈252〉
不調な　disordered〈252〉
不調和　discordance〈76〉, disharmony〈184〉, dissonance〈344〉, inconcinnity〈75〉, incongruence〈80〉, inconsonance〈85〉, nonconformity〈79〉
不調和な　disharmonious〈184〉
不調和の　inharmonious〈184〉
普通でない　abnormal〈244〉, uncommon〈66〉, unusual〈382〉, unwonted〈400〉
普通でないこと　abnormality〈244〉
普通でなく　unusually〈382〉
不都合　inconvenience〈93〉, inexpedience〈146〉
不都合な　disadvantageous〈10〉, incommodious〈66〉, inconvenient〈93〉, inopportune〈251〉, unfavorable〈156〉
物質的性質をなくす　dematerialize〈229〉
物質的に　unspiritually〈346〉
ふつつか者で　inexperienced〈147〉
不釣り合い　mismatch〈228〉

不釣り合いな　disproportionate〈286〉, ill-assorted〈27〉, ill-matched〈229〉, ill-proportioned〈286〉, incommensurate〈65〉
不釣り合いな状態で　incommensurately〈65〉
不釣り合いに　disproportionately〈286〉
不貞　infidelity〈160〉
不定の　indefinite〈109〉, indeterminate〈114〉
不定期の　nonscheduled〈325〉
不定形の　irregular〈301〉
不体裁な　undignified〈116〉
不適な　ill-suited〈357〉
不適格　incapacity〈45〉, disqualification〈291〉, incompetency〈69〉, ineligibility〈133〉
不適格性　ill-formedness〈169〉
不適格とする　disqualify〈291〉
不適格な　ill-formed〈169〉, incompetent〈69〉, ineligible〈133〉, unqualified〈291〉
不適合　incompatibility〈68〉, inconformity〈79〉, incongruity〈80〉
不適切　inadequacy〈8〉, incongruity〈80〉, irrelevance〈305〉
不適切な　ill-fitted〈162〉, impertinent〈267〉, improper〈285〉, inadequate〈9〉, inappropriate〈21〉, inapt〈22〉, infelicitous〈158〉
不適切に　improperly〈285〉, inadequately〈9〉, inappropriately〈21〉
不適当　impertinence〈267〉, improperness〈285〉, impropriety〈286〉, inadequacy〈8〉, inaptitude〈22〉, insufficiency〈356〉
不適当な　inadequate〈9〉, inappropriate〈21〉, ineligible〈133〉, insufficient〈356〉, unsuitable〈357〉
不適当な行為　inappropriateness〈21〉
不適当に　inappropriately〈21〉, inexpediently〈147〉
不手際　inefficiency〈131〉
不徹底の　nonexhaustive〈144〉
不等　inequality〈138〉
不当　unfairness〈153〉
不当な方法で得た　ill-gotten〈176〉
不当に　unduly〈127〉, unjustly〈209〉

不当表示　misbranding〈41〉
不(可)動(性)　immovability〈238〉
不同意　nonagreement〈14〉
不統一　disunion〈381〉
不同形　inconformity〈79〉
不等式　inequation〈138〉
不等質な　inhomogeneous〈188〉
不動性　immobility〈233〉
不動で　immovably〈238〉
不動の　immovable〈238〉, inexorable〈145〉, unswerving〈362〉
不導体　nonconductor〈78〉
不道徳　impurity〈289〉
不道徳な　immoral〈236〉
不道徳な行為　immorality〈236〉
不道徳にする　immoralize〈236〉
不等辺の　inequilateral〈138〉
不得策な　impolitic〈274〉, inexpedient〈146〉
不特定の　unspecified〈345〉
不慣れ　unfamiliarity〈154〉
不慣れな　unaccustomed〈6〉, unfamiliar〈154〉
不似合いな　ill-suited〈357〉, inappropriate〈21〉
不妊　infertility〈159〉
不認可　disapproval〈22〉
不人気　disrepute〈309〉
不人気の　unpopular〈275〉
不人情な　inhuman〈190〉, inhumane〈191〉
不妊の　infertile〈159〉
不燃性　incombustibility〈63〉, non-flammability〈162〉
不燃性の　incombustible〈63〉, noncombustible〈63〉, nonflammable〈162〉
不敗　invincibility〈388〉
腐敗していない　undecomposed〈107〉
腐敗する　decompose〈71〉

不爆発(性)の　inexplosive〈149〉
不払い　nonpayment〈262〉
不備　incompleteness〈71〉
不必要な　inessential〈140〉, unnecessary〈241〉
不必要に　needlessly〈241〉, unnecessarily〈241〉
不評　disrepute〈309〉
不評の　ill-regarded〈301〉
不平等　inequality〈138〉
不品行　misdemeanor〈110〉
不分割の　nondividing〈124〉
不平　discontent〈89〉
不平な　unjust〈209〉
不平を言わない　uncomplaining〈70〉
不便　inexpedience〈146〉, inconvenience〈93〉
不便で不快なこと　incommodiousness〈66〉
不便な　incommodious〈66〉, inconvenient〈93〉, inexpedient〈146〉, unhandy〈182〉
不便なことに　inconveniently〈93〉
不便を感じる　inconvenience〈93〉
不変化の　indeclinable〈107〉
不変数　invariable〈385〉
不変性　immutableness〈239〉, inalterableness〈16〉
不変に　immutably〈239〉, inalterably〈16〉, invariably〈385〉
不変の　immutable〈238〉, inalterable〈16〉, incommutable〈67〉, indissoluble〈122〉, inexorable〈145〉, invariant〈386〉
不偏不党の　nonparty〈260〉
不変量　invariable〈385〉
不法　illegitimacy〈215〉
不法行為　misconduct〈77〉
不法な　illicit〈216〉, lawless〈213〉
不法に　illegally〈215〉, irregularly〈302〉, unduly〈127〉, unjustly〈209〉
不飽和状態　unsaturation〈323〉
不飽和状態の　unsaturated〈323〉

不飽和の　nonsaturated〈323〉
不本意な　involuntary〈391〉
踏まれていない　untrod〈377〉
不満　disaffection〈12〉, discontent〈89〉, dissatisfaction〈321〉
不満な　disgruntled〈179〉, unsatisfied〈322〉
不満に思う　dissatisfy〈322〉
不満のある　disaffected〈11〉, discontented〈89〉
不満の原因となる　dissatisfactory〈322〉
不満の種　dissatisfaction〈321〉
不満を抱いている　ill-affected〈11〉
不満足な　dissatisfactory〈322〉, dissatisfied〈322〉, unhappy〈183〉, unsatisfactory〈322〉
不向き　inaptitude〈22〉
不向きな　unsuited〈357〉
不明確な　imprecise〈277〉
不明白　nonobviousness〈248〉
不名誉　disgrace〈177〉, dishonor〈189〉
不名誉な　disgraced〈177〉, disgraceful〈177〉, dishonorable〈189〉, infamous〈155〉
不名誉にも　infamously〈155〉
不明瞭　indistinctness〈122〉
不明瞭な　indistinct〈122〉, nonintelligible〈202〉, unclear〈56〉, unintelligible〈202〉
不明瞭に　indistinctly〈122〉, unintelligibly〈202〉
不滅　immortality〈237〉
不滅にする　immortalize〈237〉
不滅の　deathless〈106〉, imperishable〈265〉
不愉快　displeasure〈271〉, distaste〈366〉
不愉快な　disagreeable〈14〉, displeasing〈271〉, distasteful〈367〉, invigorous〈388〉, unpleasant〈270〉
不愉快なこと　unpleasantness〈271〉
不愉快に　unpleasantly〈270〉
不愉快にさせる　displease〈271〉

不愉快にされた　unpleased〈271〉
不要の　unwanted〈393〉
不用意な　unconsidered〈84〉, improvident〈288〉
不溶解性の　infusible〈173〉
扶養義務不履行　nonsupport〈359〉
不用心な　uncautious〈47〉
不溶性の　insoluble〈342〉
プラグを抜いた　unplugged〈272〉
プラグを抜く　unplug〈271〉
ブラシレス　brushless〈42〉
ブランド品でない　nonbranded〈41〉
不利な　disadvantageous〈10〉, untoward〈374〉
不利な立場　disadvantage〈10〉
不履行　nonperformance〈265〉
不良…　undesired〈113〉
ふるいにかけていない　unscreened〈326〉
無礼　discourtesy〈99〉, disrespect〈312〉, impertinence〈267〉, incivility〈55〉, indecency〈106〉, indecorum〈108〉, irreverence〈315〉
無礼な　discourteous〈99〉, impertinent〈267〉, impolite〈274〉, irreverent〈315〉, uncomplimentary〈71〉, uncouth〈99〉, ungracious〈178〉
無礼にも　impolitely〈274〉
プレーしない〈人〉　nonplaying〈270〉
触れてはならない　untouchable〈374〉
不連続性　discontinuity〈90〉
不連続的に　discontinuously〈91〉
不連続の　discontinuous〈91〉
不老の　ageless〈12〉
プロットなしの　plotless〈271〉
不和の　discordant〈76〉
分化していない　unspecialized〈345〉
分解　decomposition〈72〉, disassembly〈26〉, disintegration〈202〉, dissolution〈342〉
分解されていない　undecomposed〈107〉

分解する　decompose〈71〉, deconstruct〈87〉, disassemble〈26〉, dismantle〈227〉, dissolve〈343〉
分解できない　indissoluble〈122〉
分解できる　dissoluble〈342〉, dissolvable〈343〉
分割　disunion〈381〉
分割されない　undivided〈124〉
分割しない　nondividing〈124〉
分権　decentralization〈48〉
分権された　decentralized〈48〉
分権する　decentralize〈48〉
分散　decentralization〈48〉
分散された　decentralized〈48〉
分散されていない　undispersed〈121〉
分散されない　undivided〈124〉
分散する　decentralize〈48〉
紛失　disappearance〈20〉
文書化されていない　ill-documented〈125〉
分配されていない　unshared〈336〉
分配できない　indistributable〈123〉
分別のない　reasonless〈297〉
分別のなさ　irrationality〈294〉
噴霧しない　unatomize〈27〉
文明化されていない　uncivilized〈55〉
分離　disconnection〈82〉, disjunction〈80〉, dissociation〈27〉, disunion〈381〉
分離させる　disjunctive〈81〉, disunite〈381〉
分離されない　unsegregated〈330〉
分離した　disjunct〈80〉
分離する　dissociate〈26〉
分離できない　indissociable〈122〉, indissoluble〈122〉, inseparable〈333〉
分類されていない　unclassified〈56〉
分裂　disjunction〈80〉

へ

平静を失わせる　disquiet〈292〉
平然とした　unperturbed〈267〉
平坦でない　ungraded〈178〉
平凡な　indifferent〈115〉, unremarkable〈307〉
ペーパーレスの　paperless〈258〉
ベールをはがす　unveil〈386〉
へこたれない　invulnerable〈392〉
下手な　artless〈24〉
下手に　thoughtlessly〈370〉
ベルトを外す　unbelt〈37〉
弁解できない　inexcusable〈144〉
弁解の余地のない　indefensible〈109〉
弁解の余地のないこと　inexcusableness〈144〉
弁解の余地もないほど　indefensively〈109〉
変化しない　invariant〈386〉
変化のない　changeless〈51〉
変換する　disassemble〈26〉
返却されない　nonreturnable〈315〉
偏狭な　intolerant〈373〉
返金不可の　nonrefundable〈301〉
変形　deformation〈168〉
変形させる　deform〈167〉
変形した　deformed〈169〉
変形したもの　deformation〈168〉
偏見なく　impartially〈259〉, unprejudicedly〈279〉
偏見のない　colorless〈61〉, unbias(s)ed〈37〉, unprejudiced〈279〉
偏見のないこと　impartiality〈259〉
変更できない　unalterable〈16〉
弁護されていない　undefended〈108〉
弁護人のいない　undefended〈108〉
変質　degeneration〈175〉

変色　discoloration〈62〉, discoloring〈62〉
変色した　discolored〈62〉
変色する　discolor〈61〉
変装させる　disguise〈181〉
変則的な　atypical〈379〉
変動しない　nonfluctuating〈165〉

ほ

保安検査を受けていない　unscreened〈326〉
法に反した　irregular〈301〉
崩壊　disintegration〈202〉
崩壊する　disintegrate〈201〉
法外な　inordinate〈252〉
妨害　impediment〈262〉
包括的でない　incomprehensive〈73〉
放棄する　discard〈46〉
防御不可能な　indefensible〈109〉
方向感覚を失わせる　disorient〈254〉
方向感覚を失わせるような　disorienting〈254〉
方向性のない　undirected〈117〉
報告されていない　unreported〈309〉
帽子がない状態で　hatlessly〈185〉
放射能を含まない　nonradioactive〈293〉
放出された　discharged〈53〉
放出する　discharge〈52〉, disgorge〈176〉
法人化されていない　unincorporated〈197〉
包装を解く　unpack〈257〉
放置された　unattended〈28〉
法的に認められない　illicit〈216〉
放電する　discharge〈52〉, discharging〈53〉
暴動　disorder〈252〉
法令に拘束されない　imprescriptible〈279〉
飽和しない　unsaturate〈323〉

(社会的に)葬られた人　unperson〈266〉
ホームレスの　homeless〈188〉
他から強制されたものではない　unprompted〈285〉
補強材のない　ribless〈317〉
ほぐす　unbind〈38〉
ほぐれた　untucked〈378〉
ほぐれる　unwind〈397〉
保険が掛けられていない　uninsured〈201〉
保護されていない　unencapsulated〈135〉, unprotected〈286〉, unshielded〈336〉
埃のない　dustless〈127〉
星の出ていない　starless〈350〉
星回りの悪い　ill-starred〈350〉
補償作用がはたらかなくなる　decompensate〈69〉
補償されていない　uncompensated〈69〉
舗装されていない　unpaved〈262〉
舗装状態の悪い　ill-paved〈262〉
保存していない　unsaved〈323〉
保存状態が悪い　ill-presented〈280〉
ボタンが外れた　unbuttoned〈43〉
ボタンを外す　unbutton〈43〉
ほどく　unknit〈211〉, unpick〈268〉, unthread〈371〉, untie〈371〉
ほどけない　inextricable〈151〉
ぼやけている　indistinct〈122〉
掘り出す　disentomb〈137〉, unearth〈128〉
ボルトを緩める　unbolt〈39〉
本質的でない　inessential〈140〉, unessential〈140〉
ぼんやりして　inattentively〈29〉
ぼんやりする　heedless〈186〉
本を読まない人　nonreader〈296〉

ま

マイナスとなる　unflattering〈163〉

曲がっていない　unbowed〈40〉
曲がらない　inflexible〈164〉, unbending〈37〉
巻き戻す　unreel〈300〉, unroll〈317〉
まぎれもなく　unmistakably〈233〉
負けたことのない　unbeaten〈36〉, undefeated〈108〉
混ざらない　immiscible〈232〉
混ざりもののない　unmixed〈233〉
まずい　inappropriate〈21〉
まずい発想の　ill-conceived〈75〉
混ぜられていない　unadulterated〈10〉
まだ生まれていない　unborn〈39〉
瞬きしない　unblinking〈38〉
間違い　impropriety〈286〉, inaccuracy〈5〉
間違いなく　inevitably〈142〉
間違いなしに　unfailingly〈152〉
間違いのない　doubtless〈125〉, unfailing〈152〉
間違いのないこと　inerrancy〈139〉, infallible〈154〉
間違えようもない　unmistakable〈233〉
間違った判断をしない　nonjudgmental〈209〉
間違って　imprecisely〈277〉, incorrectly〈96〉
待ち切れずに　impatiently〈262〉
(政治的に)抹殺された人々　unpeople〈263〉
真っ直ぐでない　indirect〈117〉
真っ直ぐにする　unbend〈37〉, uncurl〈104〉, uncurl〈104〉
窓のない　windowless〈397〉
的外れの　ill-directed〈117〉
まとまりのない　uncoordinated〈95〉
まとまりの悪い　ill-organized〈254〉
招かれない　unbidden〈38〉
摩耗していない　unworn〈401〉
守られていない　ill-guarded〈180〉
迷いを覚ます　disenchant〈135〉
まれな　infrequent〈170〉

まれに infrequently〈171〉, uncommonly〈66〉
回り道 indirection〈118〉
満足できない unsatisfying〈322〉

み

実がなっていない unfruitful〈173〉
実入りの悪い ill-paid〈257〉
見えない invisible〈389〉, unseen〈329〉
見栄をはらない unpretentious〈281〉
見落とし inadvertence〈10〉
未解決の undecided〈106〉, unresolved〈312〉
未改正の unrevised〈316〉
未開拓の untapped〈366〉
未開発の undeveloped〈115〉
未開封の unopened〈250〉
磨かれていない unpolished〈273〉
未確定 indetermination〈114〉
未確認の unconfirmed〈79〉
身勝手な inconsiderate〈84〉
未完成の immature〈229〉, incomplete〈70〉, uncompleted〈70〉
見苦しい indecent〈106〉, unseemly〈329〉
見苦しいこと indecency〈106〉
未経験の unfledged〈164〉
未決定の undetermined〈115〉
見込みのない futureless〈173〉, hopeless〈189〉, unlikely〈217〉, unpromising〈285〉
未婚の unmarried〈228〉, unwed〈395〉
見境なく indiscriminately〈120〉
見境のない indiscriminate〈119〉
未修正の unrevised〈316〉
未熟な artless〈24〉, inapt〈22〉, inexperienced〈147〉, inexpert〈147〉, unfledged〈164〉, unskillful〈340〉
未消化の undigested〈116〉

未処理の　unprocessed〈283〉, untreated〈376〉
ミシン目が入っていない　unperforated〈265〉
水のいらない〈料理〉　waterless〈394〉
水のない　waterless〈394〉
水を抜く　unwater〈394〉
水を含まない　nonaqueous〈22〉
水先案内なしの　pilotless〈268〉
未成熟の　immature〈229〉
未成年　nonage〈13〉
未セーブの　unsaved〈323〉
未組織の　unorganized〈254〉
満たされていない　unmet〈232〉, unsatisfied〈322〉
乱されない　undisturbed〈123〉
みだらな　immoral〈236〉, indecent〈106〉
みっともない　disreputable〈309〉
未定の　unfixed〈162〉
未踏の　uncharted〈53〉, unmapped〈228〉
見通しのない　visionless〈390〉
認めない　disallow〈16〉
認められていない　unacknowledged〈6〉
醜い　ill-looking〈223〉
実りなく　fruitlessly〈172〉
見場の悪さ　unsightliness〈337〉
未発表の　unpublished〈289〉
未払いの　unpaid〈257〉
未反応の　unreacted〈295〉
未変換の　unconverted〈94〉
耳障りな　discordant〈76〉
耳によって知覚できない性質　inaudibleness〈29〉
脈拍のない　pulseless〈289〉
魅力的な　irresistible〈311〉
魅力のない　unattractive〈29〉, unglamorous〈176〉, uninviting〈206〉, unsexy〈335〉

見分けにくい　indiscernible〈118〉
見分けられない　unrecognizable〈299〉
民間の　nongovernmental〈177〉

む

無為　inactivity〈8〉
無意識に　involuntarily〈391〉
無意識の　involuntary〈391〉, unconscious〈82〉
無意識のうちに　unconsciously〈83〉
無一文の　penniless〈263〉
無意味さ　meaninglessness〈230〉
無意味である　pointless〈272〉
無意味な　meaningless〈230〉, senseless〈331〉, unmeaning〈230〉
無意味なこと　nonsense〈331〉
無益　fruitlessness〈172〉
無益に　fruitlessly〈172〉
無益の　inutile〈383〉, unfruitful〈173〉
無煙の　smokeless〈341〉
無鉛の　unleaded〈214〉
無音の　soundless〈344〉
無害　harmlessness〈184〉
無害な　harmless〈184〉, innocent〈242〉
無害に　harmlessly〈184〉
無害の　innocuous〈243〉
無過給の　unsupercharged〈358〉
無学の　illiterate〈220〉, unlettered〈216〉
無冠の　uncrowned〈102〉
無感覚　impassibility〈260〉, insensibility〈331〉
無感覚な　impassible〈260〉
無関係　irrelevance〈305〉
無関係な　irrelevant〈305〉, unconcerned〈75〉
無関係に　immaterially〈229〉, independently〈112〉
無関係の　unconnected〈81〉, unrelated〈304〉

無関心　disinterest〈203〉, incuriosity〈104〉, indifference〈115〉, unconcern〈75〉
無関心である　disinterested〈203〉
無関心な　apathetic〈261〉, careless〈46〉, feckless〈158〉, incurious〈104〉, indifferent〈115〉, unconcerned〈75〉
無関心に　apathetically〈261〉
無感性　insensitivity〈332〉
無感知　insensibility〈331〉
無感動　impassibility〈260〉
無感動な　apathetic〈261〉, impassible〈260〉
無期限に　indefinitely〈110〉
無技巧の　artless〈24〉
無機質の　inorganic〈253〉, unorganized〈254〉
無傷　faultlessness〈156〉
無傷の　faultless〈156〉, undamaged〈105〉, unharmed〈184〉, unhurt〈192〉, unscathed〈324〉
無軌道の　railless〈293〉
無給の　unpaid〈257〉
無競争[競合]の　noncompete〈69〉
無極　nonpolar〈273〉
無極性化する　nonpolarize〈273〉
無拠出の　noncontributory〈91〉
無規律　indiscipline〈118〉
無規律の　indisciplined〈118〉
無気力な　feckless〈158〉, impotent〈276〉
無垢な　innocent〈242〉
報いのない　unrewarding〈317〉
無口な　incommunicative〈67〉
報われない　unrewarded〈316〉
無形　incorporeity〈96〉
無計画の　unplanned〈269〉
無形財産　intangible〈365〉
無形にする　immaterialize〈229〉

無形の　incorporeal〈96〉, intangible〈365〉
無形のもの　intangible〈365〉
無結節の　knotless〈211〉
無血の　bloodless〈39〉
無限　infinitude〈161〉
無限である　unbound〈40〉
無限に　infinitely〈161〉
無限の　endless〈135〉, illimitable〈218〉, infinite〈160〉, limitless〈218〉, spaceless〈345〉, timeless〈371〉
無効果　inefficiency〈131〉
無香性の　scentless〈325〉
無拘束　unrestraint〈314〉
無効である　inoperative〈251〉
無効にする　disconfirm〈79〉
無効にできない　indefeasible〈108〉
無効になる　invalidate〈384〉
無効の　invalid〈384〉
無言の　unspoken〈346〉, voiceless〈390〉, wordless〈400〉
無作為でない　nonrandom〈293〉
無作為の　unselective〈330〉
無差別(的)な　nondiscriminatory〈120〉
無差別に　indiscriminately〈120〉, indiscriminatingly〈120〉
無視された人　nonperson〈266〉
無視されている　invisible〈389〉
無視する　disregard〈301〉
無視できない　nonnegligible〈241〉
無磁界の　demagnetizing〈226〉
無資格　ineligibility〈133〉
無資格の　incapable〈45〉
無次元の　dimensionless〈117〉, nondimensional〈117〉
無実の　guiltless〈180〉
無慈悲さ　ruthlessness〈319〉
無慈悲な　inexorable〈145〉, pitiless〈268〉, relentless〈304〉, remorseless

〈307〉, ruthless〈319〉
無慈悲に　mercilessly〈231〉
無私無欲の　selfless〈330〉
無邪気に　guilelessly〈180〉
無宗教の　unreligious〈307〉
無修正の　unmodified〈235〉
無臭の　odorless〈249〉, scentless〈325〉
無重力の　weightless〈395〉
無趣味に　inartistically〈25〉
矛盾　inconsistency〈85〉, nonconformity〈79〉
矛盾した　incompatible〈68〉, inconsistent〈85〉
矛盾して　incoherently〈60〉
無常　impermanence〈265〉
無条件に　unconditionally〈77〉
無条件の　termless〈368〉, unconditional〈77〉, unconditioned〈77〉, unqualified〈291〉
無症状に　asymptomatically〈364〉
無症状の　asymptomatic〈364〉
無情な　heartless〈186〉, inclement〈57〉
無消費の　nonconsumable〈87〉
無色の　colorless〈61〉
無所属の　nonparty〈260〉, unattached〈27〉
無印の　unmarked〈228〉
無神経な　indelicate〈110〉, insensitive〈332〉, undiplomatic〈117〉
無神経に　inconsiderately〈84〉
無信仰　irreligion〈307〉
無信仰の　irreligious〈307〉
無信仰の人　unbeliever〈37〉
無信心な　nonbelieving〈37〉, unhallowed〈182〉, unreligious〈307〉
無信心な人　nonbeliever〈37〉
無尽蔵　inexhaustibleness〈144〉
無尽蔵に　infinitely〈161〉
無尽蔵の　inexhaustible〈144〉, infinite〈160〉

無人の　uninhabited〈200〉, unmanned〈226〉
無神論　atheism〈369〉
無神論者　atheist〈369〉
無神論の　atheistic〈369〉
無数　incalculability〈44〉, infinitude〈161〉
無数の　countless〈97〉, endless〈135〉, inestimable〈140〉, innumerable〈245〉, numberless〈245〉, uncounted〈98〉, unnumbered〈245〉, untold〈373〉
難しくない　effortless〈132〉
結び目のない　knotless〈211〉
無声の　noteless〈244〉
無制限の　limitless〈218〉, termless〈368〉, unconfined〈79〉, unlimited〈218〉
無生物　nonliving〈220〉
無生物の　inorganic〈253〉
無責任　irresponsibility〈313〉
無責任な　irresponsible〈313〉
無責任な行為[人]　irresponsibility〈313〉
無節操に　indiscriminately〈120〉
無接続の　connectionless〈82〉
無線　wireless〈398〉
無線の　wireless〈398〉
無駄　fruitlessness〈172〉
無駄な　feckless〈158〉, fruitless〈172〉, ineffectual〈130〉
無駄に　fruitlessly〈172〉, ineffectually〈131〉
無体の　incorporeal〈96〉
無段に　infinitely〈161〉
無担保の　unsecured〈328〉
無知な　clueless〈59〉
無秩序　disorder〈252〉
無秩序な　disordered〈252〉
無秩序にする　disorganize〈253〉
無秩序の　ill-ordered〈252〉

無茶な　reckless〈298〉
無着色の　uncolored〈62〉
無調性　atonality〈373〉
無調の　atonal〈373〉
無定形　formlessness〈167〉
無抵抗　nonresistance〈310〉
無抵抗の　nonresistant〈310〉, resistless〈310〉
無敵　invincibility〈388〉
無敵の　invincible〈388〉
無電解の　electroless〈133〉
無糖の　sugarless〈357〉
無党派の　nonpartisan〈259〉
無党派の人　nonpartisan〈259〉
無毒の　innocuous〈243〉, nontoxic〈374〉, nonvirulent〈389〉
無得点の　scoreless〈325〉
無頓着　heedlessness〈186〉, unconcern〈75〉
無頓着な　careless〈46〉, heedless〈186〉, indifferent〈115〉
無頓着に　heedlessly〈186〉
無能　incompetence〈69〉, incapacity〈45〉
無能な　impotent〈276〉, incompetent〈69〉, ineffective〈130〉, shiftless〈337〉
無能の　incapable〈45〉
無能力化　disabling〈2〉
無敗の　undefeated〈108〉
無反省の　unreflective〈301〉
無反応性の　nonreactive〈295〉
無比　incomparability〈68〉
無比の　unequaled〈138〉, unmatched〈229〉, unparalleled〈258〉
無火花の　sparkless〈345〉
無表情　impassiveness〈261〉
無表情な　expressionless〈149〉
無表情な状態　expressionlessness〈149〉
無表情に　expressionlessly〈149〉

無表情の　emotionless〈134〉, impassive〈261〉, inexpressive〈149〉
無風の　nonventilating〈387〉, windless〈397〉
無分別　imprudence〈288〉, inconsiderateness〈84〉, indiscretion〈119〉
無分別な　ill-considered〈84〉, impolitic〈274〉, imprudent〈288〉, indiscreet〈119〉
無分別に　ill-advisedly〈11〉, inconsiderately〈84〉, indiscreetly〈119〉, irrationally〈294〉, unthinkingly〈370〉
無法の　lawless〈213〉
無謀な　incautious〈47〉, reckless〈298〉
無謀に　recklessly〈298〉
無防備な　armless〈23〉, defenseless〈108〉, undefended〈108〉, unguarded〈180〉, unprotected〈286〉
無味乾燥な　tasteless〈367〉
無名の　innominate〈243〉, noteless〈244〉, unsung〈358〉
無免許の　unlicensed〈216〉
無毛　hairlessness〈182〉
無毛の　hairless〈182〉
無目的　indirection〈118〉
むやみに　immoderately〈234〉
無誘導の　unguided〈180〉
無用の　inutile〈383〉
無抑制　unrestraint〈314〉
むらがある　uneven〈141〉
無理の　irrational〈293〉
無力　helplessness〈187〉
無力化する　disarm〈23〉
無力さ　ineffectuality〈130〉
無力な　helpless〈186〉, inadequate〈9〉, ineffective〈130〉, ineffectual〈130〉, powerless〈276〉
無力にも　ineffectually〈131〉
無輪の　wheelless〈396〉
無類　incomparability〈68〉
無類の　incomparable〈68〉, unmatched〈229〉, unsurpassed〈360〉

め

目に見えない　viewless〈388〉
目のない　eyeless〈151〉
目の見えない　sightless〈337〉, unseeing〈329〉
明確でない　indefinite〈109〉
明確に定まっていない　uncrystallized〈102〉
明示　disclosure〈58〉
明白で　incontrovertibly〈92〉
明白な　indisputable〈121〉, unambiguous〈17〉
明白に　unambiguously〈17〉
名誉を傷つける　disgrace〈177〉
明瞭さ　unambiguousness〈17〉
迷惑　inconvenience〈93〉, undesirability〈112〉
迷惑な　disobliging〈247〉
迷惑をかける　disoblige〈247〉, inconvenience〈93〉
目障りな　unsightly〈338〉
珍しい　uncommon〈66〉
珍しく　uncharacteristically〈52〉
目立たない　inconspicuous〈86〉, indistinctive〈122〉, unassuming〈27〉, unnoticed〈245〉, unremarkable〈307〉
目立たないように　inconspicuously〈86〉
目立って　uncommonly〈66〉
めちゃくちゃに　incoherently〈60〉
免責条項　disclaimer〈55〉

も

儲からない　profitless〈284〉, unprofitable〈284〉
申し分のない　impeccable〈262〉, undeniable〈111〉, unexceptionable〈143〉
申し訳なさそうでない　unapologetic〈19〉
盲目　eyelessness〈151〉
盲目の　eyeless〈151〉

盲目の状態で　eyelessly〈151〉
網羅していない　inexhaustive〈144〉
網羅せずに　inexhaustively〈145〉
目撃されていない　unwitnessed〈399〉
目的のない　objectless〈247〉, purposeless〈290〉
もたもたしている　inefficient〈131〉
持ち主のない　ownerless〈255〉
もつれをほぐす　unsnarl〈341〉
もてなしのよくないこと　inhospitability〈190〉
もてなしの悪い　inhospitable〈190〉
もとに戻す　uncross〈101〉, undo〈124〉, unscramble〈325〉, untuck〈378〉, untwist〈379〉
もとに戻せずに　irreversibly〈316〉
もとに戻せない　irreversible〈315〉
もとの状態に戻す　unmake〈226〉
もとの場所から移動させる　dislodge〈222〉
求めたものではない　unsolicited〈342〉
求められていない　unasked-for〈25〉
物別れに終わって　inconclusively〈76〉
問題が解決できない　inextricable〈151〉
問題なく　unproblematic(al)ly〈282〉
問題にされない　unchallenged〈51〉
問題のない　unproblematic(al)〈282〉

や

焼き入れされていない　untempered〈368〉
焼き尽くされない　inconsumable〈87〉
役に立たない　ill-served〈334〉, inconducive〈77〉, ineffective〈130〉, inefficient〈131〉, unserviceable〈334〉, useless〈382〉
安い費用で　inexpensively〈147〉
やたらに　indiscriminately〈120〉
屋根のない　roofless〈318〉
屋根をはがす　unroof〈318〉

野暮な　graceless〈177〉, uncool〈95〉
やむを得ず　unavoidably〈31〉
やりかけの　unfinished〈160〉
やりたくない　unenviable〈138〉
やる気を失う　disintegrate〈201〉
やる気をなくさせる　discourage〈98〉, discouraging〈98〉, indisposed〈121〉
やるせなく　inconsolably〈85〉
和らげられない　unmitigated〈233〉, unrelieved〈307〉

ゆ

湯あかを取り除く　descale〈324〉
由緒正しくない　nonpedigreed〈262〉
優雅でない　inelegant〈133〉
優雅でないこと　inelegance〈133〉
有害な　undesirable〈112〉
勇敢な　dauntless〈106〉, fearless〈157〉
優柔不断　indecision〈106〉, indecisiveness〈107〉, indetermination〈114〉
優柔不断な　indecisive〈107〉
夕食抜きの　supperless〈359〉
友人がいないこと　friendlessness〈171〉
友人がいない様子で　friendlessly〈171〉
融通性がない　inflexible〈164〉
ユーモアの(センスの)ない　humorless〈191〉
ユーモアを解さないこと　humorlessness〈192〉
ユーモアを解さないで　humorlessly〈192〉
遊離酸素を除去する　deoxygenate〈256〉
譲らない　unrelenting〈305〉
油断　inattention〈28〉
夢のない　dreamless〈126〉
夢を見ない　dreamless〈126〉
揺るがない　unshaken〈336〉

許しがたいこと　inexcusableness〈144〉
許せない　indefensible〈109〉, unforgivable〈166〉, unpardonable〈259〉
緩めた　unstrung〈354〉
緩める　unclench〈57〉, unfasten〈155〉, unloose〈223〉, unstrap〈354〉, unstring〈354〉

よ

用意ができていない　unmade〈225〉
用意されていない　unready〈296〉
容易に信じない　incredulous〈101〉
容易に理解できない　indigestible〈116〉
溶解　dissolution〈342〉
溶解した　dissolved〈343〉
溶解しない　incorruptible〈97〉, insoluble〈342〉
溶解する　dissolve〈343〉
溶解できる　dissoluble〈342〉, dissolvable〈343〉
要求されていない　unclaimed〈56〉
擁護できない　unsupportable〈359〉
容姿が悪い　ill-favored〈156〉
容赦できないほどに　unforgivably〈167〉
容赦ない　inexorable〈145〉, relentless〈304〉, remorseless〈307〉
容赦なく　inexorably〈145〉, relentlessly〈305〉
幼稚な　immature〈229〉
容認できずに　unacceptably〈3〉
要約されていない　unabridged〈2〉
要領を得ない　pointless〈272〉, unmeaning〈230〉
予期していない　unhoped-for〈190〉
予期しない　unanticipated〈18〉, unforeseen〈166〉, unlooked-for〈223〉
予期しなかった　unexpected〈146〉
予期せずに　unexpectedly〈146〉
抑止する　discourage〈98〉
抑制されていない　uncontrolled〈92〉, uninhibited〈200〉, unrestrained〈314〉

弱まらない　unremitting〈307〉
読んでも面白くない　unreadable〈296〉

ら

落胆させること　discouragement〈98〉, dishearten〈186〉
落胆する　discouraging〈98〉
落馬させる　unhorse〈190〉
乱雑　disarray〈24〉
乱脈な　disorganized〈254〉

り

リーダーのいない　leaderless〈214〉
利益の上がらない　unprofitable〈284〉
理解できない　inapprehensible〈21〉, incomprehensible〈72〉, indigestible〈116〉, inexplicable〈148〉
理解できないこと　incomprehension〈72〉
理解不能　incomprehension〈72〉
理解力のない　inapprehensive〈21〉, incomprehensive〈73〉, uncomprehending〈72〉
理解(力)のないこと　inapprehension〈21〉
履行されていない　unfulfilled〈173〉
利己心のない　selfless〈330〉
利己的でない　unselfish〈330〉
利己的でなく　unselfishly〈331〉
履修単位にならない　noncredit〈101〉
理数系に弱いこと［人］　innumerate〈246〉
リストに載っていない　unlisted〈220〉
理性のない　irrational〈293〉
理性のなさ　irrationality〈294〉
リセットできない　nonresettable〈310〉
立証されていない　unproved〈287〉, unproven〈287〉, unsubstantiated〈355〉, unsupported〈359〉
立証しない　unprove〈287〉

リハーサルが十分でない　ill-rehearsed〈303〉
硫化した　unvulcanized〈392〉
流行遅れの　unfashionable〈155〉
留置しない　noncustodial〈104〉
理由なく　unreasonably〈298〉
理由のない　causeless〈47〉, reasonless〈297〉, unreasonable〈297〉
領域が明確でない　unorganized〈254〉
両替できない　nonconvertible〈94〉
猟犬の資質を欠いた　nonsporting〈347〉
利用されていない　unimproved〈197〉
利用できない　unavailable〈31〉
利用不可能性　inaccessibility〈4〉
両立しがたいこと　incompatibility〈68〉
両立しない　incompatible〈68〉, inconsistent〈85〉, unsuited〈357〉
両立しないで　inconsistently〈85〉
両立不能性　incompatibility〈68〉
旅行したことがない　untraveled〈376〉
リンクを外す　unlink〈219〉
臨時の　unscheduled〈325〉
隣人らしくない　unneighborly〈241〉
倫理的に認められない[是認されない]　illicit〈216〉

る

ルール違反の　illegal〈215〉

れ

礼を失した　uncomplimentary〈71〉
例を見ない　unexampled〈143〉
例外的な　atypical〈379〉
例外的に　atypically〈379〉
例外でない　unexceptional〈143〉
礼儀作法を心得ない　inconsiderate〈84〉
礼儀をわきまえない　uncivil〈55〉

冷遇　disfavor〈156〉, indignity〈116〉
冷遇する　ill-treat〈376〉
冷酷な　inclement〈57〉
冷酷に　heartlessly〈186〉
冷静さ　impassiveness〈261〉
冷静な　dispassionate〈260〉, inexcitable〈143〉, unmoved〈238〉
冷淡さ　impassiveness〈261〉
冷淡な　apathetic〈261〉, bloodless〈39〉, unsympathetic〈363〉
冷淡に　apathetically〈261〉
霊的な　incorporeal〈96〉
歴史的視点を欠いた　ahistorical〈187〉
歴史的でない　unhistorical〈188〉
歴史と無関係な　ahistorical〈187〉
連結を解く　uncouple〈98〉
連続的な　uninterrupted〈204〉

ろ

労せずして得た　unlabored〈213〉
労働組合員を雇用しない　nonunion〈381〉
労働組合に加入していない　nonunion〈381〉
労働によって得たものでない　unearned〈128〉
狼狽させる　disconcert〈75〉
浪費された　ill-spent〈346〉
濾過されていない　unfiltered〈160〉
ロックが外された　unlocked〈222〉
ロックされていない　nonlocking〈222〉
ロックを外す　unlock〈221〉, unlocking〈222〉
論証されていない　undemonstrated〈111〉
論争の余地のない　noncontroversial〈92〉
論破できない　inexpugnable〈150〉, unassailable〈26〉
論理が一貫していないこと　incoherence〈60〉
論理が一貫しない　incoherent〈60〉
論理的でない　inconsequential〈83〉

わ

ワイヤレスの　wireless〈398〉
和解できない　irreconcilable〈299〉
わからない　incomprehensible〈72〉, unnoticeable〈244〉
わからなくなった　disoriented〈254〉
わかりにくい　unintelligible〈202〉
わかりやすくする　demystify〈239〉
わかりやすくない　unfriendly〈171〉
分けられない　unparted〈259〉
わざとらしい　insincere〈339〉
わずかな　imperceptible〈264〉, inappreciable〈20〉, inconsiderable〈84〉, insignificant〈338〉
わずかに　inconsiderably〈84〉
煩わされた　unfazed〈157〉
煩わせない　unfaze〈156〉
忘れがたい　unforgettable〈166〉
忘れる　disremember〈307〉, unlearn〈214〉
綿ぼこりの付いていない　lintless〈219〉
笑わない　unsmiling〈341〉
割り当てない　unassign〈26〉
割り当てを解除する　deallocate〈16〉
割引　discount〈97〉
悪い結果を暗示する特質　inauspiciousness〈30〉
悪い状態の　ill-conditioned〈77〉
悪気のない　offenseless〈250〉

2014年5月10日　初版発行

英語反意語辞典

2014年5月10日　第1刷発行

編　者　富井　篤
発行者　株式会社 三省堂　代表者 北口克彦
印刷者　三省堂印刷株式会社
発行所　株式会社 三省堂
〒101-8371　東京都千代田区三崎町二丁目22番14号
電話　(編集)03-3230-9411
(営業)03-3230-9412
振替口座　00160-5-54300
http://www.sanseido.co.jp/

〈英語反意語辞典・576pp.〉

落丁本・乱丁本はお取替えいたします

ISBN 978-4-385-10638-0